de Gruyter Studies in Organization 19

Organizational Symbolism

de Gruyter Studies in Organization

An international series by internationally known authors presenting current fields of research in organization.

Organizing and organizations are substantial pre-requisites for the viability and future developments of society. Their study and comprehension are indispensable to the quality of human life. Therefore, the series aims to:

— offer to the specialist work material in form of the most important and current problems, methods and results;
— give interested readers access to different subject areas:
— provide aids for decisions on contemporary problems and stimulate ideas.

The series includes monographs, collections of contributed papers, and handbooks.

Organizational Symbolism

Editor: Barry A. Turner

Walter de Gruyter · Berlin · New York 1990

Editor
Barry A. Turner
Reader in the Sociology of Organization
Department of Sociology, University of Exeter, England

Library of Congress Cataloging-in-Publication Data

Organizational symbolism / editor, Barry R. Turner.
  XII, 315 p. 23 × 15,5 cm. — (De Gruyter studies in organization : 19)
  Includes bibliographical references.
  ISBN 0-89925-635-X (U.S. : alk. paper) : $ 49.95 (U.S. :
  est.)
  1. Corporate culture. 2. Organizational behavior. I. Turner, Barry A. II. Series.
HD58.7.07464   1990
302.3′5 — dc20
                                            89-25744
                                               CIP

Deutsche Bibliothek Cataloging in Publication Data

Organizational symbolism / ed.: Barry A. Turner. — Berlin ;
New York : de Gruyter, 1990
  (De Gruyter studies in organization ; 19)
  ISBN 3-11-011051-2
NE: Turner, Barry A. [Hrsg.]; GT

♾ Printed on acid-free paper.

Printed in Germany
Typesetting: Arthur Collignon GmbH, 1000 Berlin 30. — Printing: Gerike GmbH, 1000
Berlin 36. — Binding: Lüderitz & Bauer GmbH, 1000 Berlin 61. — Cover design:
Johannes Rother, 1000 Berlin 21.

Contents

Part III. Management, Consultancy, and Metaphor 137

List of tables

List of figures

Introduction

Barry A. Turner

General

This book is intended to offer the reader a guide to some of the diversity of work emerging from the new field of organizational symbolism. After a long preoccupation with the problems of building more rational, efficient and computer-like organizations, students of administrative activities have recently become much more aware of other facets of human life which contribute to the functioning of organizations and which constitute the nature of social life as it is lived within organizational settings. This new awareness focuses attention upon the symbolic, the qualitative, the sensuous aspects of human relationships and upon the central place of these qualities in the operation of organizations.

There has recently been an abundance of writing taking a managerial view of 'corporate culture' but by intent such discussions are strongly instrumental, and start from the question of how to influence or to manipulate the corporate culture. By contrast, the present volume takes a broader, perhaps a more academic look at qualitative, symbolic aspects of organizations, drawing upon some of the multiplicity of contending approaches currently available, in studies by European, and also by some American and Canadian contributors.

Symbolism

The word 'symbol' originally meant a token of remembrance. A host would break an object in two and present one half to his guest who could use it to secure readmission to the host's house in years to come, for himself or for his descendants, if the two halves of the token could be shown to fit together. Commenting on this, Gadamer, observes that the term thus represents something, "in and through which we recognise someone already known to us," (Gadamer 1986: 32) so that the symbol is "that other fragment which has always been sought in order to complete and make whole our own fragmentary life" (Gadamer 1986: 32).

In the context of organizational studies, though, it is not so easy to convey the significance of the word 'symbol.' The term 'Organizational Symbolism' used in the title of this Reader has been used to label the discussions of a group of scholars and management specialists over the past decade. It is by no means a clearly defined term with a cut and dried meaning, and I do not think it helpful to try to specify its meaning succinctly. Neither in this brief introduction to the present set of papers, nor in the collection itself will the reader find a simple and concise specification of the term. In fact, in considering how the phrase has acted as a rallying point for some recent discussions of the cultural and qualitative aspects of organizations, it is possible to argue that its ambiguity and its diffuseness have been part of its attraction.

Thinking, however, of Gadamer's observations, it would not be unfair to describe the work of many of those connected with organizational symbolism as concerned with a search for some additional element not found in established or prevailing modes of organizational analysis. There is the possibility, or the hope, of identifying some additional factor which will make it possible to recognise those elements or organizations which are already known, but which are not yet adequately represented in analyses – the sensuous, the mythical, the aesthetic, the cultural features of organizations.

Those who have taken part in recent exchanges about organizational symbolism have thus been more unanimous in their discontent with prevailing 'main-stream' methods of organizational nalysis than in their prescriptions of what they wish to find to replace it. More united by what they already have, and are unhappy with, than by what they seek, their approaches to the problems of understanding organizations and organizational behaviour are many and various, producing a diversity which is one of the most stimulating features of the movement. Accordingly one of the purposes of this volume is to illustrate some of this variety by presenting a selection from the different approaches to organizations currently being used to deal with those symbolic aspects of organizations which are 'known but not yet fully recognised.'

As with any quest, we have to be aware that there is an element of romanticism in the search (Ebers 1985). This creates some dilemmas since a strong underlying theme of social science since the Enlightenment has been the anti-romantic concern to challenge and to unmask myths and ideologies in order to sweep away what was seen as the previous obscurantism and to help to create more realistic knowledge about society. When the sociologist Elias was asked whether people did not have a need of myths, he answered, in the spirit of the Enlightenment:

Yes, but then they must write poetry, as I have also done. I also had a need of myths and art ... People need myths, but not to give them form in social life ... It is now my view that people would live together better without myths. Myths always eventually exact a penalty of us. (Elias, quoted in Mennell 1989: ch. 1).

By contrast, MacIver (1947) argued that:

Every society is held together by a myth-system ... wherever he goes, whatever he encounters, man spins about him his web of myth as the caterpillar spins its cocoon.

Views diverge about just how true such a statement is, and just what might have to be understood as a myth in order to make it acceptable (Cohen 1976: x). There can be no reason to retain myths which are defined only as mistakes and illusions. But myths which, as MacIver would hold, are so pervasive because they are central to human social activities cannot be disposed of without disposing of social life itself.

If, nonetheless, it is the case that we always pay dearly for our myths, we should no doubt be asking whether the current interest in symbols, myths and culture is a retreat rather than an advance. Is the resurgence of interest in myths and symbolism creating a false view and a false consciousness which will exact a toll in the future? We know this century, from our experience and to our cost, that myths and symbols can readily be used to provide an appealing packaging for irrational policies. I do not think that there is any question but that we should be extremely cautious in dealing with such matters, for the ambiguity, the potency and the attractiveness of discussions of symbolism make it all too easy for such discussions to change gradually in a way which provides a cosmetic covering for the activities of those in power.

But there is also a need for some cautions to be expressed in the opposite direction. The attempts to treat organizations as rational 'authority machines,' or as computer-like assemblages of information are coming to the end of their usefulness because of those features of organizations which they fail to take into account, precisely those cultural, symbolic features with which the present collection of papers is concerned. An organization is a human creation and all aspects of human life and thought can potentially be brought to light in its activities: if human actions and relationships are more than 'communication, command and control' then so are organizations. The current concern with the sensuous and the emotional, with style and aesthetics, arises precisely because such terms refer to elements which are missing in prevailing accounts of organizational activities. With such elements absent, the accounts which existing approaches seek to offer are now seen to be inadequate for many purposes.

An early paper in this volume (Adams and Ingersoll, Chapter 1) expresses some pessimism about the possibility of finding a new approach to organizations: the prevailing culture in which we live, they suggest is so overwhelmingly characterised by its rational-technical form that even deliberate attempts to escape this mould inevitably get drawn back into it again. By contrast, the two final papers (Travers, ch. 18; Linstead and Grafton-Small, ch. 19) might be said to challenge the extent to which the rational-technical is really dominant in contemporary society — or perhaps to challenge the extent to which the undoubted ubiquity of the rational-technical actually provides dominance. The world as we deal with it is always constituted by those in it, so that, as several contributors argue in their different ways, it can always be re-viewed, re-constituted and thus transcended by making use of possibilities for reframing, or for redefining the way in which the world is understood. And thanks to the ubiquitous nature of modern technical rationality, its techniques and its equipment repeatedly present us with new possibilities for reframing and redefining which succeed one another in a bewildering spiral. Thus, rather than looking at a battle between rational and irrational systems, we are dealing, instead, with families of different types of rational systems which have the possibility of interrupting each other in an infinite regress.

Symbols then become crucial in our attempts to understand such successive transformations. The multiple possibilities for reframing which are built into them arise because symbols are objects, acts, concepts or linguistic forms which stand ambiguously for a multiplicity of disparate meanings (Cohen 1976). It is the very ambiguity of a symbol which makes it so useful. Duncan (1969) suggests that a symbol forms a bridge between different possible meanings which we can cross and recross before we finally commit ourselves to a single meaning, if in these post-modern times we are ever able to make that commitment. By the same token this ambiguity of meaning is associated with an economy of expression which is bought, of course, at the expense of precision. The possibility of compacting many appeals into a single symbol contributes to the power to evoke those sentiments and emotions which impel people to action, while at the same time the precise rationalities behind that appeal may be opaque.

A single organizational symbol can have multiple implications both within the organization and outside it, sometimes even embracing opposing ideas (Czarniawska-Joerges 1988). An emblem or a metaphor which carries connotations, for example, of continuity and community within an organization, can under certain circumstances be reinterpreted or restated in a manner which supports individualistic innovation (Cohen 1976; 1985). Symbols and symbolic actions frequently refer to issues which are central not only to organizations, but also to society and to social life. Matters of identity and selfhood on the one hand, and matters of existence, of life and death, fortune and misfortune on the other are pursued in symbolic discussions. Accordingly a number of such themes appear and recur, interwoven with the various discussions of symbolism set out in the present collection.

A Little History

Several factors seem to have combined to produce the current interest in organizational symbolism and culture (Turner 1986; Turner 1988). Specialists in social science methods over recent years have been urging caution in the application of quantitative approaches regardless of their limitations or of their unsuitability for some kinds of study (Morrison and Henkel 1970; Kriz 1988; Gherardi and Turner 1988). Critics of organizational research (Perrow 1979) have also expressed doubts about the usefulness of existing theories, but, perhaps more importantly, some leading organizational researchers who had previously espoused wholly rational-technical views of organizations, March being the most notable of these, have also shifted position, moving towards analyses which permit a more ambiguous and less machine-like view of organizational processes (March and Simon 1958; March and Olsen 1976). Such critiques found echoes in the practical experience of those who worked with organizations, either carrying out qualitative studies, or seeking to intervene and to implement change as practitioners. Since the findings of many existing studies seemed to be difficult to apply and sometimes ran counter to their own experiences of organization, and since research carried out according to existing paradigms only rarely seemed to extend their understanding, they were receptive to the possibility of new approaches which spoke more directly to their own concerns (Reason and Rowan 1981).

Over such stirrings of unease with the existing orthodoxy in organizational studies swept the wave of interest in 'corporate culture' provoked by American anxieties to find an explanation for the superior growth of Japanese industry. The clear remedies set out in Peters and Waterman's book In Search of Excellence (1982) were snapped up in America and elsewhere, making it one of the best-selling management texts ever. As a consequence, managers around the world suddenly discovered that they had to worry about the 'culture' of their organizations, and, if they did not know how to assess the state of health of that culture, they were encouraged to feel that they might consider hiring consultants to perform this diagnosis for them. The passion for 'corporate culture' is now levelling off, as a more wary view comes to be taken of the idea of 'culture' as the panacea for all organizational ills. Although as yet it is not clear what might replace it as the next managerial fashion, it is now much more acceptable than it was ten years ago to discuss myths, ceremonials and symbols in management circles.

Early in the nineteen-eighties, as these concerns were emerging, an Organizational Symbolism and Culture network was established in the United States to connect academics and others interested in cultural aspects of organization (See, e. g. Pondy et al. 1983). At the same time, a similar small study group was set up under the auspices of the European Group for Organizational Studies (EGOS). The European group was marked out by being explicitly playful, even frivolous in its outlook: it proclaimed in faintly heretical tones that 'research can be fun,' and it declared itself to be interested in 'Organizational Symbolism.' The first meeting of this study group, at Exeter University, UK, in June 1982, linked Transatlantic and European interests in the area, and resulted in the formation of the Standing Conference on

Organizational Symbolism (SCOS), which, as it grew, continued its original links as a study group of EGOS.

No one in the SCOS activities had tried to offer a specification of what Organizational Symbolism might be, but as the group moved to plan the first of a series of international conferences on the topic, it published the following manifesto:

Our starting point is the realization that an organization is a cultural and therefore symbolic reality in the life process of its members. This realization has meant that categories and discourse appropriate to the study of culture now emerge as central in this approach to our study of organizations. Thus organizations may be seen in terms of their rituals, traditions, ceremonies and 'myths', or their 'cults' and 'clans', their styles, symbols and cultural identities and so forth. The possibilities are as rich and various as culture itself and people working in many disciplines, e. g. psychoanalysis, psychology, sociology, anthropology, the arts, theatre, literature and business adminis-tration potentially have much to contribute, as well as those working more centrally in the study of organizations (Call for papers for the First International Conference on Organization Symbolism and Corporate Culture Lund, Sweden, 26 − 30 June, 1984).

As was suggested above, the SCOS Conferences seem to have functioned as a forum for those wishing to get to grips with or to understand aspects of organizations not readily catered for in the previously dominant rational-technical paradigms. From their inauguration, these conferences and associ-ated workshop meetings[1] have tried, with varying degrees of success, to retain the atmosphere of informality, the unifying 'cultural events' and the innovative approach to research-based discussions about organizations which characterised the early meetings.

Where is this 'movement' heading? There is no doubt that Organizational Symbolism constitutes 'a movement,' with recruits from academics, managers and management consultants, a string of publications and a series of confer-ences. There is not, as can be seen from the papers in this collection, a single thrust, but there is a feeling that the label of Organizational Symbolism permits a range of exploratory or 'alternative' discussions to be entered into, in an atmosphere where suggestions will be taken on their merits, and where there is no need or desire to affront in order to get others to listen to a possibility. The debates around the idea of organizational symbolism have made it possible to ask much more pertinent questions about the culture of organizations, about the systems of signs and symbols which organizations create and about the manner in which such signs and symbols also create the organization. The realisation is growing that many of the subjects consid-ered in these debates − myths, ceremonials, aesthetics − are not just

---

[1] To date there have been conferences in Lund, Antibes, Montreal, Milan, Istanbul, and Fontainebleau, and workshops in Exeter, Groningen, Trento, and Hull.

'optional extras' in the understanding of organizational life, but that they are central to much human behaviour in organizational settings. And, for those who feel that the rational-technical paradigm for the study of organizations omits some essential characteristics of organizational life, for those whose practices cannot readily be described or accounted for within existing rational technical accounts, discussions about Organizational Symbolism function as a kind of 'crucible' within which they can associate with others who are also considering alternative approaches.

Outline of Contributions

The present volume presents papers commissioned from academics and from management specialists who are members of SCOS, who have taken part in SCOS conferences, or contributed to the SCOS publications, Dragon and NoteWork[2]. They indicate some of the approaches to organizations which have been discussed at these gatherings and some of the topics which preoccupy those looking for new, more productive and more satisfying ways of accounting for what goes on in organizations. Whenever possible, the papers illustrate these approaches by reference to specific studies of organizations, offering concrete examples rather than merely taking theoretical positions.

The range of papers in the collection is wide. It varies from those presenting anthropological or symbolic interactionist studies of organizations, which are perhaps remarkable now only in the way in which they are being rediscovered by the mainstream, to accounts which see no way of discussing organizations and organizational culture without placing them in the context of the current wide ranging debates on post-modernism. Some of the papers outline carefully structured studies which are innovative in that they seek to extend their embrace to include discussion of cultural and symbolic issues, while others are more loosely structured essays which permit the authors to deal with aspects of organizational behaviour difficult to handle in conventional formats. There are many themes, and, as a consequence of the complexity of symbolic issues, these themes frequently reappear in different guises in papers which are ostensibly concerned with something else. Among other topics, the authors are concerned with leadership, with organizational style and with aesthetics in organizations, as well as with power, ethics, dominance and flirting. Also included are some discussions of organizations cast in decidedly unconventional moulds which attempt to move towards wholly

---

[2] With the exception of Ellis Finkelstein.

novel analyses of organizations. There are, finally, papers reflecting on the cultural training of managers, on the way in which the activities of consultants can be understood culturally, and on how consultants operate when dealing with cultural matters, papers which form, as a group, a reminder of the extent to which management consultants, management teachers and practising managers have been closely involved in discussions about organizational symbolism since their inception.

The Reader is divided into six sections, but this should not be taken as an indication that six topics are dealt with in six water-tight compartments. The themes of culture, symbolism, power, ideology and organization emerge and re-emerge in successive contributions, so that the reader interested in picking up a particular theme may well find it dealt with in several or even in all of the sections. The emphasis in the book upon empirical accounts of organizations, their symbols and their culture helps to ensure that organizational issues recur throughout the discussions in a series of different guises.

The first section of the book, called "Symbolic Aspects of Organizations," presents five organizational studies which offer an empirical base for the discussion of organisational symbolism and culture. Adams and Ingersoll (ch. 1), after a review of recent literature on organizational culture, discuss the changing management styles in an American state ferry company facing the challenges of being incorporated into the contemporary world of financial management. Kahle (ch. 2) takes us back to the Middle Ages to give an analysis of the manner in which a German municipality and related organizations concerned with salt production created a specific symbolic domain within which a culture could grow, pointing to the importance, not just of transaction costs, but also of transaction forms. The influence of religion upon culture forms the core of Aktouf's study of a rather unusual, Catholic-influenced company in Quebec (ch. 3) which shifts around some of our conventional thinking about the relationships of Protestantism and capitalism. The two remaining studies in this section are detailed field studies based upon participant observation: Konecki's symbolic interactionist account (ch. 4) deals with flirting and power relations in a Polish electrical engineering factory, while Finkelstein's social anthropological study (ch. 5) looks at the inter-relationship between culture and leadership roles in the setting of a British prison.

The second section, "Power as a Symbolic Domain," picks up and extends some of the concerns with power and influence discussed by both Konecki and Finkelstein. Sievers (ch. 6) looks at the symbolic links between motivation and mortality in contemporary companies and considers the opportunity which the modern employee has to transcend him or herself in work; Calás and McGuire (ch. 7) compare patterns of influence in two contrasting interorganizational networks in American health care; and Rosen (ch. 8) gives a vividly written account of the 1987 stock market crash in New

York, looking at the style of events surrounding this major upheaval in organizational life in order to develop an understanding of the relationships between events and the presentation of these events in major centres of power in our post-modernist, late capitalist society.

The third section, "Management, Consultancy and Metaphor," recognises the participation of managers and consultants in the debates about organizational symbolism, but also gives an acknowledgement of the extent to which cultural, metaphorical, verbal and symbolic issues are increasingly becoming central to current problems of management and of organizational consulting. Czarniawska-Joerges (ch. 9) deals with this point explicitly in her analysis of the language transformations involved in the practices of Swedish management consulting; while Gahmberg (ch. 10) looks more theoretically at how semiotic considerations frame and define leadership. Since symbolic issues are of such importance to the practice of management, it is sensible to ensure that managerial training refers to them, and Gagliardi (ch. 11), one of the pioneers in this field, presents some investigations into and reflections upon his experience in training Italian managers to develop an increased sensitivity to cultural matters. Even more practically, Edgren (ch. 12) gives an account of his thinking and his approach as a management consultant commissioned to carry out an extremely rapid assessment of the culture of a Scandinavian company, for which he used what he calls 'commando' techniques, which can be regarded in many respects as the antithesis of the much more long-term methods employed by social anthropologists.

Section four deals explicitly with some themes that have already been touched on, in passing, in the earlier sections: "Style and Aesthetics" in organizational settings. Witkin (ch. 13) discusses in detail the nature of organizational style, and demonstrates its dimensions in a field study of the the 'collusive manouevre' as a particular style of strategy evident in the interrelationship between managers in a British financial company, whilst Strati (ch. 14), concerned with the 'mysterious process of explaining the aesthetic dimension,' reports on a series of discussions he has had with academics in Italian universities about the significance of the aesthetic in their working lives and their organizations.

One of the issues which recurs in discussions about the understanding as opposed to the analysis of organizations, from Mary Parker Follett onwards, is a concern with a holistic approach, a concern to examine and to comprehend organization-wide processes as a whole. The fifth section, "Whole Organizations," presents three contrasting approaches to this issue. Brissy (ch. 15), having carried out several detailed studies of the impact of computers upon American and Belgian companies, feels that in order to fully extend his analysis of the effects of computers, he has to move into the metaphorical realm, discussing the 'magic' of computing and considering practitioners as 'witches' or 'magicians' in order to understand the non-rational manner in which technical innovations impact upon whole organizations. Pihlajamäki (ch. 16) draws upon a McLuhanesque model of the balance of the different senses and of different media in order to try to diagnose the sensory systems of Scandinavian organizations which she has been studying, while Koss (ch. 17) explores the assumption that it is possible to diagnose within organizations three different 'states of being' — 'vision,' 'fusion/diffusion' and 'confusion' — which reflect their current performance and future potentialities, sketching out these 'states of being' on the basis of her own research and consulting with American companies.

The final section of the collection is "Against Conclusions," where the opportunity is taken to consider some issues of theory and some of the debates of post-modernism as they relate to organizational symbolism. Travers (ch. 18) precipitates the reader through successive phases of framing and reframing in a manner which is likely to persuade us that no contemporary organizational issue can be looked at from a single, unified point of view, since the possibility of transcendent transformations is ever-present. Finally, Linstead and Grafton-Small (ch. 19) explore the organizational and other issues which can be discerned behind an advertisement aimed at British executives. The offer is ostensibly to supply a chaffeur-driven car with roses on the rear seat, but as their discussion makes clear, this is by no means all that is on offer. At the end, though, they are "against conclusions."

References

Cohen, Abner (1976): *Two Dimensional Man: An Essay on the Anthropology of Power and Symbolism in Complex Society*, Berkeley. University of California Press.

Cohen, Anthony P. (1985): *The Symbolic Construction of Community*, Chichester: Ellis Horwood.

Czarniawska-Joerges, Barbara (1988): *To Coin a Phrase: On Organizational Talk, Organizational Control and Management Consulting*, Stockholm: Economics Research Institute, Stockholm School of Economics.

Duncan, H. D. (1969): *Symbols and Social Theory*, New York: Oxford University Press.

Ebers, Mark (1985): Understanding Organizations — The Poetic Mode, *Journal of Management*, VII, 2: 51—62.

Gadamer, Hans-Georg (1986: *The Relevance of the Beautiful*, Cambridge: Cambridge University Press.

Gherardi, Silvia and B. A. Turner (1988): Real Men Don't Collect Soft Data, *Quaderno*, 13, University of Trento: Trento.

Kriz, Jürgen (1988). *Facts and Artefacts in Social Science: An Epistemological and Methodological Analysis of Empirical Social Science Research Techniques*, Hamburg: McGraw Hill.

MacIver, R. M. (1947): *The Web of Government*, New York: Macmillan.

March, James G. and H. A. Simon (1958): *Organizations*, New York: Wiley.

March, James G. and J. P. Olsen (1976): *Ambiguity and Choice in Organizations*, Bergen: Universitetsforlaget.

Mennell, S. J. (1989): *Civilisation and the Human Self Image*, Oxford: Blackwell.

Morrison, D. E. and R. E. Henkel (1970): *The Significance Test Controversy: A Reader*, Chicago: Aldine.

Perrow, Charles (1979): *Complex Organizations: A Critical Essay*, New York: Random House.

Peters, Tom J. and R. H. Waterman (1982): *In Search of Excellence: Lessons from America's Best Run Companies*, New York: Harper and Row.

Pondy, Louis R., P. J. Frost, G. Morgan and T. C. Dandridge (eds.) (1983): *Organizational Symbolism*, Greenwich, Conn.: JAI Press.

Reason, Peter and J. Rowan (eds.) (1981): *Human Inquiry: A Source Book of New Paradigm Research*, Chichester: Wiley.

Turner, Barry A. (1986): Sociological Aspects of Organizational Symbolism, *Organization Studies*, 7, 2: 101–116.

Turner, Barry A. (1988): The Rise of Organizational Symbolism, in J. Hassard and Denis Pym (eds.), *New Theory and Philosophy of Organizations: Critical Issues and New Perspectives*, London: Routledge.

Part I
Symbolic Aspects of Organizations

Chapter 1
Painting Over Old Works: The Culture of Organization in an Age of Technical Rationality

Guy B. Adams and Virginia Hill Ingersoll

Only parts of the organizational world are visible. Only some of the behaviors and motivations of organizational actors are discussable. Even though the literature has begun to acknowledge the importance of symbolic aspects of organizations, rationalism and functionalism, sometimes subtly, sometimes not so subtly, recapture our thinking. The culture at large seems primarily responsible. The 'raw material' from which organizational symbols develop is given with the macroculture in which all organizations are nested. And the propensity to shape that raw material in particular ways, that is, into stories, images, rituals, and the like, is given with human nature — with the structure and processes of human cognition (Campbell 1956; Watzlawick 1978). This implies that if one is to understand organizational symbolism fully in any particular context one must study both the pertinent forms, meanings and content of the macroculture and the predispositions of human consciousness and cognition. This article attends to the first of these.

When the concept of culture began to be applied more widely to the study of organization, it promised to reveal symbolic aspects of organizational life which, to a large degree, have been less visible. The rationalist and functionalist approaches, heretofore dominant in the field of organization studies, revealed only part of what transpires in organizations — the frontstage performance, as it were. Symbolic aspects of organizations, largely unacknowledged, but crucial to an understanding of organizational dynamics, include those aspects idiosyncratic to particular organizations, 'regional' aspects which are shared across some organizations, and elements of the macroculture which are shared very broadly across many, and in some cases, all organizations.

The culture of the modern age is a culture of technical rationality. Technical rationality is ubiquitous in the modern work organization, so much so that one can easily characterize the present day culture as the culture of organization. Consequently, when the concept of culture was applied to the study of organizations, the best intentions of researchers yielded ironic results. Culture was utilized in the study of organizations in ways consistent, for the most part, with technical rationality. That is, rather than attending to culture as the larger context of meaning within which organizations are nested, researchers quickly narrowed their focus to individual organizations, as if they each evolved their own largely idiosyncratic "culture" *de novo*. Very quickly, organizational "culture" became another *technique* for the manager's tool kit, and many companies set out to reshape their "corporate culture," in much the same way that, say, a strategic plan might be initiated. Thus, the concept of culture was essentially misplaced, as it was applied to the study of organizations, and its misplacement was a predictable, though ironic, consequence of the cultural context within which it was applied, namely, technical rationality.

1.1 The Misplacement of Culture

It is ironic and also quite revealing that the literature speaks not of the culture of organizations, but of organizational "culture." As Gareth Morgan (1986) usefully points out, culture is a modern concept, at least in the English language, gaining its first usage as "civilization" or "social heritage" only in 1871. Still, culture has an established discourse within anthropology and sociology (Kroeber and Kluckhohn 1952), a discourse which suggests that to speak of organizational "culture" misplaces the concept of culture (Guerreiro-Ramos 1981).

Guerreiro-Ramos (1981) makes an important distinction between displacement[1] and misplacement in the use of concepts outside their primary discourse to build theory in other disciplines or fields. The concept of system, for example, was usefully displaced from its origins in cybernetics to the study of organization.[2] Misplacement occurs when a concept is used inappropriately outside its discourse of origin. This has occurred quite frequently with the concept of culture as used in the literature on organizations.

The concept of culture, in its discourse of origin within anthropology and sociology, refers to a shared set of beliefs, or a context of meaning (Turner 1986: 109), of a people. One might speak of a tribal culture, a primitive culture, or a national culture, for example. But as soon as the culture of a society is characterized in a way that suggests coherence or unity, ambiguities and contradictions make themselves felt. One is quickly led to the notion of "subculture." It may be useful, for example, to speak of the subculture of class, or of industrial subculture, as Barry Turner did in his groundbreaking book, *Exploring the Industrial Subculture*, in 1971. Turner's book marked

---

[1] See Schon (1963) for the initial statement on displacement of concepts.
[2] Katz and Kahn (1978) is perhaps the best known text, representative of this useful displacement.

the first extensive use of the concept of culture in the study of organization. His work usefully displaced the concept of culture from its discourse of origin into a new one, the study of organization.

In the decade of the 1980s, however, the use of culture has burgeoned in organization studies. Unfortunately, most of the literature misplaces the concept of culture, speaking of particular organizations as if they had their own particular culture. There are several ways, at least, to think about culture and organization. First, one might construe each organization's culture as unique. In this approach, culture is particularized as something that occurs within each organization. Secondly, a researcher might examine a number of organizations' unique cultures, in order to identify those aspects that they have in common. Finally, it is possible to consider the larger culture (the macroculture, or the national culture) for those aspects which are important across many organizations. Clearly, there are elements of the larger culture (our most widely shared context of meaning) which inform all organizations' symbol systems, and for that matter, the symbol systems of organizational researchers and managers as well. The former two approaches misplace the concept of culture as something wholly emergent within the organization. The latter displaces culture in a way consistent with its discourse of origin. Both academics and managers confuse subcultures as culture, and even talk as if such subcultures were mysteriously independent of the macroculture.

The pervasive confusion of subculture as culture is, in one sense, easily remediable. Greater care and precision in the use of language, it might be postulated, could rectify the confusion. After all, one could as easily discuss the subculture of the automobile industry, or even the subculture of General Motors, as the organizational culture of General Motors.

But the confusion is not trivial, and cannot be fixed merely by shifting labels. Rather it is fundamental and symptomatic of the culture of organization within which these investigations take place. The modern age is an age of technical rationality, and it powerfully conditions not only work life in organizations, but also the research work done on organizations. Further discussion of the sustained growth of the literature on culture and organization will help illuminate how this is so.

1.1.1 Recent Literature on Culture and Organization

While there was an explosion of interest in the notion of organizational "culture" through the middle of the decade of the 1980s, this interest already shows signs of waning and is unlikely to endure beyond the end of the decade except among some few academic circles. The origins of this brief infatuation with culture among organizational researchers are clear enough. For nearly twenty years, there has been a growing sense that mainstream approaches were achieving only limited results in understanding the dynamics of human interaction in organizations. This has been accompanied by the gradual evolution of alternative, interpretive frameworks, within which the concept of culture clearly fits. As Guerreiro-Ramos (1981: 61) notes:

The field of organization theory has been so promiscuously receptive to influences from so many different areas of knowledge that it now seems to have lost a sense of its specific assignment. Although cross-disciplinary relations are in general positive and even necessary to creativity, it is time for a serious appraisal of the state of the field, lest it become a mere hodge-podge of theoretical ramblings, lacking both force and direction.

Such an assessment is a reasonable result of a period in which many new directions are tried. Rather than models or paradigms, two influential books refer instead to the field trying on a succession of metaphors (Morgan 1986; Weick 1979). Using an organic metaphor, borrowed from biology (and ecology), some researchers (Miles and Kimberley 1980) have developed the idea of an organizational life cycle (birth, adolescence, maturity, etc.). Others more recently have likened organizations to brains, using the notion of holographic systems (Bohm 1980). There are many other examples.[3]

Culture may be seen as one among this succession of metaphors. However, culture as a concept, unlike many of the other metaphors, fits within a developing, alternative framework or paradigm within social science. In the 1960s, the arrival of the post-behavioral or post-positivist era of social science was heralded, somewhat prematurely. European philosophy and social theory, in particular, phenomenology, existentialism, and critical theory, provided a foundation for the development of alternative, interpretive frameworks (Bernstein 1976). Indigenous social theory (notably ethnomethodology and symbolic interactionism) also contributed. Perhaps the landmark book in this developing subculture was Peter Berger and Thomas Luckmann's *The Social Construction of Reality* published in 1967. The most noteworthy early attempt to apply this broad, and not wholly consistent, stream of thinking to organizations was David Silverman's *The Theory of Organization* (1970).

Although the decade of the seventies saw the publication of quite a number of related articles and a few books, it might best be described as a period of incubation. The end of the decade heralded a spate of conferences and books on symbolism, culture and related topics. A 1979 conference at the University of Illinois on Organizational Symbolism led to the publication of a book under the same title (Pondy et al. 1983). This conference was preceded by the formation of the Organizational Symbolism Network, a group primarily of academics coordinated by Thomas Dandridge of the State University of New York-Albany, and in Europe, the Standing Conference on Organizational Symbolism (SCOS), an offshoot of the European Group on Organization Studies (EGOS).

---

[3] See Morgan (1986) for a useful overview of eight metaphors, as well as an extensive bibliography.

Beginning in 1981, several iterations of a summer conference on Interpretive Approaches to the Study of Organization were held through the auspices of the University of Utah. Papers from the first two of these meetings were published in a collection edited by Putnam and Pacanawsky (1983). In 1983, a conference entitled "Myth, Symbols and Folklore: Expanding the Analysis of Organization" was organized by the University of California, Los Angeles (UCLA). This was followed by another conference in 1984, the first explicitly on organizational culture, "Organizational Culture and the Meaning of Life in the Workplace," which led to the volume by Frost et al., *Organizational Culture* (1985). Two other conferences were held in 1984: "Corporate Cultures: From the Natives' Point of View," in California, and at the University of Pittsburgh, "Managing Corporate Cultures." Many others followed.

Four influential journals devoted entire issues to the topic of organizational culture. The first was the *Administrative Science Quarterly* in Fall 1983. *The Journal of Management* and *Organizational Dynamics* followed in Spring and Fall 1984, respectively. And the European journal, *Organization Studies*, devoted its second issue in 1986 to organizational symbolism.

The practitioner-oriented literature, which seeks to reach managers as well as academics, also indicated a great deal of interest in the topic. The best selling book, *In Search of Excellence*, by Peters and Waterman went so far as to say (1982: xxi—xxii):

What really fascinated us as we began to pursue our survey of corporate excellence was that the more we dug, the more we realized the excellent companies abounded in such stories and imagery. We began to realize that these companies had cultures as strong as any Japanese organization. And the trappings of cultural excellence seemed recognizable, no matter what the industry. Whatever the business, by and large the companies were doing the same, sometimes cornball, always intense, always repetitive things to make sure all employees were buying into their culture — or opting out.

Similar characterizations of organizational culture can be found in Ouchi's, *Theory Z* (1984) and Deal and Kennedy's *Corporate Cultures*, (1982). With such an outpouring of both academically-oriented and practitioner-directed literature, one might suspect that a fundamental shift in the framework of organization studies had begun.

1.1.2 The Fundamental Shift That Wasn't

However, the early promise of the culture metaphor has not been fulfilled. This is documented in a recent article in the *Administrative Science Quarterly* (Barley, Meyer, and Gash 1988). The article notes two different, and as it happens, competing conceptions of the relationship between theory and practice. The first sees the relationship as the diffusion and utilization of knowledge, following the basic research-applied research model of engineering and physical science. The second conception, which the authors term the "political" perspective, suggests almost the opposite relationship. The questions investigated by theoreticians in applied fields are framed, if not directly asked, by practitioners, who control at least some of the resources available to academics and virtually all of the settings for applications of research. The article goes on to note that actual relations between theory and practice in a particular field may lie somewhere between these two extremes, and may vary over time in one direction or the other.

Through an extensive literature review and careful application of statistical techniques, the article asks whether, over time, the academic literature followed the practitioner literature, or vice versa, with regard to writing on organizational "culture." The overall conclusion was (Barley, Meyer, and Gash 1988: 32): "... the analysis clearly suggests that conceptual and symbolic influence flowed in only one direction: from practitioners to academics." Given the almost taken-for-granted status of the diffusion model, which assumes that influence flows in precisely the opposite direction, these results are startling (Barley, Meyer, and Gash 1988: 55):

... the results are consistent with the political theorist's claim that new streams of research in organizational behavior are readily coopted by the more powerful interests of managers and consultants ... That management's symbolic and conceptual influence could derail an academic movement interested in an alternative paradigm bodes ill for any sustained attempt to construct a social science of organizations that has no immediate practical relevance ... in organizational behavior there may exist a set of social pressures strong enough to compromise a stream of pure research in less than half a decade.

The academic literature moved away from an emphasis on (the emergence of) an interpretive framework for organization studies, and toward functionalism and rational control in organizations. We arrive, then, back where we started. Reports of the demise of mainstream social science (positivism, behavioralism, functionalism) appear to have been greatly exaggerated.

What accounts for the degeneration of a rich metaphor (in this case, culture) into a passing managerial fad? How is it that we appear unable to think our way out of the dominant paradigm sufficiently to produce anything other than ephemeral results? Answers to these questions, we believe, may be found in an examination of the culture of organization.

1.2 Technical Rationality: The Culture of Organization

The culture of organization is fundamentally modern. The modern age is an age of technical rationality. Technical rationality, as a way of thinking, has its antecedents at least as far back as Aristotle. However, as the foundation of the culture of organization, the cornerstone of technical rationality was laid down during the Progressive Era (1896 – 1916) in the United States. A confluence of two streams occurred during this period. The first stream is the scientific-analytical mindset that was the particular legacy of enlightenment thinking. The second stream was the product of the Great Transformation of the nineteenth century, and comprised the technological progress characteristic of this period of industrialization with its unparalleled succession of technological developments. Technical rationality is the convergence of the scientific-analytical mindset and technological progress. Beginning in the Progressive Era, it was applied to the social world and placed on the political agenda.

Technical rationality is quite similar to "functional rationality" as it was described by Karl Mannheim (1940). He saw functional rationality as the logical organization of tasks into smaller units, originally in the interest of efficiency. Mannheim contrasted this with "substantive rationality," the ability to understand the purposeful nature of the whole system of which a particular task is a part. Technical rationality is also closely akin to the notion of "instrumental reason" as it was discussed by Max Horkheimer (1947). Instrumental reason is the narrow application of human reason solely in the service of instrumental aims. Until the modern era, reason was conceived as a process incorporating ethical and normative concerns as well as the consideration of merely instrumental aims.

During the Progressive Era, technical rationality became the vehicle of hope in the social and political world.[4] It created a wave that before World War II had prompted new professionals, managers, behaviorists, social scientists, and industrial psychologists toward a world view in which human conflicts appeared as problems fit for engineering solutions. By the present time, as William Barrett states (1979: 229):

... it would be silly for anyone to announce that he is 'against' technology, whatever that might mean. We should have to be against ourselves in our present historical existence. We have now become dependent upon the increasingly complex and interlocking network of production for our barest necessities.

Some would suggest that the Progressive Era was merely an historical phase. According to some contemporary writers, we have had, since then, a "systems revolution" and an "information revolution" at least. Even if we have not made great strides in our understanding of organizations, we have at least evolved more and more sophisticated and complex theories and models to bring to bear on the study of organization.

---

[4] See Bendix (1956), for example.

These myriad attempts to capture the nature of organizations in words remind one of *pentimenti*, an Italian word which refers to a practice of artists. Because canvas and stretcher bars are expensive, it has been a common practice for centuries for artists to paint over their earlier paintings in an effort so save money. Over the years, though, an image — a *pentimento* — from the earlier painting often bleeds through what has been painted on top. Likewise, over the years organizational theorists have painted new versions of organization theories over the old, the organizational "culture" approach being among the most recent. While "culture" is thought of as affording an entirely new view of organizations, the old images continue to bleed through. These old images — images of technique and rationality — are part and parcel of the modern age, and they are not so easily covered over.

What accounts for the staying power of technical rationality? Why is water somehow central for fish? Just as water simply *is* the milieu, the surround of the fish, so culture simply *is* the milieu and surround of the human. The fact that there is wide variation across the cultures of humankind, and the fact that human action constructs and enacts culture (even as that culture in turn shapes human action), does not mean that culture is easily malleable, or even malleable at all within the extremely shortened time horizons of the present.

It is not easy to think our way out of technical rationality, the culture of organization; it is more difficult still to act our way out, to behave as if a different context of meaning, an alternate culture, were true. Argyris and Schon (1976) make a useful distinction between espoused theory, what we say we do, and theory in use, what we do in practice. Our espoused theory of organizational life has undergone a great deal of change in just the last twenty-five years, as noted earlier, but our theory in use has remained safely within the framework of the technical-rational mindset.

1.3 The Managerial Metamyth

We have been especially interested in aspects of the macroculture relevant to organizations. In earlier work (Ingersoll and Adams 1986), we discussed technical rationality as a set of beliefs found in management and organizations, and referred to it as the managerial metamyth (the prefix "meta" means "situated behind," and describes a myth that operates behind the scenes — backstage, as it were). The managerial metamyth includes the following beliefs: 1) eventually all work processes can and should be rationalized, i. e., broken into their constituent parts and so thoroughly understood that they can be completely controlled, 2) the means for attaining organizational objectives or ends deserve maximum attention, with the result that the ends quickly become subordinated to those means, even to the extent that the ends become lost or forgotten, and 3) efficiency and predictability are more important than any other considerations in managing an organization. Note that there is no suggestion that this is the way things actually work. Rather, this metamyth represents a set of shared beliefs — a context of meaning — about how things ought to be, about what is good and worthwhile. As such, the managerial metamyth tends to be used as a justification and a guide for organizational action. In the process it takes on the character of self-fulfilling prophecy.

The Managerial Metamyth is present in the academic and managerial subcultures, but these arenas are not its primary home. As we have emphasized throughout, the Metamyth is embedded in the macroculture, and that is precisely what makes it so pervasive, and accounts for its tenacity and persistence in our thought and action. As people cross the boundaries from one organization to another, they carry with them a set of symbolic baggage that includes all the images, words and routines associated with technical rationality. This symbolic baggage is an accretion based on life experience, some of it idiosyncratic, but all of it built on symbolic messages transmitted through various means to members of society. These pervasive symbolic messages include the mass media and literature of all kinds, among others.

1.4 The Culture of Organization: A Case Example

The themes embedded in the managerial metamyth are not just apparent in reflections of the symbolic environment, as discussed above. The same themes were found in field research on an organization conducted recently (Ingersoll 1987). The situation examined, involved the attempt of one organization to impose cultural elements on another organization. This was an instance in which the managerial metamyth itself constituted the overt content in the imposition of cultural elements, although the principals involved did not think of it in that way.

The focal organization had been self-sustaining for many years. However, in time of financial distress, it came increasingly under the control of another organization which manifested vastly different traditions, approaches to problem-solving, and norms of behavior. Indeed, this second organization was a strong adherent of modern management methods embodying the managerial metamyth. The story of this case illustrates that the imposition of culture is not accomplished easily, that people guard their prerogatives almost literally with their lives, and that the imposition of cultural elements is a decidedly political process.

The research began as an investigation of the impact of data processing installations on cultural aspects of organizations. Automation of an organization's practices and procedures require that those practices be made very explicit and that people reach agreement of the meaning of terms in the data bases on which the automation depends. Therefore, the act of automating at the very least makes a portion of the cultural ethos explicit.

Furthermore, since there is not likely to be complete agreement on language and practices once they are made explicit, automation represents a form of cultural conflict and change. Somebody's set of meanings needs to be adjusted if everybody's meanings are to be brought into agreement. If automation is imposed from above, as it most often is, it represents the imposition of cultural elements. As it turned out, the data processing installation was part of a much larger organizational change, one which resulted in a serious realignment of one organization's cultural ethos.

1.4.1 The Washington State Ferry System

The focal organization of this research was the Washington State Ferry System, which is the largest in the United States. It operates 22 vessels over 9 routes on Puget Sound and serves 20 terminals. During fiscal year 1984, it carried 17 million people and 7 million vehicles. The ferry system employs more than 1200 people, 97% of whom belong to one of 14 labor unions. Most of the riders use the ferries to commute between the various islands and peninsulas of Puget Sound and mainland cities, such as Seattle and Tacoma, but in the summers there are large numbers of tourists who ride the vessels for pleasure through the exquisitely beautiful Puget Sound waters.

Until 1951, the ferry system was privately owned by the Puget Sound Navigation Company, also called the Black Ball Line, a company which had grown up with Washington State and which had descended from an east coast firm that sailed large packet ships across the Atlantic during the nineteenth century and that was renowned for its reliability. The ferry system operated successfully under the Black Ball flag for the first half of the 20th century, although it came to be a regulated industry in such the same way that utilities are today in the United States. But after World War II, when costs went up and the state refused to allow the Black Ball Line to raise its fares to what the Company considered an adequate level, the state bought the ferry system — though the process was by no means as simple as we must portray it here. For the next 20 years, the system operated much as it had under Black Ball ownership — that is, like a privately owned enterprise which recovered its operating costs at the farebox. The only major difference under state ownership was that capital costs were met by the state through various bond issues. Once each year, the general manager of the ferry system would drive the 60 miles to Olympia, the state capital, to present the ferry system budget, but for the rest of the time the system was run from Seattle, at Colman Dock which is located at Pier 52.

During this era people were proud to work for the ferry system. People who worked in the offices at Colman Dock, where much of the research took place, reflected this pride, as well as the roots the system had in the family-owned Black Ball Line. The sense of a marine heritage was strong, and it was evident in management. As recently as seven years ago, people from the fleet (as opposed to "professional" managers) were still running the system. People who worked for the system at that time describe the situation as "one, big happy family."

Office practices and procedures gave evidence of their Black Ball roots, long after the state had bought the system. The accounting system reflected the fact that the ferry system had previously been a family-owned business and not a government entity. A home-grown system of accounting was used, and the books were kept manually. Until 1979, nothing in the ferry system was automated, with the exception of a partially automated payroll system that required a lot of manual entries and manual reporting. Managers had risen through the ranks, either in the offices or in the fleet; there were no so-called professional managers. It should be carefully noted that during these years, despite the merry-making and the old fashioned approach to management, the work always got done, the ferry system operated suc-cessfully — especially compared to other public transportation systems, and the staff was small. There were 18 or fewer management people, depending on how one counts these and on who is counting. Today, there are 47. (During the 1970s the number of vehicles carried by the ferries doubled and the number of passengers increased by 75%. However, the number of vessels and routes have changed very little.)

1.4.2 Setting the Stage for the Imposition

But all was not well. Beginning in 1972, the ferry system was beset with the rising costs that afflicted all public transportation systems. Fuel prices were skyrocketing, and labor costs were on the rise. This latter was of special concern in the ferry system where nearly everyone belonged to a union. From 1951, when the state took control of the ferry system, until 1972, the state had paid the system's capital costs, but ferry operations were self-sustaining. The Washington State Toll Bridge Authority acted as the ferry system's bonding authority for their capital needs, and the system was technically an appendage of the State Department of Highways, though nearly an autonomous one. Then, in 1972, the system needed operating money for the first time, and with the money came a kind of outside accountability the ferry system had never faced.

During the mid-70s the forces in Olympia, the state capital, were coalescing. Until this time, the ferry system had been but a loose appendage to the state. In an effort by the governor to get more control over the highway department, as well as to encourage an integrated transportation system statewide (and to jibe with federal funding strategies), the Department of Transportation (DOT) was formed. DOT became an operating entity in 1977.

1.4.3 The Imposition Begins in Earnest

The Department of Transportation (DOT) is predominately a highways organization. Its headquarters in Olympia are of massive concrete, the acrylic paintings in the hallways depict highways in a spare and dramatic way, and the heavy-looking sculpture on the grounds suggests primitive stone carving. Understandably, DOT management tends to have been trained as engineers, and, partly as an artifact of Olympia's proximity to the army base at Fort Lewis, many members of DOT have been retired Army men. Elements of military subculture are reflected in DOT's authority structure. As one person put it, "If the boss says jump, people jump." Someone even described DOT as a paramilitary organization. It was this professionally, even "scientifically" managed, engineering-oriented organization that would try to change the way things were run at Colman-Dock — and thereby to change the ferry system's ethos, at least in the offices and maintenance shops.

Several forces came together to favor DOT's ascendency over the ferry system. First, when state money is being spent, the law requires that it be accounted for in very specific ways and that purchases be negotiated according to explicit regulations. Second, some say that the ferry system had outgrown the antiquated system of accounting and the old-fashioned procedures that it had used since the days of the Black Ball Line. Third, with the local press eager for interesting copy, to say nothing of the fact that one of the local editors is a ferry commuter, any mistake within the ferry system made it immediately vulnerable to fickle public opinion. And fourth, the ferry system made mistakes. As one man put it, "We kept shooting ourselves in the foot."

The period from 1978–1981 was marked by crisis. First, the Hood Canal Bridge blew down in a storm, making it necessary for the ferry system to devise transport for the people across that waterway — a difficult feat when the ferry system's resources were already taxed to the maximum. Second, the state commissioned six new ferries, called Issaquah Class ferries after the name of the first such vessel to be built. In an effort to save money during a time when state revenues were thin, the Department of Transportation deviated from the usual method of bidding and building ferries, which called for bids to be made on complete plans that had been designed by a naval architect in full consultation with the ferry system. Instead, the ferries were bid on a design-construct contract, which resulted in the ferries being built with numerous deficiencies. This led to a third crisis, a strike. As vessel engineers with the ferry system became more and more concerned about the quality of the new ferries, they began to petition Olympia to take action. When Olympia seemed unresponsive to their expressions of concern, the engineers went on strike. This seemed to be the first of several incidents in which the expertise of ferry system personnel — that is, key elements of their cultural ethos — was discounted by DOT. It left many ferry system people very bitter. The strike had drawn attention to the issue of the Issaquah Class ferries, but the vessels were still built in a way that the engineers couldn't countenance. Today ferry system people and commuters refer to them as the "Citrus Class" boats — lemons one and all.

1.4.4 Enter: The Managerial Metamyth

New, professional management was brought to the ferry system in 1981, and one of the first actions was the commissioning of a study to be done on the ferry system by a Big Eight accounting firm. As is usual with such management audits, the firm recommended that the ferry system automate many of its management information systems and adopt less reactive management styles. That is, they should institute modern management techniques, including setting objectives, making long range plans, gathering information more systematically, and evaluating performance.

What the consultant's report called for and the process it set in motion to achieve those ends both fully embodied the principles of the managerial metamyth. Its recommendations called for development of "planning and performance measurement," for instance, which required rationalizing work processes, as well as automation, which demanded that implicit work steps be made explicit so that a program could be written to embrace them. The introductory paragraph to the report said, "In recent months questions have been raised as to whether the Washington State Ferry System (WSFS) has the management structure and systems to efficiently administer the approximately 1200 person organization which provides such a vital public service." That is, the drive for efficiency was a *raison d'être* for the study. And, as the study recommendations became implemented, especially in automated systems, the systems took on a life of their own. That is, the means became paramount and the objectives, while sometimes mentioned, became secondary. The managerial metamyth was fully manifested in the consultant's report and its outcomes.

1.4.5 The Role of Automation

During the next four years, the leading edge of DOT's attempt to gain ascendency over the ferry system comprised the new management, the efforts to implement the consultant's recommendations, and the replacement of existing ferry system personnel, many of whom had come from the fleet. All three of these seemed to coalesce in the automation effort.

Automation projects were considered for a number of ferry system operations: dispatching of crews, toll collection, payroll, traffic statistics, inventory control, maintenance management, and finance/accounting. (Five years later, the only automated system fully operating is payroll — and what's operating there is an update on the old NCR system that was undertaken in 1979, two years before the consultant was hired. The payroll system considered in 1982 was a version which would run on the DOT computers, instead of the computer local to the ferry system. But the effort continues.)

1.4.6 Aspects of DOT Ascendency

Meanwhile, DOT was exerting its influence elsewhere. In the fleet it was installing bell loggers, called Black Boxes and Tattle Tales by the men who installed them. The bell loggers record all the operations a captain performs in the wheelhouse, so if there's an accident it can be determined whether the captain exercised poor judgment or not. In an effort to monitor how fast captains were running their boats — since the vessels burn more fuel at higher speeds — fuel monitors also were being installed. Both of these devices were costly, and the men who installed them resented the cost at a time when the ferry system was under strong pressure to reduce costs. The devices represented management's distrust of the captains, and they may have been the result of captains' efforts to maintain their autonomy from DOT. They also are indicative of the managerial metamyth, for they provide means of measurement in an effort to gain greater control. Atop each vessel now rides the "Flying T," the logo of the DOT, something which galls the people in maintenance and in the fleet, but which also symbolizes DOT's ascendency over the ferry system.

1.4.7 The Imposition of Cultural Elements

The initial impetus for this research had been the question about how installation of automated systems might affect cultural aspects of organizations. It quickly became apparent that the question was much too narrow. The meaning of automating, at least in this situation, lay in power relationships that transcended issues of technical advancement and even cost. DOT was interested in making the ferry system more accountable for the money it was getting, but the accountability was going to be expressed in DOT language and in terms of DOT's computers, despite the fact that the fit between highway construction and a ferry system — to state the contrast in its most simple and direct form — is awkward even in such rudimentary management activities as accounting.

The ferry system was getting ugly publicity over such items as the Issaquah Class ferries crisis and the budget problems, and if DOT was going to have to suffer public displeasure, to say nothing about embarrassment, it was going to shape the system up. To institute a system of top down accountability, in which every expenditure could be traced to a person, would give DOT a lot of control. Automating was a way to achieve this aim. And to adopt and use the automated system *de facto* required a much different way of articulating ferry system activities, that is, the imposition of ascendant cultural elements upon a necessarily submissive organization. This change is understandable only through reference to elements of the macroculture — in this case technical rationality and its offspring, the managerial metamyth.

The presence of the managerial metamyth seems to indicate that there is one stream of cultural content that transcends organizational boundaries and that informs the culture of many organizational groups. The metamyth was evident in the consultant's report, it is manifest in DOT (though there wasn't space to treat that in detail here), and it is part of the language of managers who have come from DOT to the ferry system. Some might say that such language — replete with words such as accountability, planning, evaluation, performance review, and efficiency are what management is all about, and that the words represent an essential approach to the successful operation of large, complex organizations. The very acceptance of the necessity of an approach that embodies this language is evidence that it is indeed part of a culture that transcends particular organizations. And the fact that it becomes embodied in procedures and activities, such as automation, which are not resisted without great cost indicates that the metamyth can become embedded in a group's ethos, even though it includes values alien to the group's initial tradition.

1.5 A Culture-Sensitive Approach to the Study of Organization

We have attempted here to expand the visible in the realm of organizational dynamics, by shedding light on aspects of organizations which are not easily seen. It is ironic to note that aspects of the macroculture, such as the managerial metamyth, are not visible, or only partially visible, in our thinking about organizations. The macroculture, as a context of meaning is ubiquitous; it should be everywhere visible. It is a paradox of the age of technical rationality, which urges us to analyze, to isolate figure from ground, object from context, that the context itself, culture, becomes submerged, invisible as it were.

Attention to the symbolic environment of organizations represents an attempt to bring what is hidden to light. As we have seen, it is far easier to espouse the centrality of symbols than it is to alter one's theory in use, one's world view. We have seen already how the literature on organizational culture lapsed back into functionalism and technical rationality. Organizational researchers, it must be obvious, are hardly immune from the surrounding culture.

In earlier work (Adams and Ingersoll 1985), we described the difficulties of developing a culture-sensitive approach to the study of organizations. A culture-sensitive approach suggests a different conception of the research enterprise; a conception which understands research as aesthetic, as the bringing forth of concealed aspects, and as a manifestation of both care and projection. Such an alternate conception of research may not be an easy mental task for the traditionally trained academic. And it is perhaps even more difficult to actually *do* research differently than we have been taught to. The lesson suggested by the pentimenti recurs, and recurs again.

References

Adams, Guy B. and Virginia Hill Ingersoll (1985): The Difficulty of Framing a Perspective on Organizational Culture, in Peter J. Frost et al., *Organizational Culture*, Beverly Hills, CA: Sage Publications.

Argyris, Chris and Donald A. Schon (1976): *Organizational Learning: A Theory of Action Perspective*, Reading, MA: Addison Wesley.

Barley, Stephen R., Gordon W. Meyer, and Debra C. Gash (1988): Cultures of Culture: Academics, Practitioners and the Pragmatics of Normative Control, *Administrative Science Quarterly*, 33 (March): 24–60.

Barrett, William (1979): *The Illusion of Technique*, Garden City, NY: Anchor Press/ Doubleday.

Bendix, Reinhard (1956): *Work and Authority in Industry*, New York: John Wiley.

Berger, Peter and Thomas Luckmann (1967): *The Social Construction of Reality*, Garden City, NY: Doubleday/Anchor.

Bernstein, Richard (1976): *The Restructuring of Social and Political Theory*, New York: Harcourt, Brace, Jovanovich.

Bohm, David (1980): *Wholeness and the Implicate Order*, London: Routledge and Kegan Paul.

Campbell, Joseph (1956): *The Hero With a Thousand Faces*, Cleveland: World Publishing.

Deal, T. E. and A. A. Kennedy (1982): *Corporate Cultures*, Reading, MA: Addison Wesley.

Frost, Peter J. et al. (eds.) (1985): *Organizational Culture*, Beverly Hills, CA: Sage Publications.

Guerreiro-Ramos, Alberto (1981): *The New Science of Organization*, Toronto: University of Toronto Press.

Horkheimer, Max (1947): *The Eclipse of Reason*, New York: Oxford University Press.

Ingersoll, Virginia Hill (1987): *Strapped On: Modern Management and the Washington State Ferries*, Unpublished manuscript, Olympia, WA.

Ingersoll, Virginia Hill and Guy B. Adams (1983): *The Child is 'Father' to the Manager: Images of Organizational Behavior in Children's Literature*, Paper presented to the First International Imagery Conference, Queenstown, New Zealand.

Ingersoll, Virginia Hill and Guy B. Adams (1986): Beyond Organizational Boundaries: Exploring the Managerial Metamyth, *Administration and Society*, 18 (November): 360 – 381.

Ingersoll, Virginia Hill and Guy B. Adams (1987): A Trip into Deep Water: Imposing Cultural Elements Across Organizational Boundaries, *Dragon*, 2 (April): 11 – 41.

Katz, Daniel and Robert Kahn (1978): *The Social Psychology of Organizations*, New York: John Wiley.

Kroeber, A. L. and C. Kluckhohn (1952): *Culture: A Critical Review of Concepts and Definitions*, Cambridge, MA: Harvard University Press.

Mannheim, Karl (1940): *Man and Society in an Age of Reconstruction*, New York: Harcourt, Brace, Jovanovich.

Miles, R. H. and J. R. Kimberly (1980): *The Organizational Life Cycle*, San Francisco: Jossey-Bass.

Morgan, Gareth (1986): *Images of Organization*, Beverly Hills, CA: Sage Publications.

Ouchi, William (1984): *Theory Z*, Reading, MA: Addison-Wesley.

Peters, Thomas J. and Robert H. Waterman (1982): *In Search of Excellence*, New York: Harper and Row.

Pondy, Louis et al. (eds.) (1983): *Organizational Symbolism*, Greenwich, CT: JAI Press.

Putman, Linda and Michael Pacanawsky (eds.) (1983): *Communication and Organization*, Beverly Hills, CA: Sage Publications.

Schon, A. Donald (1963): *Displacement of Concepts*, London: Tavistock Publications.

Silverman, David (1970): *The Theory of Organization*, New York: Basic Books.

Turner, Barry A. (1971): *Exploring the Industrial Subculture*, New York: Herder and Herder.

Turner, Barry A. (1986): Sociological Aspects of Organizational Symbolism, *Organization Studies*, 7,2: 101 – 116.

Watzlawick, Paul (1978): *The Language of Change*, New York: Basic Books.

Weick, Karl (1979): *The Social Psychology of Organizing*, Reading, MA: Addison-Wesley.

Chapter 2
Interrelations Between Corporate Culture and Municipal Culture: The Lüneburg Saltworks as a Medieval Example

Egbert Kahle

2.1 Introduction

The intention of this paper is to demonstrate through the example of the Lüneburg saltworks and its medieval form of organization the influence of municipal culture on organizational culture and vice versa and to indicate that the possible forms of transaction — not only the costs of transactions — which involve special institutional symbolisms provide the set of conditions within which special forms of organizations can evolve. For this purpose it is necessary to give a sketchy overview of the general conditions of the saltworks and the production of salt in a medieval town in Northern Germany.

2.2 The General Conditions

It is documented since 956 A.D. that there has been a fountain of brine in Lüneburg from which salt is produced. This brine is fully saturated and without pollution from other minerals. So it can be cooked into salt without any cleaning and thickening which cost labour and energy. According to German common law mineral resources, including brine, were owned by the crown, i.e. the Dukes of Lüneburg and Brunswick. The crown leased the fountain and the privilege of the production of salt to the townspeople, the citizens of Lüneburg. The town was characterized by two other features: a fortress on a dominating hill (or mountain) as a border fortification against the neighbouring tribes of Slavonians and the northernmost ford across a river which opens into the unfordable Elbe (Reinecke 1977: 8 ff.).

According to the first recorded accounts of saltern organization the production of salt was organized in the following way until 1800:
All the brine fountains — numbering 8 to 12 — gave their supply to a general fountain called *Sod* by means of a subterranean canal system. Special

labourers heaved the brine from this *Sod* with buckets and distributed it to huts, where it was cooked or boiled. The saltern consisted of 52 huts. They were all alike. In each hut there were four boiling pans of nearly square form and a metre length and breadth and 25 cm height. The pans were all alike, made from lead and procured by a forge which belonged to the saltworks. Each pan sat on a wood-fired hearth. In full production the saltworks needed 50 000 cubic metres of wood per year (Kahle 1987: 1 ff.). As early as 1200 and presumably much earlier the ownership of the brine had been distributed from the crown to different persons and institutions; the persons were the gentry of the surrounding area, whose duty was the manning of the fortress, and some townspeople; the institutions were all kinds of clerical ones: churches and abbeys all over Northern Germany and parts of Northern Europe (Reinecke 1977: 41 and 191 ff.). These clerical institutions made up the greatest number of owners, so that owners as a whole were called the *Prelates*. Ownership was measured in pans or part of pans; each of the four pans in each hut had its specified place (the left front pan, the left rear pan, etc.); each hut had its own name (Reinecke 1977: 191). By this means of identification each part of ownership was defined; the ownership of a pan gave the right of getting the due part of the brine.

The process of boiling the brine into salt and the selling of the salt was permitted only to citizens of Lüneburg. Like all other crafts and industries in medieval times these saltmakers were incorporated in a guild. They called themselves *Sülfmeister*, that is "independent masters," because they worked on their own; working for another person, especially for strangers, was strictly forbidden (Reinecke 1977: 396). In each hut were five workers, each with special duties. This number, added to the brine bearers, the forge workers and some central staff for cleaning and watch duties and for administration, gives the number of employees of the saltern, that is 300; in a town of 14 000 inhabitants that is a recognizable part. The saltwork, consisting of the fountain, the salt-cooking huts and the forge, was surrounded by a wall; it lay within the walls of the city of Lüneburg and was therefore a part of it, but a distinguished one. The wall between saltworks and habitation area of the city was a defence against the stealing of salt and against the dangerous fires which more than once consumed the cooking huts.

2.3 The Organizational Symbolism

By location and membership rules, the saltwork as an organization was therefore a part of the city; but due to the mostly foreign ownership of the basic production supply there were special organizational forms and a special organizational culture. Before dealing with these regulations I have to explain some organizational symbols and symbolic transactions connected with the saltwork.

In the Middle Ages the German law was a declaratory one; transactions had to be done publicly to be valid. The written record of a transaction was only a reminder of the real transaction. This legal feature was important for the organizational form and regulations of the saltwork. As I have described above there were a great number of owners of pans or parts of pans and 52 huts in which salt was cooked. To be a saltmaster one had to get the right to get the brine from four pans at a minimum by leasing them from the owners. The leasing contract was fixed for one year and could be prolonged every year. The saltmaster had to pay a fixed sum per quantity of brine for the leasing. This sum increased over the course of time by the addition of extra payments called "friendships," "beneficiaries" and so on.

To get the sum of four pans one would possibly need ten or more contracts and these contracts would belong mostly to different huts. It would have been impossible to organize the production in different huts, if every contract had been actually executed in the hut it was assigned to. Therefore the saltmasters chose one of their own as the Master of Barter (*Bütemeister*); when the production year ended, about the 10th of December, renewing or changing of contracts took place; until Christmas everyone who wanted to be a saltmaster had to show his contracts to the Master of Barter; he assigned to them the huts; contracts which didn't sum up to four pans "went into the barter," that means, they were executed by others and the contractor got a fixed sum (Zenker 1906: 27). If there was a newcomer to the contractors he had to gain acceptance to the guild of the saltmasters; otherwise he was not allowed to execute his contract. He could only be rejected if he was not a citizen of Lüneburg or not of an honourable profession; women were generally rejected. The announcement of companionship in the guild and of the newly assigned huts took place in a chapel outside the saltworks, just opposite the gates. This chapel was the assembly room of the saltmasters guild and their special worship chapel. In these contract and membership affairs the public meant the members of the guild.

The public of the transfer of ownership in the saltworks was the general public. There was a special judgement stone on the outside of the saltmasters chapel, which was the only place where legal commitments concerning the saltworks could be done. To transfer ownership of a pan or part of a pan the former owner had to take a burning log from the pan which belonged to him and give it to the future owner in front of the judgement stones. Only this public declaration made the transfer valid, and even the Duke of Lüneburg followed this regulation when he transferred one of his pans to the cathedral of Lübeck (Reinecke 1977: 194).

Another special form of personal transaction took place in the buying of firewood. The great demand for firewood, which is said to be the cause of existence of the Lüneburg heath, led to a strong competition between the saltmasters to get enough firewood. The sale could only be contracted by personal agreement of buyer and seller. The firewood came by carts from the surrounding villages and the farmers who delivered it came to the saltwork to sell it. There the saltmaster was allowed to negotiate with the oncoming farmer; no other buyer was allowed to give his offer while the first one was negotiating.

Only when an agreement between the first in line and the seller had failed the next had his try. It was forbidden to negotiate with the oncoming farmers at another place or to buy the wood in the villages and have it delivered. Wood that was bought against the regulations was either confiscated or the buyer was heavily fined (Volger 1956: 47). Similar to the regulations for the supply of production factors (brine, pans, firewood) there were regulations concerning the selling of the salt. The saltmasters were producers and dealers *en gros*; they were not allowed to sell salt in small quantities. The selling *en detail* was done by a special shop owned by the guild. The minimum quantity to be sold by the saltmasters was a barrel; mostly they sold it by the shipload. There was a special kind of ship matching the measurements of a canal from the Elbe to the Baltic Sea (Lübeck), which could load 10.6 metric tons (Witthöft 1976: 2f. and 31 f.). The barrels for stowing the salt were standardized by the coopers guild; they had a stamp showing that they contained good Lüneburg Salt. This stamp was a symbol of the city and the saltworks. It included the initials of the three features of the city and looked like a map of the saltworks.

2.4 The Interrelations of Corporate and Municipal Culture

The connections between city and saltworks may be easily and clearly derived from these technical and legal conditions. In medieval times, when salt was the only means of preservation for meat and vegetables, producing and selling salt was a most profitable industry. The saltmasters got very rich and so did the town itself. As in other medieval cities, the members of the richest and most important industry were the men of council and mayorship. But it was not quite that simple. The guild of saltmasters did not simply constitute the council of the city or choose it; the coming into office was a more complex process. There were different offices in saltworks and city, as is shown in figures 2.1 and 2.2. In the saltwork there was the above mentioned Master of Barter, there were two Masters of the Forge who had to direct the works in the forge and supply it with the necessary lead and there was

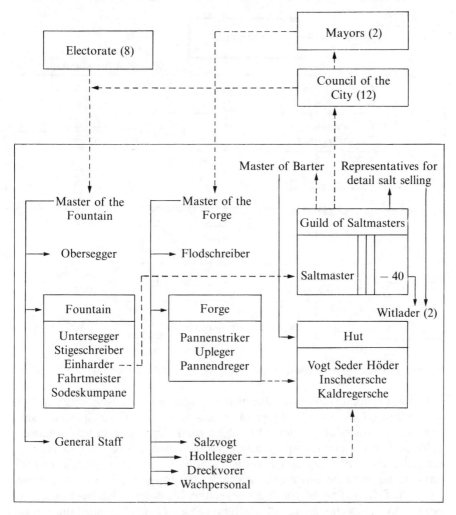

Figure 2.1 Organizational chart of the medieval Lüneburg saltern

the Master of the Fountain, who was the Chief Executive Officer of the saltworks; he represented the saltworks in all matters and had to regulate the bookkeeping and accounting of the saltworks, the distribution of the brine and the registration of sales prices. In the city there were twelve members of council, in pairs responsible for taxes, fire regulations, jurisdiction, defense and commerce, and two mayors, one of them the Speaking Mayor: he was head of the town. The officers in the saltworks were appointed for one year and reappointment was possible; the council membership and mayorship was for life.

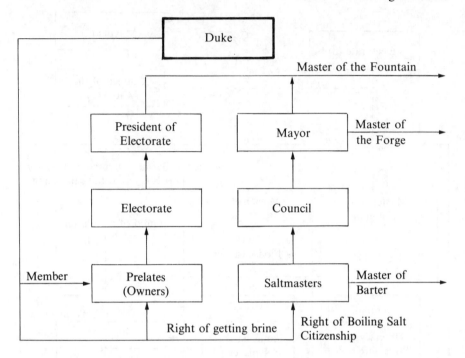

Figure 2.2 The corporate constitution of the medieval Lüneburg saltern

In the beginning saltmastership was open to anybody who was a citizen of Lüneburg. Later on it became more or less hereditary. Council membership required membership in the saltmasters guild; but there were saltmasters belonging to the council and saltmasters not belonging to the council. The council was filled up by cooperation. Usually, becoming a council member required having held office as a Master of the Forge for one year or more. The Chief Executive of the Saltworks, the Master of the Fountain, was elected by a special group of electors consisting of the most important owners and the two mayors of the city. This office required knowledge in accountancy and in all matters of the saltwork; therefore mostly council members with experience in taxes became Masters of the Fountain. In the year of his office, this master was not allowed to execute his contracts as a saltmaster. The mayors, whose concern was the well-being of the city and its biggest trade, were chosen by the council from their own ranks and very often were former Masters of the Fountain (Reinecke 1977: 253 f.).

The saltworks and its labourers and the saltmasters and their guild were integrated in the city, but they were something special. So their organizational rules, especially the implicit ones we try to recollect under the aspect of organizational culture, were part of the municipal culture which made it different from municipal culture in other cities. One element was the role in the municipal defence system: the guilds were not only commercial coalitions, but a modified continuation of the pre-historic and early German fighting community. The Germans fought together in clans; kinsmanship was the bond of helping each other in war. In the medieval city this bond of kinsmanship was replaced by the guild, which regulated the commercial problems between guild members and their co-workers, in which the members held their festivities and their worship and which was the basic unit of the defence system of a city. Each guild had its assembly place and a part of the wall to defend. The saltmasters and their workers defended the outer walls of the saltworks which were in that part the city wall. The saltmasters were the reigning group of the city and in the course of time they became a hereditary gentry, who led the whole defence system of the city. In many a strife and war, in defence of the city and in giving assistance to the Hanse, saltmasters were the leaders of the troops of the city, which consisted of citizens and of hired mercenaries.

So it was a special feast when the young saltmaster got his first office in the saltworks; he had to show his ability as a nobleman, his horsemanship, in a special way. A big barrel, of three metres length and two metres diameter, filled with rocks had to be drawn through the streets of the city by his horse; this had to be done as fast as possible. This obligation was an opportunity for showing riding ability as much as richness of garment, and in the course of time this event became a kind of carnival with a great number of adjoining people in different costumes. After the show in the streets the new Master of the Forge entertained the fellow members of his guild in the chapel with a big meal and the public got its due part of eating and drinking (Reinecke 1977: 370 f.).

Another special feature of the organizational and the municipal culture was the way both communities enforced conformity to regulations. There was a criminal law and criminal court, but most smaller offences against regulations were solved with fines and in heavier cases with house confinement. Everybody knew everybody, so there was no need for confinement in a prison; only foreign trespassers and people accused of capital crimes were held in prison. The same kind of social control was efficient enough to bring about tax honesty. Each citizen had to show up before the tax accounting council member and to estimate in public his own property; from this self-estimation he had to pay his due tax (a penny from a mark, the mark having 192 pennies) (Reinecke 1977: 176). The self-esteem was enough to create honesty, perhaps more an over-estimation than an under-estimation. If someone tried to cheat, he would have been cut from all social relations; nobody would speak, eat or have commerce with a cheater.

In similar way the guild regulated its own affairs, strictly and without great commotion. Smaller offences — like being late for a guild session and so on — were punished with fines which filled the treasury of the guild. Heavier offences and not paying fines led to exclusion from the forge — a new pan was needed every four to six weeks — or from the fountain. Without pans or brine production was impossible (Reinecke 1977: 362, 367). So there never were successful offences against guild regulations except those which went undetected; but that was nearly impossible in a production that went on in public.

Another point of interrelation is the strategy for securing the markets for the salt and the supply of wood. Today it would be the duty of the Chief Executive of the Saltworks to define politics in opening and securing the markets for salt and the supply of wood. Instead of this, the council and especially the mayor of the city worked out contracts with the foreign dignitaries, the Kings of Denmark and Sweden, the Electors of Brandenburg and Saxonia, the Dukes of Mecklenburg and the neighbouring counts, and with the emperor himself. This was necessary because the saltwork was no institution according to the medieval law and the saltmasters guild — as important and powerful it was — was in no way a partner for earls, kings and emperors. So the city acquired privileges for selling salt in a monopoly all over Northern Europe. They acquired the privilege that all commodities going from areas south of Lüneburg to the north had to go via Lüneburg and there they were taxed and stapled for three days. These privileges were bought with much money which came from taxes paid in the city and from direct contributions from the saltworks. Similarly the supply of firewood was sustained by supply contracts the city transacted with neighbouring cities and countries; there was a special canal built in the Dukedom of Mecklenburg which connected the Elbe with the deep forest of this dukedom, from which much wood was imported. These contracts and the canal were financed by special payments from the saltworks (Reinecke 1977: 290 f.).

On the other hand, it was necessary for such a rich city to be properly defended. There was a great amount of armour and cannons in the arsenals of the city; in normal times there was a troop of "riding servants" or *gens d'armes*" to secure the gates. To secure the ways and roads around the city, many castles were bought or leased within a circle of more than 40 kilometres around the city. These military actions were financed not only from the city treasury but by special payments of the saltworks. The discussion about these payments became heated at the beginning of the 15th century and led to a hundred-year-conflict between the city and the saltmasters on one side and the saltprelates on the other side; in the end the city came off the better (Reinecke 1977: 203 — 243).

So the duties and the goals of the city and the organization were not divisible. All this ended with the year 1800, when the saltworks became a government plant under the direct supervision of the government of the Kingdom of Hannover.

2.5 Conclusions

The relationship between the municipal and the corporate culture in this case can be described in general terms by following features:

The corporate culture was a subculture of the municipal culture, restricted to economic affairs, whereas the municipal culture contained various kinds of relations. Both cultures were semi-closed, that means, admission was granted by cooptation; the corporation had a limited number of possible members. Regulation and control in both cultures used the same means: social control by the peers and arbitration of differences by a code of standard behavior or by voting of the peers. Representatives of the city as well as the corporation were elected; in the majority of offices there were two men in one office for mutual control. As usual in medieval Germany the codes of standard behavior were not written down in a constitution or law but handed down by habit and repeated practice.

The corporation of the *Sülfmeister* was not a rational planned enterprise but a way of living in this city; rationality is found only within the limits of the opportunities these ways of living offer.

References

Kahle, E. (1987): Die Organisation der Saline Lüneburg vom Mittelalter bis ins 19. Jahrhundert, *Zeitschrift für Unternehmensgeschichte*, 1: 1 – 22.

Reinecke, W. (1977): *Geschichte der Stadt Lüneburg*, (2 vols., reprint of original from 1933). Heinrich-Heine Verlagsbuchhandlung, Lüneburg.

Volger, F. W. (1956): *Die Lüneburger Sülze*, Museumsverein, Lüneburg.

Witthöft, H. (1976): Struktur und Kapazität der Lüneburger Saline seit dem 12. Jahrhundert, Offprint from *Vierteljahresschrift für Sozial- und Wirtschaftsge-schichte*, 63, 1: 1 – 112.

Zenker, L. (1906): *Zur volkswirtschaftlichen Bedeutung der Lüneburger Saline für die Zeit von 950 – 1370*, Hannover und Leipzig. Forschungen zur Geschichte Niedersachsens 1, 2.

Chapter 3
Corporate Culture, the Catholic Ethic and the Spirit of Capitalism: A Quebec Experience

Omar Aktouf

3.1 Foreword

Over recent years a great deal of writing and discussion has been generated about what are called "new work methods," covering a number of topics, from Japan, IBM, third-wave companies, shared ownership, "company projects" to freedom of expression, profit sharing, emergence of new social agents in the company ....[1] The principles and models being advocated constitute a veritable jungle of new work methods, though, especially in North America, various attempts to save the status quo and its systems of privileges predominate. Still, as concerns the basic problem being addressed, there is complete consensus: work relationships now prevalent in the West must be revised in view of the stunning impact of Japanese and West German models.

But the question I would here like to examine and answer is: To what extent does Cascades Inc., a Quebec pulp and paper company started from scratch in 1963, owe its brilliant success during the 1979—84 recession and its current spectacular rise as a multinational to an almost radical transformation of work relationships, accomplished quite spontaneously through on-the-ground activity? The executives of this company never tire of saying that there is an open secret: Workers can expect fair treatment, treatment based on honesty, openness, listening and sharing; an almost total absence of hierarchy; this is what they call the "Cascades philosophy."[2]

I have been studying the Cascades phenomenon since 1985. My research has consisted in numerous visits to the company's plants, on-site interviews and participatory observations. And I have bowed to the growing conviction that the spontaneity of this attitude on the part of Cascades executives somehow springs from the resurgence of a feudal and Catholic strain of

---

[1] See Bosche 1984; Nizard 1983—4; Sainsaulieu 1983; Vogel 1983; Wegnez 1984; Archier and Sérieyx 1984; Peters and Waterman 1982.

[2] I have presented all the details and principles related to this system of management — its philosophy, its concrete impact, etc. — in Aktouf and Chrétien 1987.

civilization and the new encounter of its particular ethic with the spirit of capitalism.

3.2 Genesis of Capitalism and Evolutionary Differences Between the Ethics of Northern and Southern Europe from the 13th to the 18th Century

Schumpeter (1979), along with Cooke (1950) who is supported by Braudel (1982: 5), is, I believe, closer to the truth than we might like when he states that Italian scholastic philosophers were quite right to condemn the scientific "progress" taking place between the 15th and 17th centuries. In it they instinctively felt the rising tide of individualistic rationalism and its companion, capitalism – the movement that Cooke (1950) calls the "capitalist metaphysics." I agree with Schumpeter (1979) that, as early as the period between the 15th and 17th centuries, the utilitarian charm of the sciences (especially in the almost exclusive application of mathematics to problems of commercial accounting and architecture) marks the birth of a new mentality in Western Europe. Weber would dub this mentality the "spirit of capitalism."

According to common elements gleaned from authoritative sources,[3] this spirit is rooted in progress in the use of money and its corollaries: cost accounting and double entry bookkeeping (Weber 1971). Moreover, these authors almost all agree that the post-Renaissance rationalization of scientific thought concurs with the doctrinal principles of Lutheranism, the Calvinist dogma of predestination and the soon-to-appear Puritan revolution to provide a lasting foundation for what may be called the system of symbolic and moral representations of the promoters and artisans of Northern European capitalism.

Double entry bookkeeping was already being practised in 13th-century Florence and in 1494 Luca Pacioli published his *Summa di arithmetica*, containing the "complete model of double entry accounting." (Braudel 1982: 555) Calvin's pronouncement on usury dates from 1545, and, according to Braudel, in 1517 Matthäus Schwartz, bookkeeper for the Dutch Fuggers, is already condemning, in the name of double entry accounting, "transactions recorded on scraps of paper and stuck on walls by merchants." (ibid.: 572)

Meanwhile, Lutheranism was, as we know, provoking a turmoil of intense emotions in Christendom, especially in Northern Europe. With Luther the

---

[3] These include Schumpeter; Sombart; Weber.

notion of *"beruf"* adds to its usual connotations of trade, profession, vocation, and calling the concept of "task imposed by God." According to Weber (1958: 79 – 80), this new meaning is transferred to the social sphere and generalized as the rationalistic and moral precept by which the West viewed: "fulfilment of duty in worldly affairs as the highest form which the moral activity of the individual could assume." (Weber 1958: 79 – 80) The way to become more acceptable in God's sight was not through monastic asceticism but rather through the fulfilment of the obligations imposed by one's station in the world. Weber sees this religious shift in the meaning of *beruf* as one of the milestones of "capitalist civilization," by which "everyday worldly activity (acquires) a religious significance" (Weber 1958: 80).

But, in Weber's assessment, it is Calvinism and, in particular, its puritanical aftermath which would stamp the capitalist mentality of Northern Europe. Calvin contributes what Weber calls the "puritan dogma" and, of course, an almost unequivocal acceptance of usury, or, to be more precise, of "licit" interest on loans involving a "risk." Usury can be licit if it is moderate and used among merchants. Only when it goes against the rule of charity is it clearly illicit. While officially opening the door to lending at interest, this interpretation, by its prescription of "moderate" interest rates, also paves the way for the broader social acceptance of such loans.

Weber points to Calvin's dogmatic declaration that each man's destiny has been established by "divine decrees", since the foundation of the world. Contrary to Catholic beliefs, no act, confession, or repentance can hope to "alter God's will." One is either elected or not, and one must follow the predestined path alone. Each man who is passionately dedicated to his *beruf* is an instrument of God's divine power acting through him. (ibid. 90 – 103)

Sombart states unequivocally that "rationality" is the essence of "western evolution" and that "without double entry accounting capitalism would be inconceivable," the former being the "form" of the latter's content.[4]

The main point to be noted is the degree to which classical management doctrine enshrines these principles, from the self-confidence and materialistic individualism of Calvinism (the conviction that material success and winning place one safely among the elect) through Lutheranism's *beruf* and solitary destiny to the accounting mentality of technocratic and managerial rationalism. Alexis de Tocqueville (*Democracy in America*) and Weber (*Economy and Sociology*) both clearly predicted the triumph of this new form of domination.

In corporate life this has led to dehumanized relationships and the chilling control of technical accounting over organization, division of labour, decision-making, management methods, recruitment and so forth. Everything — qualifications, training, hiring, personnel — pays tribute to this cost/benefit

---

[4] Quoted by Braudel 1982: 573.

logic which, with its arithmetic infallibility, treats the employee like a simple investment. Already made a marketable commodity by the wage economy (as Marx showed), the employee is now only an abstraction to be periodically aligned in income statements. For the traditional capitalist employer, this is the essential meaning of labour.

Nothing has influenced the practice and teaching of modern management more than the science of economics, and this marks another triumph of double entry accounting. We are reminded of this by Granger (1976: 1020): starting with Quesnay "economics will consist in describing, in the manner of accountants, the circulation of global quantities of products and money . . . ." Society is reduced to "producers," "consumers," and "services," all three henceforth considered mechanisms for the circulation of money and sites for calculating costs and benefits. Similarly, the "nation" is transformed into a series of "corporate endeavours."

Yet, as Braudel (1982) points out, the logic and practice of accounting were scarcely confined to Northern Europe and protestant countries. Why is it that the triumph of the "spirit of capitalism" was so much weaker (or slower) in the regions of Southern Europe?

To answer this question we must perhaps go back to Aristotle and the widespread hostility to money as: "an intrusion of impersonal exchange into the old agrarian economies" (Braudel 1982: 561). Yet, despite this hostility, these economies based on growing seasons had a need for credit and, for them also, money was a factor of progress. Money, credit and usury have inspired ambivalent attitudes throughout the centuries, but it seems impossible to do without them.

The Aristotelian position, which spreads throughout 13th-century Christendom and strengthens its hold through the writings of St. Thomas of Aquinas, radically condemns usury because it distorts the original function of money which is to facilitate exchange. The Greek term "*tokos*" (off-spring) that was used to designate usury reflects the scorn it aroused. The formula "money is barren" will be insistently proclaimed at the Council of Trent. The formula from Deuteronomy (23: 19) is just as unequivocal: "Thou shalt not lend upon usury to thy brother." According to Braudel (1982: 560), this explains why the Jews, who considered themselves a "minority surrounded by dangerous enemies," would practise usury on a large scale with non-Jews. And, the Church, while proclaiming all men brothers, would still permit, even at the time of St. Ambrose of Milan (4th century), usurious loans "to the enemy during a *just* war." (Braudel 1982: 560)

The second Lateran Council, in 1139, took the firm decision to deprive "the unrepentant usurer" of the sacraments and refuse him burial in hallowed ground. But it later fell to the scholastics to soften the harshness of this view. For while condemning usurious interest as a "sale of time" which belongs only to God, they conceded that the practice would be justified "when the lender was running a risk (mannum emergens) or failing to gain (lucrum cessans)." (Braudel 1982: 562)

It would seem reasonable to agree with Weber, Schumpeter and Braudel that capitalism's greater success in the northern regions of Europe can be ascribed not only to the absence of these stormy quarrels over usury but also, and perhaps above all, to a certain climate of violence (which Marx, Engels and Lenin were not slow to point out) that brought a more rapid and complete destruction of traditional social, moral, economic and political structures.

Weber explicitly states that the rise of "accountancy" would increase the lure of individualism, separate households (no longer places of "common productive life" but now "consumption units") from the workplace and dissolve the forms of "domestic communism" which, from *an economic point of view*, had become irrational. "Profit-oriented activity ... becomes a distinct profession ... leading to the formation of a separate society ...," (Weber 1971: 403) one which Weber opposes to the domestic community and the ancient Greek *oikos* (household living in economic autarchy and not concerned with profit). It is not the physical separation between private dwellings and workplaces that is decisive (this already existed in Oriental bazaars, souks and casbahs), but rather "the *accounting and legal* distinction between household and profit making and the West's invention of a special legal system based on this separation" (Weber 1971: 404).

Paradoxically (and this is what I would now like to demonstrate), there are currently signs that a return to ethical values associated with "home," trust, charismatic leadership and Mediterranean Catholic culture would be the only path of recovery for our present, faltering Western-style industrial and post-industrial economies. Using our Quebec example, with very occasional references to Germany and Japan, I shall attempt to develop preliminary elements and hypotheses for use in a debate which is now inevitable.

3.3 The Unorthodox Management Style of the Cascades Company of Quebec: Crystallization of Elements of Another Capitalist Ethic?

Although Braudel dismisses as "disconcerting" much of the evidence Weber advances to show the differences between the protestant and catholic ethic, I still maintain that the latter's deductions often retain a basic descriptive value.

For example, the distinctions Weber (1958: 10) deduces from the writings of Benjamin Franklin (the 18th century American doctor, philosopher, and stateman referred to in the opening chapters of *The Protestant Ethic and the Spirit of Capitalism*) and from the work of his own student, Martin Offenbacher, are still significant. Franklin's cult of money and his desire to use time, credit and personal reputation for gain are easily recognized (as they were by both de Tocqueville and Nietzsche) as that greed and "savage pursuit of money" so characteristic of the 19th century American. By contrast, Offenbacher, in his 1895 statistical studies on the distribution of wealth and economic activity between Catholics and Protestants in Baden, finds that Catholics are more interested in a "calmer life," with less thirst for profit and less devotion to the cult of money (Weber 1985: 188). The Catholic mentality was torn between the triumph of money and old values associated with awaiting the Parousia ("the eschatological" outlook with its relative indifference to economic activity) as preached by St. Paul, with the condemnation of usury and profit as *turpitudo* (depravity) by Aquinas, with the disdain for worldly activity inherited from Pascal, one of Jansenism's most brilliant defenders. (Although it was at Port Royal that ideas close to Calvinist predestination also found expression.)

These things considered, we should scarcely be surprised that it should be Quebec which sees the appearance of a business style entirely imbued (almost without the knowledge and will of its promoters) with the resurgent vitality of social attitudes and relations marked, in the Weberian sense, by a more Catholic and community-oriented spirit.

One should, I believe, start with a look at the situation of Quebec. Briefly and from a broad perspective, one may say that this region of the modern world is one upon which the weight of the Church, until very recently (up to the 1960s), rested the most heavily. It is also, and above all, a veritable island of Latin, French and Catholic culture in an ocean of English-speaking Protestantism, self-confident and intrusive in character. As a result, Quebecers have even recognized themselves in Albert Memmi's *The Colonizer and the Colonized*. Hence, there is nothing extravagant in presuming that the traditional and ancestral values of Southern Europe's Latin culture would offer a refuge, anchor and defense for Quebecers' identity. The Quiet Revolution (to be broadly characterized as the movement, starting in the second half of this century, by which Quebecers regained social and economic power from anglophone business interests) would place a growing number of Quebecers in the ranks of business and industry. It was in the context of these developments that the three Lemaire brothers and their father, natives of a small country town, acquired ownership of an old, abandoned pulp and paper "mill" in 1963. Started from scratch, their business had close to a onebillion-dollar turnover by 1988. This spectacular success involved reviving and restoring a large number of bankrupt business to top performance. Some of these businesses were located outside Quebec, notably in the USA and France.

I have given elsewhere (Aktouf and Chrétien 1987) a very detailed account of the amazing features of this firm's management style summarised briefly below. Here, I shall focus on the aspects that illustrate my observations regarding the resurgence of a feudal-Catholic ethic, which, I believe, is the key to understanding Cascades' strong "corporate culture," with its conviviality, commitment and productivity.

As mentioned above, I have spent the last three years conducting participatory observation in Cascades' various plants, several of which are unionized. I would also mention that many other Quebec businesses are successfully following the Cascades model. My major findings with respect to the Cascades phenomenon are presented below. They are based on my research to date of more than 80 days spent in the field; more than two hundred in-depth interviews conducted and twelve plants studied (the Cascades group has close to 4000 employees and about thirty plants).

On first visiting a Cascades plant, the outside observer is struck by an almost total absence of the rationality of classical management so pervasive in the North American milieu: no organization charts; almost no distinctive titles or official positions; no job descriptions; no time sheets; at most three or four symbolic levels of hierarchy; self-management in everything; no supervisory function or control; systematic avoidance of hierarchy; direct and informal relations at all levels; frank exchange at all levels; tolerance of human error; open-book policy on all information including financial information; access to executive offices for all employees; self-managing work teams; universal profit sharing unrelated to individual productivity; position of foreman abolished at all levels ... At first sight, one has the impression that the whole mentality and "metaphysics" of double entry accounting with its mechanistic capacity for formalizing every aspect of life, and especially corporate life (as Weber and Schumpeter make abundantly clear) have almost completely vanished at Cascades. The frenzied need for cost/benefit analysis is absolutely not required dogma, which is especially striking in this period of recession and widespread intensification of the passion for squeezing and cutting salaries and expenses.

At Cascades, there are a number of significant facts which clearly reflect the revival of Catholic[5] concerns about usury and profit as *turpido*. The prime example is the systematic biennial sharing of profits in each plant. Profits are shared prior to deductions for depreciation and taxes, meaning that, from the accountant's point of view, the company risks experiencing losses at the end of its financial year, after having distributed profits to the

---

[5] I am using the term "Catholic" in the present discussion, but these positions could just as well be called Mediterranean, Arabic, Islamic. It is well known that the writings of Aristotle penetrate the West in the 10th century by way of Arab translators.

workers. This is nothing less than a means of returning a share of their work directly to employees.

As concerns social relations and "management" style, the Cascades model leans relatively more in the direction of the ancient *oikos*, the feudal-charismatic impulse, and the domestic community than toward the accounting-centred firm. The profit sharing example is a clear indication that "maximum profit" is not the firm's overriding goal. As the general director himself confided to me in a taped interview: "I am ready to give up profit to keep an employee." This firm seems to have escaped from the reigning economic rationality which, as Schumpeter (1979: 188) observed, lets "ledgers and the calculation of profits absorb and isolate their servants." Work at Cascades seems rather to be an occasion for an intense, almost community life which reaches beyond the workplace. From top management down, almost everyone faithfully attends the many celebrations, sporting activities, excursions and ceremonies willingly financed by the company.

Employees at all levels refer to the president as if he were a superman: he is the "hero" that Schumpeter accuses prosaic, bourgeois business of having eliminated from the scene. The president's brothers and daughter (she is also a part of the company's top management) — though to a lesser degree — also inspire the same loyalty and praise. Interestingly enough, employees clearly connect the president's heroic aura with personal qualities such as simplicity, availability and concern for others, particularly including the most humble ... Each and every Cascades employee can tell several stories illustrating the charismatic and generous acts of Bernard Lemaire or one of his brothers. "They care about us and respect us," "they take care of us," "they don't think they are better than we are," "they don't think they are God's gift to the world," "they know they were born of a mother just like us" ... this is typical talk among Cascades workers.

Schumpeter would surely be astonished by the mythical dimensions of such leadership. The power to violate taboos is known to be the primary characteristic of the mythical hero, and the Lemaire family has violated one of the West's most powerful taboos, the one establishing an unbridgeable gap between capitalist bosses and workers (Schumpeter 1979).

The Lemaires need no instruments or contrivances to show their authority, its recognition is a foregone and unshakable conclusion. It might even be said that this authority is more readily accepted and even stronger because it is not overbearing but open to contestation. The Lemaires do not command obedience but rather, by directing their own desires and projects toward what is conceived as a common good, they implicate others in their project and obtain their eager co-operation.

Also to be found at Cascades are numerous signs recalling the basic values (described by Weber (1971: 399—410)) of the *oikos* and the domestic community. One detects in countless ways the presence of a healthy paternalism, paternalism in the strong, feudal sense of the term. The directors are treated like *pater familias* and local lords. They may even be consulted regarding matters of social life in Kingsey Falls. "We feel secure here," "we know that we won't be thrown out like old socks," "Cascades is not like other companies," "there is nothing I wouldn't do for Bernard Lemaire," "these people are really human," "they don't have to share, but they do!" ... Such comments from the majority of workers are an undeniable expression of feelings of loyalty and security which strongly smack of feudal values.

Obviously, this reflects a situation where personal relations and "quality of life" take precedence over the pursuit of maximum profit. President Lemaire is quick to explain how this came about: "When we were still just a handful of men at the old mill, I quickly realized that sharing (both the good and the bad) with others, and treating them openly and honestly as part of a whole will earn their whole-hearted support and make them just as interested and concerned about the company's success as you are ... I just generalized this realization, as simple as that." Weber would have easily recognized in this attitude some of the key elements of the *oikos*: a familial, personalized, paternalistic and protective approach to human relations which chooses the common good as a final goal. (This last point is also a basic element in Aristotelian and Thomistic philosophy.) Schumpeter would also see in this attitude the reappearance of that "personal ascendancy" formerly exercised by the lord and the lack of which he deplored in bourgeois entrepreneurs. Once again, we have, in Aristotelian terms, an attitude which is more "economic" than "chrematistic," one which goes against the grain of Western management's hyper-rationality.

Hazarding a comparison with other high-performance models on today's scene, the Cascades model would seem to share at least some common features with those in Japan, West Germany and Sweden.[6] Without concocting any rash theoretical claims, we cannot help but notice that, despite their concrete differences, all these models repose, in varying degrees, on modes of personal relations which predate industrial capitalism, specifically those related to Weber's domestic community. In Japan, is it not true that many of the traditional values associated with rural and feudal life have been preserved by Shintoism and channeled into modern economic and social life? And, in Sweden and West Germany, was the Reformation not more Lutheran than Calvinist?[7] Remember Weber's explicit claim that both Catholics and Lutherans were "horrified" by Calvinism's "valorization of life in this world" through its attachment to work and material success (Weber 1958: 98–107).

---

[6] See, among others, Bellemare and Poulin-Simon 1986, which gives a partial review of the Swedish, West German and Austrian models.

[7] As is well known, Calvinism has always been more influential in Switzerland, the Netherlands, the United Kingdom, France and the United States of America.

3.4 Conclusions

Cascades teaches a lesson for our times: business firms can no longer ignore the necessity of casting in their lot with workers. This was one of the least understood and most ardently resisted of Marxist rallying cries. Weber advocates similar reform when he observes that: "human conflict is the precondition for any rational market calculation" and "appropriation of supplies and control over one's own labour are the strongest incentives to ceaseless individual work" (Weber 1971: 94, 157).

Finding ways of encouraging the employee "to work ceaselessly" is not one of my intentions, but I would like to show that the worker can be truly motivated if allowed to reappropriate, if not the means of production, at least functional and decision-making powers in the workplace (Weber [1971: 71] seems to include production and transportation in the concept of "supplies."). In the same vein, it is rather surprising to find an economist from the renowned Massachusetts Institute of Technology, Weitzman (1984), using his pen to advocate: abolishing salaries and linking remuneration to business performance ... in somewhat the same way as do the Japanese.

Finally, one cannot help but be struck by the similarity between the attributes both Weber and Schumpeter use to describe pre-capitalist, socio-economic life (community-oriented, romantic, charismatic ...) and the fondest aspirations of the devotees of "corporate culture": firms and leaders with mythical dimensions, whose heroic and symbolic virtues would inspire unity and enthusiastic commitment ... These are certainly worthy goals, but are those who advocate them ready to understand that, as in the *oikos* and the domestic community, applying community values to the firm would mean renouncing individualism and the strict law of cost/benefit metaphysics?[8]

References

Aktouf, O. and M. Chrétien (1987): "Le cas Cascades: comment se crée une culture organisationnelle", *Revue Française de Gestion*, 65 – 66, novembre – décembre: 156 – 166.

[8] The author wishes to acknowledge his warmest gratitude for all the advice, comments and bibliographical information provided to him by Mr. Maurice Dufour. "L'École des Hautes Etudes Commerciales de Montréal" benefits from a subvention granted by the "Fonds pour la Formation de Chercheurs et l'Aide à la Recherche" (FCAR) for the publication of its research papers.

Archier, G. and H. Sérieyx (1984): *L'Entreprise du troisième type*, Paris: Seuil.

Bellemare, D. and S. L. Poulin-Simon (1986): *Le défi du plein emploi*, Montréal: Ed. St. Martin.

Bosche, M. (1984): "Corporate Culture, la culture sans histoire", *Revue Française de Gestion*, 47 – 48, septembre – octobre: 29 – 39.

Braudel, Fernand (1982): *The Wheels of Commerce, Civilization and Capitalism: 15th to 18th Century*, Vol. II, translated by Sian Reynolds, New York: Harper and Row.

Cooke, C. A. (1950): "Corporate Trust and Company" in F. Braudel *Civilization and Capitalism: 15th to 18th century*, Vol. II, translated by Sian Reynolds, New York: Harper and Row.

Granger, G. (1976): Epistémologie économique, in J. Piaget (ed), *Logique des connaissances scientifiques*, Paris: La Pleiade.

Memmi, Albert (1972) *Le portrait du colonisé*, Montréal, L'Etincelle.

Nizard, G. (1983 – 84): "Identité et culture de l'entreprise", *Harvard-L'Expansion*, 31, hiver: 90 – 106.

Pacioli, L. (1494): *Summa di Arithmetica*, translated by R. G. Brown and K. S. Johnston. New York: McGraw Hill, 1963.

Peters, T. and R. Waterman (1982): *In Search of Excellence*, New York: Harper and Row.

Sainsaulieu, R. (1983): "La régulation culturelle des ensembles organisés", *L'Année Sociologique*, 33: 195 – 217.

Schumpeter, J. A. (1979): *Capitalisme, socialisme et démocratie*, Paris: Payot.

de Tocqueville, Alexis (1961): *De la démocratie en Amérique*, Paris, Gallimard.

Vogel, E. F. (1983): *Le Japon médaille d'or: leçons pour l'Amérique et l'Europe*, Paris: Gallimard.

Weber, M. (1958): *The Protestant Ethic and the Spirit of Capitalism*, translated by Talcott Parsons, New York: Charles Scribner's Sons.

Weber, M. (1971): *Économie et société*, Paris: Plon.

Wegnez, L. F. (1984): *Le miracle japonais: source d'inspiration pour une nouvelle gestion*, Bruxelles: Office International de Librairie.

Weitzman, M. L. (1984): *The Share Economy: Conquering Stagflation*, Cambridge: Harvard University Press.

Chapter 4
Dependency and Worker Flirting

Krzysztof Konecki

> This heart is sore and sad.
> Crossed in love?
> — James Joyce

4.1 Introduction

The problem of structural dependency in a formal organization and the shape of this dependency, as it emerges from interaction, is created in the particular culture of the organization. Structural dependency means that one worker or group of workers is dependent on other workers because the second group has some special power originating from the organizational hierarchy or from the system of work and production which enables them to influence the behavior of the first. Every organization creates its own specific way of using this power, with practices specific to the organization. Moreover, each organization creates its own culture.

In the following account the culture of an organization is viewed as a 'family of concepts,' made up of such ideas as symbol, language, ideology, beliefs, ritual and myth. Symbol is the most inclusive category (Pettigrew 1979: 574), but language permeates all categories. Try as we might to change it any analysis of symbolism is usually made through an analysis of language.

Interaction is the sphere in which symbolic meanings are realized on the level of language. The meanings are strictly combined, according to relatively durable interactional rules, which are worked out in particular social groups. Hence they are common social artefacts of the culture of the organization. The rules are frequently unconsciously applied and difficult to observe. Nevertheless, they govern the social life of the organization. They are implicit rules since many of them are inscribed into the colloquial language which is the main safeguard of social order in worker groups and formal organizations. The rule matrices become explicit whenever new workers or 'strangers' make interactional errors. New workers are entering a culture which is made up of many interactional games, such as, for example, those connected with the sporadic face-to-face contacts described by Turner (1971: 62 – 63) in terms of the so-called norms of 'continuity of contact' and 'establishment of common ground.'

Turner is mainly concerned with explicit rules of interactional behavior such as the 'norm of reciprocity' (op.cit.: 63 – 68), as he speaks of the necessity of paying back when something has been intended, with full awareness, as a gift (op.cit.: 64). Moreover: "Some continuing reciprocal relationships may be attached to a job-role rather than to a person, and in these cases it then becomes necessary to induct the new incumbent into the rights and duties which he has acquired in this regard" (op.cit.: 68). The same deliberatedness is connected with the norms of 'continuity of interactional contact' (op. cit.: 62 – 63) and norms of 'establishing common ground' (op.cit.: 63). Generally, however, people are not fully aware of these norms because the norms of language are taken as a *matter of course* (Wittgenstein 1953). There are many rules in language which we are made to 'follow.' Yet following a rule implies meaningful action:

Our language and our social relations are just two different sides of the same coin. To give an account of the meaning of the word is to describe how it is used and to describe how it is used is to describe the social intercourse into which it enters … .
The use of language is so intimately, so inseparably bound up with the other non-linguistic activities which men perform, that it is possible to speak of their non-linguistic behavior also as expressing discursive ideas (Winch 1967: 123, 128).

Moreover, "understanding rule involves understanding contradiction too" (op.cit.: 65). Intersubjectivity is connected with the evaluation of an event and, at the same time, with the application of a rule in a given context. Norms, in this sense, exist only if in applying them we can observe, reflectively, their alternatives. They exist only in action strictly connected with the usage of language or talk.

Thus, norms are especially visible in the difficult situation of a new worker joining the game of 'the interactional ritual of ridiculing.' Since he or she does not recognize the rules of ritual linguistic exchange and reacts to them in an incompetent way (not to be confused with Chomsky's usage), he or she will therefore frequently 'lose face' (Goffman 1967; 1971). The newcomer rarely perceives 'deceit through insinuation,' one of the linguistic devices of ridicule, and even if it is perceived, the newcomer is unable to react to maintain or to regain face. The situation is similar in another form of ritual, a ritual which we will call "worker flirting."

The present paper concentrates on 'worker flirting' as one of the forms of interactional ritual in the culture of an organization. It is thus *only an illustration* of the interactional dimension of the culture of an organization.

The paper[1] deals with interactional ritual in an industrial organization and is based on an empirical study carried out in a radio-electrical plant, "Z,"

---

[1] A version of this paper was presented at the 'Standing Conference on Organizational Symbolism' (SCOS) in Milan, Italy, June 24 – 26, 1987.

which employs 1,500 workers. The author carried out a period of three-months covert participant observation and recorded 139 free-interviews. These were supplemented by three months of covert participant observation by the author's collaborator, himself a worker at the plant. The study also included 21 one-week periods of covert participant observation in other plants.

The research and analytical procedures utilized in this study have been taken mainly from the work by Glaser and Strauss, *The Discovery of Grounded Theory* (1967; see also Glaser 1978; Turner 1981; and Martin and Turner 1986).

4.2 Flirting

Our observations in Plant Z revealed the frequent occurrence of parasexual interaction between men and women workers, most frequently in the production units, but also among clerks. Its non-verbal aspect consisted of the pinching of women workers by men, mutual embracing between men and women, flirtatious self-exposure by women, the simulation of sexual behavior or of sexual intercourse in close contacts, and the undressing of women by men, with the women's passive or active consent. The verbal part consisted of veiled or open references made to the sexual life of a particular person, making sexual offers or asking questions about a woman's menstrual cycle. The language of flirting is saturated with vulgarisms, especially in the production units, and makes use of a specific sexual vocabulary. Both men and women are initiators of this kind of interaction, irrespective of age in a given sex category or of age differences between sexes[2], so that we are justified in concluding that relations within this ritual interaction were, for the most part, symmetrical.

---

[2] Cultural anthropologists have pointed out that flirting and joking among men and women in primitive societies are accepted only when the persons are potential sexual partners, i. e., they are not bound by some prohibition of contact, taboo, restriction, etc. (Brant 1948: 160; Lowie 1949: 97; Radcliffe-Brown 1952: 100). A different situation was observed in an industrial plant, a printing house, in Glasgow, Scotland, by Sykes (1966) where flirting, usually obscene, ocurred most frequently between older men and women, who were not potential sexual partners. Obscene jokes were made also between old women and younger men, though it was the women who initiated flirting, and no physical contact (or petting) was possible. Here flirting was a sign of exclusion from potential sexual relations. Jokes with sexual overtones occurred also between old men and younger women. As in the previous case, the jokes precluded any serious sexual relations between these social

It should be noted that the behavior in question has a jocular character. It is not serious, but is full of coquetry and its sexual content is not taken literally. We have, therefore, called it *'worker-flirting.'* The 'worker' part refers to the contextual aspects of work-situations in which flirting occurs — the description below refers mainly to the mechanical department F-1 of Plant Z.

Parasexual interaction was observed between:
1) Press operators (women) and fitters (men);
2) Press operators (women) and internal transport workers (men);
3) Press operators (women) and quality inspectors (men);
4) Press operators (women) and other workers (men).

Figure 4.1 presents a diagrammatic representation of these types of interaction.[3]

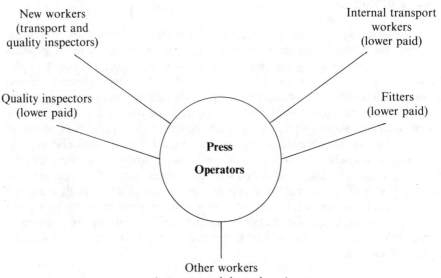

New workers
(transport and
quality inspectors)

Internal transport
workers
(lower paid)

Quality inspectors
(lower paid)

Fitters
(lower paid)

Press

Operators

Other workers
(no structural dependency)

Figure 4.1 Diagrammatic representation of the main actors in the flirting ritual and their relations

categories. On the other hand, public flirting or petting between young men and women was entirely prohibited. Modest behavior of the women was a sign of sexual availability (Sykes 1966: 188–193).

We have encountered a quite different situation in Factory Z, department F-1 and F-2, where the flirting relations were symmetrical with regard to social and age categories. This situation is best accounted for by the structural relations described below.

[3] I should like to thank B. A. Turner for this suggestion.

Flirting occurs mainly between those occupational groups whose relations to each other are determined by the technological process, and whose interactional contacts are most direct. Thus, the flirting which we observed is all a property of an occupational group, and not of a couple of people engaged in the game of coquetry at any particular moment. Worker flirting always takes place in the presence of other workers who form an audience. That is, the *rule of observability by others* is an essential part of it. Workers flirting away from the group in dyads were negatively sanctioned by their co-workers. Another rule of the ritual seems to say that *flirting cannot continue outside the workplace*. If it does, it is sharply branded with humorous comment and malicious gossip. Certainly there were cases when flirting continued outside the plant, but it was sanctioned negatively and the audience refused to accept it unless it ended up in the marriage of the flirting couple: "They got married because the machine broke down." Flirting which went on outside the plant threatened yet another rule of worker flirting which can be put as follows: *worker flirting has its limits* — it does not lead to sexual consumation.

Worker flirting may occur where there is a *hierarchy of power and dependency* of one group on another. In our case it was an informal power relationship in which the press operators' flow of work depended on the previous performance of other groups of workers, as described below. These groups had a discretionary power over the press operators (Crozier 1964). The structural relationship, a necessary condition for flirting, became in this case one of the rules of flirting, since its recognition was essential if both parties to the interaction were to participate smoothly in it.

4.3 Parasexual Behavior in the Relations Between Press Operators and Fitters

The women press operators, who work at air-operated and circular cam presses, make various parts for transformers and stabilizers. Their flow of work and their wages — they are paid on a piece-work basis — depend on the other groups of workers. Their dependency upon the fitters arises from the frequent need to fit new jigs to their machines due to mechanical wear, and to the technical requirements of different parts. For the sake of simplicity we shall initially concentrate on this particular relationship with the fitters. The nature of the relationship can be expressed in the following hypothesis: The more resistance there is from the women to the flirting of fitters, the less likely the fitters are to deal with their machines quickly. Or, conversely: If flirting proceeds undisturbed, the fitters get to work immediately after receiving information from a press operator about the need to change a jig.

We have thus seen that worker flirting has a structural basis and that it is performed relative to a particular technological cycle and a particular system of paying the press-operators (by piecework) and the fitters (by the hour). Moreover, the fitters' wages are lower than the women press operators', even though their flow of work depends upon the fitters. We may then be seeing the consequence of a desire on the part of the fitters to compensate for their lack of status, most frequently manifested in direct interaction on pay-days, when women boast of their higher wages. The men may try to win back their status through the degrading practices which sometimes occur in worker-flirting, and which symbolize their discretionary power over the press operators.

In the factory units observed, matters of sex, prevailed in break-time conversations. At the foreman's table workers constantly talked of the past, about "what fine women they used to have in the unit, and what they used to do on the night shift!" They often cursed and swore and supplemented their stories with gestures which symbolized sexual intercourse. The main story-tellers at the table were the fitters, then the foreman, then the transport workers.

The themes of physical force and fights, together with sex reflect a 'macho' ethos cultivated by the male-workers which emphasised physical and sexual ability as factors of male supremacy over women. Dependency flirting becomes more understandable against such an ideological background. Moreover we should add that the workers mainly come from the country or are first generation industrial workers of peasant origin.

The problematic side of the press operator's situation at work is well indicated in the following excerpt from the researcher's notes:

(Some) women (press operators) were complaining again that they had no work to do. One of them ... was crying because a fitter was so slow in fixing her machine that she had to be transferred to another one (which reduced her output below the daily rate, since she rarely worked at the machine and was not used to it). In the end the fitter fixed her machine but some other woman was assigned to it. When E. refused (weeping) to work at the other machine the foreman cursed and scolded her. After ten minutes of 'sitting' protest E. went to the new machine. Yesterday she didn't manage to reach her daily rate again.

This woman was sometimes opposed to the flirting practices. The fitters and foreman disagreed with this ambiguous attitude to flirting and tried to punish her for it.

Thus we come to worker flirting. Below are some examples from field notes:

I noticed later that all cart drivers (transport workers) were drunk. A few fitters and women press operators were drunk, too. The fitter M. started flirting with the press operator E. and two other women (press operators). E. was lifting her dress and showing her thighs and the fitter looked at them expertly and made comments. ... He told me later that he would go to bed with her if she bought him a bottle of vodka.

I once saw a press operator come to a fitter asking him to fit the press at which she was working. She started by embracing him by the neck and hugging him. After a short while he went to fit her machine.

Below is a quotation which clearly points to the structural interrelation between the work of press operators and the work of fitters:

When I was sitting with other workers (fitters among them) at the junk-yard — they had called me there — "Come and have a rest" — two press operators came running and urged two fitters (without cajoling or courting them) to fit new jigs on their machines. "We're coming," they said. But they did not go for the next ten minutes. In the end the foreman came and said to the fitters: "The women are yelling. Go and do those jigs for them." They did not go for another ten minutes and commented that those particular women were always in a hurry and yelling. Others were much better. You could go an hour and a half later and they would be there, sitting quiet and saying nothing.

The structural dependency was most frequently manifested in the contexts preceding the fitting of new jigs by a fitter, or the mounting of a new belt by a transport worker. However relative, the compulsion to engage in the flirting ritual by both parties to the interaction, and especially by the women, seemed to be a principle. Only a few women did not participate in this ritual and they were excluded from the communication network of the worker group.

Nevertheless, flirting also occurred in other contexts which did not immediately precede the changing of jigs by a fitter, for example at the foreman's table at breaktime:

One of the fitters pressed one of the operators hard with the front of his body. The 'Big Girl' laughed flirtatiously — it looked as if she was enjoying it.

Sometimes in the course of the coquetry-game, the degrading aspects of flirting became manifest:

I've got a loose pin. Come and fix it." "What have you got loose?" asks the fitter. "Well, that thing on the side of this ..." says the woman. "Then what do you call it?" asks the fitter. "Well, the screw-thread, I think ..." answers the press operator. "That's a different story" said the fitter and winked at us workers sitting at the foreman's table. Only then did he go to fit the machine.

The fitter took advantage of his superior qualifications and his superior technical knowledge. This component of work organization, the technical qualification, is manifest in the above interaction and changes its character.

However, worker flirting may also have an integrating function in the worker unit (see the first hypothesis above) as the following note suggests:

This morning O. came to a fitter and asked him to fix her machine. The fitter who serviced her machine (he was also her charge-hand) immediately went to fix it ... Later I noticed that the fitter was 'feeling up' O. The press operator was laughing (she seemed to enjoy it).

In some respects, flirting reinforces the internal bonds of the group and creates a good atmosphere for work. Many workers (men and women) expressed such an opinion during interviews and confirmed that flirting had such a meaning for them: "We are one family, so that we can behave like that".

Similar patterns of behavior, in accordance with both of our hypotheses occurred in the interaction between press operators and *internal transport workers*. The transport workers' job was to supply the strip and to mount it on a reel from which it was fed into the press operators' machine. Whenever a press operator is reluctant to engage in coquetry the transport workers seem to be slow to do their work.

In some ways the press operators were also dependent on *quality inspectors*. This dependency rested on the inspectors' freedom to refuse a quality pass to parts made by a particular press operator. The formal quality standards could not always be used by the inspectors in their work because of the low quality of metal strip supplied by the foundry and because the quality of production was generally sub-standard. As a result the quality inspectors applied their own kind of quality standards in order to satisfy the need to 'keep the production going.' This may well influence their behavior since they have a ready way to participate in worker flirting, arising from the possibility of using their discretionary power.

There were also instances of flirting between press operators and *other categories of workers*, from other departments or machine bays. These were, however, isolated cases which took place mainly at break time, unlike the cases previously discussed, when flirting occurred mainly in the machine bays, during work-time. It seems that flirting with other categories of workers was not structurally based and could be interpreted in two ways, either as an activity which might break the monotony of work or as part of a more general pattern of sexual harassment.

4.4 New Workers and Worker Flirting

New workers must become fully aware of the rules of flirting before they can enter the system of communication of a given working group. For a new worker, worker flirting sometimes looks like sexual foreplay which leads up to a culmination in the form of intercourse. Many new workers were caught in this trap, by getting involved in the perplexing affairs which entail a loss of face and which often place them at the bottom of, or even outside the social hierarchy of the group:

A new transport worker (two weeks of work) was making a pass at one of the press operators by painfully hitting her on the back and feeling various parts of her body. It went on for some time with tacit acquiescence from the woman. At one point, however, when his behavior became more intense the press operator asked him to stop. Suddenly, she hit him hard in the back and kicked him below the waist saying, "F... off!" She later added, "It's a pity I didn't get him in the balls".

In the above case the structural basis was present but the new worker did not recognize the essential feature (one of the rules) of worker flirting: that is, that 'flirting has its limits.' The initiator of the flirting episode was too aggressive, his flirting lasted too long and the balance of acceptance and rejection was then unsettled by the total rejection given by the press operator. Its meaning was misinterpreted by the new worker.

A second observation:

I talked to a new worker (aged 21, 1.5 months of work in the transport department) about an incident on the second shift when he had been beaten up by a woman-worker (an assembler in another bay). "What, have you messed about with that woman?" I asked. He said "Well, it went all right at the beginning, but then she went nuts ..." "Were you pressing her too much?" I asked. "Well, you see, I could have hit her, even killed her, but what for? ... Anyway, she was stoned too".

It would seem that this new worker did not recognize another rule of worker flirting, according to which the work of the assembler should have depended on his. It did not: the assembler worked in a different bay and had no reason to accept his passes or to participate in the game of flirting with him. It is difficult to be definite about this, but it seems probable that we see here a breaching of the rule of the common pattern of behavior.

The flirting of new workers with press operators refers not only to transport workers but also to quality inspectors:

I noticed that a new quality tester was taking a liking (reciprocated) to some press operators. He is especially close to one of them. Their conversations are saturated with erotic allusions. The tester once said to me, "She is that kind of girl that if I pressed her a little harder she would go for it".

Here again the new worker fails to recognize one of the rules of flirting, namely that 'flirting has its limits,' although he did not go on to breach this rule in action.

A further quotation from my field notes:

I saw how a new transport worker (5 weeks at the plant) who was mounting the strip, delicately hit the press operator above the hips with the fingers of both hands. The woman sprang up and squeaked. They were both happy (laughed). Other men and women workers who saw the incident were also laughing.

In the above example the flirting followed all of the rules. There was a dependency of the press operator's work upon that of the transport worker. The flirting was a public fact, since it was observable by other workers. The essential features of flirting are recognized and the flirting is performed in the workplace.

Getting used to the worker flirting ritual is an important element in the initiation of new female workers who are employed as press operators. This is especially true with regard to the touching of their bodies in public. The male workers accomodate the women (both mentally and physically) to the novel situation. They introduce them to the new intimate spheres, those which the women have previously treated as inaccessible to others but which are now made accessible. The social delimitation of the new spheres of intimacy frequently comes as a shock to the neophyte, since particular regions of the body have strictly defined meanings, which may have to be reinterpreted when the cultural milieu or context is changed:

A press operator once told me that men were harassing her a lot when she first came to work here (they would pinch and feel her up, etc.). She couldn't stand it and she would often go to the ladies room to cry. In the end she gradually got used to it and changed her tactics. She started behaving in the same way, 'snapping back' at them and using the same kind of language (vulgarisms) in order to survive and bear up against her situation in the plant.

Getting used to worker flirting is thus associated with the socialisation process for newcomers: "A sexualized workplace may depress the number of behaviors labelled as sexual harassment because workers may become habituated to sexual behavior at work due to constant exposure" (Konrad and Gutek 1986: 424).

Women in our case study may, of course, be accustomed to such a pattern of behavior in the factory but outside the workplace they are still likely to treat such behavior as sexual harassment. The general perception of worker flirting in Factory Z is a male 'perception.' Men usually have different orientations than women to sexual behavior and they may not perceive many of these activities as sexual harassment (Konrad and Gutek 1986: 430−431). If women accept the male interpretation of these behaviors they will suppress their own interpretation desired from a more ideal world and will move to behave according to the male definition of worker flirting, in which 'worker flirting is not sexual harassment.' But this shift of perspective, that is the redefinition of parasexual behavior, is made under the pressure of the male definition of the situation. Real sexual harassment may thus sometimes be hidden under the surface of a male definition of flirting as normal behavior, or, alternatively, as appeared at many points in our case study, it may also develop into a pattern which takes on the appearance of a normal mode of cooperation at work.

4.5 Conclusions

Worker flirting has all of the features of a dependency ritual, since it reflects the direction of dependency and the presence of social distance (Turner 1971: 23−26). Its form is the result of negotiation and adaptation on both sides of the interaction, a negotiation to which the various parties bring differing types of resources. It is a product of interaction which takes place in given working groups. It is not 'forced upon' workers by the organization or executed according to formal rules. The only 'forced' part is the condition necessary for the occurrence of the ritual — the structural dependency. This holds true not only for the technological dependency which we have seen in worker flirting, but also for formal dependency, associated with, for example, 'informing,' 'making gifts,' 'manifesting discontent with a subordinate' and other forms of dependency rituals. Nevertheless, this condition of dependency must enter the interaction as an 'interactional resource' related to the will and tendencies among the working groups concerned. Sometimes workers do not want to participate in the rituals, but in such a situation, they are excluded from the social network and become marginal to the group. Hence the dependency ritual, treated as an element of the culture of an organization, arises 'from the ranks' as an outcome of shared subjective interpretations of members of the formal organization.

Observing the interactional rules of the dependency rituals helps all participants to maintain face once such a system has been established. Those who do not observe the rules usually lose face, and this frequently has far-reaching consequences for their participation in the every-day life of the working group, for persons who have lost face may be excluded from the group and become outsiders.

References

Brant, Ch. S. (1948): On Joking Relationships, *American Anthropologist*, vol. 50: 160–162.

Crozier, M. (1964): *The Bureaucratic Phenomenon*, London: Tavistock.

Glaser, B. G. and Strauss, A. L. (1967): *The Discovery of Grounded Theory*, Chicago: Aldine.

Glaser, B. G. (1978): *Theoretical Sensitivity*, Mill Valley, CA: Sociology Press.

Goffman, E. (1967): *Interaction Ritual: Essays on Face-to-Face Behaviour*, New York: Anchor.

Goffman, E. (1971): *Relations in Public: Microstudies of Public Order*, New York: Basic Books.

Konrad, A. M. and Gutek, B. (1986): Impact of Work Experiences on Attitudes toward Sexual Harassment, *Administrative Science Quarterly*, vol. 31: 422–438.

Lowie, R. (1949): *Primitive Society*, London: Routledge and Kegan Paul.

Martin, P. Y. and Turner, B. A. (1986): Grounded Theory and Organizational Research, *The Journal of Applied Behavioral Science*, vol. 22: 141–157.

Pettigrew, A. (1979): On Studying Organizational Culture, *Administrative Science Quarterly*, vol. 24: 570–581.

Radcliffe-Brown, A. (1952): *Structure and Function in Primitive Society*, London: Cohen and West.

Sykes, A. (1966): Joking Relationship in an Industrial Setting, *American Anthropologist*, vol. 68: 188—193.

Turner, B. A. (1971): *Exploring the Industrial Subculture*, London: Macmillan.

Turner, B. A. (1981): Some Practical Aspects of Qualitative Date Analysis: One Way of Organizing the Cognitive Processes Associated with Generation of Grounded Theory, *Quality and Quantity*, vol. 15: 225—245.

Winch, P. (1967): *The Idea of a Social Science*, London: Routledge and Kegan Paul.

Wittgenstein, L. (1953): *Philosophical Investigations*, Oxford: Blackwell.

Chapter 5
Culture and Crisis Management in an English Prison[1]

Ellis Finkelstein

The notion of culture has recently come into fashion among students of organizational behaviour. Although culture may be defined in different ways I do not want to become involved in a debate over a definition which might be seen as inflexible. For my empirical purposes culture exists in the minds of men; it is an abstraction which gains significance once attempts are made to align norms with behaviour. Here, and in the following pages, I do not mean to imply that all actors adhere equally to the cultural imperatives of their group. People have different feelings about the society in which they live and work so that their attachment to a group can be revealed only through behaviour. In this paper I argue that some actions take place within an historical context so that history affects the ways in which some members of staff understand the prison in which they work and the part which it plays in the wider organization; culture generates expectations among prison officers for those in superordinate positions, especially prison governors. Thus, the aim of this paper is to show the part which culture plays in the way that two prison governors managed crises at a particular prison.

A prison is not a total institution[2] but part of a large, complex organisation directed from the Home Office. Divided into four operational regions the Prison Service employs around 20,000 staff (prison officers and others) in

[1] Material for this paper was gathered when I worked as a seconded probation officer at the prison. I am grateful to Michael Banton and John Arnott for their comments on previous drafts.

[2] Goffman (1961) suggested that certain institutions, such as monasteries, mental hospitals and prisons so emotionally overwhelm their residents that they lose their identities. Sometimes this concept has become perverted in that attempts are made to use the concept for sociological purposes so that these institutions are seen as standing alone and as self-contained. From the perspective of network analysis prisons are not total institutions because prisoners may be transferred from one institution to another and also receive visits and correspondence during the course of the sentence. Members of staff are affiliated in associations which span the prison service. The ability to relate to others outside the prison diminishes the heuristic value of Goffman's concept from a *sociological* perspective.

some 150 prisons containing roughly 50,000 prisoners. The size and geographic spread of the organization contribute to difficulties in coordinating and fulfilling departmental objectives. Occasionally policy imposed from the top of the organization will fail to take effect at an individual prison where local conditions and procedures are given preference. Similarly, issues and events at individual prisons may have an adverse effect upon the wider organization. The reader may be familiar with a number of problems which have beset the Prison Service during the past decade; overcrowding, escapes, riots and industrial action at a few prisons receive regular attention in the national press. Rather than dwelling on all of these issues I intend to focus upon certain events at a specific prison.

5.1 The Prison

Located in the north of England the Fortress[3] occupies a unique position in English penal history. Constructed in the mid-Victorian period the prison occasionally has been used for purposes other than the containment of adult prisoners. By the turn of the century it established a reputation of being able to control and contain prisoners who could not be controlled elsewhere so that for much of this century it was full of long-serving incorrigibles. Thus the Fortress became the subject of folklore as a tough prison for hard men. To some extent prison officers appear to have enjoyed the reputation and status they earned from working in such an establishment. However, following the publication of the Mountbatten Report[4] in 1966 the Fortress was downgraded. Many of the dangerous, high-risk prisoners were dispersed[5] to other, more secure facilities. Some members of staff encountered difficulty in accepting the change in the status of the Fortress to that of a closed training prison[6]. Similarly, Prison Service administrators appeared uncertain of the part which the Fortress would play within the new scheme and for a while local rumours predicted the closure of the prison. By 1980, however,

---

[3] A number of facts have been changed to alter the identity of the prison and to protect members of staff employed by the Prison Service.

[4] The report recommended, *inter alia*, that prisoners should be classified according to the danger they present to the public.

[5] The Mountbatten Report recommended that the most dangerous prisoners should be dispersed to a few highly secure prisons around the country. The Fortress did not meet the stringent criteria established for those prisoners placed in the most dangerous category.

[6] The report recommended that prisons should be classified according to function, viz, Local, Dispersal. Closed Training and Open.

the future of the prison had been clarified; regional administrators began to transfer younger, shorter-serving prisoners to the Fortress anticipating that its regime would change to meet the needs of its population.

In an attempt to further encourage change in the regime of the prison a Governor was appointed in 1981 who broke the mould established for that position at the Fortress. Martin Jones lacked the military background of his predecessors and the associated ability to command men. Unexpectedly the planned change in type of prisoner and prison Governor did not yield a change in regime. Staffing levels stayed high when compared to similar institutions elsewhere and there remained a number of posts peculiar to the Fortress which contributed to its unique character. Attempts to bring staffing into line with other prisons precipitated a crisis because many members of staff viewed the proposed changes in manning levels as a threat to their reputation of maintaining a tough regime for hard men. The character of the prison had been retained by staff who appear to have ignored changes in the population of the prison which no longer housed dangerous offenders. The staff acted as though the contemporary population was similar to that of bygone days, so keeping alive the prison's culture.

Externally directed change is inevitably accompanied by problems of acceptance among the workers. Such problems are manifested in two ways. First, workers look to the past idealizing the institution and its key personnel so that nostalgia generates myths about how things were[7]. Second, change and the threat of change produce dilemmas between what is and what should be. These dilemmas tend to cause insecurity which Blau (1964) suggests leads to intolerance.

Before the publication of the Mountbatten Report the Fortress had established a reputation for controlling dangerous and hard men. Inside the prison officers reputedly stood with their backs to the wall rarely engaging prisoners in conversation. Local stories tell of young prison officers who dipped their chains in acid to wear off the shiny metal coating: — the chains of established officers were dull. There are also anecdotes about new officers who had to work five years at the prison before their longer-serving colleagues would talk to them. Outside the prison many inmates worked on nearby farms where they were shackled to avoid escape; prison security patrols were noted for exercising repressive methods of control over their charges. But if the staff were considered hard on prisoners they were equally so with their Governors (and Prison Service administrators) with whom there were regular and frequent confrontations; the staff had become accustomed to Governors who were able to manage industrial conflict and believed that Governors of their prison possessed special qualities.

---

[7] See Gouldner (1955) for his discussion of the Rebecca Myth.

5.2 The Role of the Governor

Expectations assume a central place in role theory. In his elegant statement about role Mitchell tells us that

... role is the behaviour to be expected between two people in the ... content of their interaction ... Content becomes the normative framework of the role relationship encompassing the expectations of ego and alter of each other. The concept of role, therefore, becomes relevant in networks; role relates essentially to dyadic behaviour in terms of the content of the partial network (1969: 46).

Mitchell's position has profound implications for role theory because he takes the notion of expectations from the general to the specific. The importance of specific meaning in terms of content will be illustrated in the incidents discussed below.

For a number of years the Fortress was governed by retired military officers, some of whom became legendary figures. These former military officers were strong-willed men who governed by force of personality. Throughout the 60's and 70's the prison repeatedly was disrupted by industrial action which tested the mettle of its Governors. On one occasion, for example, a Governor was recalled from his annual leave when officers refused to enter the prison. By the time he arrived military units were already in the vicinity and awaiting orders to enter the prison. The Governor mounted some steps and began to harangue the staff. An informant recalled the following conclusion to the Governor's speech: "O.K. you bastards! You know how I operate. First you take care of them (inmates), then I take care of you." Staff then entered the prison so averting the crisis which was imminent. He was followed by another former military officer whose short-temper with Prison Service administrators was legendary. He was well known for his sharp tongue and confrontational style when dealing with those located in administrative units distant from the prison. But in so far as the staff were concerned he had a reputation for taking care of the 'boys'.

The appointment of Martin Jones broke with the past and almost immediately some members of staff began to question his ability. He did not act as the staff had come to expect; he seemed reluctant to take decisions and appeared remote. Additionally, and perhaps more importantly, many members of staff thought that he was more interested in prisoners than in the problems which were encountered by those who worked in the prison. Over the months individual members of staff and the local Prison Officers Association (POA) branch became increasingly disenchanted with the Governor and in the summer of 1982 the POA expressed "no confidence" in him. Several months later, when he failed to ensure that the prison would be properly manned over the Christmas holiday, Martin Jones precipitated a crisis which led to his removal. He refused to allow the staff to work the holiday rota which they negotiated with the administration. A brief discussion of this incident will be followed by a discussion of the problems encountered over the implementation of the Manpower Report and the way in which Jones's replacement was able to operate in culturally acceptable ways.

5.3 The Christmas Rota

The Christmas holiday period invariably poses problems for administrators responsible for staffing the prison. Members of staff want to spend more time with their families but both they and the inmates expect that the latter will receive extra privileges associated with the holiday season, such as additional association and recreation. Because of the special demands of the holiday period the normal duty rota is suspended and replaced with one tailor-made for the occasion. In mid-October 1982 the Chief Officer instructed the Principal Officer/Detail to draw-up a holiday rota.

For around a fortnight the Principal Officer/Detail consulted with individual members of staff and members of the POA Committee to achieve a rota acceptable to all parties. In discussion with staff the Detail PO needed to balance the needs of individuals against those of the prison. He needed to know which members of staff did not want to work and also to consider who had worked previous holidays. His task was made easier by those who requested to work for the generous financial premiums paid. Members of the POA Committee were available to mediate between the Detail PO and individual members of staff who had certain preferences which appeared to cause difficulty.

To some extent the various parties involved in the construction of a rota made an investment in the staffing of the prison for the holiday period and so they were angry when Governor Jones refused to sanction the rota for financial reasons. The staff were fully aware that the Governor had the authority to refuse to accept the rota but when they volunteered for certain duties and shifts they did so in the belief that the approval of the Governor would be *pro forma*. After all, this is the way that the rota always had been constructed so the staff had grown to regard the process as 'traditional', meaning that they viewed the process as inflexible.

When employees feel able to volunteer their time they do so on the basis of trust. Rather than working to a set schedule members of staff are offered a choice, not completely free of constraints, but one which allows individual members of staff to trade-off today's institutional needs against tomorrow's contingencies. In principle, when working becomes voluntary *ego* trusts *alter* to abide by agreements. But there is another aspect of trust which needs to be considered; members of staff had come to trust that the procedures of the past would persist into the future. Trust in others with whom agreements are reached and in the 'customary' way of doing things create sets of expectations so that when agreements are broken belief systems are attacked on a cognitive level.

A few days after the Governor refused to approve the rota the POA met to consider its position. The Chief Officer, also a member of the POA attended the meeting to explain the reasons why the Governor did not accept the rota. In a series of heated exchanges he was accused of failing to keep staff informed about financial limits, and as the meeting wore on he was subjected to personal insults from several prison officers.

Some of the difficulties inherent in this incident suggest a major problem of communication on various staffing levels; between the Governor and Chief Officer, between them and the POA and between the Chief Officer and members of the uniformed staff. But for the purposes of this paper my concern is with the expectations which staff had created for their Governor. They had come to expect that Governors were men of action and decision; they were surprised when Governor Jones suggested that the Regional Office construct the holiday rota rather than to instruct the Chief Officer to submit another, more financially acceptable rota. How could an administrator located a considerable distance from the prison construct such a rota? This action confirmed the view of the staff that Jones was indecisive and lacking in the ability to lead men. The Regional Office also was faced with the spectre of an unmanned prison, so arrangements were made for a regional administrator and a member of the POA National Executive Committee (NEC) to visit the Fortress later in the month. The staff now entered a period of limbo; officers could make no plans for the holiday weekend because no rota was available to them.

During this hiatus the members of the local POA branch voted to accept the Report of the Manpower Team (discussed below) whose existence they had refused to acknowledge. The Chief Officer apparently linked this action to the difficulty over the Christmas rota and, with the approval of the Governor, instructed members of the uniformed branch to follow the 'Vee' scheme[8] duty rota for the holiday period. At first staff were bemused and then dumbfounded by this instruction which meant that from the evening meal on 24 December to the morning of 27 December the prison would be staffed by volunteers; staff cannot be directed to work overtime. What purpose now could be served by throwing open the rota to allow for voluntary overtime when a rota constructed for that purpose had been rejected by the Governor?

---

[8] The 'Vee' Scheme was created for local (remand) prisons. The Fortress normally operated the FGS Scheme for training prisons.

The implications for the prison were serious indeed. While staff were unclear about what would be expected they could take no action. Now they could act in unison against those administrators (the Chief Officer and Governor) who they felt had breached trust. The staff decided that they would withhold their labour over the Christmas holiday; what began as a cooperative effort between members of staff and administrators turned into an organizational shambles.

The instruction to work the 'Vee' scheme placed both the POA and the Regional Office in positions where neither could work toward a settlement. How could the staff negotiate with the Governor in good faith? Could the Regional Director *trust* the Governor to manage the prison? The difficulties over the Christmas rota proved the 'straw that broke the camel's back'. The only possible solution available to the Regional Director was to replace the Governor. This was done the following week.

5.4 The New Governor

Within three days of arriving at the Fortress Arthur Bold had agreed a rota for the Christmas holiday. He met with members of the POA Committee who showed him copies of the rotas for the previous five years; these were similar to the one which had been rejected by Martin Jones. Bold approved the rota which had been drawn up initially.

When Arthur Bold replaced Martin Jones the latter had isolated himself from his staff and appeared to encounter difficulties in making decisions. Some members of staff thought that Jones could make decisions only when the appropriate circular instructions were available. This characteristic led some members of staff to refer to him as "Sir Circular". They could not understand how a Governor could not make routine decisions quickly as had previous Governors at the Fortress who had earned reputations for making decisions with apparent reckless disregard for relevant circular instructions.

During his first few days at the Fortress Bold took a number of actions which indicated to staff that he could make decisions quickly and that he was in charge of the prison. He dealt with prisoners' requests with considerable dispatch. On his fourth day at the Fortress he disciplined a member of staff for leaving a party of inmates unsupervised. His movements around the prison were brisk and during the course of the day he would stop to have a brief word with members of staff. In terms of the 'business' of running the prison, Bold quickly earned the respect of the staff which he enhanced by frequenting the Prison Officers' Social Club where he seemed to mix with considerable ease. These, as well as some other actions, placed him in a favourable light with the staff; but his main concern was to restore the authority of his office so that he could tackle the major problem confronting the prison — the implementation of the Manpower Report.

5.5 The Manpower Team

From time to time the Regional Director forms a manpower team whose members are drawn from several prisons within the region. This small group of supervisory level personnel work together for around a year travelling to each prison in the region to report on whether it is making the best use of available manpower. Because of the increasing cost of the operation of the Prison Service administrators are under pressure to exert greater financial control over costs. Since salaries and wages are the most significant cost factor in the running of prisons it is also the item which could contribute the greatest savings. Be that as it may many members of staff, especially supervisory level personnel who had worked at other prisons, were aware that some of the posts at the Fortress were peculiar to the prison. How many of these posts came into being were the subject of speculation and rumour, but their elimination could be achieved only by a study of staffing levels.

After assembling the Manpower Team a schedule is issued so that each prison knows when the Team will visit. Staff are invited to meet the Team, cooperate with the investigation and present arguments to preserve posts or for increases in establishment due to special conditions arising since manning levels were last determined. Despite attempts to encourage the participation of staff in the production of its report officers at the Fortress refused to cooperate; the local POA branch voted to 'black' the investigation. Why was the Fortress the only prison in the region which did not cooperate with the Manpower Team?

I suggested earlier that the Fortress had established a reputation as a tough prison for hard men. Many members of staff gained some status from working at the prison and presented a veneer of 'hardness' to maintain this reputation. Staff demonstrated their hardness not only by their brutal control over prisoners but also by their intractability in dealing with Prison Service administrators. The investigation of the Manpower Team provides an opportunity to see how the tough prison myth became operational as a component of the culture of the Fortress.

In 1977 the first Manpower Team arrived at the Fortress. The members of the local POA branch refused to cooperate. Although in the event their refusal probably was not complete, the lack of cooperation was so significant that the Team left the prison without completing its task. Five years later, when another Manpower Team was scheduled to investigate the use of manpower, many members of staff believed that they had 'beaten' a Team before and they could do so again. Why was it so important for the staff to adopt this position?

While part of the answer to this question might be found in the 'nature' of the relationship between the staff at the prison (and their perceived image) and the wider Prison Service, I prefer to look at the more pragmatic issues which were relevant to the staff, viz, availability of overtime and opportunities for promotion. Whether in private industry or public service the call for greater efficiency creates anxieties in the workforce whose members fear redundancy, changes in demarcation lines or a reduction in wages through reduced overtime. Changes in manning levels affect staff in a variety of ways, but in order to analyse the resistance to the Manpower Team we must first understand how the present manning levels were arrived at before the establishment of the Manpower Team.

Many of the prisons in use today formerly were county jails or other facilities (such as disused military camps) which gradually came under the control of the contemporary Prison Service through various legislated amalgamation, purchase and/or lease of facilities from the Ministry of Defence. Before the strengthening of the regional offices in 1979, methods for determining manpower were not clear. Some members of staff at the Fortress suggest that one of the prison Governors in the last decade increased the number of staff by eighteen during the seven years of his service at the prison. A number of supervisory positions were created as his way of 'taking care of the boys'. It is unclear how he was able to do this but in 1982 many officers at the Fortress realized that a number of posts would be eliminated by the Manpower Team. Some of the staff occupying these positions retired either shortly before the arrival of the Team or during the course of its investigation. These posts could not be eliminated immediately but they were left unfilled so that staff were promoted to fill them on a temporary basis enhancing the salaries of those 'acting-up' (i. e., promoted temporarily). Historically prison officers have received low wages which may be enhanced by plentiful overtime, free accommodation and opportunities to act-up. To some members of staff the Manpower Team symbolized the contracting manpower needs of the Prison Service and the reduced opportunities for promotion.

An equally important issue concerned physical safety. Many officers thought that a reduction in manpower could endanger safety to both staff and inmates. The staff exercised tight control over the prisoners, so a reduction in manpower could adversely affect the level of supervision. Resistance to the Manpower Team could not be based on the historical precedent of beating a Team in 1977. The POA had to fight the Manpower Team based on issues important to the staff — wages, promotion and safety. The battle was joined over these issues which effectively united staff opposition to the Manpower Team.

Before the Christmas holiday Governor Bold met several times with members of the POA Committee and members of the Manpower Team. The POA remained opposed to the implementation of the Team's recommendations so shortly after the Christmas holiday the Governor announced that the report would be implemented at the end of January. The target date then was altered several times to give the POA additional opportunities to negotiate further with the Manpower Team. These negotiations proved fruitless and the Governor instructed that new manning levels would come into operation during the second week of March; the Detail Office was instructed to allocate work assignments accordingly. Now the POA had to reach a decision; they could agree to the new working arrangements or take some form of industrial action. The latter course was decided upon and, taking advice from their NEC, officers worked to a state of maximum control. This meant that prisoners would be allowed out of their cells in a ratio of three prisoners to two prison officers. Thus, if six prison officers were present on a wing nine inmates were permitted out of their cells.

The tactical application of the maximum control state effectively slowed down the routine of the prison. Except for certain essential areas of work, such as the kitchen and laundry, most prisoners were unable to work. Because the routine was operating so slowly staff were unable to complete their duties on the wings, such as the serving of meals, supervision of exercise and 'slopping-out'[9] within the prescribed schedule; therefore some members of staff had to work voluntary overtime to ensure that prisoners were fed, and so on.

With the onset of industrial action the Governor was informed that a head office department would negotiate a settlement with the POA NEC. Although he was not directing the negotiating process Arthur Bold nonetheless approached the members of the POA Committee to seek a relaxation in the industrial action over the forthcoming Easter weekend, but this request was refused. At the conclusion of the long and uneventful holiday weekend he had a notice distributed to each inmate thanking them for their cooperation; he then left the prison to take a week's annual leave. Later that evening a group of young men who lived in a nearby village went to a low perimeter wall close to one of the wings and taunted the prisoners who shouted back and kicked their cell doors. This created a considerable racket within the wing and some staff became concerned that in the present industrial climate

---

[9] Many English prisons lack sanitation facilities within the cells. Prisoners are provided with plastic buckets for use as toilets which they are allowed to empty when the cells are unlocked.

the noise could lead to greater problems. The Governor was telephoned at home and advised of the situation. He returned immediately to the prison, declared a state of alert and called-in all staff informing them that the prison would now operate normally. Any officer who disagreed could hand in his keys, he said. How could the Governor take charge of the prison in this way when the authority to negotiate had been taken from him? The answer may be found in the way that he managed his image to fit into the expectations of the staff.

When Bold was transferred to the Fortress his home and family remained around a hundred miles away. He temporarily lived in lodgings near the prison and his personal circumstances facilitated visits to the social club where he could be seen drinking with some of the officers and where he earned a measure of respect for buying his share of the rounds. He thus developed an easy rapport with members of staff on whom he tried to impress the importance of goodwill in operating the prison. After the Christmas holiday, however, his visits to the Club reduced and socially he began to distance himself from the staff. However, when the POA initiated industrial action Bold returned to the Club at lunch time where he could be seen standing at the short end of the 'L' shaped bar with a dozen or more officers at the long end. These daily visits were somewhat tense occasions marked by a lack of communication between the Governor and the prison officers who frequented the club. But unlike his predecessor Bold was not denigrated by the staff for appearing to confront them in public.

The way that a Governor conducts relationships with his staff is part of a wider issue connected with his intermediate position. Staff at the Fortress were accustomed to Governors who *acted* as though *they* were in control of the prison and took decisions accordingly. This clearly was not the case with Martin Jones who appeared to prevaricate and procrastinate, creating problems for members of staff who became unsure about who was in charge of the prison. Since insecurity leads to intolerance, so staff denigrated Jones; intemperate and derogatory remarks about the Governor gave way to personal slurs, reflecting the intolerance of the staff. Rumour and innuendo degraded the position of the Governor creating difficulties in obtaining cooperation and compliance from the staff. There were no such attacks on Bold who exuded an attitude of hardness and continued to confront staff both within and outside the prison. Why did he project this kind of image? Since the staff were aware that negotiations were taking place away from the prison it would have been convenient to maintain an easy rapport with the staff rather than to project a confrontational style.

Regardless of the outcome of the negotiations, Bold would remain as Governor of the Fortress. He was clearly in favour of the recommendations of the Manpower Team which was demonstrated by the several instructions he issued for its implementation. He (and I suspect all members of staff) knew that eventually the manning levels at the prison would be changed to those recommended by the Manpower Team. As Governor of the prison Bold would have to shoulder responsibility for the implementation of the report and during the industrial action any sign of friendliness toward the men could be construed as taking their side against the recommendations of the Team. Thus, Bold had to maintain an image that left no room for misinterpretation. He made known publicly that he wanted the manning levels changed and had to act accordingly so that staff would not think that there was a difference between his public statements and his actions. The silent 'confrontations' with staff at the Prison Officers' Social Club suited this purpose. When he was called to the prison because of the disturbances he already had an image of someone who would take charge and deal with the men in a way that they could understand.

Prison Governors lack the authority to dismiss members of staff so his threat to officers to "turn in their keys" or resume a normal work routine was hollow. He conducted himself in the manner expected of Governors at the Fortress; he took charge of the prison without *apparent* reference to regional administrators and by so doing acted in culturally acceptable ways. His actions also moved the centre of negotiations away from the regional office and the POA NEC back to the Fortress where he could now take charge. This meant that he effectively minimised the influence which the regional office exerted over events at the Fortress; regional administrators were forced into a position where they supported Bold or removed him. The latter course of action would have been impractical following the removal of Martin Jones four months earlier.

After the staff returned to normal working Bold set into motion negotiations which would allow some extra manning levels which marginally would increase the number of staff on duty during weekends. This effectively allowed the local POA Committee to 'save face' with its members and with the NEC whose recommendation to the local POA branch was for a six month trial of the new system. Bold was able to manage the manpower crisis effectively through the use of culturally acceptable behaviour suggesting that a knowledge of institutional culture may provide solutions to certain issues at individual prisons.

5.6 Conclusion

A knowledge of the culture of the Fortress would appear to suggest that the staff will continue to encounter difficulties in accepting changes which are not defined and introduced in culturally acceptable ways. Although the power of a Governor may ebb and flow according to his personality, members of staff appear to have a vested interest in perpetuating the character and reputation of the prison. Governors unable to meet the expectations of staff will encounter difficulties in exercising control and in obtaining compliance. However, those who are able to exert their influence may be able to promote change in ways that are culturally acceptable.

References

Blau, P. (1964): *Exchange and Power in Social Life*, New York: John Wiley.

Goffman, Erving (1961): *Asylums: Essays on the Social Situation of Mental Patients and Other Inmates*, Garden City, New York: Anchor Books.

Gouldner, A. W. (1955): *Patterns of Industrial Bureaucracy,* London: Routledge and Kegan Paul.

Mr. Justice May (Oct. 1979): *Report of the Committee of Inquiry into the United Kingdom Prison Services*, H. M. Stationary Office. London:

Mitchell, J. Clyde (1969): The Concept and Use of Social Networks, in Mitchell, J. Clyde (ed.), *Social Networks in Urban Situations: Analyses of Personal Relationships in Central African Towns*, Manchester: Manchester University Press.

Earl Mountbatten (Dec. 1966): *Report of the Inquiry into Prison Escapes and Security*, H. M. Stationery Office. London:

Part II
Power as a Symbolic Domain

Chapter 6
Zombies or People — What Is the Product of Work?
Some Considerations About the Relation Between Human and Nonhuman Systems in Regard to the Socio-Technical-Systems Paradigm

Burkard Sievers

In the epilogue of his book 'Socio-Technical Design' Herbst (1974: 212 ff.) states the often repeated phrase that "the product of work is people". Unlike countless others this author is in no doubt that "contentment, peace of mind, happiness, and wisdom ... are not obtainable from the environment, but they determine how we are able to relate ourselves to our environment". They can only be "found in oneself and to achieve them involves a different form of work" (Herbst 1974: 216). Our contemporary economic, industrial, scientific, and technological achievements are not goals in themselves; their ultimate and enduring value can only be found in regard to the extent to which they are contributing to the further "exploration and cultivation of previously unknown modes of human potentiality and in the conditions provided for the development of human qualities, intellectual, social, and moral" (Herbst 1974: 216).

Although I share Herbst's postulate and the *homo mensura* principle (cf. Glasl 1980), it is based upon, it seems to me that in comparison to the majority of contributions, both theoretical and applied, which have created and maintained the last four decades of the socio-technical systems tradition such a position is not a predominant one.

The *work hypothesis* which, therefore, will be presented and elaborated here is that the socio-technical systems paradigm, despite the enormous challenge and contribution it has provided for new designs of the organization of work as well as for the improvement of working conditions for countless employees, has to quite an extent colluded with or been dominated by an image of man (and woman) through which people are deprived of one of their predominant human preconditions, that is the awareness of the inevitability of their own individual death. The question which has to be raised is whether the widespread use of the socio-technical paradigm, quite contrary to its original intent, has caused or contributed to a development in our contemporary work enterprises which converted the product of work into zombies, i. e. humanlike creatures but ultimately automatons because of their lack of a soul (cf. Dewisme 1957; Seabrook 1932).

Offering and adopting such a working hypothesis could easily be misunderstood as a proposal to abandon the socio-technical systems paradigm in order to search for a new organizational theorem which would provide the employees of organizations, workers and managers alike, with a higher probability of humanity both in their work and their lives. It, therefore, has to be emphasized that the following thoughts are guided by the attempt to inspect both this paradigm and its application in order possibly to improve its contribution to the quality of working and living conditions in our contemporary work enterprises. This attempt is guided by the conviction that the use of this paradigm obviously is undergoing a major transition; a transition from our elder colleagues like Trist, Emery, Herbst or Thorsrud who, among various others, have had a predominant impact on the constitution and further development of this paradigm, to those of us who have more or less taken it over as an important conceptual framework during our socialization processes as researchers, consultants or managers. To take over this inheritance in order to become their potential successors is not primarily a matter of adoption and perpetuation; in order to become heirs we have to scrutinize with our own authority and responsibility what we want to accept and what we have to reject (cf. Sievers 1988). Thus to reflect upon what our predecessors were concerned about may help us to derive a better vision of what our task for the future may be.

It is my understanding that by having contributed the relations between "the technical as well as the social system in the factory" as "a new field of inquiry" (Trist 1981: 7) the socio-technical-system approach did not only offer a new paradigm which "entailed a shift in the way work organizations were envisaged" (Trist 1981: 10); in addition, it opened a new philosophy of work and altered the perception and conceptualization of the social world we are working and living in. Although the main target of this approach obviously has been the relationship between the social system and various kinds of technical systems (which include not only our production technologies but the electronization of information and communication processes, as well as our financial and economic tools, our architecture etc.) the devotion towards this kind of orientation has enabled many of us to develop a further insight into "the relations between a nonhuman system and a human system" (Trist 1981: 12) which exceeds the traditional concerns of designing or redesigning a particular work setting or enterprise. The main impact of the socio-technical system framework, therefore, is not only a new way of managing the interfaces between the social system and our various technologies; it also has led us into a new symbolization of the relationship between man and his work.

With the concept of symbolization I am referring to its original sense of the Greek '*symballein*' i.e. to relate, to put together, to unite, which is the opposite of '*diaballein*' which means to separate, to split and to fragmentise (Sievers 1989). In this sense the socio-technical system framework means the unrenounceable demand to overcome many of the 'diabolic' fragmentations and splittings through which, in our western history of industrialization, men have been and to an enormous extent still are segregated from the work they are producing. The symbolization which crucially is inherent in the socio-technical paradigm is that men and their man-made world are related and can be related. Our technical civilization and its various revolutions have, from a macro-social level, to be regarded as men's product. As Eric Trist (1981: 13 referring to Singer 1959) has stated, "the technological choices made by a society are critical expressions of its world view." And I would add, the extent to which these choices and the application of their respective technologies are understood as the outcome of human activities or as nonhuman givens is in itself a matter of human responsibility and/or fatalism.

From a symbolic perspective I regard it as the main task and vision of the socio-technical paradigm to manage the relations between a nonhuman system and a human system in such a way that people in an enterprise, through the use of nonhuman systems are able to establish meaning through their work which keeps them from alienation and allows them to live a human life. Although it very often appears to be difficult if not impossible to qualify what is meant by 'human' or 'humanity', it seems easier somehow to describe the opposite and to specify nonhumanity or nonhuman systems. One crucial difference between human and nonhuman systems, however, lies in the fact that nonhuman systems or things are nonmortal; although they may be consumed, worn out or destroyed they miss the ability to die and to be aware of their potential death as a precondition of life.

Despite its obvious tendencies to overcome organizational splitting and fragmentation (cf. Sievers 1986), however, it seems to me that the socio-technical systems paradigm, over the years, has initiated another splitting of organizational reality through the predominant emphasis on its social dimension as against the psychic one. This split and the nearly total ignorance of the latter dimension finds its most evident expression in terminological changes in how the human system is described and specified. Whereas the literature on the early projects in coal mining put the emphasis on the psychological situation of the miners *in relation to* the social structure and technological content of the work system (e.g. Trist and Bamforth 1951; Wilson, Trist, and Bamforth 1951) thus mirroring the psychoanalytic tradition of the Tavistock Institute which, for example, finds its expression in the works of Jaques (1953), Menzies (1970), Miller and Rice (1970) or Lawrence (1979 a), this focus in the later works, primarily in Scandinavia and the U.S., has fallen more or less into oblivion. Contrary to the origin of the socio-technical approach when the action researchers, as Mumford (1986: 338) put it, "needed to understand both themselves and the individual worker" the more recent work within this paradigm almost exclusively seems to be concerned with the social dimension of the organization, with an increasing emphasis on its political implications; a shift of perspective which from the theory of object relations (cf. Guntrip 1961) can be described as one from the relatedness of man's inner and outer world to the ignorance of the former. This reduction of social reality into a mere concern for the outer world also can be seen as a consequence of the further development of social systems theory of which e. g. Luhmann (1984) and his emphasis on a system of actions is one of the most predominant examples.

The fact that, for example, this particular author, to whom I have been indebted for much of my own scientific development (cf. Sievers 1971), does not even mention the soul in the index of his fundamental outline of social systems theory may serve as a further indication for the working hypothesis I have stated. The frame of reference upon which this social systems approach, in particular, and the majority of social systems theories, in general, seem to be based is determined by the one central metaphor that every other metaphor, and that of the soul in particular, is lacking any further significance for the social sciences. It somehow appears to me that the contemporary mainstream approaches of the socio-technical systems theory are nearly exclusively referring to theories of social reality which reduce men, their work "and organizations as well as their interrelatedness into reified derivatives"; the understanding of work derived thereupon further seems to neglect "any relatedness of work to the human existence" (Sievers 1986: 335 and 342).

Even in the broader context of the social sciences it often occurs to me that holding on to the notion of a soul, although as a metaphor it is as old as mankind (cf. Rank 1930; 1950), predominantly appears to be antiquated if not out-of-science. Nevertheless, I am convinced that the notion of man's soul is a constituent concept and metaphor for any symbolic orientation in general, and that of organizational symbolism, in particular, because it stands for man's existential capacity to transcend himself both in a more functional as well as in a spiritual sense. If it makes sense that the symbol, as Winnicott (1974: 211) states, "is in the space between the subjective object and the objectively perceived object" it then can be understood as transcending the gap between the inner and the outer world.

In a metaphorical sense the soul then can be regarded as man's capacity to reach beyond the narrow frame of his subjective existence in order to establish and maintain a meaningful relatedness to his environment. Thus the more 'functional' transcendence is referring to man's capacity of managing his relatedness both to human and non-human objects which, for example, in the frame of work enterprises chosen here, are the social and technological systems with their various components. In comparison to this social and material dimension, man's capacity of transcendence in time does not only include his relatedness to an immediate past or future but also a transcendence which goes beyond the narrow frame of his own existence (cf. Lawrence 1985), i.e. the beginning as well as the end of his own life, points which according to our contemporarily agreed upon social construction of reality are marked by the moment of one's birth and death. This capacity of the soul to transcend the time of a man's subjective and limited existence has to be regarded as a spiritual one, regardless of whether one shares a belief in a life after death or not.

And it is the evident loss of the spiritual capacity for transcendence of man's soul, through which the human system in the contemporary use of the socio-technical-systems paradigm is predominantly characterized, which led me to the hypothesis that the product of work has become zombies. As I have tried to elaborate on previous occasions (Sievers 1986; 1987) such a derivation of the result of the production process in our working enterprises and employing institutions is mainly caused and facilitated by the societal split of life and death which in our contemporary organizations is continuously sustained by the enormous split of life into a work life and a remainder. To the extent that our employing institutions, in a way similar to ancient cities or kingdoms (cf. Dunne 1965) are tending to represent timeless survival as an equivalent to immortality (cf. Sievers 1985) the notion of work, as well as those who in their various roles as workers or managers are supposed to perform it, can nearly exclusively be perceived in the contribution they are making to the enterprise's growth and survival. Both the notion that all work one is doing is necessarily based upon the work of predecessors (cf. Marcuse 1933) as well as the idea that every employee — with some certainty — will be succeeded, have totally fallen into oblivion. Collectively we have got used to such an extent to the conviction that death will occur neither at the workplace nor during work life, that human mortality no longer can be perceived and related as a constituent part of the human system in the work context.

The ignorance of death as such has become primarily the fate of the worker in so far as the predominant split of work and life is accompanied and enforced by a further split in our contemporary work enterprises between those at the top, commonly called managers, and those at the bottom.

Although, for example, many greenfield-sites, which, over the years, have been set up in the tradition of the socio-technical paradigm (cf. e.g. Sievers et al. 1985) are providing quite an integration of the managerial function into the workforce they nevertheless ultimately cannot obscure the fact that it is the managers who are supposed to have a career whereas even multi-skilled workers face rather a limited range of development. This only seems to mirror the more general split according to which managers tend to identify themselves, as well as being identified by others, with the employing institution, whereas the workers themselves as they are no longer able to equal the perfection of their products tend to identify with their product thus becoming products themselves (Anders 1987). To the extent that managers are deified and workers reified both sides are deprived of their mortality.

Although it may appear rather frightening or even macabre, the following example from my experience may further elucidate how Herbst's (1974) phrase "the product of work is people" can receive quite the contrary meaning to its intention. When I was involved some years ago in a socio-technical design project for the greenfield site of a new petfood plant we were visiting another plant of the same company. Observing a worker at a huge cracking machine breaking deep frozen meat blocks into smaller pieces which then were processed either into dog cakes or canned food I suddenly became aware of my own anxiety about staying in front of the giddy opening of the machine. When I then turned to the manager who was guiding us and asked him how he thought that this particular worker would deal with his own anxiety about falling into the cracker, I had to realize from the immediate answer which excluded any possibility of such an accident that these feelings had to be denied.

When, however, I, insisted and asked what really would happen if a worker actually did fall into this machine which was part of a highly automated process, the quite lapidary answer I got was that in such a case one probably would have no other choice than to bury a whole palette of dogfood as a substitute for the dead body of the worker. The underlying denial of mortal anxieties and the contempt towards the worker had, on this occasion, to be contained by a joke. I wonder, however, how the colleagues as well as the management in another case, which, according to newspaper reports happened recently, were able to cope with the sudden death of a young worker who actually had fallen into a soya bean cracker in a fodder plant in France.

After what has been stated so far one may easily object that what I am propagating is just a too idealistic or too demanding notion of humanity, which not only goes beyond the possible reasonable range of social science but is an idea which was never intended to be realized since the socio-technical paradigm was originated in the early fifties. The former objection seems to be based on a rather pragmatic notion that science, in general, and social science, in particular, can't reach beyond the obviously obvious. And neither do I agree with the latter although, at first sight it might even appear to be accurate. Referring to my limited knowledge of the socio-technical literature in its narrower sense, I cannot recall any explicit reference to mortality which would have any direct impact on the theories built upon this paradigm. This does not, however, mean that this work has not had any relatedness whatsoever with the inevitability of death in work enterprises.

If one does not regard it as a mere accident but as a constituent historic event that the socio-technical paradigm originated from action-research in coal mines a further understanding may be derived. With the exception, probably of soldiers in the wars of this century almost no other occupation than the miner's faced death as an almost daily fate. Thus mortal anxiety and its related defences not only have an immediate impact on the social structure of a pit but also on the surrounding community. The arrival of a husband, father or son is always uncertain for his family, even "lateness caused by overtime might mean that an accident has happened" (Wilson, Trist and Bamforth 1951: 19). Although the quality of the description of the working conditions of the miners by these researchers of the early coal mine projects is rather abstract and can as such not be compared with how poets like e. g. Orwell (1937) or von der Grün (1962) describe their experience in the pit, there can be no doubt that the pertinent threat of severe and even mortal accidents as a constituent factor of the miners was taken into account by these researchers; the fact that Bamforth had been a miner himself for 18 years before he joined the research team seems to be not the least evidence for such an assumption. It seems that in this particular research, from which the socio-technical concept and its theory originated, work, death, and life itself were so narrowly interrelated for the miners, their families, as well as the researchers that it had not to be made more explicit.

The socio-technical paradigm since these early studies has represented hope through the conviction that the alienation of our industrial work, in particular, and the potential destruction of our contemporary civilization, in general, may be overcome. This paradigm is, above all, based on two postulates: on the microsocial level it is assumed that the immense destruction of the unity between man and his work, or, as Berger and Pullberg (1966) put it, between the producer and his product, can be reversed; on the macrosocial level, on the other hand, we may have a reasonable chance that we will survive as human beings instead of ending up as mere homunculi, robots or zombies. As such the socio-technical paradigm does not give rise to catastrophic images of the end of man or of mankind; it unquestionably enforces the vision of a livable future.

However, it seems to me that during the subsequent development of this framework and its application to various enterprises and their respective production processes: paper, cars, chemicals, and food, the concern with new designs, improvements, and changes in work conditions colluded quite considerably with the predominant contemporary social dynamic. Through its primary concern for increased effectiveness, economic growth, rationalization, automation and world wide competition this seems to be devoted exclusively to the principles of the Olympic games: faster, higher, wider! It thus appears that the inherent social hope of the socio-technical paradigm,

through its collusion with our contemporary illusions, may finally be perverted into just another social technology. I am worried about my impression
that often enough the success stories of socio-technical projects and experiments seem to exceed the description of their limitations and failures; these
projects seem to be guided by such a level of aspirations that the various
attempts to improve the design of work systems are often replacing real hope
by instant hope. Disillusion, depression, and despair both on the part of the
employees and on that of action-researchers or consultants have become
experiences which not only remain unmentioned in the literature but which
seem to have fallen into oblivion. To ignore these and other similar dimensions and qualities of human experience ultimately reinforces the reduction
of human beings to customers as their predominant or nearly exclusive role
in the various markets of our capitalistic economy.

There can be no doubt that Herbst's expression "the product of work is
people" is a constituent concern of the socio-technical paradigm and the
work based thereupon. There can, however, be no doubt that the realization
of this postulate is not a matter of theory. Despite the fact that "the system
concept ... is a useful heuristic construct ... for making sense of what seems
to be the reality of enterprises" (Lawrence 1979 b: 51) neither the system
concept nor the theory are able to grasp the dialectic of mortality/immortality
which the above presented working hypothesis is based upon. The probability
of whether the final results of our contemporary work enterprises ultimately
are human beings or soulless automatons will, therefore, fundamentally be
determined through our practice which not least includes the practice of
theory (cf. Luhmann 1969). To the extent that we as practitioners in our
various roles as workers, managers or researchers are either reducing ourselves or letting ourselves be reduced by others to mere agents of or substitutes
for a theory we should not be too surprised that what we are creating or
just reproducing are homunculi, i. e. "human beings who (are) willing to
act as substitutes for machines and ... to subordinate themselves to the
requirements of authoritarian hierarchical work organizations" (Herbst 1974:
185).

The fact that some of the most prominent early protagonists of the socio-
technical paradigm recently have died may make us, as their potential or
actual successors, aware anew that not only do we have to die, too, but that
it is our mortality and the meaning we give to it individually as well as
collectively, which determines the quality of the product of work. Thus we
may be able to determine whether the socio-technical paradigm is merely a
useful tool for the engineering of work conditions or whether it is rather a
symbol which "is in the space between the subjective object and the objectively perceived object" (Winnicott 1974: 211). If it is the latter case the
socio-technical paradigm could then not only be seen as a useful image of
organizations and their potential changes and necessary improvements but

also of their relativity and their further completion, because every image as a way of seeing is at the same time a way of not seeing (cf. Morgan 1986). The metaphor chosen here of the zombie thus may serve as a helpful discriminator to qualify both the people which work is producing and our image of man upon which it is based. We have, doubtless, to be aware that zombies and people are not alike.

References

Anders, G. (1987): *Die Antiquiertheit des Menschen*, Vol. 1, Über die Seele im Zeitalter der zweiten industriellen Revolution, München: C. H. Beck.

Berger, P. and S. Pullberg (1966): Reification and the Sociological Critique of Consciousness, *New Left Review*, 35: 56—71.

Dewisme, C.-H. (1957): *Les zombies ou le secret des morts-vivants*, Paris: Edition Bernard Grasset.

Dunne, J. S. (1965): *The City of Gods: A Study in Myth and Morality*, New York: Macmillan.

Elden, M. (1979): Three Generations of Work-Democracy Experiments in Norway: Beyond Classical Socio-Technical Systems Analysis, in C. L. Cooper (ed.), *The Quality of Working Life in Western Europe*, 226—257, London: Associated Business Press.

Glasl, F. (1980): Das Homo-Mensura-Prinzip und die Gestaltung der Organisationen, in B. Sievers and W. Slesina (eds.), *Organisationsentwicklung in der Diskussion: Offene Systemplanung und partizipative Organisationsforschung*, 99—133, Arbeitspapiere des Fachbereichs Wirtschaftswissenschaft der Gesamthochschule Wuppertal No. 44, Wuppertal.

Grün, M. von der (1962): *Männer in zweifacher Nacht*, Recklinghausen: Georg Bitter.

Guntrip, H. (1961): *Personality Structure and Human Interaction. The Developing Synthesis of Psychodynamic Theory*, London: The Hogarth Press and the Institute of Psycho-Analysis.

Herbst, P. G. (1974): *Socio-Technical Design: Strategies in Multidisciplinary Research*, London: Travistock Publications.

Jaques, E. (1953): On the Dynamics of Social Structure. A Contribution to the Psycho-Analytical Study of Social Phenomena, *Human Relations*, 6: 3—24.

Lawrence, W. G. (ed.) (1979 a): *Exploring individual and Organizational Boundaries. A Tavistock Open Systems Approach*, Chichester: John Wiley & Sons.

Lawrence, W. G. (1979 b): *Making Life at Work Have Quality*, Tavistock Institute Document No. 2T281, London.

Lawrence, G. (1985): Beyond the Frames, in M. Pines (ed.), *Group Psychotherapy*, 306—329, London: Routledge & Kegan Paul.

Luhmann, N. (1969): Die Praxis der Theorie, *Soziale Welt*, 20: 129—144.

Luhmann, N. (1984): *Soziale Systeme. Grundriß einer allgemeinen Theorie*, Frankfurt: Suhrkamp.

Marcuse, H. (1933): Über die philosophischen Grundlagen des wirtschaftswissenschaftlichen Arbeitsbegriffs, *Archiv für Sozialwissenschaft und Sozialpolitik*, 69/ 3, repr. in H. Marcuse (1965): *Kultur und Gesellschaft*, Vol. 2, Frankfurt: Suhrkamp, 7–48.

Menzies, I. E. P. (1970): The Functioning of Social Systems as a Defence Against Anxiety. A Report on a Study of the Nursing Service of a General Hospital. Research Report, *Tavistock Pamphlet No. 3*, London: The Tavistock Institute of Human Relations.

Miller, E. J. and A. K. Rice (1970): *Systems of Organizations. The Control of Task and Sentient Boundaries*, London: Tavistock Publications.

Morgan, G. (1986): *Images of Organization*, Beverly Hills: Sage.

Mumford, E. (1986): Helping Organizations Through Action Research: The Socio-Technical Approach, *Quality of Work Life*, 3: 329–344.

Orwell, G. (1937): Down the Mine, in G. Orwell (1972): *Inside the Whale and Other Essays*, 51–62, Harmondsworth, Middlesex: Penguin.

Rank, O. (1930): *Seelenglaube und Psychologie. Eine prinzipielle Untersuchung über Ursprung, Entwicklung und Wesen des Seelischen*, Leipzig: Franz Deuticke.

Rank, O. (1950): *Psychology and the Soul*, Philadelphia: University of Pennsylvania Press.

Seabrook, W. B. (1932): *L'île magique*, Paris: Firmin-Didot.

Sievers, B. (1971): System – Organisation – Gesellschaft. Niklas Luhmanns Theorie sozialer Systeme, *Jahrbuch für Sozialwissenschaft*, 22: 24–57.

Sievers, B. (1974): *Geheimnis und Geheimhaltung in sozialen Systemen*, Opladen: Westdeutscher Verlag.

Sievers, B. (1985): Participation as a Collusive Quarrel over Immortality, *Dragon*, 1,1: 72–82.

Sievers, B., H. Rieckmann, W. G. Lawrence and M. Foster (1985): The Role of the Parties Concerned in the Design and Setting Up of New Forms of Work Organization. A Comparison of Six Greenfield Site Projects, in European Foundation for the Improvement of Living and Working Conditions (ed.), *The Role of the Parties Concerned in the Design and Setting Up of New Forms of Work Organizations: Germany/United Kingdom*, Dublin: Shankill, Co.

Sievers, B. (1986): Beyond the Surrogate of Motivation, *Organization Studies*, 7: 335–351.

Sievers, B. (1987): Work, Death, and Life Itself, *Arbeitspapiere des Fachbereichs Wirtschaftswissenschaft der Bergischen Universität – Gesamthochschule Wuppertal*, Nr. 98.

Sievers, B. (1988): *"I Do Not Let Thee Go, Except Thou Bless Me!" (Genesis 32, 26). Some Considerations About the Constitution of Authority, Inheritance, and Succession*, Paper presented at 'Contributions to Social and Political Issues', The First International Symposium on Group Relations, July 15–18, 1988, Oxford.

Sievers, B. (1989): The Diabolization of Death. Some Speculative Thoughts on the Obsolescence of Mortality in Organization Theory and Practice, in J. Hassard and D. Pym (eds.), *The Theory and Philosophy of Organizations. Critical Issues and New Perspectives*, Beckenham, Kent: Croom Helm, (forthcoming).

Singer, E. A. (1959): C. W. Churchman (ed.), *Experience and Reflection*, Philadelphia, Penns.: University of Pennsylvania Press.

Trist, E. L. (1981): *The Evolution of Socio-Technical Systems. A Conceptual Framework and an Action Research Program*, Issues in the Quality of Working Life. A Series of Occasional Papers No. 2, (Ontario Ministry of Labour; Ontario Quality of Working Life Centre) Toronto.

Trist, E. L. and K. W. Bamforth (1951): Some social and psychological consequences of the longwall method of coal-getting. An examination of the psychological situation and defences of a workgroup in relation to the social structure and technological content of the work system, *Human Relations*, 4: 3—38.

Trist, E. L., Higgin, G. W., Murray, H. and A. B. Pollock (1963): *Organizational Choice*, London: Tavistock Publications.

Wilson, A. T. M., Trist, E. L. and K. Bamforth (1951): *The Bolsover System of Continuous Mining. A Report to the Chairman, East Midlands Division, National Coal Board*, Unpublished manuscript, London: The Tavistock Institute of Human Relations.

Winnicott, D. W. (1974): *Reifungsprozesse und fördernde Umwelt*, München: Kindler.

Chapter 7
Organizations as Networks of Power and Symbolism

Marta B. Calás and Jean B. McGuire

7.1 Introduction

Interorganizational networks in American management literature are often considered as a separate level of organizational analysis with its own particular characteristics stemming from the complexity of the system (Aldrich 1971). But in contrast with the consistent emphasis on intraorganizational issues, the study of interorganizational phenomena is fragmented (Galaskiewicz 1985), the focus on intraorganizational activities relegating what happens outside the more or less narrowly defined "organization" to that most useful of residual categories: "the environment."

Lately, however, the study of interorganizational networks has gained new interest, perhaps because of the wide acceptance of the open system approach for organizational analysis, and the recognition of growing turbulence in the environment where organizations operate (Cook 1977). There is an increasing rate of interconnection among the organizations in any system (Terreberry 1968; Emery and Trist 1965), and interorganizational relations, as a primary unit of analysis in complex social systems, are thus of increasing importance.

Conceptually these ideas have been widely accepted, but empirical approaches that could capture the complexity of interorganizational systems have been generally lacking (Hall 1987). In this chapter we propose that the difficulty of developing adequate empirical analysis for these systems resides first and foremost in the manner in which interorganizational networks and relations have been conceptualized. We review some of these approaches and contend that their conceptualizations of the networks as bounded, predictable, and rational entities fail to capture the ontological status of interorganizational relations. We then propose a different approach, derived from social anthropology, where interorganizational relations are understood as socially constructed on-going processes, and where networking activities are the focus of analysis.

7.1.1 Literature Review

To date, most analyses of interorganizational network relations have used an exchange or resource-dependence framework, often seeking to identify the conditions leading to particular network characteristics or forms of exchange (e. g. Halpert 1982; Boje and Whetten 1981; Van de Ven and Ferry 1980). Another focus has been on the consequences of particular network characteristics, for example, those characteristics leading to conflict or better coordination among members (e. g. Aldrich 1971; 1976; Provan 1984).

In general this research has emphasized the objective and static nature of networks, their instrumental and functional nature, and the expectation of finding universal patterns that could explain network "behaviours." Researchers have assumed that networks are relatively stable organizational phenomena with measurable objective characteristics such as formalization (e. g. Aldrich 1971; 1976; Hall et al. 1977; Litwack and Hylton 1962), centrality in the network (Boje and Whetten 1981; Provan et al. 1980) and frequency of contact between members (Aldrich 1971; 1976; Hall et al. 1977).

These assumptions explain the development of network characteristics by implicitly taking for granted their purposive, rational nature. The problematic nature of coordination among organizations thus becomes salient, and coordination and conflict become particularly important areas of interorganizational research (e. g. Aldrich 1976; Hall et al. 1977).

Network power-structure research focuses on the role of network centrality and control of resources and finances as important influences on power assessment (e. g. Aldrich 1976; Provan 1984; Boje and Whetten 1981; Pfeffer and Long 1977; Provan et al. 1980). While it sometimes departs from the purely functional and instrumental orientation found in other network structure research (e. g. Benson 1975; Zeitz 1980) it has generally emphasized that power rests in the control of resources needed by organizations for their survival (e. g. clients and financial resources) implicitly retaining assumptions of organizational stability and purposive rationality in the networks.

Such research also rests on strong assumptions about homogeneity of perceptions and orientations among network members, and about the universal validity of "correct" orientations. For example, it has assumed that formalization is seen as beneficial to cooperative relations, or that particular resources are seen as equally important by network members (Pennings 1981; Gottfredson and White 1981).

7.1.2 From Networks to Networking

Some organizational literature − mostly European − has proposed that in organizational situations the *status quo* is determined by a plurality of interests (e. g. Crozier 1964; Pettigrew 1973; Silverman 1971; Crozier and Thoenig 1976; Mason and Mitroff 1981). This perspective has seldom been represented in mainstream interorganizational research, where pluralism should be thought of as a natural ocurrence (e. g. Hellgren and Stjernberg

1987). The diversity of organizations and individuals composing a network creates the possibility of continuous differences of objectives and perceptions, making assumptions of homogeneous understanding and of rationality questionable. Network relations are not merely an arena where organization members exchange resources and come to agreements, but also a context where they must constantly reinterpret what is ocurring around them and attempt to re-structure their relations.

Some researchers acknowledge that the field of interorganizational literature has been oriented to coordination and stability, rather than coercion, bargaining, conflict of interest, and subversion of system goals by members (e. g. Aldrich and Whetten 1981) and suggest that more research should be conducted on the use of power and exploitation. What escapes these views, however, is the understanding that any research emphasizing the regulation of social affairs, and the instrumental rationality of social systems — typical of the functionalist view of organization — can hardly be expected to address issues of conflict in a non-positivist manner (Burrell and Morgan 1979).

The typical epistemology and methodology within the dominant paradigm of organizational research would only consider conflict and inconsistencies in the context of order and regularities. In that sense, the discovery of organizational phenomena outside these norms would only be considered "organizational pathologies," or "noise" in the research process. On the other hand, if approached from a pluralistic point of view the research must face a shift of emphasis; one must question the appropriateness of viewing network relations as objective and instrumental phenomena with a rational purposive essence, rather than as processes by which certain organizational forms may come into existence and be maintained. Simply stated, in the latter case *instead of studying networks one must study the process of networking* (Johannisson 1987; Melin 1987).

Unfortunately, most approaches chosen by interorganizational researchers do not seem adequate for understanding networks as continous processes. A network is a static entity when represented in a graph or matrix (Aldrich and Whetten 1981). The pattern of relations observed in a cross-sectional study is of little importance unless the investigator is able to understand the processes that brought the network to its current state. Aldrich and Whetten suggest the use of an evolutionary framework to understand the changes in the network from simple to complex states. A similar understanding could be attained by a natural selection or ecological model (e. g. Aldrich and Pfeffer 1976; Beard and Dess 1988).

These models, however, are based on strong epistemological assumptions, on a biologizing metaphor of organizational systems, which is difficult to maintain when the organizations in the system do not behave with the expected regularities, when the processes by which variation, selection and retention are expected to occur are subject to considerable alterations, and when the interconnecting processes in the system are basically ignored.

We present below an alternative approach to studying organizational networks which assumes that network structures are typically constituted by dialectical relationships between power and symbolic action. The ontological status of the network is seen as a precarious situation where ambiguous expectations and roles, and changing conditions of interaction are the norm rather than the exception. Here the important questions change from a focus on the current state of the network to a focus on how network members order and interpret contacts with each other, how they make sense of the network, and how they may *or may not* arrive at a state of relative stability and consensus whilst still maintaining "organization."

7.2 Interorganizational Relations as Networks of Power and Symbolic Action

As we have seen, some traditional approaches to interorganizational relations emphasize network interactions in the context of resource dependencies, where the transactions provide perceived *control over uncertainty* and carry the meaning of power (Hickson et al. 1971). Network properties then become associated with the distribution of power and influence within social structures (e. g. Salancik 1986). Crozier (1964) provides a different explanation when he argues that individuals in bureaucratic organizations *may create uncertainty* about their actions to maintain their own power within the system. Following this logic, one may say that the "management of uncertainty" is more plausible in interorganizational relations, where the typical loose coupling of the system blurs the attribution of actions to any individual actor.

These views, however, still assume the necessary rationality of systems and actors. It might be more appropriate to say that interorganizational members *confront equivocality* (Weick 1979) rather than *manage uncertainty*. From this perspective, most organizational events are overdetermined, more things operate on one event than are really necessary to produce it, and the significance of any event is plural. People in organizations, having selected and imposed meaning to one event, often discover that additional meanings are just as plausible.

The organizational culture literature has paid attention to the ways in which meanings may be selected and enacted as shared meanings in symbolic formations and symbolic activities by organizational members (e. g. *Administrative Science Quarterly* 1983) and some interorganizational literature has also adopted this perspective (Johannisson 1987; Ritti and Silver 1986). But these symbolic "systems of meaning" have more recently come to be seen as fairly opaque and precarious formations, constantly undergoing constructions and destructions (Donellon, Gray and Bougon 1986; Gray, Bougon and Donellon 1985). Here symbols are considered as objects, acts, relationships, or linguistic formations that stand ambiguously for a multiplicity of meanings, evoke emotions, and impel members to action (Cohen 1976).

From a postmodernist point of view (e. g. Lyotard 1984) such understandings about "meaning-making" are increasingly important. The current condition of Western society, with its multiplicity of discourses and "floating" units of signification, makes it quite unlikely that any particular theory proposing stability of content or process would account for the experiences of most organizational members. Indeterminacy rather than definition, difference rather than singularity, represent the current state of affairs (Calás 1987; Cooper and Burrel 1988; Smircich and Calás 1987). Interorganization rather than organization is the context of action for most members of society (Johannisson 1987).

This line of argument leads to the issue of the ontological status of the networks. People select and impose meanings on their situations as they socially construct reality (Berger and Luckmann 1966). But given the precarious and ambiguous nature of our signifying practices, "reality" must be constantly constructed and reconstructed between and within social system members. To consider interorganizational networks as socially constructed realities is to consider that their essence resides in the social processes which allow for the constant renegotiation of their system of meanings.

These symbolic processes could be defined as "political" (Pfeffer 1981) but only as a result of the broader cultural agreements of modern western society. As paraphrased by Sahlins:

… we have a kind of empirical society which precipitates organization out of the play of real forces. Ours too may be a culture, but its form is constructed from events, as the system gives people license to put their means to their best advantage and certifies the result as a genuine society. Thus the nature of man seems 'a perpetual and restless desire for power after power that ceaseth only in death,' and society but the collective effect, miraculously ordered out of private contention 'as if by an Invisible Hand.' Organization is the socialized realization of desire. (1976: 52).

Thus, it is the proposition of this chapter that interorganizational networks are socially constructed realities which enact typical organizational experiences of today's complex societies. The networks are "structured" in transactions; and the transactions serve to negotiate the favoured cultural meaning or "ground" of that reality (Perrow 1986) as power and as a political process. Networking is constantly re-enacted through symbols and symbolization rather than through specific resources or other "objective facts."

In the following pages we suggest an investigative approach which facilitates understanding the dynamics of power and symbolism as they define diverse networking organizations.

7.2.1 Power Relationship and Symbolic Action as Dynamic Interdependencies

Cohen (1976) has developed an approach in social anthropology which could offer an important heuristic in the analysis of networking activities. The researcher observes and tries to understand the enactment of power by informal groups in complex societies, focusing on activities which are typical of "westernized" cultures. In these societies symbolic action and power relationships stand in dialectical relationship to one another, confirming and reproducing the order of society. Only when the relations between the two domains are studied can a significant analysis of these societies be made.

From Cohen's perspective symbolic action in complex societies serves to resolve people's continuous struggles to achieve personal identity and selfhood. People interpret their "world" and these interpretations result in a political economy of the symbolic domain. Most people depend on the symbolic patterns of the groups to which they belong; and the groups may try to manipulate not only the symbols that they offer to individuals but also the need intensity for those symbols.

This approach thus focuses on comparative analyses of different groups within different structural situations. In Cohen's words:

The organizational potentialities of different symbolic forms can thus be analysed. In this way, different symbolic forms are compared within similar structural situations and similar symbolic forms within different structural situations (1976: 131).

Cohen (1976) identifies these symbolic and political activities as follows:

a) *Distinctiveness*: To operate effectively a group must define its membership and its sphere of operation by defining its identity and its exclusiveness within the political field in which it operates. Groups adopt one or more of a number of symbolic forms to define their distinctiveness, creating myths and ritual practices, for example, which are legitimized by the moral exclusiveness and style of life of the participants.

b) *Communication*: Distinctiveness alone is not enough to create a functioning political group. Members of the group should exchange messages, pool their separate experiences, and identify problems by which they would then develop some kind of common denominator or agreement.

c) *Decision Making*: Even though distinctiveness and communication contribute to the emergence of political groups, a more powerful vehicle is necessary to enable the group to act. The group must have a procedural pattern for the regular collection and exchange of important messages, for discussion, and for deciding the appropriate action.

d) *Authority and Leadership Process*: Decisions will be implemented only if they are backed by some type of authority, and by the exercise of power. Authority is seen through its symbolism and ceremonials, and leadership is fulfilled as leaders manipulate symbols through power given to them by the group itself. Power is essentially symbolic and leadership is a process of mutual stimulation between the members of a group.

e) *Ideology*: The articulation of the organization requires the mobilization of different kind of myths, beliefs, norms, values and motives. These different elements, which are employed in the development of a political system, become so interdependent that they tend to be seen in terms of an integrated ideological scheme related to problems of the individual members of the group and his/her place in society. Thus, an ideology of this kind is itself a significant element in its own right, contributing further to the development and functioning of the group.

f) *Socialization*: An ideology will function only if it is maintained and kept alive by continuous indoctrination, conditioning of moods and sentiments, and affirmation of beliefs. This is achieved by ceremonials which should be frequent and repetitive to fulfil their purpose of maintaining the organization of the group.

These inseparable activities could be observed to understand the process of the creation and maintenance of organizations as social constructions. Each activity is not a "variable" but part of the dialectical processes of power and symbolization making "organization". These relationships are represented in Figure 7.1.

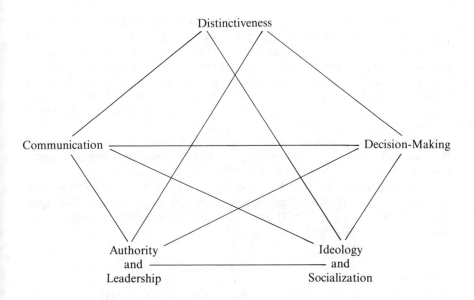

Figure 7.1 Network defined by the dialectics of its symbolic and power activities

In the following pages we analyze two interorganizational networks by means of this framework, and demonstrate the usefulness of this approach in the understanding of equivocal organizational arrangements.

7.3 A and B: Two Networks of Mental Health Organizations

7.3.1 The Organizations

The two networks in this study comprise mental health service providers within two areas of a New England state mental health system. This particular system was required to decentralize its provision of services by legislative mandate in the early 1970s. The state agencies had to stimulate private organizations to offer services previously provided by the public system, and do so on a competitive basis following from the assumption that better and less expensive services could be provided in this manner.

The state office in each area puts out an annual request for proposals (RFP's) which are the core item in the competition. Providers are expected to make clear-cut proposals which show their ability to offer quality services at a reasonable cost. Funding for the system comes from the state budget, according to the legislature appropriations, but it is not "earmarked" for each area.

The services provided cut across client needs so that often the same person might be a client of different agencies. Also, many of the services rendered by different vendors complement each other. Even though this situation seems to require extended and close interactions between agencies, when the system was decentralized a network of services was never formally established, nor was any particular organizational structure followed. It now appears that the system was shaped over the years through the activities of individuals and organizations in each area.

For the purpose of analysis the two networks will be labelled *A* and *B*. Both networks are composed of vendors (service providers) with continuous contracts with the state system since 1972, the most recent vendors coming into the system in 1980. Twelve (12) agencies — 65% — plus the Department of Mental Health (DMH) area office in Network A, and twenty (20) agencies — 65% — plus the DMH area office in Network B participated in the study and were analyzed.

7.3.2 Method

An interview was administered to the vendors and the DMH area director in each area. Twenty four open-ended questions requested information about the respondents' perceived role in the network, their perceptions of network relations, and their understanding of major strengths, weaknesses and problems faced by themselves and the network as a whole.

In most cases the respondents were the executive directors of each agency since it was expected that these were the principal actors in the interactional processes among organizations, and also the most influential persons in the political processes.

Each interview was content-analyzed to extract information on political and symbolic activities which would indicate distinctiveness, communication, decision-making, authority and leadership process, ideology, and socialization, as previously discussed.

The following analytical description of the two networks under consideration will illustrate how power and symbolic action conform and maintain each "organization" in a system that promotes, in appearance, both competition and cooperation.

7.3.3 A and B: Power Relationships and Symbolic Actions

a) Distinctiveness

Network A. Most comments regarding distinctiveness tended to separate the vendors from the state area office. A general feeling of "them vs. us" permeated most of the interviews: for example, respondents compared dealing with the DMH area office to "bridging the fortress," and repeatedly couched their responses in "us" and "them" terms.

The two most apparent symbolic forms used to differentiate service-providing agencies from the area office were the "ignorance" of the area office and their concern for finance. The state agency was seen as being confused about its role within the network and unaware of critical issues influencing care providers. Moreover, the state agency was represented as being primarily concerned with finances and bureaucratic procedures, and less concerned with (or unaware of) the client issues the vendors felt most important.

In essence, agency directors did not feel that the DMH shared their concerns, so that they were not working together towards a mutually acceptable goal. Rather than viewing their relations with the DMH as a collaborative effort, it was perceived as an instrumental and necessary endeavour, which sometimes "got in the way" of their true function: client service.

Network B. In contrast to the previous network, this area achieved distinctiveness by emphasizing the unity of the area as an entity, distinct from the state-wide Department of Mental Health organization and bureaucracy. The DMH area director attempted to work with contract agencies as colleagues, and repeatedly emphasized that developing a long-term rapport and a feeling of trust between the area office and agencies was critical to the success of the area.

Agency directors, on their part, tended to perceive the area office as basically "on our side" regarding most issues. Any problems were seen as emanating from the state level, placing the area office in an uncomfortable "middle man" situation.

As will be discussed later, the area office maintained this unity by strongly advocating and imposing a particular treatment ideology to which all agencies had to subscribe. This ideological solidarity was an important means of maintaining unity among agencies and between agencies and the DMH.

b) Communication

Network A. Communication between agencies and the DMH was frequent, but primarily focused on contract administration and fiscal matters, as already indicated. These concerns, of course, are congruent with the agencies' view of the DMH area office as being primarily a fiscal and bureaucratic entity.

Communication among vendors in this area was frequent only when required by specific client-related issues. Otherwise, agencies did not maintain close contacts, and while they might in theory have wished otherwise, they did not feel these contacts to be critical.

These communication patterns reflected and reinforced beliefs regarding the distinctiveness between the agencies and the DMH area office. While the dominant issue in the communication process was "client needs," it was also clear that they often saw little need for agencies to work together to meet these needs.

The nature of the contracting system — which established relatively independent agencies to serve the specific client populations described in the contract — allowed for communication patterns that reinforced this fragmentation of the network. In general, the agencies thought that their goals in serving the client could be best met by focusing attention on their own agency, and by minimizing DMH interference in the provision of services.

Network B. Communication in this network contained a large amount of bureaucratic and financial information which was perhaps greater than anything found in Network A. While the DMH area director saw great value in these contacts, the agencies' staff were less enthusiastic about the dominance of fiscal and bureaucratic reporting required by the DMH.

However, network communication extended well beyond these issues. All agency directors mentioned the weekly or monthly meetings as an important communication mechanism, although they disagreed over the usefulness of these meetings. They noted, nonetheless, that the meetings gave them an opportunity to discuss wider-ranging issues that would have been otherwise possible.

c) Decision-Making

Network A. DMH officials saw their decision-making processes as legitimate and well regimented. The assistant area director described at length the processes used to evaluate contracts, including examination of financial data, qualifications of staff, clinical evaluation of the proposed programmes, and consideration of the agency's past experience and potential.

She flatly denied any possibility of manipulation, describing such charges as "sour grapes." She was similarly adamant about evaluation procedures, emphasizing both the qualitative and quantitative monitoring and information obtained by the area office.

Agency directors, in contrast, perceived the process as inherently political, and one over which they had little control. They perceived it as a political tool used by the DMH to control the network, and thus as illegitimate. Moreover, they saw this political process as detrimental to their concern for client services and well-being.

Network B. In keeping with his emphasis on collegial relations with agencies, the DMH area director portrayed the contracting decisions as intense and comprehensive, but with politics and negotiation playing a minor part. He emphasized that contracting was not the time at which major problems should arise, since they should have been addressed as soon as they arose. He repeatedly commented that as a result of his knowledge of agencies and of the intensity of the monitoring procedure used by the area office, there should be "no surprises" on either side during recontracting.

The terms of the contract also reflected the collegial theme. The area director did not necessarily see a lot of competition as beneficial to the system for this might destroy collegiality. Thus, the specialization of agencies in certain area of service such as residential programmes helped to attain complementary togetherness of the agencies, which he favoured.

While proposals were extensively evaluated on twenty criteria by a selection committee, the area director admitted that the area staff's familiarity with an agency did play a role in this decision, and felt that this knowledge was used fairly to assure the quality of patient care. Agencies saw this personalization of the decision process as slightly less neutral but had confidence that the area office was making decisions for the benefit of the system.

d) Authority and Leadership

Network A. Authority and leadership processes in this area were seen to be lacking. It was not clear who provided the leadership, if any, or how power was negotiated. The system was seen as a bureaucracy, mostly symbolizing an organizational pathology.

Network B. Several agencies resented the strength and centrality of the area office, and believed this role to be harmful. However, here the flavour of the comments pertained to a feeling that the system would "get you" if you did not knuckle under.

Agencies saw themselves as becoming part of the system established by the area director, although this did limit petty vendettas and politics. Still, power was symbolically associated with the capability to get funded by the state system, even though the area has only denied renewal of contract to one vendor since the system was decentralized in the early 1970's.

e) Ideology and Socialization

Network A. This area did not seem to share a general ideology of any type apart from its concern with client needs. Given the lack of socialization activities within the area, this concern was not institutionalized.

On the other hand, the frequent complaint of "lack of clear mission in the system" kept more than one agency going. It appeared that many felt compelled to be more responsible for the client's welfare since they perceived deficiencies in the system at large.

Network B. Ideology was very important in this network. There was no doubt that in this network a common value and philosophy was shared by the members: "normalization."

Even though "normalization" was the intention of the whole state system, which was established to keep as many patients as possible out of the institutions and leading a "normal" life in the community, there was only one vendor in Network A who addressed the issue.

However, all the interviewees in Network B were clear about the ideology they shared, often mentioning it as a consistent set of values between area offices and vendors. Their clarity about this shared ideology appeared to be related to the socialization process. Socialization occurred very frequently in their meetings but, more important, it was designed into a 5-day training programme at the area office for all members of the agencies. These work-shops were offered at regular intervals and served to re-enact the symbolic meaning of the "normalization" belief.

In general, then, both networks indicated a dialectical relationship between power and symbolic activities. Following an analysis of networking activities similar to that suggested by Cohen (1976), it appeared that the success of attaining "organization" and maintaining it did not depend on perceiving a lack of conflict or competition in the system — an issue which was similar in both networks — nor on differences in perception about the content of relationships between the vendors and the state system, for these were perceived as mainly political in both networks.

The apparent success of Network B over Network A — in terms of perceived effectiveness of the "network" from the actors perspective — stemmed from the interactional dynamics of power and symbolization. Net-work B members saw themselves attaining distinctiveness, maintaining com-munication, decision-making, and leadership processes, which were met by an ideological commitment kept alive by continuous indoctrination. Even though Network B was not "rationally" designed, its functioning appeared to have the "consistency" resulting from a traditionally structured organizational system. Tables 7.1 and 7.2 summarize each network's state at the time of the study.

The interesting point, however, is that Network A did not seem to be any less effective than Network B. Clients were well attended, and received the

Table 7.1 Summary of results for Network A

Activity	Actual State of the Network
Distinctiveness	Two groups within the same area: state area office and vendors. Clear separation between the two.
Communication	Between area office and vendors: focused on contract administration and fiscal matters. Between vendors: focuses on client-related issues.
Decision-Making	Perceived as legitimate and well-regimented by the area office; based on administrative and fiscal monitoring. Perceived as a political process by the vendors; detrimental to their concern for client services.
Authority and Leadership	Perceived as unknown or in a decaying state.
Ideology and Socialization	Weak; based on concern for client needs; lack of clear mission; lack of socialization processes.

Table 7.2 Summary of results for Network B

Activity	Actual State of the Network
Distinctiveness	One group within the area; distinct from the state DMH and its bureaucracy.
Communication	Frequent between area office and vendors, and between vendors; day-to-day as well as in scheduled meetings; focused on bureaucratic and financial information as well as on wider range of issues.
Decision-Making	Personalized on the area office director; based on strength of "buying into" the area ideology.
Authority and Leadership	Granted to the area office director in view of "effectiveness" of results attained when dealing with the larger state bureaucracy and in sustaining the ideology; centralized in the area office.
Ideology and Socialization	Strong; based on philosophy of normalization; maintained by constant socialization through workshops.

necessary services from the providers; and the organizations in both systems had the same longevity, and similar probabilities for recontracting with the state system. Thus, what have we learned? What was the point of this study?

7.4 Conclusion

Our investigation illustrated the development of an interpretive approach derived from social anthropology, which ascertains the dialectics between symbolic and political activities within the *cultural meanings* of the organizations studied.

Gaining this "closer-to-the-phenomena" perspective of interorganizational systems implies that one must take into consideration the "ground" as well as the "figure" while defining each network as a whole (Perrow 1986). A social anthropological perspective, especially one which focuses on complex social systems in western societies, is particularly well suited for such an endeavour.

Our position in this chapter, however, goes one step beyond the interest of an appropriate description of networking activities. The possibility of describing "ground" (power and political activities) and "figure" (symbolic action), and the ways in which they configure each other and "organize" the networks, allows us to illustrate another position: that organizational research should be undertaken in an appreciative rather than a regulative mode (Gadalla and Cooper 1978). In their words: "The epistemological nub of this position is *appreciation*, the condition of being fully sensible of all the good qualities in a situation" (355).

This view – that organizations should be viewed as systems or contexts management, rather than systems that manage goals or tasks – requires, first, an acknowledgement of the illusion of "management," particularly in the "unmanageable" world of the postmodern. Second, it requires the valuation of relationships instead of "things." The primary relationship, being in this case that of the organizational actors and their environments, requires that the actors acknowledge their participation in enacting their own systems and environments (Zeitz 1980; Smircich and Stubbart 1985). Thirdly, it requires the understanding that what can be appreciated in any context is *difference*. That is, the understanding that a rich territory is composed of "altitudes" and "declines" rather than flatness would allow for an appreciation of the unevenness of organizational life. The quest for "management" is often the quest for the "flattening" of this life.

Finally, the appreciative view requires us to map and make explicit the "context languages" or discourses. For the actors to understand and appreciate their situation and actions, it is necessary that they "see" their "territory" through their own discourses.

The approach we have taken here could provide a "baseline networking topography" as a starting point for the actors' appreciation of their enacted relationships, and for further "mapping" of their networking activities over time. The matrices of relationships below are possible examples of these "topographies."

Table 7.3 Matrix of Relationships — Network A

Symbolization \ Power	D	C	D−M	A & L	I & S
D		Reinforces differences	Reinforces differences	Ignorance maintains separation	Weak within the system; maintains separation
C	Impaired flow by perceived distance		Impaired flow by distrust	Impaired flow by lack of direction	Impaired content by lack of mission and indoctrination
D − M	Opportunity for opposing views	Perceived as political influence		Multiple interpretations by participants	Lack of action maintains multiple views
A & L	Opportunity to deny recognition	Reduced by denial	Questioned legitimacy		Prevents emergence
I & S	Contributes to lack of clear mission	Prevented by lack of clear patterns	Differences in view prevents clarification	Prevents definition of mission	

The heuristic value of this approach is that it permits the researchers and actors to jointly map "the differences that matter" in the actors "world" without prescribing a normative "organizational view." However, the illustrations we provided in this chapter for Networks *A* and *B* fell short of completing this research strategy.

Table 7.4 Matrix of Relationships — Network B

Power \ Symbolization	D	C	D−M	A & L	I & S
D		Reinforces negotiated agreements	Reinforces compliance	Recognition maintains common-alities	Strong within the system maintains common-alities
C	Adequate flow by perceived closeness		Adequate flow by confidence	Augmented flow by clear direction	Adequate content based on common philosophy and frequent socialization
D−M	Oppor-tunity for agreements	Perceived as a political process		Similar inter-pretation by the participants	Continuous action maintains similar views
A & L	Oppor-tunity to recognize "a leader"	Augmented by re-cognition	Legitimi-zation by personali-zation		Sustain position and leadership
I & S	Contributes on the strength of ideology	Maintained through clear patterns	Negotiated agreements sustain ideology	Re-enacts definition of mission	

Our investigation's primary concern was to present a specific framework that could allow for the "mapping" of "territories," and to suggest a methodology based on its usefulness for interorganizational research. Our "mapping" metaphor, nonetheless, permits us to do some further traveling. We consider that once the networking topographies have been developed by the researcher, she or he should return to the organizational participants, and analyze *with them* how well the "map" reproduced their systems of meaning. Moreover, that would also be the time for the researcher to help the actors appreciate the systems which they have enacted *together*. "Disorganization," and "conflict" may attain new and positive meanings through these strategies.

We believe that only in this manner can a valuable understanding between the organizational researcher and the organizational participant occur: as a form of "discourse" to attain a better organizational world.

Nonetheless, we cannot leave this writing without reflecting on our own "ground" as researchers. Our first lines in this chapter acknowledged the fragmentation in and limitations of the American literature about interorganizational networks. One may attribute this lack to the favoured research epistemologies and methodologies, as we did, or one may further ask: is there anything about "networks" that violates American researchers' value systems? Ending this discussion on an exploratory note we want to advance the possibility of the latter. Could individualism as social doctrine (Meyer 1986) in that most individualistic of societies (Hofstede 1980) be violated by accepting as desirable the interdependencies promoted in the networking contexts? Perhaps it is here that we have to start questioning our own inattention to networking ... while further reflecting on the fact that we are writing these words now.

References

Administrative Science Quarterly (1983): Special issue on Organizational Culture, 28: 331 – 495.

Aldrich, H. E. (1971): Organizational Boundaries and Inter-Organizational Conflict, *Human Relations*, 24: 279 – 293.

— (1976): Resource Dependence and Inter-Organizational Relations, *Organizations and Administrative Science*, 8: 23 – 40.

— and J. Pfeffer (1976): Environments of Organizations, in A. Inkeles (ed.): *Annual Review of Sociology*, 2, Palo Alto, CA: Annual Reviews, Inc.

— and D. Whetten (1981): Organization Sets, Action Sets, and Networks: Making the Most of Simplicity, in P. C. Nystrom and W. M. Starbuck (eds.), *Handbook of Organization Design*, vol. 1, London: Oxford University Press.

Beard, D. W. and G. G. Dess (1988): Modeling Organizational Species' Interdependence in an Ecological Community: An Input-Output Approach, *Academy of Management Review*, 13: 362 – 373.

Benson, J. K. (1975): The Interlocking Network as a Political Economy, *Administrative Science Quarterly*, 20: 229 – 249.

Berger, P. and T. Luckmann (1966): *The Social Construction of Reality*, New York: Anchor Books.

Boje, D. and D. Whetten (1981): Effects of Organizational Strategies and Constraints on Centrality and Attributions of Influence in Inter-Organizational Networks, *Administrative Science Quarterly*, 26: 434 – 448.

Burrel, G. and G. Morgan (1979): *Sociological Paradigms and Organizational Analysis*, London: Heinemann.

Calás, M. B. (1987): *Organizational Science/Fiction: The Postmodern in the Management Disciplines*, Doctoral dissertation, Ann Arbor, MI: University Microfilms.

Cohen, A. (1976): *Two Dimensional Man*, Berkeley, CA: University of California Press.

Cook, K. S. (1977): Exchange and Power in Networks of Interorganizational Relations, *Sociological Quarterly*, 18: 62–82.

Crozier, M. (1964): *The Bureaucratic Phenomenon*, Chicago: University of Chicago Press.

— and J. G. Thoenig (1976): The Regulation of Complex Organized Systems, *Administrative Science Quarterly*, 21: 547–570.

Cooper, R. and G. Burrel (1988): Modernism, Postmodernism and Organizational Analysis: An Introduction, *Organization Studies*, 9: 91–112.

Donellon, A., B. Gray, and M. G. Bougon (1986): Communication, Meaning and Organized Action, *Administrative Science Quarterly*, 31: 43–55.

Emery, F. E. and E. L. Trist (1965): The Causal Texture of Organizational Environments, *Human Relations*, 18: 21–32.

Gadalla, I. and R. Cooper (1978): Towards an Epistemology of Management, *Social Science Information*, 17: 349–383.

Galaskiewicz, J. (1985): Interorganizational Relations, *Annual Review of Sociology*, 11, Palo Alto, CA: Annual Reviews, Inc.

Gottfredson, L. S. and P. E. White (1981): Interorganizational Agreements, in P. C. Nystrom and W. H. Starbuck (eds.), *Handbook of Organizational Design*, vol. 1, London: Oxford University Press.

Gray, B., M. G. Bougon, and A. Donellon (1985): Organizations as Constructions and Destructions of Meaning, *Journal of Management*, 11: 77–92.

Hall, R. H. (1987): *Organizations: Structures, Processes & Outcomes*, 4th edition, Englewood Cliffs, NJ: Prentice-Hall.

— J. Clark, P. C. Giordano, P. Johnson, and M. Van Roekel (1977): Patterns of Interorganizational Relationships, *Administrative Science Quarterly*, 22: 457–474.

Halpert, B. P. (1982): Antecedents, in D. L. Rogers and D. A. Whetten (eds.), *Interorganizational Coordination: Theory, Research, and Implementation*, Ames, IA: Iowa State University Press.

Hellgren, B. and T. Stjernberg (1987): Networks: An Analytical Tool for Understanding Complex Decision Processes, *International Studies of Management and Organizations*, XVII: 88–102.

Hickson, D. J., C. R. Hinnings, C. A. Lee, R. E. Schenk, and J. M. Pennings (1971): A Strategic Contingency Theory of Interorganizational Power, *Administrative Science Quarterly*, 16: 216–229.

Hofstede, G. (1980): *Culture's Consequences: National Differences in Thinking and Organizing*, Beverly Hills, CA: Sage.

Johannisson, B. (1987): Beyond Process and Structure: Social Exchange Networks, *International Studies of Management and Organizations*, XVII: 3–23.

Litwack, E. and L. Hylton (1962): Interorganizational Analysis: A Hypothesis of Coordinating Agencies, *Administrative Science Quarterly*, 10: 395–420.

Lyotard, J. F. (1984): *The Postmodern Condition*, Minneapolis, MN: University of Minnesota Press.

Mason, R. O. and I. I. Mitroff (1981): *Challenging Strategic Planning Assumptions*, New York: John Wiley.

Melin, L. (1987): The Field-of-Force Metaphor: A Study in Industrial Change, *International Studies of Management and Organizations*, XVII: 24–33.

Meyer, J. W. (1986): Myths of Socialization and of Personality, in T. C. Heller, M. Sosna and D. E. Wellbery (eds.), *Reconstructing Individualism*, 208–221 Stanford, CA: Stanford University Press.

Pennings, J. M. (1981): Strategically Interdependent Organizations, in P. C. Nystrom and W. H. Starbuck (eds.), *Handbook of Organizational Design*, vol. 1, London: Oxford University Press.

Perrow, C. (1986): *Complex Organizations: A Critical Essay*, 3rd edition, New York: Random House.

Pettigrew, A. M. (1973): *The Politics of Organizational Decision-Making*, London: Tavistock Publications.

Pfeffer, J. (1981): *Power in Organizations*, Boston: Pitman.

– and A. Long (1977): Resource Allocation in United Funds: Examination of Power and Dependence, *Social Forces*, 55: 775–790.

Provan, K. G. (1984): Technology and Interorganizational Activity as Predictors of Client Referrals, *Academy of Management Journal*, 27: 811–829.

– J. M. Beyer, and C. Kruytbosch (1980): Environmental Linkages and Power in Resource-Dependence Relations between Organizations, *Administrative Science Quarterly*, 25: 200–225.

Ritti, R. R. and Silver, J. H. (1986): Early Processes of Institutionalization: The Dramaturgy of Exchange in Interorganizational Relations, *Administrative Science Quarterly*, 31: 25–42.

Salancik, G. R. (1986): An Index of Subgroup Influence in Dependency Networks, *Administrative Science Quarterly*, 31: 194–211.

Sahlins, M. (1976): *Culture and Practical Reason*, Chicago: The University of Chicago Press.

Silverman, D. (1971): *The Theory of Organizations*, New York: Basic Books.

Smircich, L. and M. B. Calás (1987): Organizational Culture: A Critical Assessment, in F. M. Jablin, L. L. Putnam, K. H. Roberts and L. W. Porter (eds.), *Handbook of Organizational Communication*, 228–263 Newbury Park, CA: Sage.

– and C. Stubbart (1985): Strategic Management in an Enacted World, *Academy of Management Review*, 10: 724–36.

Terreberry, S. (1968): The Evolution of Organizational Environments, *Administrative Science Quarterly*, 12: 590–613.

Van de Ven, A. H. and D. L. Ferry (1980): *Measuring and Assessing Organizations*, New York: John Wiley.

Weick, K. (1979): *The Social Psychology of Organizing*, 2nd edition, Reading, MA: Addison-Wesley.

Zeitz, G. (1980): Interorganizational Dialectics, *Administrative Science Quarterly*, 25: 72–78.

Chapter 8
Crashing in '87: Power and Symbolism in the Dow

Michael Rosen

On October 19, 1987 the stock market crashed. I lived the minute-to-minute events of this great drama in the midst of stunned stock traders bailing out of positions, frantically calling other traders who hang up under the pretense of faulty phone connections, not wishing to transact business to avoid yet more debilitating loss. Others take orders they never execute. Traders holding hundreds of millions of dollars of positions in stocks that minute by minute lose their value, lifetimes of accomplishment dwindle to nothing. Successful seasoned veterans panic under fire. The "Big Board" of the capitalist world, the New York Stock Exchange *de facto* creasing to exist on Tuesday, October 20, 1987 near noon, players sitting befuddled next to their banks of never yet now quiet phones and unmoving computer screens. We feel the palpable terror of the end of life as we know it in the West, on the brink of unimaginable catastrophe, a giddy terror of apple carts and soup lines, of the high brought low and the low crashing the bottom. I stand in the midst of hundreds of traders in the gargantuan hyperspace of a corporate trading room, banks upon banks of instantaneous all financial markets information screens, beyond the leading edge computerized telephones, capital markets global markets muni-salesmen munitraders[1] risk managers futures traders foreign currency traders all-instrument hedgers risk arbitrageurs rocket scientist computer modelers all apparently between twenty-two and thirty-five, blue shirt white shirt grey suit pants blue suit Hermes Brooks Brothers Ralph Lauren ties Anglophile suspenders the New York Stock Exchange ticking away larger than life lights overhead the American Stock Exchange slower cousin mimicking the action nearby Dow-Jones news across the wall blinking away now no doubt about it on the edge of what is Standard-and-Poors keeping pace any bit of information otherwise unnoticed hundreds of traders synced into their two story cathedral ceilinged open space phones ringing names calling deals happening you are it more revolutions per moment than any competing line. Breathless. And social construction looms all around, consent writ large in the logic of interaction from the corporate construction of social space.

---

[1] Municipal bond salespeople and traders.

8.1 Introduction

This paper explores the relationship of power and culture in formal organizations, its moment of departure being the presumption that social life may
rewardingly be conceived as organized in terms of symbols, the meaning of
which we must make sense if we are to more deeply understand such
organization and formulate its principles (Geertz 1983: 21). But the work
here is largely conducted at the industry and society levels of analysis through
an investigation of the great stock market Crash of October 1987. This
framing has been selected since the internal contradictions of multinational
capitalism tend to play themselves out at various levels of the social structure.
A wide net has been cast to explore a complex phenomenon inherent in the
totality of our social system.

Being about power, this paper is also about control, for control is the
central problem of advanced administrative organization. And being about
control, this paper is also ultimately about consent, for consent to the labor
process is the principal mode of control in contemporary formal organization.
And extending this long-linked relationship by extending levels in dialectical
argumentation, consent is achieved within the dialogue of meaning systems
through the interaction of symbols, through the manipulation of the culture
order, just as the shared meaning system of culture is achieved ultimately
over the manipulation of power.

Further, any discussion here of the interrelationship and interpenetration
of power by culture and culture by power is framed within a postmodern
understanding of western, bourgeois culture. Postmodern culture itself de-
notes consent to that which is, to the present, to "what's here now." Any
statement on culture is also simultaneously a statement on the nature of
power in postmodern, multinational capitalist society. For embedded within
the meaning system of any social group are assumptions legitimating the
power of some, and matrices channeling/enabling the social enactment of
such power. In the instance of the Crash explored here, believing in the
normative value of the stock market — assuming it to be a critically necessary
component of the wider economy, accepting its stock price pronouncements
as measures of corporate efficiency, of its health as indicative of the overall
economic health of the nation, of its winning players as honor due powers
in the state — helps reproduce the existing social and economic order, and
thus the power of those who dominate in this order. And if the institution
of the stock market were to lose the moral commitment of the community
of which it is part, so too would the power recede of those behind the
institution. Thus, when dark stirrings appear suddenly on the horizon
threatening disaster, a response for institutional survival must be choreo-
graphed, whose steps and relationships should appear unflappably reasonable

to system players. The perceived plausibilities of danger's cause, an institution's response, and the resulting social effect are all ultimately anchored in the moral fabric of a social system, for the credibility of any environment's reaction to threat is secured by the moral commitment of a community to a particular set of institutions. Beliefs will remain intact insofar as the institutions which the beliefs support command loyalty, while beliefs will change as institutions lose support (Douglas 1975: 241).

Of the Crash, if the curtain were pulled back and the mysterious Great Oz of the market were revealed only as the traveling showman Professor Marvel from Omaha, the institution might lose support, the beliefs behind it might change, and the power of capital might be imperiled. Engendering the reproduction of power thus becomes a process of securing support for the market by plausibly broadcasting its position of centrality, by securing support for its continued workings through political and symbolic action.

8.2 The Falling Sky: On Power, Culture, Control, and Consent

The reality of any social process, Berger and Luckmann (1966: 121) remind us, is constructed in the face of chaos. Culture is built on the edge. That which appears to be objective — the naturalness of organizations, the structuring of hierarchies, the immutability of economic laws, the stability of order — is illusory, where fronts are maintained through the management of common backstages of meaning. Nevertheless, at times disorder raises its head, the mask of everydayness fades, we peer over the edge into the abyss of uncharted terror.

This is the case with the events dominating the news throughout and beyond the third October week of 1987. On Monday October 19 the stock market crashed, or more to the point, a string of financial market crumbles rippled west as the earth rotated in time-space, bringing the first market day of the week to the stock exchanges in Sidney, Tokyo, Hong Kong, Frankfurt, Paris, Zürich, London, New York, Los Angeles, and the electronic synapses of the thousands of computers scattered across the country that are the NASDAQ[2] Over the Counter market.

The losses preceding and including Monday were astounding. They were totally without precedent. Over one trillion dollars of stock value was lost

---

[2] NASDAQ stands for National Association of Securities Dealers Automated Quotation.

in the United States alone. On Tuesday the stock markets appeared near total collapse.

In an episode of "Adam Smith's Money World" — public television's popular program hosted by "Adam Smith" — entitled "The Great Crash of '87: Could It Happen Again?" (February 1, 1988), the introduction included the following exchange:

Announcer: "Black Monday swept away a trillion dollars' worth of stock value. On Terrible Tuesday the financial markets almost ground to a halt. Just how close did we come to a total meltdown?"

Buzz Geduld (partner in Herzog, Heine, Geduld, Inc.): "I think we came to the brink, I really do."

Announcer: "What would that have meant?"

Mr. Geduld: "We could be very close to a financial collapse of the Western Hemisphere."

Heady stuff for anyone vested in the "Western Hemisphere," or more correctly, the multinational capitalist countries. A trillion dollars lost! The financial markets grinding to a halt! The civilized world on the brink of financial collapse! What is the story behind such a cataclysmic event, one that occurred without a blink in the day as automobiles continued to roll off assembly lines, farmers tended their crops, Bloomingdales remained perfume-sprayingly crowded, and the San Francisco Giants lost in seven games to the Minnesota Twins. The American preoccupation with its baseball World Series did not evaporate on account of pending financial doom.

In August 1982 the Dow Jones industrial average (the "Dow") began a sustained climb. It marched from 800 points to a crescendo of 2,722.42 points on August 25, 1987, an increase in market value of 340 percent over a five year period. Through the remainder of August and September and into October, however, the Dow began to decline in a rather peaceful and relatively un-newsworthy manner. The popular press did not speak of impending doom. The Boys of Summer took front page as the Penant races thickened. Then suddenly, on Wednesday October 14 the Dow slid 95.46 points. It gave up an additional 57.61 that Thursday. On Friday the market behaved in a relatively orderly fashion, at least throughout most of the day. It was, according to seasoned traders, negative but not particularly agitated. At 3:00 P.M., with only one hour left to the trading day, the Dow was at 2294.88, already sixty points down on the day. Then the "once-in-a-lifetime" slide began. In one hour the Dow gave up forty-eight points, eight-tenths of one point for each minute of trading. It closed 108 points down on the day. "I've never seen anything like it." said one senior partner at a long-established firm. "There was no market late Friday, and it was terrifying. There wasn't a bottom."

Friday's 108 point drop made the evening's headlines as the largest single-day decline in the history of the New York Stock Exchange, but commentators continued to advise that the bull market was not yet finished. The market could yet conceivably hit 3000 or beyond before December. Optimism notwithstanding, the Dow was down 235 points on the week, an astounding drop in a business where a ten point swing in any one day was till recently considered significant.

Adam Smith: "October 19th and 20th, 1987, are now etched into the minds of investors the way Black Thursday was in 1929. In one day the Dow Jones industrial average dropped 508 points, 23%, 604 million shares, astounding. More shares traded in that day than in all of the year 1957. One trillion dollars of market value washed out."

Late Sunday night the financial watchers were already aware that the markets in Hong Kong, Australia, and Japan were down sharply. London was already down 10% by Monday's dawn in New York. One key piece of news was that a significant U.S. mutual fund, reportedly Fidelity, tried to beat the expected stampede in New York by selling $ 95 million in stock on the London exchange. And even before the New York market opened at 9:30 A.M., the NYSE's state-of-the-art main computer system, the DOT (for data order transmission) was already clogged. Fidelity reportedly dumped another $ 500 million in New York within the first half hour of trading. Wells Fargo reportedly sold more than $ 1.3 billion dollars worth of stock that Monday in thirteen waves of $ 100 million each.

By 10:30 A.M. the market was already down 104 points. Within thirty minutes it plummeted another 104 points. Even the vernacular used by traders and commentators to describe the ensuing events resounded of military catastrophe, of wagontrains drawn round as the enemy establishes its onslaught. As Michael Steinhardt, of Steinhardt & Partners said,

"I tried to pick moments of rallies to trade around the positions I had already acquired, but I wasn't particularly successful, because they didn't rally for more than a few moments or a few minutes at any particular time" (Smith, 1988).

At 11:46 A.M. the Dow Jones had risen to 2140 after a brief rally, but suddenly it began a dramatic reversal. By 12:55 P.M. it had sunk to 2053. Index arbitrageurs, those hightech traders who make money by playing the difference in price between stocks in New York and index futures traded mostly in Chicago — trading figured out by computers and limited to those who can play with huge numbers — saw a gap between Chicago and New York. But instead of stepping into the gap as they normally do, they fled to the sidelines.

At the same time, the specialist firms — those firms on the floor of the New York Stock Exchange with a monopolistic franchise through which all purchase and sale orders for any stock must be transacted — found themselves in conflict with the very task with which they are charged. This is the mandate of keeping the trading in any particular stock "orderly," a task incongruous with a full scale market rout. In normal times a stock is offered for sale, the specialist buys at least a minimally reasonable amount to give the impression of a two-sided market, even if no ultimate purchaser is in sight. But on Monday, as hundreds of millions of shares flooded onto the market specialists were faced with one sided buying at ever lower prices, each time reducing the value of all they purchased before. By following the rules of keeping an orderly market, however, they were imperilling the minimum capital requirements the Exchange demands they maintain. Long established firms were literally driving themselves out of business. A. B. Tompane & Company, for example, a specialist firm that had survived the crash of 1929, had a franchise to trade in USX, the U.S. Steel Company. On Monday, as the price of steel dropped, Tompane bought. Pete Haas of Tompane stood at his post crying "Steel, 250,000 steel for sale." But buyers stayed away. That evening Tompane's huge inventory of unwanted USX was marked to the close on Monday night, that is, to the lowest price Tompane had tried to sell this unwanted stock at all day. Such dramatic discounting impaired the firm's capital, and by Thursday Tompane had disappeared, purchased by Merrill Lynch.

In this sense, unlike the index arbitrageurs and most other traders, specialists had nowhere to hide. As the tide swung undeniably against the market and other players fled to the sidelines to hope and survive, specialists watched nervously as their capital dwindled and their survival was imperilled.

Exchange officials were acutely aware of this dangerous situation. Earlier in the day John Phelan, Chairman of the New York Stock Exchange, had established open lines to the Federal Reserve, the White House, the Treasury, and the Securities Exchange Commission. That is, to the critical loci of state financial power. According to Mr. Phelan,

"What you try to do is set up a control center, to keep watching, to keep monitoring to see where the pressures are, you know. Talk to the firms sometimes, go down to the floor some other times, keep base with this communications net ..." (Smith 1988: 5).

At 2:45 P.M. the Dow had settled near 2000, but waves of intensely heavy selling by portfolio insurers and others cracked any temporary semblance of equilibrium, and the market suddenly erupted into free fall. Throughout the remaining hour and a quarter of trading the Dow sank at the rate of one point every seventeen seconds.

"The interesting part about all this is that the theoretical capacity of the Street at that point in time was about 450 million shares. By the end of the day and certainly by 2:00 in the afternoon, we were running at a clip that was — eventually turned out to be 160 million beyond the theoretical. All right, so we were in a — almost in a free fall in space as far as volume was concerned" (Phelan, in Smith 1988: 5).

The allusion to order, to etiquette and honor that underscores the normal transaction of business in the stock market, gave way under the onslaught. As Muriel Siebert of Muriel Siebert & Co., Inc. noted of her attempts to do business on Monday,

"One firm slammed the phone down on us three times when we said 'Sell. We have stock to sell.' They just slammed the phone down, they said 'We are disconnected.' So we tried again. It was a very tough, nasty day." (Smith 1988: 5).

Buzz Geduld spoke of onslaught, of the power of mass panic in the crowd:

"This was a continuous onslaught of sell order after sell order after sell order, and it never stopped. And it's all we knew was, we were seeing a big panic, and we were just hopeful and praying that somewhere this was going to stop" (Smith 1988: 5).

Unlike the largely uncontrollable disasters of an earthquake, hurricane, or nuclear fallout, however, the Exchange runs on clockwork. At precisely 4:00 P.M. the bell rang, closing the market exactly as the piece of social construction it is frequently forgotten to be. The Dow closed at 1738, with the drop of 508 points being the largest single day decline ever.

And it is here, perhaps, where the real story of consent and falling skies begins. A thread of this may be seen in Muriel Siebert's statement that

"Normally, we don't get that many walk-ins. I saw people coming to the office just to see, and there was fear in their faces" (Smith 1988: 5).

There was fear throughout many sectors of America Monday night. By numerous popular accounts the world had changed. The economic foundations had been jostled. "The End of Business as Usual," the headlines of the *New York Times* notified us. The freefall market tailspin was "a little like seeing the atom bomb go off," observed Richard West, dean of New York University's Graduate Business School. "Once you've seen it, you know it could happen again. The world has changed" (*New York Times* 10.25.87, Section 3: 1).

"It was like being on a beach and the waves are coming at you, and you can't get away. There was no place to run. It was a very eerie, scarey feeling," said Muriel Siebert (Smith 1988: 2).

What this meant in real terms was readily reported in the press. All Americans are likely to be hurt, the *New York Times* announced, even those who own no stock, unless the market somehow miraculously "bounces back quickly" (10.20.87: 1). Businesses, hurt by the decline in the value of their shares and the predicted drop in consumer spending, will shy away from building new plants, and even from buying new equipment. Widespread unemployment will then occur. Universities, churches, hospitals and other nonprofit institutions, considered to be relatively immune to the vagaries of the stock market, will also all be hurt. The value of their endowments shrunk dramatically through the Crash and might continue to do so, and they too will be required to cut back on spending. Those close to retirement, among those who can least afford to be hurt, will be because the value of their retirement plans disappeared as the prices of stocks plummeted. Esteemed university professors were widely quoted, pronouncing that recession was inevitable if the market did not turn around. Similarly, housing values would drop, and because most home owners have the vast bulk of their personal wealth tied up in their homes, significant personal hardship would be experienced nationwide. "My 55-year-old mother called me twice today to ask if we're going into a depression, and she doesn't own a share," an economics expert was quoted in the *New York Times* (10. 20. 87, Section D: 34).

In another article entitled "The Market: Why does it Matter?," Leonard Silk of the *New York Times* wrote that when the market drops by one trillion dollars, "that plunge is enough to wipe out decades of savings" (*New York Times* 10. 21. 87: 1). Beyond that, "equity" in a corporation — understood here as the market value of all shares owned in a corporation — "is vital to the functioning of the capitalist system" (*New York Times* 10. 21. 87: 1). If equity dwindles corporations must borrow less, stifling expansion and possibly necessitating business cutbacks. Thus, because the market value of shares plummeted during the Crash, "corporations find themselves on thin ice and could crash through," as would the economy, the whole capitalist system, all life as we know it.

In a wonderful reproduction of the legitimating myth of the market, Silk writes that

The stock market holds every company, however lofty or lowly its product or purpose, to the same daunting standard. It honors the enterprise that knows how to make a buck. Executives learn that the market takes their measure.

Its constantly fluctuating prices pronounce them effective managers, irresistible salesmen, inspirers of others, daring innovators, maybe geniuses — or sluggards, milquetoasts, wrong-guessers, incompetent turkeys whose inaction has left their companies ripe for sharp-eyed, sharp-penciled raiders (*New York Times* 10. 21. 87, Section D: 17).

It is precisely this myth which gives the market its centrality. The market is endowed with a life of its own, its own objectivity. It is understood to be the measure of each company and each manager, to be the measure of the health of the entire nation.

"The economy will never be the same," William Glaberson told us in the lead story on the front page of the *New York Times*' Business Section on the Sunday following the Crash (10. 25. 87, Section 3: 1).

No matter where the stock market heads in coming months, the whole process of doing business, making a living, choosing investments — even buying a house — has been radically transformed. Last Monday's market collapse was one of those pivotal events that shape everything that comes afterward.

This legitimating myth, just as it denies the possible unconnectedness of the market to the economy, also posits not the market's social constructedness, but its objective independence. It is presumed to have a life of its own, or at least one independent of individual direct intervention. Such independence is also seen in the reported responses to Monday's Crash. Said Dudley Eppel of Donaldson, Lifkin & Jenrette:

"The fundamentals of the market changed. We became part of a computer instead of part of a system, and the liquidity in our marketplace was taken out of the hands of the professionals and run through a computer" (Smith 1988: 2).

Eppel even blamed the extent of Monday's drop on computerized trading programs, stating

"That is, I think, the thing that turned a 200-point rout into a 500-point rout. Yeah. I just think it − I don't think a computer should be running our business" (Smith 1988: 4).

Said Muriel Siebert, concurring with Dudley Eppel on machine control of the market,

"You know, computers have to be managed by people who have a little more experience and know the value of stocks, not that know cold-blooded numbers" (Smith 1988: 4).

This view of a stock market out of the hands of humans who understand value and the basis of its creation, and instead controlled by machines programmed by people who understand only cold numbers, fundamentally contradicts the conception of the market as an arbiter of such corporate value and the efficiency of its creation. Yet even those who espoused this critical view following the trading on Monday and Tuesday might well disagree with its radical conclusions of the disconnectedness of the market from the creation of value. It is safer to repeat corporate efficiency as the market's key legitimating myth rather than to open the Pandora's box of marginalist economics and let the chips fall where they may. The newspapers, television broadcasts, and politician's speeches continued to speak directly or indirectly of market efficiency and corporate value.

8.3 Postmodernism, Commodities, and Consent

It is in the nature of capitalism, Marx notes (1977: 967), to constantly expand, where this expansion holds a dual nature. The capitalist market grows insofar as it includes ever new producers and consumers. Simultaneously, it grows as ever more facets of social existence are commoditized and exchanged. Herein, as capitalist production is increasingly highly developed, more products take on the nature of commodities, that is, their production and exchange is predicated on a valorization process separate from the service they ultimately perform as use-values. There nevertheless exists an "indissoluble union" (Marx 1977: 952) within the same commodity between this valorization process and a labor process, and it is here that control through consent becomes pervasive in advanced multinational capitalism. Market logic becomes so extensive that control of the labor process through domination becomes superfluous. As actors in an economy transact as producers or/and appropriators of surplus value, and always as consumers of valorized commodities, self-evident market logic prevails. Everything is naturally bought and sold. People sell their labor, buy their entertainment, pay others to raise their children, and occasionally to bear them. And when nearly all facets of human social existence are bought and sold, that is, when nearly all participants in an economy are buyers and sellers of valorized commodities and perceive themselves naturally to be so, control is achieved through consent. The perception of naturalness in this commoditized social existence is precisely the essence of such control.

In a postmodern understanding of U.S. culture, American life is seen to have taken a turn, arguably somewhere in the 1960's, towards a "decentralized, superficial, amnesic, consumptive desperation" (Latimer 1984: 127). Ours is an era, Jameson proposes, where a particular depthlessness prevails. A weakening of history, a waning of affect, and a poststructuralist abandonment of depth models of understanding form part of and give rise to a social existence sundered from any roots and disconnected from any future. In such space the concepts of anxiety and alienation are no longer appropriate coordinates, where "alienation of the subject is displaced by the fragmentation of the subject" (Jameson 1984: 63). Within the realm of formal organization, this "death of the subject" can readily be perceived as the once-existing centered subject in the period of classical capitalism and the presumed nuclear family giving way to the fragmented subject of contemporary formal organization (Jameson 1984: 63). But if control was hegemonic in the dominant ideas of a ruling class, such domination gives way in the postmodern to a "field of stylistic and discursive heterogeneity without a norm" (Jameson 1984: 65). In advanced capitalism there are yet the powerful who "inflect the economic strategies which constrain our existences," but they no longer need or perhaps are unable to impose their "speech" upon us (Jameson 1984: 65). The Crash of October 1987 may be interpreted as the inflection of such economic strategies.

In the postmodern world the place of the legitimation experts and engineers of consent is thus to recreate those conditions the sum total of which amounts to − here borrowing from Jameson himself borrowing from Kant − the "hysterical sublime." For Kant the sublime was that state achieved whenever the mind attains the limits of its own ability for conception. "The result was a sense of speechlessness, of being overwhelmed by the divine, or at least by the metahuman. One underwent experiences of the sublime most often on the tops of mountains or in contemplating the sea" (Latimer 1984: 123). For Jameson, however, this sublime is transcended in postmodern culture by individual subjects suspended "in some vast network of international business, blinking, clicking, whirring incessantly to transmit, like transistorized Jedi knights, the power of the Force" (Latimer 1984: 123). This is the spirit of postmodernism, where a sublime may be conceptualized which abounds in decentered, depthless relations transacted in the whirl of a dehistoricized context. And it is in this sublime that resistance may be understood to be negated and consent to reside, synonymous with the postmodern emotional ground tone that things are what they are. Depths and absences subside into an experience of "pure presents in time," a cultural style Latimer identifies as Lacanian schizophrenia (1984: 120). Resistance to what? — if again following Latimer, himself borrowing from James Brown the King of Soul — "It is what it is, that's what it is" (1984: 120).

It must be understood that the very concept of resistance is built on a proposition of authenticity, one found incomprehensible in postmodernism. There is no subject to resist in the "depthless, styleless, dehistoricized, decathected surfaces of postmodern culture" (Eagleton 1985: 61). Instead, one goes with the flow of a social reality that has abolished all alienation, and thus the reason of resistance.

Postmodernism is thus a grisly parody of socialist utopia, having abolished all alienation at a stroke. By raising alienation to the second power, alienating us from even our own alienation, it persuades us to recognize that utopia not as some remote *telos* but, amazingly, as nothing less than the present itself, replete as it is in its own brute positivity and scarred through with not the slightest trace of lack. Reification, once it has extended its empire across the whole of social reality, effaces the very criteria by which it can be recognized for what it is and so triumphantly abolishes itself, returning everything to normality (Eagleton 1985: 61).

Through the reification of everyday life in postmodernism, everything becomes part of the capitalist marketplace, coextensive with commodification and thus with the market logic of exchange. Here, consent exists in going with the flow, for flow is what is. The reproduction of this ground tone involves immersion in the vortex of postmodern existence, its flat and positive essence. But it may also involve periodically peering over the abyss, experiencing the terror represented by change and presumed loss, and being reassured that chaos would therein abound and should be avoided. This peering over the abyss is the great Crash we have begun to witness.

8.4 Setting Your Own Stage

Experts had feared that many firms might begin collapsing on Tuesday if Friday and Monday's rout continued, and it started to appear that their prescience might materialize as the morning of "Terrible Tuesday" played itself out. Soon after its 9:00 A.M. opening the market soared 200 points, but the tide ebbed and began fading. By 12:30 P.M. the market was at 1711, below Monday's close.

Felix Rohatyn, the renowned general partner in the top flight investment banking firm of Lazard Freres & Company, thinks the stock market "came within an hour" of disintegration. "The fact we didn't have a meltdown doesn't mean we didn't have a breakdown. Chernobyl didn't end the world, but it made a terrible mess," he told the *Wall Street Journal* (11.20.87: 1), setting the metaphoric table with clearly high priced examples, pivotal happenings, events the world might spin upon. We were not in the Woolworth's of bargain basement occurrences of insignificance, and the *Wall Street Journal* readily concurred.

But it was on Tuesday, Oct. 20, that the stock market — and by extension all of the world's financial markets — faced one of their gravest crises (*Wall Street Journal* 11.20.87: 1),

the Journal announced, highlighting the market and the centrality it feeds on.

Not all stocks opened for trading Tuesday morning. Some specialists refused to do business until they had sufficient buy orders to enable their stocks to trade at higher prices than at Monday's close. Other stocks traded only briefly, closing soon after opening in the face of intense selling pressure. Shortly after 11:00 A.M. a wave of closings occurred among the bluest of the blue chip firms. Sears closed at 11:12 A.M.; Eastman Kodak at 11:28 A.M.; Philip Morris at 11:30 A.M., 3M at 11:31 A.M.; USX at 12:51 P.M. Nearly forty-five minutes earlier, at 12:15 P.M., the Chicago Mercantile Exchange — the "Merc" — halted trading in Standard & Poors 500 futures contracts, that security central to most programmed trading. By 12:30 P.M. trading in nearly 170 stocks had shut down, with rumors floating that the major exchanges themselves were considering closing.

Major players gathered in John Phelan's office at noon to consider the consequences of closing the "Big Board," a move of unprecedented proportion. Those gathered included Robert Birnbaum, President of the Exchange, key Exchange officials, and the directors of primary specialist firms.

The White House made it clear to Mr. Phelan that it did not want the Exchange to close, and he was apparently convinced, responding by announcing that "if we close it, we would never open it." Business as usual — cowboy bravado — would go on.

Business did go on, but not as usual. Many specialist firms surviving Monday ended the day with stock inventories several multiples higher than their average holdings, all of which had to be paid for within five business days. Prestigious firms turned to their normal lenders, similarly prestigious New York banks, only to find that the banks were not interested in lending. With phone calls from major securities firms pouring in to officials at the NYSE and the Federal Reserve Board complaining that without extended credit they could no longer continue to conduct business, the Fed made an astounding intervention, announcing that they would in effect guarantee loans. The Fed would provide desperately needed liquidity, standing behind those banks lending money to specialist firms, enabling them to play out their trading functions.

At 12:38 P.M., in what has come to be described as a probable manipulation of the market, the Major Market Index futures contract (the "MMI") began a magnificent rise. Like the Standard & Poors 500 index mentioned earlier, the MMI is a contract for future delivery of a specific amount of cash, based on an index — in essence a basket — of stocks. At this juncture, with essentially all other options and futures trading at a standstill, in a span of approximately six minutes the MMI rose from a discount of 60 points to a premium of 12 points over the Dow. And since each MMI point represents about 5 points in the Dow, this surge was equivalent to a 360 point Big Board rally. "Some believe that this extraordinary move set the stage for the salvation of the world's markets," reported the *Wall Street Journal* (11. 20. 87: 23).

As the MMI was forced to a premium over the cash value of the underlying index, a near instantaneous round of purchasing occurred in New York, with index arbitrageurs buying the separate stocks constituting the MMI and selling the futures.

"And so when I left the floor and came back up, I began to watch the machine again and look at the statistics, and sure enough, I mean, we weren't getting that pressure anymore, and she was beginning to round and to turn around ... And you could almost feel it crawling, trying to feel its way through the bottom. And it began to gain a little strength, and so it wasn't off 100 points, it was off 70; and then it was off 65 and then 50, and then 40 and then 35, and you could see it was beginning to get a new life. It was almost like for an hour, and the wind had been knocked out of it, and suddenly but slowly it was beginning to breathe again, and to get back up and going" (Phelan, in Smith 1988: 6).

This turnaround was orchestrated, the *Wall Street Journal* speculated, by a "small number of sophisticated buyers" deploying relatively little cash.

Nearly simultaneously early Tuesday morning, a number of major corporations throughout the country announced stock buy back plans. "This, too, appears to have been encouraged by major investment banks, many of which spent Tuesday morning frantically calling chief executives of major clients urging them to buy back their stock" (*Wall Street Journal* 11. 20. 87: 23). First Boston, for example, called approximately 200 clients. Major companies created a buying pressure of hundreds of millions of dollars where only sell orders had previously existed. If major corporations believed strongly enough in the market to dive in and purchase, perhaps the economy was not disintegrating, so the intent of the symbol went.

8.5 Let's Listen to Dad

As proposed earlier, power in a system is maintained during crisis by, among other things, orchestrating a rally around the symbolically critical institutions in that system, by reinvesting them with meaning. In this manner, a community is endowing its environment with credibility, selecting dangers to fear and rules to follow to preserve tranquil life within. The institutions safeguarded within a system are both a mask and a support for a particular form of power structure (Douglas 1975: 247).

As also proposed earlier, the credibility of any calculus of how the environment will react is thus ensured by the moral belief of a society in a particular set of institutions. Beliefs will remain insofar as the institutions which the beliefs support command loyalty, and beliefs will change as the institutions themselves lose support (Douglas 1975: 241).

The deepest emotional investment therefore lies in the assumption that there is a rule-obeying universe, and that its rules and behavior exist independent of human process. Danger exists in threats to this system, in threats to its conceptual base (Douglas 1975: 243).

Rather than giving credence to any thought that the market might not be central to the economy, or worse, that the economy might not be central — or might even be antagonistic — to the play of significantly worthwhile moral community bonds, we see the stock market at this time of crisis reinvested with meaning, reendowed with credibility. This emphasis upon centrality has been seen repeatedly in the dialogue by market experts quoted here. It is seen in the place accorded to the crash in the media outlets of the powerful, such as the *New York Times*, the *Wall Street Journal*, and "Adam Smith's Money World." It is seen in the total lack of countervailing dialogue, of any credibly placed voice intimating that falling rates of profit and crises of capitalism might be inevitable, or that the market might be disconnected from product value and its creation. These beliefs are kept totally in the background, endowing capitalist production with a relatively tranquil existence and capital with power.

If the market were to crash, go to zero, there is scant doubt that the sun would shine the next day, people would not have forgotten their languages, farmers would yet retain the secrets of farming and bricklayers the miracles of curtain walls and perfect arches.

And if the market had gone to zero during Monday or Tuesday, if the price of every outstanding share of stock traded on every exchange throughout the world had fallen to zero, absolutely no value would have been destroyed, not one iota. The value of every corporate asset would remain as before the cataclysmic Crash, as would each asset's use-value in the process of production. Thus we see the ultimate disconnectedness of the stock market from the underlying economy, from the production of goods. The Crash does not threaten the fundamental processes of production, but the relations of production. These must be kept wrapped tightly round in the *bricolage* of the Crash, lest we completely demystify high finance.

Unless we support the institution, sing its praises and bemoan the devastation which would arise given its demise, life as we know it would surely end, we are told. Without a smoothly functioning stock market, Adam Smith warns us, "you have Argentina or Mexico ... If money leaves our markets, our money, we would be a different poorer country. There is a lot at stake" (Smith 1988: 7). Images of Third World proverty and insecurity detract from the possibilities of transcending capital, of liberation from class strictures and from wage labor oppression. Protecting what is becomes paramount for Everyman.

With leaders desiring to lead and legitimation experts and engineers of consent plying their trade, crisis emerges as an exceptionally visible arena for the public enactment of secularized rituals of calm, trust, and compliance. Such intent possibly underlay the two press conferences conducted by the Reagan administration on the Crash, and the panel of luminaries, the Presidential Commission, subsequently assembled to establish blame for what happened and procedures to follow to insure that it would not again. A decisionist undertaking.

The first press conference took place on the White House lawn after an hourlong meeting between Reagan and his two top economic advisors, a meeting the *New York Times* described as "extraordinary" apparently only because Reagan met with both advisors for a full hour. Dressed in a dark suit and diagonal striped tie and standing alongside a youthful Marine in full military regalia, Reagan delivered a short prepared address, shouting "over the din" of an awaiting engine-on-and-roaring helicopter (*New York Times* 10. 21. 87, Section D: 12), the helicopter in Reagan's administration being elevated to a particular symbol of the Presidency.

The President stated that the market was up on the day and looked stable. Key administration people were in "constant contact with financial leaders" world wide. Reagan had ordered meetings with bipartisan leaders from Congress, a "summit meeting" on the budget, to find ways to remedy the record high government deficit and the international trade deficit, both which experts thought contributed substantially to the Crash.

Reagan's statement of bipartisan cooperation was Presidential, positing unity as the leader of the entire nation, one whole community.

"The economic fundamentals in this country remain sound, and our citizens should not panic. And I have great confidence in the future." (*New York Times* 10. 23. 87: 8)

A moment after preaching national unity, however, Reagan could no longer apparently withstand the competitive urge honed over years of professional politics. Rather than maintain the formal facade prepared by speechwriters, he launched an impromptu attack on the Democrats, stating that "I have never gotten a budget that I asked for ... And [therefore] the Congress is responsible for the deficits." And the Crash. And the President stepped into the whir of the bird and flew away.

The next day Reagan again delivered a prepared text and fielded questions from pre-screened reporters, this time at a press conference inside the White House. The tacking Reagan enacted between the clear and already cataclysmic volatility yet existing in the market and the reinvestment in the credibility of the system the administration sought to build was breathtaking. There was no Crash *per se* in Reagan's world. Instead, Americans watched the stock market "toss and turn" but largely come about. "There were a couple of days of gains after several days of losses," and there is, inexplicable, "excess volatility" in the market. But most importantly, "it does appear the system is working." Have faith, pull together, and we all will survive, his message said.

"When we've faced challenges before, this country has resolved them by pulling together." (*New York Times* 10. 23. 87: 8)

The President announced that he would form a commission to study "stock procedures and make recommendations on any necessary changes," what would come to be known as the Brady Commission. Blue chip to the core. The President would also meet with the bi-partisan leaders of Congress to begin deficit reduction discussions.

The traditional Question and Answer period included the following working of the fundamental ambiguity of symbols to convey this or that and this and that all simultaneously:

The President of the United States of America:
1. The only thing that "could possibly bring about a recession would be if enough people, without understanding the situation, panicked and decided to put off buying things."
2. "I think this was a long overdue correction, and what factors led to its kind of getting into the panic stage I don't know, but we'll be watching it very closely."
3. "Mr. President," one reporter shouted, "would you buy stocks now?" No response. Several more questions asked and answered. Again shouted, "Mr. President, would you buy stocks now?" No response. (*New York Times* 10. 23.87: 8)

Beneath the works was the clear message of the centrality of the market to the economy, to the whole social system. The man went on national television twice in two days to speak indirectly towards this centrality, which he then simultaneously denied in a brilliant sleight of symbols. Important indices measuring economic strength are up. Employment is "great." Inflation is down. Citizens are enjoying "the prosperity that is ours out there." Wondrously, however, we need not be concerned with the event which was a

non-event in a market which is volatile yet strong and working, because the
market does not matter. It is, after all, disconnected.

"But this is, I think, purely a stock market thing, and there are no indicators out
there of a recession or hard times at all." (*New York Times* 10.23.87: 8)

8.6 Smart Guys Don't Lose and Corporations Can't

American capitalism readily rewards those who combine hard work, intelligence, and talent. Such is the nature of laissez-faire social relations. Most
obviously, then, American capitalism most rewards those who work the
hardest, are the most talented, are the brightest. It therefore comes as no
surprise that our media star businessmen − including Carl C. Icahn, T.
Boone Pickens Jr., Sir James Goldsmith, and Donald J. Trump − did not
lose even a penny in the Crash. "After selling everything in August and
September, I got back in this Tuesday," Donald Trump, the famous real
estate developer and Atlantic City gambling casino owner told us. "I sold
on Wednesday afternoon. I made about 20 percent." A phenomenal one-day
return, equivalent, if it could be sustained, to a 7,300% yearly return,
somewhat better than the average bank deposit.

"I have been out of the market, too, for some time personally − out of
it from the long side; I've been in it from the short side," T. Boone Pickens,
the renowned owner of Mesa Petroleum and consummate corporate raider
told us. That put him in an even smarter position than Trump because, being
"short" stock, he had invested strongly in the market going down. He must
have reaped huge profits in a downturn so dramatic as the Crash.

In contrast to this astounding smartman/richman acumen, Trump recommended that the mere average investor stay out of the market and let those
serious men so interested do battle. "I suggest that the little guys just sit on
the sidelines. Instead of playing the market, they should go to Atlantic City."
And gamble in Mr. Trump's casinos, one presumes.

Pickens, who has gained national attention through his daring merger and
acquisition efforts, proposed an interestingly egocentric interpretation of the
Crash. He attributed the event to the then current Congressional proposal
which would make mergers and acquisitions more costly. A view the *New
York Times* called "perhaps ... somewhat parochial."

There is here in the antics and untruths of these super-rich an enactment of
the dehistoricized, depthless present, the flat positive essence of postmodern
society. T. Boone Pickens had in truth been joined by associates shortly
before the Crash in stock purchases of Newmont Mining, Boeing, and Singer.
Donald Trump was making substantial purchases of Resorts International

stock shortly before the Crash. These were commonly known investments in the small and tightly coupled world of high finance, particularly where these prominent players stood to reap increased profit through others belatedly following their lead, driving up prices through expectation.

The motive to reenvision truth, to position themselves as "winners" with the public, standing with impunity in the clear face of facts, only highlights the attendant myths of capitalism. These men are winners, and because winners win, they must have won, and because we want them to win, because we want the system to work, they did win. They told us so.

In contrast to the fantasies of today's financial elite, and in contrast to the flat amnesic essence of our postmodern society, the financial elite during the Crash of 1929 did not brag of their trading acumen. Modesty, and occasionally even philanthropy, characterized the 1929 post-Crash ground tone. For example, in October 1929, Julius Rosenwald, Chairman of Sears Roebuck, promised to guarantee the stock market accounts of over 40,000 Sears employees who suffered losses during the Crash.

Not only did our individual financial heros deservedly flourish during the Crash, but the financial institutions that participated directly in its enactment instantaneously reframed the very events they played out. Such reframing is seen clearly in the extensive newspaper advertising campaign run by Fidelity — the mutual fund company mentioned earlier in the context of London and early New York trading — the week of the Crash. In tone and content the Fidelity ads are similar to television commercials run by others, such as Merrill Lynch and the Shearson, Lehman, Hutton, American Express conglomeration, all stressing continuity and security. All reassuring.

These firms presided over the dissolution of hundreds of billions of dollars of market value, only to coax people to stay in for the long run. Again there is no Crash here, only equilibriums being tested, recessions and wars won, and something called "this week."

The Fidelity text:

We've heard from many of our long-term investors this week, some of whom have been invested in our funds for over thirty years. They've maintained faith in the long-term outlook for America, our economy, and the markets through recessions and wars.

Yet the question that even many of the most seasoned are asking is: Does what happened last week somehow change all that? Should I really think about selling everything?

Fidelity's immediate response to these concerned questions is — *don't overreact*. We believe a long-term approach has been and still is a prudent mutual fund strategy.

Every day buyers and sellers are actively competing in the stock markets. This last week, the usual equilibrium of buyers and sellers was undeniably tested, but the long-term individual investors who form the heart of Fidelity maintained their belief in the fundamental soundness of the stock market.

Fidelity believes your mutual fund investment philosophy should be based on long-term convictions. And Fidelity believes short-term trading and market timing for quick profit will more often than not work against the individual investor. Whether you're investing for a child's education or your own retirement, Fidelity is totally committed to working with you to achieve your long-term goals. (*Wall Street Journal* 11. 23. 87: 23)

This is the same Fidelity which rushed to unload 95 million dollars of stock in London on Monday, seeking to beat the anticipated U.S. downturn by taking advantage of time zones, and it is the same company which reportedly dumped another 500 million dollars of stock during the first half hour of trading once the New York market did open that day.

But the post-modern terrain is marked by a weakening of history, and in the aftermath of the Crash Fidelity characterizes itself as it will, rewriting — as did other firms and substantial individuals — that which occurred almost instantaneously in the face of countervailing facts. Consent in the postmodern "now" lies in going with the flow, the discourse of popular expectations and interpretations partially molded by those in a position to do the shaping.

8.7 In the Aftermath: Theory Redux

The Crash of 1987 is not taken as a cause of consent in the labor process of formal organizations. Instead, this wonderfully dramatic event has been explored in relationship to such consent, as a microcosm in which the reproduction of capitalist relations of organization — and also simultaneously the reproduction of consent — may be viewed as if from the outside. And standing as if from the outside, the fiction of the market has been highlighted, its gaming aspects understood as socially constructed. In normal times, this construction acts as a facade behind which we may live, warding off chaos. But chaos may emerge occasionally from behind the screen, as it did during mid-October 1987. When this occurs, the subtle contracts with which we have constructed our world become more palpably apparent, enabling us to more readily understand how we have structured our own environment.

We invent our world and then endow it with an independence, an objectivity beyond our control, a world controlling us. But by looking upon such exceptionally dramatic events as performance, we may gain access to some of the rules by which we live. As the Broadway producer Joseph Papp stated, there has been "no greater theater than the stock market" since the Dow Jones Industrial Average plunged 508 points on Monday, October 19, 1987.

The symbolism of the Crash conveys the idea that we are all tied into the market. We are all dependent on this great institution, which is our jobs and our country, and which is then capitalism itself. We are tied not only into this stock market, but into the market of the production and consumption of commodities, of valorized products. Accordingly, in addition to any gaming at this level (Burawoy 1979; Rosen 1985; 1988), consent to the labor process at the immediate point of production resides, also in the wider market of commodities, in the indissoluble union within the commodity between the valorization process and the labor process.

We see in the Crash a clear instance of the hysterical sublime of Jameson, the sublime of postmodern culture in which the subject is clearly deconstructed. The common individual is restrained from any autonomous steps in the playing out of this ground rocking drama, in a great multinational cataclysmic whirling electronic transmutational obliteration of wealth, nation, job, and security.

And we see here again that any study of the dialectical inter-relationship and interpenetration of power and culture involves to some extent what Jameson terms the "underside of culture," that is, "blood, torture, death, and horror" (Jameson 1984: 57). For the Crash communicated significant terror, raw fear over the possibility of the market collapse leading to extensive personal hardship and quite possibly to national and international catastrophe. Fear was a constant emotion underlying the Crash, first sowed through prediction and conjecture. Then work began to quiet it in such a way as to reproduce the power and meaning structures characterizing the terrain before the advent of crisis.

Here again there was no rupture with the mode of existence underlying the Crash, no immediate move toward transcendence motivated by anxiety from "what is" towards another "is." There was no sense of the humanist self, of the subject as free, active, autonomous, self-identical. Instead, there was a dramatic search to re-assert the present as it slipped past.

References

Berger, Peter and Luckmann, Thomas (1966): *The Social Construction of Reality*, Garden City, New York: Anchor.

Burawoy, Michael (1979): *Manufacturing Consent*, Chicago: University of Chicago Press.

Clifford, James (1986): Introduction: Partial Truths, in Clifford, James and Marcus, George E. (eds.), *Writing Culture*, 1—26, Berkeley: University of California Press.

Douglas, Mary (1975): *Implicit Meaning*, Boston: Routledge & Kegan Paul.

Eagleton, Terry (1985): Capitalism, Modernism, and Postmodernism, *New Left Review*, 152: 60—74.

Geertz, Clifford (1983): *Local Knowledge*, New York: Basic Books.

Jameson, Fredric (1984): Postmodernism, or the Cultural Logic of Late Capitalism, *New Left Review*, 146: 53–93.

Latimer, Dan (1984): Jameson and Post-Modernism, *New Left Review*, 148: 116–128.

Marx, Karl (1977): *Capital, Volume One*, Fowkes, Ben (transl.), New York: Vintage Books.

New York Times (October 20, 1987): Market Plunge 508 Points, A Drop of 22.6%, 1.

New York Times (October 20, 1987): Who Gets Hurt?, 1.

New York Times (October 21, 1987): The Market: Why Does It Matter?, 1.

New York Times (October 21, 1987): Reagan Says He is Open to Budget Talk, Section D: 12.

New York Times (October 22, 1987): Stocks Fall, But Avert Plunge, 1.

New York Times (October 23, 1987): Reagan's News Conference, 8.

New York Times (October 25, 1987): The End of Business as Usual, Section 3: 1.

New York Times (October 25, 1987): Financiers React to the Plunge, 6.

Rosen, Michael (1985): Breakfast at Spiro's: Dramaturgy and Dominance, *Journal of Management*, 11,2: 31–84.

Rosen, Michael (1988): You Asked for It: Christmas at the Bosses' Expense, *Journal of Management Studies* (forthcoming).

Smith, Adam (1988): *Adam Smith's Money World: The Great Crash of '87: Could It Happen Again? Part I*, February 1, 1988. Transcript New York: Journal Graphics, Inc.

Tyler, Stephen A. (1986): Post-Modern Ethnography: From Document of the Occult to Occult Document, in Clifford, James and Marcus, George E. (eds.), *Writing Culture*, 122–140, Berkeley: University of California Press.

Wall Street Journal (November 20, 1987): The Crash of '87 Proves Fortunate for 'Serious Money,' 1.

Wall Street Journal (November 20, 1987): Terrible Tuesday: How the Stock Market Almost Disintegrated a Day After the Crash, 1.

Wall Street Journal (November 23, 1987) Fidelity Investments Advertisement, 23.

Part III
Management, Consultancy, and Metaphor

Chapter 9
Merchants of Meaning: Management Consulting in the Swedish Public Sector

Barbara Czarniawska-Joerges

9.1 Organizational Talk and Organizational Control

The essence of organization is a repetitive collective action. In order to accomplish any collective action, the involved actors must have at least a rudimentary common framework, some shared meaning. It does not have to be much. If we are to carry a table together, we can belong to different political parties, as long as we agree upon what is "up" and what is "down," where is "left" and where is "right," which are the legs and what is the table-top[1]. Of course, even these matters can be challenged and subsequently negotiated, if the parties are equal, or imposed by one person (or a group), usually called a leader. These negotiations and introjections of meaning constitute, to large extent, *organizational talk* (Czarniawska-Joerges and Joerges 1988). In that sense, organizational talk is a kind of organizational action: it is a prerequisite for material action, it can substitute it, and it gives meaning to the past and future material action.

In this context one can say that what managers really manage is meaning (Smircich and Morgan 1982). Aiming at producing shared frameworks, they introduce world views, ideologies, ideas, rationalizations and interpretations. All this displaces the more traditional forms of organizational control, like force, or incentives, which become more and more decoupled from actual performance and linked to positions. Talk remains the best tool of operational organizational control. "This is the table; you take the top; we go to my left."

Managers tell their subordinates what is what (they *label* things), what things are like or what they could be like (they use *metaphors*), they tell them what is normal and acceptable (they utter *platitudes*). Labels, metaphors and platitudes are building blocks for more complex control machinery: world views, philosophies, ideologies, cosmologies, business ideas.

---

[1] This is not so obvious as it might seem, as I noticed once observing a girl and a boy in a Swedish sauna, involved in a quarrel over where was the right and where was the left (they stood facing each other). Eventually, the patriarchal society had won and the remaining children accepted the boy's definition.

Where do labels, metaphors and platitudes come from? Partly, leaders and managers produce them themselves; it is one of the keys to their success. Partly, from the mass media, a mass producer of such linguistic artifacts. But there is a new profession, increasing in volume and significance, which specializes in production and delivery of linguistic artifacts: management consultants.

These observations, accumulated in the course of several studies on organizational control, led to a study of consulting in Swedish public administration organizations, reported here[2]. The choice was dictated by the fact that the phenomenon of management consulting in and for the public sector is relatively new, and rapidly expanding, and that the novelty of the field requires from consultants the production and application of new approaches, therefore making the process more transparent both for the actors and for the external observers.

9.2 The Study

Starting with the point of interest thus formulated, I undertook an empirical study of consulting projects in public administration organizations in Sweden. The aim of the study was to reconstruct the substance and the proceedings of such projects and not to present a general picture of the scene (for this, see Premfors et al. 1985; Brulin 1987). The main approach was that of grounded theory — a constant comparative analysis guided by theoretical sampling and exhausted by a theoretical satiation (Glaser and Strauss 1974).

However, reality, as often happens, interfered with the purity of the method. My intention was to begin with consultants as a "natural" source of information; ask them to describe various projects and then follow the projects to the clients using the principle of minimizing (similar projects) and maximizing differences (different projects).

The collection of material turned out to be almost self-controlled. My two talented and dedicated interviewers, Anna Nilsson and Birgitta Schwartz, came back from the field with long and exhaustive interviews which showed distinct regularities. The consultants talked, basically, about two kinds of projects. One type concerned "internal" organizational matters: reorganizations, issues of control and leadership, strategy changes, etc. I have called these "restructuration," or RS projects. The consultants told us much about

---

[2] This paper is based on the study reported in a book *Att handla med ord*, Stockholm, Carlsson 1988. The study was financed by The Study of Power and Democracy in Sweden and an English report entitled *To Coin a Phrase* can be obtained from the author.

these, but in most cases did not want us to contact their clients. The reasons differed: company policy, project unfinished, sensitive project and so on. The other type of projects dealt with problems which can be seen as "external": located in the environment, or concerning the relationships between the client organization and other organizations. I have called these industrial policy, or IP projects, and we were allowed to follow them which, I think, is easy to understand. Nevertheless, it boiled down to the fact that projects we were allowed to study in detail were very similar to each other and the theoretical satiation was reached very soon.

Altogether, seven management consultants and nine of their clients were interviewed, speaking about ten different projects[3]. The comparative analysis of the interviews was completed with documentary analysis: we received consulting company brochures, reports, official commentaries, press cuttings and similar texts concerning the projects.

In the analysis, I used all the ten cases. However, when analyzing projects reported by one person only (RS projects), I compared them across projects to achieve the intersubjectivity equivalent to that created by various reports on the same project. Consequently, only experiences which were repeated in several RS projects were included in the analysis.

One should bear in mind that the clients we contacted were the closest collaborators of the consultants and, as a rule, were very contented with the consultants' work. As this study was aimed at a reconstruction of what happened where consultants were at work and not at an evaluation of the effects of their work, this limitation was accepted, especially as it did not mean that the clients were uncritical.

9.3 Diagnostics and Labels

It is commonly known that the first, and maybe the most important phase of consulting work is that of making a diagnosis. I do not want to question the obvious validity of this statement, but I would like to point out that it is formulated in a metaphorical way and there is no need to accept the metaphor unreflectingly. There are two professions in which diagnostics are extremely important: medicine and engineering. I suppose both metaphors can be accepted, depending on whether one sees organizations as organisms (a doctor) or as machines (a technician).

---

[3] Not that it matters; reporting numbers is a sort of tribute to the positivist tradition. From theoretical sampling and theoretical satiation perspective, numbers are irrelevant.

The present analysis, however, is based on an alternative metaphor: that of the travelling merchant, who sells tools for producing the meaning, and therefore the control, which is needed for the collective action. Some of them are so powerful, that they do not travel themselves, only send their salespeople around. The merchants not only sell, but also teach their clients how to use the tools. And so the next two sections will concentrate on tools, and the following two on teaching services.

At the first contact with the organizations, merchants have to establish what can be sold and what is needed (these might or might not be the same things). In order to do that, a merchant/consultant must categorize the most important matters, must introduce an order in the existing system of meaning by giving proper names to its important elements. And so the first step is to be able to say:

This is what you do/are ...
You are our client.
Your *problem* is ...

And so, for example, they might say: you used to be an "appropriation authority" but now you are an "assignment authority." Your problem is the misfit of goals and functions. Your internal organization did not follow the change in your identity. Our main target will be the accounting system.

How does one arrive at a set of successful labels? There appear to be two schools of thought. The "doctor/technician" school claims that labels must be authoritatively attributed by consultants. The rationale behind this approach is that "patients" do not like to face unpleasant truths. Also, there may be some labels already in place and in conflict with each other or with the consultants' picture. This has much to do with deciding who is the client. In one case, a chairperson of a Public Agency called the consultants in. At the first meeting between the chairperson, the consultant and the Agency's Director the following exchange took place:

Chairperson: "You must *do* something!"
Director: "But *I* am doing something: ..."
Consultant: "This is too narrow. This requires a holistic approach".

The consultants decided to select the director and the other related management groups as the main clients, even if they might have been the main problem. Remaining in contact with the chairperson was considered to be ineffective.

Another school, more of the merchant type, claims that labeling must be done by clients themselves. Labeling gives understanding, and this is what it is all about.

But no matter which school, the way of proceeding is the same: a thorough scanning of the organization by consultants or by organizational actors

directed by consultants. The aim is, "an authentic picture of the organization". All this is then interpreted, as historical documents might be, in a
search for meaning.

The point is, the labeling already merges with the next step; and good
labels are half way towards metaphors, and collecting information is already
a form of training for the client. No matter how, they must learn what is
going to happen. And apart from knowing what is ahead of them, the actors
also learn to cooperate with the consultants, which is a necessary preliminary
step for continued learning. And, last but not least, this is the way for the
consultants to show their prowess to the client: as they go around and
present their samples, the client watches them carefully.

Which labels are effective? Labels which produce an "aha!" experience, a
feeling that important but somehow hidden knowledge and understanding
has been released with the production of the label. In this sense, labels
operate just like metaphors.

9.4 Modelling and Metaphors

Metaphors are rarely presented separately: they tend to come in systems, or
kits of metaphors. There are at least three types of kits: analysis, identity
(organizational and personal) and construction kits. The kits are more or
less ready-made: again, the consultants who work as "doctors" usually have
complete kits, whereas the "merchants" might have various elements which
are then assembled for a specific purpose.

The analytic kits contain concepts like: strategy, market, resources, information systems, etc. − which are supposed to guide the analysis of the
problem. The analytic kits are usually the least flexible. The opposite is true
of construction metaphors, which are the most attractive and the most
important. These are also what the consultants are known for: metaphors
that permit building, the creation of something new. The kit can be assembled
or ready-made and merely presented to the client.

Where do metaphors come from? From reading the work of other consultants in the first place, and from researchers in the second. From public
lectures, from seminars. From fiction. Then, in the large consulting companies, the metaphors are tried on and polished and ornamented in internal
seminars. Toffler, Näsbitt, and Peters and Waterman are widely read. This
also applies to theoretical works, as some of the consultants are either active
researchers or else have a research background.

When the choice of constructive metaphors has been made, the active
promotion starts. I attempted to produce a schedule of major steps:
1) deliver an instruction for use and check first reactions;

2) create (or choose) a metaphor's referent in reality: a group of people, a project, a unit to which the metaphors refers;

3) facilitate its accomodation into the existing system of meaning by finding or creating links between this metaphor (kit) and other labels and metaphors, used by other groups and units;

4) weaken the potential opposition by localizing it, finding out its possible motives (envy, threat, competition) and try to either incorporate it ("you will also join the group in the future") or isolate it ("the two ideas are really complementary").

Let us say that the leading constructive metaphor is "market tigers."[4] I shall insert this fictitious example into descriptions of actual processes, based of course on other (but functionally equivalent, so to say) metaphors.

The series of seminars usually starts the process. The metaphor kit is. presented verbally and visually (overheads, films, etc.). The introduction is cautious, step-by-step, watching reactions closely. (Compare the process to traditional teaching, where usually a model, totally external to the audience, is dropped like a hot potato among students and left there). Before or after, these one-way communication occasions are completed with personal contacts. Then the time comes for subsequent steps: creating referents, setting them in a friendly network, feeling for potential animosities.

We invited people to an information meeting for the whole of X, together with few external people who happened to be there. 20 to 25 people were there, and 18 of them from X. We have fixed up appointments for selection interviews. This was at some time in the winter ..., then we got started some time in April and in May we had the selection and took the decision in [the market tiger board] about who would get a chance to be [market tigers] ... and then in connection with that we also did some intensive training ... [A meeting] led to a discussion in a cross-section group, with the board, the management group and the union, where we drew up the criteria, guidelines, rules of the game and the general emphasis of the [market tiger operation] in X. To start with, we based everything purely on [market tigers]. But we realized that there had to be a close link to the whole organization because otherwise it doesn't work. We had some links already in place, but we reinforced them. We have also realized that giving support and understanding to what the [market tigers] − are doing, means at the same time working towards a management development program for executives. But it was a massive reshaping, and there were plenty of discussions and a certain amount of jealousy.

So, how do metaphors work? If a label introduces order, certainty, by giving a name to things, a metaphor has an almost opposite effect: it breaks through

---

[4] I am not quoting original metaphors because this would reveal the identity of our respondents. That would mean, at best, an unevenly distributed marketing attempt (I could not possibly reproduce them all); at the worst it would certainly be a breach of anonymity promised, which helped us to obtain interviews where others had failed.

old labels, creating a hope for change, for something new. Labels say what things are; metaphors say what they are like and what they could be like. The effects of metaphors are specially visible where there is a feeling of a trap, exhaustion and a cul-de-sac as a result of prolonged difficulties.

Some metaphor kits are famous; this is why the consultants are called in — to get the access to their kit. The effective, constructive metaphors become labels: the ineffective die, or become platitudes. That is, when the force of the first, unexpected association wears off, a good metaphor becomes a name (this is not *how* it is, this is *what* it is!) and a bad one winds up, at best, as a platitude to be repeated in times of anxiety. I came round to this observation via another: in the interviews, clients used more metaphors than the consultants. However, the clients' metaphors lacked the strength of concentrating attention on a clear image. "It mustn't be the case that when you fire off a project or an experiment that it ends up like a flare which is shot off and then dies out." The image lasts about as long as this imaginary flare. Compare it with "market tigers" (to the extent that I managed, in my metaphor, find the equivalent of the original one).

I should also add that, although when I speak about metaphors I usually mean verbal ones, meaning does not only lie in words. Pictures and numbers are also languages, and some people are much more susceptible to these two non-verbal languages. Consultants as a rule support verbal messages with other languages, in order to reach as many people as possible.

But the strength of the metaphor lies not only in its aesthetic appeal, or rather its appeal is not limited to individual reactions. A powerful metaphor initiates and guides social processes.

9.5 Creating Talking Networks

Creating networks of people and/or organizations who can and want to speak to each other in the same language was of crucial importance in all projects. And metaphors played an important role here.

A network-creating metaphor must have magnetic properties — it must attract many various actors, and, possibly, be able to release an action — action-coupled metaphors are of high value. But a single action is not enough. What is needed, and what consultants help to create, is a "magnetic field" — an aura around the network which ensures that many spontaneous actions start, all of a sudden. This is difficult, not only because it is difficult as such, but also because, in the case of the public sector, there is a public which is waiting for the results. The help of local newspapers is very important in gaining the patience and understanding of the public: somebody who can explain that what is happening is invisible for the time being, even if it is happening. A magnetic field is invisible, after all.

In networks, a straight "management of meaning" is impossible, or at least very difficult, and it is therefore replaced by the "management of expectations". Creating a belief that small projects will grow big, presenting the metaphor of growth may be one way of achieving "management by expectations". But "managing the expectations" does not only mean making them grow. It means keeping them under control. Exaggerated expectations are just as dangerous as those which are too low. Frustrated expectations are destructive.

It is easy to make mistakes when trying to create networks: seminars fail because the lecturers are too "mighty" for the audience, even (or rather because) they are world-famous consultants. At other times, the network might be forced upon groups who did not know how to talk to each other because they had never tried.

But then, finally, it works. The network falls into place. For example, one of the great successes in one of the IP projects was a discovery that the employers, municipality representatives and union representatives could meet and *not negotiate*, which they almost automatically did at the beginning. They realized that it was possible to speak about matters of common interest, after all, to discuss and not to bargain.

In this case, this was talking among strangers. But a major part of the user instructions, especially in RS projects, is to teach people within the organization to use another language to analyze the situation they are in.

9.6 Teaching Languages

Which languages are taught? For example, the creativity training language is very popular. But this was not the only one. For instance, one consulting company came to the conclusion that in order to be economically minded, one must be economics-minded first. They trained all of the personnel to count — a group which by profession was very unnumerically minded.

A new language then gives an opportunity to see new things and, consequently, also an opportunity of seeing oneself in another light, of acquiring a new self-image. It is only in French that one can be called "*gourmet*" (or at least it sounds as good as it tastes in French only). New language usually offers a range of personal metaphors, belonging to the "identity kit." But not only personal metaphors: identity can have a wider meaning ("There has been a [regional] identity which has been reinforced with the help of the training program").

The training is over when the trainees can manage independently what they were supposed to do, without consultants' help. In other words, when they can go out and start using the new language to communicate, to shape and influence the reality which resides outside the "classroom."

But will the others understand them? Consultants do not only teach foreign languages; they often try also to fill in the communication gaps. To be able to accomplish a collective action, it is necessary that people communicate with each other, no matter whether they agree or not. That can be difficult — for example because of a generation gap. Thus a consultant serves as an interpreter and a mediator between the two sides. But sometimes no communication is possible. Then the consultants serve as vicarious communicators, and say what others, trapped together in the same organizational scheme for life, cannot.

Being a coach, a mentor, a mediator or a catalyser to idea-producing groups may become a fulltime job for a consultant, a job which then goes on for years rather than months. Nevertheless, at some point the consultants have to leave, but with the work well established and anchored. This depends to a large extent on whether there is somebody who will continue to "spread the gospel." Some missionaries, or local service persons for the tools that are left behind, must be trained.

And so we arrive at the end of the "affair": the deal has been concluded, the tools are in their place, the merchants have gone home. But what has really happened?

9.7 What Do Consultants Do?

According to whom? The consultants themselves? The clients? Or me, usurping a right to a meta-interpretation over and above everybody else's? It is perhaps best to separate and juxtapose the three sources of opinion.

Let us start with consultants themselves. Here is the most succinct normative definition of consulting:

Consultation is getting somebody else — the client — to realize what development might be and to achieve the will and the power to extract whatever individual potential there is and to do it.

This is done by playing many roles simultaneously or by choosing some of them. The choice depends partly on one's repertoire, partly on the needs of the client. Consultants establish clients needs in a way that closely resembles empirical research: out of many pictures they reconstruct one which is more complete and complex than anybody else's; and they use similar techniques (interviews, document analysis, group discussions). But if researchers very often get a Sunday-school type of an account, it seems that people are more open with consultants.

Which roles do they play? Some of them still speak about the "company doctor role," but this is clearly not in fashion any more, and the clients will not accept it, either. The *ingénue* role, that of the child who saw through the emperor's new clothes, is accepted by all sides. After all, it is all there, waiting to come out. Not so much a doctor, but a midwife, one might say. Or perhaps an amplifier — for those who whisper and do not dare to say something out loud.

But it is not only a question of what exists and must be extracted. Maybe there are things that exist potentially, but they need external stimulation in order to emerge. So, consultants serve as sparring partners, but not necessarily as passive sparring-partners. What they have to offer are ideas and metaphors. "They do not have metaphors" said one of consultants "We bring them in." The consultants are "idea-makers" or "idea-cultivators".

The clients also had a succinct definition. "It's really a question of stirring up the pot — and that's difficult to do internally". Indeed, it is difficult to stir a stew if one is sitting in the pot. But it is clear that consultants do not come to an empty table. Organizations are full of labels and metaphors which, with time, wither into platitudes. Somebody must stir the stew and add fresh vegetables to it.

Both consultants and clients present the process as an almost natural development, triggered off by consultants. The possible difference is that, if we follow this military metaphor for a while, consultants tend to believe they have aimed the gun, whereas the clients see it as relieving a natural phenomenon by producing vibrations with a random series of shots.

The extreme "stirring the stew" strategy is to simultaneously employ consultants known to have different and conflicting viewpoints. This is good for an organization where "everything is so stiff and jammed that it is a major step to ease things up". But it is not recommended for an average organization: it creates chaos and frustration. That is because it is never just a question of stirring the stew, but always adding new ingredients as well. Here is a direct question from the interviewer:

"What had the greatest effect?"
"New patterns of thought. It is fresh thinking which always has the greatest effect, there's no doubt about it".

Using the legitimate functionalist language of organization theory, one could say that consultants are needed to replace the old staff functions, as the creativity and ingeniousness, openess and freshness of a permanent staff is of a limited duration (Brulin 1987). Smaller companies, especially, could never think of permanently employing a staff representing all the specialities they could potentially use.

But, once we are in a functionalist frame of mind, how can one evaluate the consultants' work? There must be good consultants and bad consultants, surely? There must be projects which end with a success and those which end in failure?

As to any formal evaluation, both sides are very skeptical. One consultant said:

"I don't think there is any objective way of measuring it. We try to understand it by going out and interviewing people, both now and later. And then we follow up what progress has been made here. But it is not possible to take such things into account".

Clients agree. Success and failure in consulting work are very close. In a very successful project, people said: "They showed us that we can do it ourselves!" And, in the same organization, in another project which became a failure, "part of the criticism was that 'we could have managed that on our own'". What is the difference? Perhaps the answer lies in a feeling of surprise, which is close to an aesthetic pleasure, as when we read good poetry, and say, happily: "This is exactly what I think," and when we read bad poets, and say, disappointedly: "I could have written it myself." In this context, March's advice is particularly valid:

... good consulting, like good theory and good art, emphasizes aspects of events and interpretive schema that may be, by themselves, quite misleading or overstated, but that lead in combination with what is accessible to ordinary knowledge to improvements in understanding. From this perspective, the extent to which a speculation is non-redundant in an interesting way is likely to be as important as whether it is precisely true (...). Thus, it calls for an appreciation of the role of surprise, evocativeness, and beauty in interpretation (March 1984: 19).

But how to recognize a failure? By observing the effects, especially when the consultants are no longer there: "... if there isn't some sort of anchorage and no one responsible for pushing things ahead consequently, then everything collapses rather rapidly like a house of cards". Labels and metaphors are tools. If nobody learned how to use them by the time merchants have departed, then they will soon rust away, unused.

Thus I return to my own metaphor in the end. Although my respondents did not use this metaphor as a whole, there were bits and pieces of it, and, all in all, I did not find anything contradicting it or challenging its validity. I still tend to see consultants as travelling merchants, with their kits of tools for producing action through meaning.

In market places they might meet a leader of an organization and let him glimpse their goods, or else their fame is such that everybody has heard about the wonders stored in their bags. So they are invited and come, first to show all they have, and while they are demonstrating their wares, they are learning as much about the place they came to as the buyers about their goods. The transaction includes instructions for use: they hold demonstrations and they teach people how to use their tools. As people become more and more fascinated with the tools, they forget the merchants and want to put the tools to a real use.

If this picture seems too romantic, I would like to remind the reader that, as with all metaphors, this one also entails potentially ugly sides to the story. In other words, metaphors should be used not only for construction but also for analytic purposes. A good metaphor for consulting (be it merchants or something else) should create a potentiality of reflection and self-reflection.

References

Brulin, G. (1987): *Konsulten — en kunskapsförmedlare?*, Working Paper, May, University of Uppsala, Department of Sociology.

Czarniawska-Joerges, B. and B. Joerges (1988): How to Control Things With Words. Organizational Talk and Organizational Control, *Management Communication Quarterly*, 2, 2: 170–193.

Glaser, B. G. and A. L. Strauss (1974): *The Discovery of Grounded Theory. Strategies For Qualitative Research*, Chicago: Aldine.

March, J. G. (1984): *Organizational Consultants and Organizational Research*, Talk delivered at the annual meeting of the Academy of Management, August, Boston.

Premfors, R., A.-M. Eklund and T. Larsson (1985): *Privata konsulter i offentlig förvaltning*, Department of Political Science Working Paper No. 9, Stockholm.

Smircich, L., and G. Morgan (1982): Leadership: The Management of Meaning, *The Journal of Applied Behavioral Science*, 18, 3: 257–273.

Chapter 10
Metaphor Management: On the Semiotics of Strategic Leadership[1]

Henrik Gahmberg

The recent vogue of corporate culture among practising managers and the corresponding activity of studies on organizational symbolism within the organization and management field may be interpreted as indicators of a longer term shift in attitude and research paradigm.

The shift of emphasis from rational planning models in strategy formulation to organizational aspects of strategy implementation − to a more balanced strategic management, in Ansoff's terms, was the preceding phase.

The critical views of managerial work and strategy-making and alternative views offered by Mintzberg (1973), Miles and Snow (1978) and Miles (1982) were other "overtures" that led us all into the age of corporate cultures. They showed how a certain persistent strategic style may be identified, which is deeply embedded in the managerial processes of the firm and in its response pattern to environmental demands.

In strategic management research a reorientation seems evident: Bennis (1984; 1985) and Greiner (1983) may be regarded as representatives of the new school of thought of strategic management, that Alvin Toffler has touched upon in his *Third Wave* visionary work. This school seems to originate in the studies of the Silicon Valley phenomenon and others mainly in California.

10.1 Strategy Shaping as Culture

Greiner has presented this "revolution in management" in a nutshell. He shows in his critique of formal strategic planning, how even strong advocates of formal strategic planning have serious doubts about its working and about the premises it is built on. Greiner notes that "the values of Western

---

[1] An earlier version of this chapter appeared as a paper in the TIMS XXVII Conference, Gold Coast City, Australia, July 20 to 23, 1986. It was based on a presentation given in the Strategic Management Society Conference, Barcelona, Spain, October 1985.

Rationalism have permeated the field of strategic management" (Greiner 1983: 12) and that we, therefore, have been using false assumptions. Based on this Greiner presents an alternative set of assumptions to replace the false, traditional ones. The new assumptions state that strategy evolves from inside the organization — not from its future environment; that strategy is a deeply ingrained and continuing pattern of management behavior that gives direction to the organization — not a manipulable and controllable mechanism that can be easily changed from one year to the next; that strategy is a non-rational concept stemming from the informal values, traditions, and norms of behaviour held by the firm's managers and employees — not a rational, formal, logical, conscious, and predetermined thought process engaged in by top executives; and, finally, that strategy emerges out of the cumulative effect of many informed actions and decisions taken daily and over the years by many employees — not a "one-shot" statement developed exclusively by top management for distribution to the organization (Greiner 1983: 12−13).

Accepting the new assumptions means for Greiner that strategy making should be viewed as a shaping process that gradually moves the organization along a particular path.

> What is at stake in strategy-shaping is the 'deep structure' of the firm. Any real change in strategic direction must address this deeper value core; a proposed change that is contrary to the core values will likely be rejected (Greiner 1983: 13).

Greiner's own experience and research suggests that the senior executive's leadership behaviour has the single most powerful effect on shaping a firm's strategic direction. He, therefore, develops a picture of a strategic manager of the Third Wave — the "strategic actor" as opposed to the "trapped executive". Greiner's arguments show that he sees strategy making as a cultural phenomenon.

The following extract shows how the semiotic aspect is strong in Greiner's argument, even if he nowhere specifically refers to this aspect:

> Why do I call the first executive a 'strategic actor'? Senior executives, whether they like it or not, are 'on stage', with a surrounding cast of subordinates and an audience of hundreds, often thousands, of employees. Every action taken by the senior executive, verbal or non-verbal, carries cues with 'symbolic meaning' to the cast and audience. They are looking for signs that indicate what is important to the senior executive, what will be rewarded, where they are going, and if they want to invest their efforts in expressing the specific behaviours that seem to be valued by top management (Greiner 1983: 15).

Davis (1984: 7), reflecting on his own work on strategy and culture in corporations, places, likewise, strong emphasis on the role of top management in "giving direction". The guiding beliefs of an organization are, in his experience, always set at the top and transmitted down the ranks. Such guiding beliefs are only few and they are broad enough to accommodate any variety of circumstances. Davis' guiding beliefs are equivalent to the central values forming the core of an organizational culture. His daily beliefs are, again, the situational applications of those overall values.

10.2 The Management of Meaning Paradigm

In addition to Greiner's views, the four competencies of leaders as documented by Bennis would suggest a view of strategic management as the "management of meaning". Such a view has been elaborated, in more conceptual depth, by Smircich and Morgan (1982) and, further, by Smircich and Stubbart (1985), who consider the above reviewed ideas to represent a reorientation and a paradigm shift.

According to the new paradigm, organizations are socially constructed systems of shared meaning. Organization members, thus, actively form (enact) their environments through their social interaction. A pattern of enactment establishes the foundation of organizational reality, and further effects the shaping of future enactments. The task of strategic management in this view would then be organization making — to create and maintain systems of shared meaning that facilitate action (Smircich and Stubbart 1985: 724).

How, then, can strategic managers generate context for meaning(fulness) in an organization? Smircich and Stubbart refer to recent studies, where "management-of-meaning" has been shown to be accomplished through values and their symbolic expressions, dramas and language (1985: 730). According to them, research has only begun to explore such symbolic realities. They refer to Broms and Gahmberg (1983) and Peters (1978) as such new research.

In managers' creation of a meaningful context for the organization members we have found examples of classical myths used in a situational application. Such are, for instance, the myth of rebirth, or the story of the Phoenix bird, at occasions of crisis and during turnaround operations, or the myth of the Argonauts in life histories of famous leaders.

10.3 Metaphors in Strategic Decision-Making

An illustrative example of the power of the metaphorical representation of issues in decision situations is given in Alice Sapienza's (1984) study of top management in two U.S. teaching hospitals.

A major change occurred in their environment, a new state law to counter-
act rising hospital costs: one negative incentive was now, that, if actual
expenses exceeded the prospective target, managers would have to make up
the difference from hospital reserves; on the positive side, if a service were
implemented that yielded marginal revenues, a surplus, managers could keep
the difference and invest it over the term of the legislation without affecting
future rates. At both institutions a certain language evolved to handle the
matter.

First, for a number of weeks managers discussed their individual perceptions of the
law: what it was, why it came about, how it would impact the institution, and so on.
The second stage involved development of a common language with which managers
described the stimulus and understood it. At institution A, the definition of the law
was understood metaphorically as a box. At institution B, one impact of the law was
understood metaphorically as pain and suffering for the employees. The third stage
was marked by a perceptible shift in the focus of discussions to institutional response.
In this stage the influence of the reigning metaphor appeared to be most striking. At
institution A, if the law were a box, then reducing expenses to fit in organ transplants
(in the box) would be logical. Strategy was expressed metaphorically as 'cutting back
other programs by 100,000 dollars each year to give room to organ transplants.' At
B, if one impact of the law were suffering for employees, then avoidance of this
hurting would be logical. Strategy was again expressed metaphorically: the 'least'
painful way to meet the budget was to leave employee perquisites intact by finding
marginal revenues (Sapienza 1984: 11 – 12).

10.4 "Tangibilitation"

The results of Bennis' (1984; 1985) study of 90 American leaders with the
four areas of competence match well with the above and emphasize the role
of symbolic, indirect communication in true leadership:

... One of these leaders was described as making people want to join in with him; he
enrolls them in his vision. Leaders manage attention through a compelling vision
that brings others to a place they have not been before ...
To make dreams apparent to others, and to align people with them, leaders must
communicate their vision. Communication and alignment work together ...
In his first budget message, for example, Reagan described a trillion dollars by
comparing it to piling up dollar bills beside the Empire State Building. Reagan, to
use one of Alexander Haig's coinages, 'tangibilitated' the idea. Leaders make ideas
tangible and real to others, so they can support them. For no matter how marvelous
the vision, the effective leader must use a metaphor, a word or a model to make that
vision clear to others. In contrast, President Carter was boring. Carter was one of our
best informed presidents; he had more facts at his finger tips than almost any other
president. But he never made the meaning come through the facts ...

Leaders integrate facts, concepts and anecdotes into meaning for t'
the leaders in my group are word masters. They get people to under
their goals in a variety of ways. The ability to manage attention a
from the whole person. It is not enough to use the right buzz word
or to hire a public relations person to write speeches (Bennis 198

10.5 The Roots of Leading Symbols

Metaphors, like simple symbols, allegories or myths, signify something other
than themselves. In the above case of leaders, they are signs of outcome,
goal or direction. They always include both a cognitive and an affective
aspect; they signify some underlying belief, attitude or a fundamental value.

Thus, we may find in the core of a multi-layered corporate culture the
general, persistent symbolic representations of the very few core values that
the culture builds upon.

Similarly, the individual manager or leader may have thousands of beliefs,
hundreds of attitudes, but only a dozen fundamental values. As these value
orientations or tendencies reside in the subconscious deep structure of the
mind, the person may not constantly be aware of them.

Individual character traits, type of education and environment certainly
have an influence on a person's skill to be able to communicate through
"indirect" symbols. However, there seem to be seasons in a person's life,
when one is sensitive to such modes of communication.

In our own research, we have been guided by Carl Jung's adult psychology
and by a more recent study by Levinson (1979) to focus on the mid-life
transit process (age 40 to 45), where a person meets his inner self. This
process of individuation, as Jung called it, is the start of a new, more mature
world view, and, what is particularly important here, a first acquaintance
with the archetypal images resident in one's unconscious. By becoming
gradually aware of that symbolic content, one is offered an opportunity to
enrich one's "vocabulary" with metaphors, mythical entities that people will
grasp instantly through some sort of mechanism that goes beyond the
standard rational comprehension.

Our assumption has been that strong leader personalities undergo this
individuation process in an open and daring way, facing and accepting the
revealed, undeveloped, perhaps shocking side of self. As strong personalities
they will then learn to develop and master some parts of their former
subconscious and will, thus, be able to redirect that untapped psychic energy.

As managers they are now able to make their ideas appeal to both the
conscious and the subconscious of their peers and subordinates. We consider
this one of the decisive moments on the way from management to leadership.

10.6 A Study of Values Behind Symbols

My more recent research has been focused on the deep value orientations of strategic managers (Gahmberg 1986). In my search for a methodology in order to undertake such a task, I became familiar with structural semiotics, an approach with a long scientific tradition, but seemingly far removed from management research. Generally, semiotics may be called the science of signs and symbols. It studies the signification process, the generation of meaning.

In Europe and in the French-speaking world the methodology of structural semiotics has moved from its original field of linguistic and literature research to new fields of application in the social sciences. In cultural anthropology, the applications in the work of Levi-Strauss, for instance, have become well known.

The general framework of the Paris school of semiotics, or Greimas' theory of the generation of meaning, was followed; particularly the actant model and the canonical narrative structure (in this case the recurring narrative syntagm of life test). I studied the discourse of four managing directors and the material was gathered for the most part in several in-depth interviews. My study focused on the main blocks, or the narrative sequencies, and on the general intention of the entire discourse of each manager. The interested reader may find a review of my analytical method in Gahmberg (1987) or the detailed report of the research in Gahmberg (1986). Based on the distribution of generalized actors, or actants, in the subsegments of the narrative sequences (independent sub-stories), the nature of the relations between key actants were established and, thus, the subject's underlying modal value could be discerned.

In this framework four universal fundamental modal values influence a subject (person) and, thus, modalize all his doing and being. The four modal values determine the subject's modal competence, his intentionality. They are "having-to" or obligation (*devoir*), "wanting-to" or volition (*vouloir*), "being-able-to" or power (*pouvoir*) and "knowing-how-to" or knowledge (*savoir*).

So my journey to the deep roots of symbols in the managers' narratives resulted in the identification of such modal values. What makes leaders tick, then, is a deep subconscious personal modal value orientation.

In the first manager's narrative, the subject person's doing and being was clearly modalized by a *savoir* modal value; in the second, the subject was a *devoir* man with a deep mid-life transfer into a *pouvoir* man. In the third "text" the subject was driven by a strong *vouloir* of being somebody, which was accomplished by an ability to do (*pouvoir*). In the fourth text the subject person turned out to be driven by a combination of *savoir* and *pouvoir* modalities.

The link from such underlying personal values to their metaphorical communication in visions comes through human growth in the doings and beings of life, in the initiations and acceptances, in the successes and failures of a managerial career.

References

Ansoff, Igor, Roger P. Declerk and Robert Hayes eds. *From Strategic Planning to Strategic Management*, London: Wiley, 1976.

Bennis, Warren (1984): The 4 Competencies of Leadership, *Training and Development Journal*, August: 15 – 19.

Bennis, Warren and Burt Nanus (1985): *Leaders — The Strategies for Taking Charge*, New York: Harper & Row.

Broms, Henri and Henrik Gahmberg (1982): *Mythology in Management Culture*, Helsinki: Helsinki School of Economics Publications D-58.

Broms, Henri and Henrik Gahmberg (1983): Communication to Self in Organizations and Cultures, *Administrative Science Quarterly*, 28: 482 – 495.

Davis, Stanley M. (1984): *Managing Corporate Culture*, Cambridge, MA: Ballinger Publ. Co.

Gahmberg, Henrik (1986): *Symbols and Values of Strategic Managers — A Semiotic Approach*, Helsinki: Acta Academiae Oeconomicae Helsingiensis, Series A: 47.

Gahmberg, Henrik (1987): Semiotic Tools for the Study of Organizational Cultures, in Sebeok, Thomas A. and Jean Umiker-Sebeok (eds.), *The Semiotic Web '86 An International Yearbook*, 389 – 403, Berlin: Mouton de Gruyter.

Greimas, Algirdas J. (1966): *Semantique Structurale. Recherche de methode*, Paris: Larousse.

Greiner, Larry E. (1983): Senior Executives as Strategic Actors, *New Management*, vol. 1, no. 2: 11 – 15.

Jung, Carl G. (1980): *The Archetypes and the Collective Unconscious*, Princeton: Princeton University Press.

Levinson, Daniel J. (1979): *The Seasons of a Man's Life*, New York: Ballantine Books.

Levi-Strauss, Claude (1979): *The Raw and the Cooked* (orig. 1964), New York: Octagon.

Miles, Robert H. (1982): *Coffin Nails and Corporate Strategies*, Englewood Cliffs, N.J.: Prentice-Hall.

Miles, Raymond E. and Charles C. Snow (1978): *Organizational Strategy, Structure, and Process*, Tokyo: McGraw-Hill.

Mintzberg, Henry, *The Nature of Managerial Work*, New York: Harper and Row, 1973.

Sapienza, Alice (1984): *Metaphor and Management Decision Making*, Conference paper. Boston: School of Public Health.

Sapienza, Alice (1987): 'Image making as a strategic function' in Thayer, Leed ed. *Organization-Communication: Emerging Perspectives II* Norwood, N.J.: Ablex Publishing Corp. 1987.

Smircich, Linda and Gareth Morgan (1982): Leadership: The Management of Meaning, *The Journal of Applied Behavioral Science*, vol. 18, no. 3: 257–273.

Smircich, Linda and Charles Stubbart (1985): Strategic Management in an Enacted World, *Academy of Management Review*, October, vol. 10, no. 4: 724–736.

Toffler, Alvin *The Third Wave*, New York: William Morrow, 1980.

Peters, Tom J. (1978): 'Symbols, patterns and settings', *Organizational Dynamics* 7, 3–22.

Chapter 11
Culture and Management Training: Closed Minds and Change in Managers Belonging to Organizational and Occupational Communities

Pasquale Gagliardi

11.1 An Introduction: The Impact of the Cultural Approach on a Management Centre

In recent years corporate culture has attracted the interest of a growing number of scholars. Moreover, it has become the latest fashion among managers: *Fortune* (October 17, 1983) devoted its cover to culture as if it was a business star and *Business Week* (January 20, 1986) listed culture among the things which are currently "in" in business corporations.

In 1977, some years before the topic was in fashion, a few of the faculty members of ISTUD — an Italian Management Institute specializing in in-service training courses for executives — started a number of seminars on the problems of cultural analysis and change. The messages which basically the teachers wanted to transmit to the trainees were the following:

a) culture, understood as a coherent system of assumptions and basic values — mostly taken for granted by organization members — constitutes the framework and the root of organizational behaviour;

b) the culture of each particular organization appears through expressive strategies which support and justify instrumental strategies in a success-reinforcing "virtuous circle": culture is then a resource for organizational integration;

c) when the instrumental strategies needed for organization survival are not consistent with the existing culture, the virtuous circle becomes a vicious one, the chances for a cultural change are very few and basically depend on skillful leadership creating the conditions for the idealization of new successful experiences and promoting a mythical retrospective interpretation of success.

The reaction of our managers — at the same time fascinated and shocked by this proposal — revealed that the new approach was not simply a new topic of the curriculum: on the contrary, it challenged their self image as rational managers who use scientific rather than mythical knowledge and who reject the use of symbolic persuasion and ideological suggestion as tools of management. We realized that the cultural approach challenged the "managerial culture" that we ourselves were proposing in other seminars or in other classes of the same course. This traditional culture, mainly derived from psychosociological literature on management, emphasizes logical reasoning, negotiation and development of interpersonal competence, without analyzing or really debating value orientations.

The anthropological perspective appeared to our trainees, and to ourselves, as a "subversive" intellectual instrument. In fact — as Postman and Weingartner pointed out (1969: 17) —

this perspective allows one to be part of his own culture and, at the same time, to be out of it. One views the activities of his own group as would an anthropologist, observing its tribal rituals, its fears, its conceits, its ethnocentrism. In this way, one is able to recognize when reality begins to drift too far away from the grasp of the tribe.

It is not an accident that this book by Postman and Weingartner became one of the main ideological points of reference for the faculty.

The cultural approach comes to be a sort of boomerang for those who use it: it compels scholars of culture to reflect on their own culture and ideology. That is what happened to our School. We were compelled to become aware that education is a particular kind of cultural engineering. In most cases this engineering is done without being aware of it: teachers usually know what information they want to transmit and which attitudes or behaviour they want to induce, but very rarely are they aware of the basic values and assumptions they actually refer to. The anthropological perspective "subverted" our Institute, originating reflections which involved the entire faculty and led us to review and define explicitly the kind of "culture" that ISTUD wanted to transfer to executives attending the most demanding of the courses offered by the Institute, the "Programma di sviluppo delle abilità direttive", referred to hereafter as PSAD.

The PSAD, an intercompany residential programme lasting 9 weeks and divided up into three-week blocks, is offered to executives with a professional background in one or more functional areas (marketing, production, personnel, finance, purchasing, etc.), who are preparing to take on more general management tasks. Some firms made systematic use of it as a way of developing the management skills of their own executives who were about to take on overall management responsibility in subsidiaries, divisions, profit centres or complex organizational units. The course was thoroughly overhauled by the entire teaching faculty in 1978 and those firms which had become the main users of the course took part in the lengthy debate and detailed analysis. When the work had been completed, the basic objective of the Programme was defined as follows: to endow its participants with greater freedom and critical scope towards both their own professional group — so as to be able to act as integrators of various professional cultures rather than as specialists — and the firm they belong to — so as to be able to help their own firm to adopt new strategies as and when needed.

The revision of the course confirmed and strengthened a series of house-keeping and management rules concerned with the running of the course and designed to encourage the assumption of attitudes and values consistent with the basic aim of the course:

a) there should be the greatest possible range of age, present functional area, firm and economic sector in the course group;

b) extensive use would be made of active teaching methods, particularly the case method, as laid down by the orthodox Harvard Business School tradition (McNair 1954; Andrews 1956);

c) participants would be rotated in different work sub-groups;

d) a wide range of background and experience would be actively encouraged in the faculty itself and in its teaching style.

The intention was not only to encourage contact between different social, professional and corporate cultures and a reassessment of cognitive and operative paradigms whose assumptions and validity had been taken for granted, but also to affirm publicly the Institute's belief in the value of criticism and the tolerance of cultural and professional diversity. In this sense, the authority of the Institute (and its ability to influence course members) was deliberately used to reinforce these rather than other values. During the debate which took place during the revision of the course, several faculty members often quoted the slogan written by an unknown student on the walls of Nanterre University during the protests of 1968: "*La seule attitude dogmatique qu'il faut reapprendre et conserver c'est l'attitude critique*". Many faculty members were also by no means unaware that this anti-ideological statement constituted an ideology in itself, but this ideology was advanced in all seriousness as a distinctive feature of the sort of manager the firms using the course actually needed or would need in the future.

During the revision of the PSAD, an attempt was also made to tackle the problem of how to make a systematic and credible assessment of the effect the course had had on its participants and so also of the extent to which its aim — the cultural transformation of participants — had actually been achieved. After lengthy debate, it was decided to set up a longitudinal research project which involved administering three tests to all participants before the start of the course (Time 1) and then later on at the end of the course (Time 2). The tests included Rokeach's mental openness/closedness test[1] which had been specially revised and adapted to reflect the features of a managerial population in Italy.

---

[1] The other two tests were for, respectively, change in how the manager's role was defined and the acquisition of management concepts and methods. They were designed to measure the attainment of important teaching objectives which were secondary, however, to the basic aim of reducing dogmatism in course participants.

The test was taken by 184 executives who had completed the Programme during the three-year period from 1982 to 1984 and had attended 9 different sessions of the course.

In the following pages the research project will first be illustrated. Then two sets of findings will be presented and discussed:

a) the difference between dogmatism levels at the beginning and at the end of the Programme, in connection with some traits of the learning experience;

b) mind openness (and its tendency to change through the Programme) in managers belonging to different organizational or occupational communities.

11.2 The Research Project

Dogmatism was studied by Rokeach as a particular mental structure or form which distinguishes individuals along a mental "openness/closedness" continuum. Rokeach (1960) defines dogmatism as "a closed way of thinking which could be associated with any ideology regardless of content, an authoritarian outlook on life, an intolerance toward those with opposing beliefs, and a sufferance of those with similar beliefs" (1960: 4 – 5). According to Rokeach, dogmatism can be analyzed in relation to three dimensions: the "belief-disbelief" dimension, the "central-peripheral" dimension and the "time perspective" dimension.

As regards the "belief-disbelief" dimension,

a system is defined to be closed to the extent that there is a high magnitude of rejection of all disbelief systems, an isolation of beliefs, a high discrepancy in degree of differentiation between belief and disbelief systems, and little differentiation within the disbelief system (1960: 61).

Rokeach defines three regions within the "central-peripheral" dimensions: the central region, which is the seat of primitive beliefs (the nature of the physical world, the nature of the "self" and of the "generalized other"), the intermediate region which contains beliefs about the nature of authority, and the peripheral region which contains beliefs deriving from authority and completing the world-map of the individual. As regards this dimension,

we assume that the more closed the system, the more will the world be seen as threatening, the greater will be the belief in absolute authority, the more will other persons be evaluated according to the authorities they line up with, and the more will peripheral beliefs be related to each other by virtue of their common origin in authority, rather than by virtue of intrinsic connections (1960: 62).

Finally, about the time dimension:

the more open the system, the more the immediate future should be in the service of confirming or not confirming predictions about the present. It is the other way round in closed systems. Things that happen in the present should be in the service of "confirming" the remote future. For this reason, a narrow, future-oriented time perspective, rather than a more balanced conception of past, present and immediate future in relation to each other, is also seen to be a defining characteristic of closed systems (1960: 64).

Although insisting on the "formal" nature of dogmatism i. e. on its independence from the actual content of beliefs, Rokeach himself maintains that intermediate and peripheral beliefs emerge from primitive beliefs which are formed early on in the life of an individual, "as walking and running emerge from crawling" (1960: 42). And yet, Rokeach offers no specific hypothesis regarding the relationship between dogmatism as the "mind-set" of an individual and the "nature" (the quality of beliefs and values) or "strength" (stability, homogeneity, distinctiveness) of the social cultures the individual was reared in or now belongs to.

The study of these relationships was not one of the main objectives of those involved in the research project, who were concerned above all to measure the effectiveness of the Programme in "opening the minds" of course members. Moreover, to have made an accurate survey of their "home" cultures (organizational and occupational) would have been both difficult and impracticable given the large range of firms to which they belonged and the difficulty of identifying and delineating possible reference groups. Nonetheless, the research group decided not to let slip entirely the possibility of investigating these aspects, both because of the theoretical interest of the subject and because the results would be of some practical use in establishing criteria for selecting participants and putting together classes and sub-groups in the future. It was decided, then, to correlate degree of individual dogmatism (and its propensity to change after the course had been taken) with a number of known and so classifiable features of the past experience of course members which could be used as indicators of cultural typologies. This would then throw some light on the relationship between dogmatism and culture — or, at least, would allow rather more accurate hypotheses to be formulated.

The known and classifiable features of the past experience of course members were:

a) the professional/functional area they belonged to at the time;

b) the economic sector of the firm they belonged to at the time;

c) whether they had always worked in one single firm or in a number of different firms;

d) whether they had always worked in the same professional area or in a number of different professional areas;

e) whether the firm they belonged to was publicly or privately owned.

The research design assumed that those who had spent the whole of their working lives in the same firm (working in different functional areas) would have the firm itself as their primary reference community, while those who had worked in the same professional area in a number of different firms would have their professional group as their primary reference community. Finally, the research team felt that the possibility of assessing dogmatism in individuals who could be regarded equally as members of both an organizational and an occupational community (having always worked either for the same firm and in the same professional area, or else in many firms in many professional areas) would assist in the interpretation of any possible relations between dogmatism and culture.

Thus, the research programme made it possible, on the one hand, to measure absolutely the variation in individual dogmatism upon completion of the course, and on the other, to answer the following sorts of questions:

a) Which occupational cultures tend to produce a higher degree of dogmatism in their members?

b) In which economic sectors do organizational or occupational cultures encourage a higher degree of dogmatism in their members?

c) Does the level of individual dogmatism tend to be higher in individuals who adopt the firm as their primary reference community, or in individuals who adopt their professional group as their primary reference community?

The findings also make it possible to explore whether these variables, apart from the influence they have on the absolute level of dogmatism, also have an effect on the tendency of dogmatism to increase or decrease in individuals exposed to an executive training programme whose explicit purpose is to reduce the level of dogmatism in those attending it.

The answers to these questions may throw some rather more factual light on a controversy that is at present creating a rift between scholars of culture. Some authors maintain that organizations tend to construct a relatively unified base culture i.e. a system of shared basic beliefs and values which functions as a means of integrating the organization as a whole (Gagliardi 1982). If we exclude counter-cultures — which openly challenge the values of the dominant culture — sub-cultures could only be reinforcing in relation to organizational culture (Martin and Siehl 1983), or else represent minor variations of the dominant culture (Turner 1986). Other authors (Alvesson 1984; Louis 1983) maintain that organizations are simply containers of sub-cultures, and of professional and class-based cultures in particular. If this is the case and we exclude clans (Wilkins and Ouchi 1983) and total institutions, it is unlikely that organizations can ever be said to have a unified culture.

The second group of authors sees the very concept of organizational culture as in itself highly debatable, and the analytical approach they envisage is the one which Van Maanen and Barley used to brilliant effect in their essay on occupational communities (1984). In all fairness, it should be said that they themselves are rather more cautious than some of their more enthusiastic supporters. In a footnote to their essay (1984: 353 – 354) they clearly state:

Occupational cultures may, of course, reside more or less peacefully within (and as part of) organizational cultures, may exist alongside and in opposition to them, may be buried by them, or may even contain them. Within organizations, occupational cultures are subcultures harboring segments of relative diversity within a generally approved organization plan; alongside organizations, occupational cultures compete with the plan, offering to its membership alternative goals; when buried by organizations, occupational cultures cease to exist; and, when containing organizations, the occupational and organizational cultures are one and the same. This crude taxonomy ... only begins to suggest the kinds of interactions possible. The main point is, however, the need to explain each rather than assume the priority of one over the other.

This argument can, on the whole, be accepted. It is pointless to try to define in the abstract which type of culture has priority over another, but it can be assumed that if the priority of one system of beliefs and values over another is not clearly recognized and defined, the organizational and psychological cost will be extremely high. The degree of coupling between conflicting systems can sometimes be reduced (Van Maanen and Barley 1984) to the point where distinct and sufficiently separate cultural unities may be created. If this is not possible, it becomes important to know which mechanisms and variables result in one culture prevailing over another in specific situations. We shall return to this notion in the light of the research findings.

11.3 The Main Findings of the Research Project

Dogmatism was measured using a scale of 28 items located along the three dimensions of dogmatism and their specifications, the overall structure of the scale being more or less similar to Rokeach's own dogmatism scale. Values were calculated by awarding points for the answers to each item, ranging from $+6$ (maximum agreement) to $+1$ (maximum disagreement) and then adding up the points. Since the statements in each item were "typical" of closed mental attitudes, the score shows the level of dogmatism in the subject taking the test (the higher the score, the more closed the mind).

In the 184 subjects who took the test, the average individual dogmatism index fell from 75.03 at the beginning of the course to 70.98 at the end of the course, a decrease of 4.05 points. Since it was impossible to compare these indices either with general averages and standards or with control readings in other groups of executives, we are unable to decide whether the average initial dogmatism of our subjects was relatively high or low, or whether the variation recorded at the end of the course was relatively moderate or high. However, internal analysis of the results does provide assessment parameters and allows a number of interesting comparisons to be made. The three tables given below summarize the main results of the research project. They show, in order:

a) the average dogmatism index of the group at Time 1 and Time 2 in the nine sessions of the Programme (Fig. 11.1);

Session*)	Time 1	Time 2	T2−T1
1	75.47	71.60	− 3.87
2	77.07	71.84	− 5.23
3	74.43	68.91	− 5.52
4	74.21	69.94	− 4.27
5	73.55	72.73	− 0.82
6	71.86	69.96	− 1.90
7	77.13	73.05	− 4.08
8	80.63	70.26	− 10.37
9	71.78	70.31	− 1.47

*) The courses during which tests were performed are given here in temporal order. Course 1 was the 35th held since the founding of the Institute, and Course 9 was the 43rd.

Figure 11.1 The Average Dogmatism Index of the Group at Time 1 and Time 2 in the Nine Sessions of the Program

b) initial dogmatism levels cross-referenced with age, the economic sector of the firm to which subjects belonged, the type of ownership of the firm (public or private), the functional/professional area subjects belonged to at the time, and whether they had always worked for one single firm or for a number of different firms (Fig. 11.2);

c) the degree of change after the course (the difference between the dogmatism index at Time 1 and Time 2), cross-referenced with the variables given above (Fig. 11.3).

The results can be used both to examine to what extent the individual dogmatism of a subject was affected by having attended the course, and to examine the relationship between individual dogmatism (and its tendency to be modified over the course) and the previous experience and assumed culture of course members. The results of these two analyses are discussed separately below.

	High ←————————— Average ————————→ Low		
Age	Over 45 (82.45)		36/45 (72.13)
			Up to 35 (73.01)
Economic Sector	Public Services (83.39) Banking/Insurance (83.23)	Textiles/Clothing (75.06) Foodstuffs (75.1) Commerce (76.01)	Engin./Metall. (66.88) Electronics/Elec. Eng. (72.02) Chemicals/Rubber (73.40)
Ownership	State-Owned Firms (81.85)		Private Firms (73.13)
Functional/ Professional Area	Admin. Finance (78.25) Personnel/Ind. Relations (76.74) Planning (76.06)	Inform. Systems (74.94)	Engineering/R & D (69.72) Marketing & Sales (70.68) Production (72.46)
Experience	Only One Firm (77.91)		Several Firms (70.70)

Figure 11.2 Level of Dogmatism at Time 1

	Low ←————————— Medium ————————→ High		
Age	Over 45 (− 2.22) Up to 35 (− 2.69)		36/45 (− 5.33)
Economic Sector	Foodstuffs (− 0.59) Chemicals/Rubber (− 2.38) Public Services (− 2)	Textiles/Clothing (− 3.74) Banking/Insurance (− 3.51) Engin./Metall. (− 3.42) Electronics/Elec. Eng. (− 4.52)	Commerce (− 10.96)
Ownership	State-Owned Firms (− 1.34)		Private Firms (− 4.71)
Functional/ Professional Area	Marketing & Sales (− 1.27)	Personnel/Ind. Relations (− 4.49) Admin. Finance (− 3.69) Planning (− 3.70) Production (− 3.29)	Engin./R & D (− 6.22) Inform. Sys. (− 5.39)
Experience	Only One Firm (− 3.03)		Several Firms (− 4.84)

Figure 11.3 Difference between Dogmatism at Time 1 and Time 2

11.3.1 The Effect of the Programme on Individual Dogmatism

There can be no doubt that attending the course did reduce the mental closedness of participants (Fig. 1), presumably due to the tendency of individual participants to change. And we have seen that this is correlated with a series of personal, company and professional attributes of the individuals themselves (Fig. 3). But we should note that while the average dogmatism index at Time 1 in the nine groups who attended the nine course sessions fluctuates over a range of around 9 points, the average dogmatism indices at Time 2 fluctuates over a range of little more than 4 points. It would seem that groups (and individuals) tend to align themselves with the standard of mental openness explicitly or implicitly expected of them by the Institute itself, no matter what their specific personal or group characteristics may be.

It will be obvious that the various results obtained in each course could have been influenced by the particular way in which new values were transmitted and received by course members, and that the way in which this occurred differed, perforce, from course to course. Each group constructed — through the dynamic interaction between participants and with teachers — its own particular culture, i. e. its own particular way of perceiving, structuring and living the social and learning experience it was confronted with. This means that we would have to analyze the particular features of each course in order to identify which conditions hinder or promote change.

Such a qualitative analysis was in fact carried out by the faculty research team for internal purposes. Some of the more important conclusions the faculty arrived at were that the courses which furnished the best results (in terms of decrease in dogmatism in participants) were also those in which members 1) demonstrated greater emotional *commitment* to and *participation* in the course; 2) emphasized the *social* nature of the learning experience and attained high levels of interpersonal cohesion; 3) and finally, *idealized* the social and learning experience, seeing it as a unique and unrepeatable event in their professional lives. This seems to confirm that the idealization of a collective successful experience is a basic condition for incremental cultural change (Gagliardi 1986). It is also interesting that the conditions did not include meek acceptance of the Institute as such (indeed, course members were often highly critical of it) or the establishing of good relations between participants and faculty (they were often stormy in the extreme).

11.3.2 Individual Dogmatism and Reference Cultures

In the population we studied, the highest level of dogmatism at Time 1 (Fig. 2) was found in executives 1) belonging to firms in the transport industry and other public services, banking and insurance or to state-owned firms, 2) who worked in administration/finance, personnel/industrial relations and planning, 3) who had always worked for the same firm, in the same functional area or in different functional areas. The lowest level of dogmatism was found in executives 1) belonging to firms in the engineering/metallurgical and electronics/electrical engineering industries, or to private firms, 2) who worked in engineering/R & D, marketing or production, 3) who had worked in a number of different firms, whether in the same profession or in different functional areas.

If we assume that the primary reference community of those who have always worked for the same firm is the firm itself, and that, correspondingly, the primary reference community of those who have worked for several different firms (while still usually performing the same tasks) is the professional group to which they belong, we might conclude that corporate cultures are more likely to encourage dogmatism than professional cultures.[2] Could this be due to the greater importance of mythical and pre-scientific beliefs, beyond the influence of critical appraisal based on reason and experience, in corporate cultures than beliefs of scientific or technical origin?

However, corporate cultures do tend to produce in their members attitudes which are more or less dogmatic according to two basic factors: 1) the exposure of the firm to competition; 2) the importance of technical and scientific knowledge in defining the distinctive competence of the firm.

This interpretative framework suggests that there is a high level of dogmatism in members of firms which are protected from competition in a way which allows organizational behaviour to be based on a rather uncritical view of the situation of the firm. State-owned firms, public service corporations, and banking and insurance organizations are examples of this phenomenon in Italy. Correspondingly, in firms which have to have fully updated and so constantly monitored technological resources at their command in order to survive and be competitive, we find that scientific knowledge holds pride of place in the culture and competence of the firm. Such is the case in engineering and electronics firms and, more generally, in all firms dependent on the transformation of inputs into outputs by means of processes whose efficiency and effectiveness can be empirically measured.

This could also explain why certain occupational cultures produce higher dogmatism levels than others. Even if technical and scientific knowledge is more important in most occupational cultures than in most corporate cultures, the fact remains that the cultures of certain occupations are based on "conventions" rather than on empirically confutable knowledge (administrative jobs in comparison with R & D and production jobs), or on ideologically

---

[2] This would not be the case if we accept Rokeach's thesis that the primitive beliefs which strongly influence the level of dogmatism in an individual are established in the earliest years of life. Even if we do accept this, the present argument remains basically unaltered if firms select or co-opt people who match the dominant attitudes of the organization.

conditioned knowledge (personnel management) rather than on ideas and views that are constantly exposed to the scrutiny of market forces (marketing).

Thus, the results of our research project suggest not only that corporate cultures do in fact exist, but also that they tend, more than professional cultures, to discourage critical awareness in their members by offering more simplified and dogmatic versions of the real state of affairs. These "sketch maps" promoting stability and consistency in shared systems of meanings are a way of integrating organizational structures, but they may also prove a hindrance to organizations when they need to formulate new strategies and revise their visions of reality.

Do these results allow us to say anything definite about the relationship between professional and corporate culture? More specifically, which of the two cultures would concede pride of place and allow itself to be framed by the other?

Our findings show that people who have always worked for the same firm have high levels of dogmatism compared with those who have worked for a number of firms, regardless of whether they have always worked in the same or in different functional areas. In our population at least, a person who has two equally stable and consolidated reference cultures at his disposal (his organization and his occupation) will tend to identify with the organization rather than with his occupation.

It has been observed that an organization wins the loyalty of its employees by promotion opportunities which serve to break up occupational communities (Van Maanen and Barley 1984). From this point of view, the fact that our course members were career executives with further promotion prospects ahead of them was probably not without influence. In more general terms, however, our findings would seem to suggest that an analysis of professional and organizational cultures and their inter-relations would benefit from more explicit recognition and consideration of mythical knowledge on the one hand, and technical and scientifical knowledge on the other. When incompatible cultural systems cannot be managed by weakening the coupling between them, the need for internal consistency within the symbolic field (Berger and Luckmann 1966) will probably result in the cultures in question assuming a hierarchy. It is theoretically plausible that technical/rational expertise will be put at the service of ideology and not *vice versa*, and that such expertise will be applied within the range of options the "available" myths allow (Gagliardi 1986).

Acknowledgments:
This paper couldn't have been written without the help and support of Frediano Di Rosa, team leader for the research on the evaluation of PSAD, and senior faculty member at ISTUD.

I am also grateful to my colleagues of SCOS for the helpful comments received at the 2nd International SCOS Conference (Montreal, June 1986), where an earlier version of the paper was presented.

References

Alvesson, Mats (1984): *On the Idea of Organizational Culture*, Paper presented at the 1st International Conference on Organizational Symbolism and Corporate Culture, June, Lund, Sweden.

Andrews, Kenneth R. (1956): *Human Relations and Administration*, Cambridge, Mass.: Harvard University Press.

Berger, Peter L., and Thomas Luckmann (1966): *The Social Construction of Reality: A Treatise in the Sociology of Knowledge*, Garden City, N.Y.: Doubleday.

Gagliardi, Pasquale (1982): *L'identité, ressource pour l'intégration et la motivation*, Paper presented at the International Seminar on Corporate Identity Building, March, CERAM, Sophia Antipolis, France.

— (1986): The Creation and Change of Organizational Cultures: A Conceptual Framework, *Organization Studies*, 7/2: 117—134.

Louis, Meryl R. (1983): Organizations as Culture-bearing Milieux, in L. R. Pondy, P. J. Frost, G. Morgan, and T. Dandridge (eds.), *Organizational Symbolism*, vol. 1, Greenwich, CT: JAI Press.

Martin, Joanne, and Caren Siehl (1983): Organization Culture and Counterculture: An Uneasy Symbiosis, *Organizational Dynamics*, 12/2: 52—64.

McNair, Malcom P. (1954): *The Case Method at the HBS*, Cambridge, Mass.: Harvard University Press.

Postman, Neil, and Charles Weingartner (1969): *Teaching as a Subversive Activity*, Harmondsworth, England: Penguin Books.

Rokeach, Milton (1960): *The Open and Closed Mind*, New York: Basic Books.

Turner, Barry A. (1986): Sociological Aspects of Organizational Symbolism, *Organization Studies*, 7/2: 101—115.

Van Maanen, John, and Stephen R. Barley (1984): Occupational Communities: Culture and Control in Organizations, in B. M. Staw and L. L. Cummings (eds.), *Research in Organizational Behavior*, vol. 6: 287—365, Greenwich, CT: JAI Press.

Wilkins, Alan L., and William G. Ouchi (1983): Efficient Cultures: Exploring the Relationship between Cultures and Organizational Performance, *Administrative Science Quarterly* 28: 468—481.

Chapter 12
The 'Commando' Model: A Way to Gather and Interpret Cultural Data

Lars D. Edgren

12.1 The Concept of Organizational Culture

The following description consists of two parts, the first one describing how an uninitiated observer can "read" the culture of an organization by searching for culture-specific phenomena. The second part is about a *concrete working method* where you alternately gather and interpret cultural data.

There is however a question we have to tackle before we explain how we work when we study the culture of an organization:

How do we define the concept of organizational culture?

Our work originates from the following notion. Just as a society, a certain population, a tribe or whatever it may be, can be said to constitute a culture, an organization in itself can be a culture. An organization maintains boundaries, has its symbols, carries out rites and lives with its rituals.

The reality that the members of the organization experience is formed by its history and the norms it has developed, but also by the organizational goals and the different ways they are achieved.

12.2 Some Starting-Points and Foundations

Before we continue, let us take a brief look at where we stand theoretically and explain the foundations that rule the way we work.

The method is qualitative and we emphasize interpretation and understanding of the data collected. We ourselves are the instruments when we step inside an organization to gather and interpret cultural data. We make, as it were, a qualitative valuation of the culture in a specific organization.

The way we study organizational cultures resembles how ethnologists work when they study different societies and cultures. Just as they do, we interpret and put together what we see and hear as entireties. Together, these entireties form an image of the thinking and acting of the organization. When we at a certain point of time draw out, or uncover dominating ideas and traits that powerfully affect life in an organization and document them, we catch an instant picture of the culture.

Later on, this picture is given back to the organization. In this way we open up for the organization's own interpretation what we have found — i. e. what we think we have seen and heard. This is important since the difference between a correct interpretation and more common opinions sometimes seems to be subtle.

In addition to drawing out hidden meanings in what is said and done and thereby giving the reality a meaning, we also let dead things send their messages to us. Buildings, interiors, colours etc. — what do we learn from them? What other noticeable things give us coded messages about the culture we study?

12.2.1 Perspective

Our perspective is not like that of the actor-researcher's in the way that he classifies and interprets a reality defined by the organization members. His way to work is characterized by an attempt to see reality through other people's eyes. Instead, we are guests or uninitiated contemplators who "open ourselves up" to the culture of the organization for a very short period of time. We are careful not to stay too long and become a part of the culture ourselves. We come as strangers and deliberately call everything we see and hear in question.

So, if the actor-approach means to interpret what people mean by the things they say and do, our uninitiated approach — or peep-hole perspective — implies that we interpret words and ways acting independently of what the members of the organization themselves mean by them. The experience we already have from different organizational cultures is a part of our frame of reference. This knowledge directs our search like a compass.

12.2.2 Level of Abstraction

Our level of abstraction is the entirety. We start there and return to it when relating the parts. If we, for example, study solely one division within a company, we define this division as the entirety to which we relate. There is a big risk of going astray and losing your way in details if you do not constantly ask yourself how much meaning the parts have in the whole context. Another approach is to study different subcultures and whether they interact or not.

12.3 Data Gathering

12.3.1 Interviews

Interviews are our most important method for gathering data. We use private interviews almost exclusively. The questions are more suitable for person-to-person dialogues, though we have tried group interviews a couple of times.

Regarding the interviews, it is important that the procedure in itself should encourage the organizational culture. This happens when we make underlying values and norms obvious for those we interview. The questions are different in the way that they create a distance from everyday life and make it necessary for the interviewee to stretch, or even to receive shocks in his conceptual frame. We create a situation where the interviewee becomes aware of the organizational culture through a series of "Aha!-experiences."

It is therefore important to create a friendly atmosphere that opens up the dialogue from the start of the interview. It is also important for us as interviewers to feel the rhythm and pulse in every situation. Some people get inspired very suddenly while others need to think for a little while before they give their answers.

To trade small against big is also important. As soon as we notice we are involved in small unimportant details, not of interest for our project, we change this by going from details to entirety. This is done without giving priority to one thing over another. Instead we relate them to each other.

We also try to interview those who are willing to share their thoughts and feelings about different situations in everyday life in the organization. But sometimes an interview fails; it gives nothing and a dialogue is not achieved. Both parties feel it is wasted time. No matter whose fault it may be, we have to end such an interview rapidly and in an appropriate way.

What different categories do we choose to interview? We look for two groups:
— people, who mould public opinion (persons who have great influence, regardless of their position),
— other employees.

The public opinion moulders are often managers, trade-union leaders or specialists with a high status.

Among the category "other employees", we often choose to interview incoming order clerks, switchboard operators, receptionists and manager's secretaries, all examples of groups that usually have special access to the cultural keys.

All the voices from "the floor" also have to be considered, to speak in management terms. Different interviewing themes are discussed below under the title "The cultural keys."

12.3.2 Observation

As a complement to our interviews, observation also forms part of our techniques of collecting data. The spirit, cooperation and commitment in the organization can also be registered if we expose ourselves to a broad range of contacts. Information of this kind can, for example, be found in the reception area, if we sit down in some of the visitors' chairs and study all the meetings that take place there. For example how are visitors received or directed to a new place? The way people are welcomed is an important cultural element. Another approach is to have lunch in the staff restaurant. To wait in a line, sit down among the employees and chat informally, also gives us a unique possibility to take a bearing on the spirit of this culture.

Here our outlook is open. We do not expect this or that to occur. We are prepared for anything to happen. Curiosity and a willingness to discover things guides us.

Observation also includes a study of the physical localities: buildings, interiors, colours and so on. A camera is very useful. Striking differences in size and interior of offices may offer an example of contradictions in the organization's attitude towards managers and other employees.

12.3.3 Secondary Data

Advertising leaflets, videos, staff-magazines, product-brochures and annual reports are all secondary data revealing how the organization chooses to appear towards employees, customers and other significant groups. In a large organization it is usually easy to find information since it is accessible through the archives. If you cannot find an archive, it is always possible to ask the person responsible for information to give you relevant prints.

In sum, when we gather cultural data, the guiding principle is that: All possibilities to collect relevant information should be utilized and documented.

12.3.4 The Cultural Keys

It is not our purpose to describe the questions we use or why we use them. Different questions have to be chosen to suit every single organization. However we have found some particular points to be of importance in our cultural diagnosis, and these points, which are mapped in personal interviews, are listed below:

1) The saga
   - The creation of the organization, i. e. how did it all start?
   - Why the organization was created.
   - The founder and his personality.

- Epochs, milestones and critical events.
- Heroes, i. e.historically important personalities and their influence.

2) The primary task
   - Is the task still the original one?
   - How deeply rooted is the task among the employees?

3) Rituals
   - What is the significance of everyday work, for example test- and controlroutines, meeting routines, decision-taking, cooperation forms?

4) Ceremonies
   - Celebrations, parties, appointments etc.

5) Spirit and pride
   - How is the atmosphere?
   - Do the employees feel proud of their organization?

6) Rewards and punishment
   - What is understood as positive, or as negative?

7) The soul
   - A couple of questions derived from other worlds, for example, the family, the vegetable kingdom, the animal kingdom or the world of cars helps us to catch the deeper features of the character of the organization.

12.3.5 Selection

Since the investigation is qualitative, we try to work with an assortment of people, as widespread as possible. Concerning the interviews, we usually finish a successful dialogue by asking the interviewee if he/she can suggest any other employee who is willing to be interviewed. In this way our investigation to a certain extent becomes self generating.

How broad should the choice be? It is very hard to specify the number of interviews needed beforehand. We ought, if possible, to continue until we are theoretically satisfied, i. e. until further interviews do not give us any essential new information.

Since the collected material hardly can be data-processed, the number should not produce more material than can be worked with manually. By experience we know that one person can handle around 25 interviews, which means that a group of three persons is able to evaluate 75 interviews. This calls also for daily meetings throughout the process where we report the results to each other. More is said about this in the section "Interpretation", but before that some words about our interrogation-technique.

12.3.6 Simulated Situations and Metaphors

We use questions that deal with simulated situations, because they create a distance from the interviewee's culture. The goal is to make them step out of their own culture and look at it from a distance. This is made possible by using questions which encourage people to take a stranger's seat, to be able to discover their own culture, as we indicated when we discussed "Interviews."

A question simulating a situation might be as follows: "Imagine you are reading the newspaper on Sunday morning and suddenly you think you discover a big headline about your company. How does the headline read?"

Another example: "Imagine it is Saturday night, you are at a party and happen to hear some people you do not know talk badly about your company. How do you react?"

We use metaphors to obtain summary valuations of the organizational "soul," topics which otherwise are hard to express. Metaphors help us to reveal the concealed, hidden side of the organization, the core itself, but also the opposite — the obvious, which is too familar to be noticed.

A metaphor aims to characterize a phenomenon with the assistance of something totally different. An example is this type of question is: "If the company were a tool, what kind of tool would you choose it to be?" The instant, spontaneous answer is rather uninteresting. The more interesting thing is what different qualities the employee associates with the tool. Therefore the first question has to be followed up by asking, for example: "Would you like to describe the tool thoroughly?" The hidden aspects are only revealed when the tool is described in more detail.

A questionnaire copy is given at the end of this chapter.

12.4 Interpretation

Let us be clear that our interpretations have to be related to the primary task to make sense. How to relate the things we hear and see to the organizational task is a continuing question. The difference between the culture we are studying right now and all the other cultures we have already studied *is* the culture.

We are not aware of our own culture until we are confronted with other cultures. People react to differences. As long as all of our actions are "normal" and accepted within our culture, we do not react. This is the reason why our questions aim to make the interviewee pretend to be a stranger.

If data collecting is easy and stimulating, interpretation is demanding and takes time. We have already mentioned how much pre-understanding means. Openness is another important aspect. We have to be aware that our own understanding of cultural phenomena may alter. This includes not least the dialogues we have with those we are "interviewing," and our immediate interpretation of what is said during these dialogues.

We try to find the features and elements in the culture that forcefully influence behaviour. We are looking for cultural patterns when we know how the parts cooperate with the entirety. We focus on central conceptions and manifestations.

As uninitiated observers, we can mediate a snapshot of the culture. With taperecorders and cameras we "freeze" the culture at a specific point of time, interpret it and reflect it back to the organization. This can only be a snapshot because our view of reality changes through continuous communication processes. This means we cannot lay claim to the picture we mediate of the culture, beyond exactly the point of time when we analysed it. Our view of culture alters and the way the organization mediates its own culture also changes.

12.5 Presentation

How to present cultural data is as important as the quality of the result of the study in itself. Our investigation instruments are very effective and sometimes there is a risk of embarrassing the organization if we present our data too directly. For that reason it is our duty to balance what data we feed back with that which we refrain from feeding back.

There is commonly resistance to the presentation of all cultural data. If we start to nibble at what people really do, at their fundamental valuations, we really find strong information, information that the organization's representatives might be inclined to deny. This makes it harder to present.

Another aspect is that the people of the organization usually try to construct and uphold an image or a front in relation to the outside world. Good cultural studies will penetrate this front and expose both good and bad sides of the organization. By going under the surface we will, as it were, unmask the organization. We will drive ourselves down to the essence of the question, of why people act in a special way. It is the unmasking itself that can appear threatening. Since it is important to present data without being threatening or condemning, how do we do that?

One way is to rewrite the diagnosis in the form of a fairy-tale. The fairy-tale or saga has the advantage of not being threatening. The dominating actors within the organization can be allowed to step forward in the saga. They can, whenever they want to, relate themselves to the characters in the fairy-tale. But they do not have to, they can always say to themselves: "I am just listening to a fairy-tale." But the thing of importance — the message of the fairy-tale — will reach out. Light and sound effects can also be used in the presentation to create a fairy-tale atmosphere.

Another "trick" is to use quotations from persons interviewed which are typical of the culture itself — for example something that describes the message or essence of what most people have given an expression to. In a strongly profit-oriented company, the division-managers statement to one of the profit centres, is an example: "I don't give a damn if you have soap in the bathrooms — the main thing is, you show me some results!"

Pictures offer a third way to describe the culture vividly. They often provide a stronger way to express oneself than with words. We could for example use cuts from the organization's own printed matter, mixed with the photographs we have been taking during the process.

A fourth way is to use dramatic sketches. These will not be seen as threatening either, although you need some acting talent if such a presentation is to be successful. Five to six short character-plays that humorously describe some typical situations with a clear message is all that is needed.

Video-techniques can also be used to make a short film, preferably with some help from the people in the organization, again highlighting some typical culture scenes. This exciting option can also be used in study-circles afterwards.

The content of our message, and the psychological profile of the audience help us to decide what kind of presentation we use. Unfortunately, we usually find that it is only the organizations in the front line of development that really dare to confront their own culture.

12.6 Operation Hot Cat

12.6.1 The Task

In the beginning of April, 1983 I was commissioned to perform a sensitive and strongly time-limited task. In three weeks I was to personally lead a culture diagnosis project in a Scandinavian service company with 7000 employees and 2 billion Swedish Crowns in total turnover. The result was to be presented for the company's Top Executive Committee at their next meeting during the first week in May. Among other things the diagnosis was to form a basis for discussing and specifying organizational goals and fundamental views or attitudes to different important questions.

The project needed to be manned with a couple of discerning, not easily stressed collaborators who could travel together, mostly in Scandinavia, to collect data. To succeed, we would have to work with concentration, fast and methodically and in a, for the client, somewhat unusual way. We had a very short time at our disposition, in total 15 working days from the start to the presentation of our results.

12.6.2 The Birth of the Commando Model

How would it be possible in such a short period of time, to carry out a culture diagnosis without drowning in all of the actions and behaviour that manifest the essence of a culture?

We realized that a detailed study, similar to that of the ethnologists, would require too much time and risk us being engulfed by the culture we were to critically interpret. We might get lost in details instead of finding overall pictures.

However we considered that a passable way to work would be to use the same principles as commando soldiers do when they prepare and carry out their actions.

This is how the commando concept was born. A commando force is a group of individuals, specially trained for raids, stormings, and other "lightning actions." The troop acts independently under its leader. The leader himself works tactically and independently to reach the strategic goal. To become successful the performance has to be unexpected and surprising to the target group.

To give a feeling of how a commando group organizes its work, we present a realistic description. The interesting thing is the methodology, the way they act, not the result.

The hijacking of Lufthansa's Boeing 737 flight 181 from Palma had lasted for 12 hours when the West German Government decided to put in the anti-terrorist combat-force "Grenzschutzgruppe" (GSG 9). Every man in the group was a skilled marksman, knife-expert, karate-expert, diver and alpinist.

A couple of minutes after the Government decision is taken, the commander of the force, Ulrich Wegener and his 28 hand-picked soldiers are flown away to trace the hijacked plane. The force immediately starts to prepare for their task — a rush attack towards LH 181 as soon as it has landed.

The hijacked 737 finally lands, after a couple of ordered touch downs, in Somalia on Mogadishu airport. The murder of the captain that took place during the intermediate landing in Dubai speeds up the preparations for the German commando force's effort.

Somalia's President, Muhammed Siad Barre receives two telephone calls from the Federal Chancellor, Helmut Schmidt. Finally he gives his signal to Schmidt: "Your men can start." The force who are waiting on Crete get the message by telex.

Right after nightfall the commando-force's Boeing 707 lands, with just the tail light lit, on Mogadishu airport as far away as possible from the hijacked 737. Then it slowly rolls away towards the far end of the runway.

The commando soldiers, dressed in dark blue and green and with blackened faces, sneak over to the tail of the hijacked plane without being seen. Now their skills really will be tested. Inside the plane are 82 passengers, crew and four wild terrorists. The storming has to be fast and methodical to avoid a big massacre.

Metallic ladders are soundlessly put against the plane and magnetic explosive charges are placed on the left side around the doors. A moment later the doors are blown out simultaneously. The soldiers who have climbed on the wings suck out the windows by the emergency exits with very low pressure equipment from the British army.

Each of the two soldiers throws a hand grenade of phosphorus into the plane. When they explode the cabin is filled with a forceful bang and a blinding white light. The grenades do not produce any splinters. The commando soldiers with protective goggles enter the plane. The two first hijackers are shot down as they, paralyzed by the blinding light, stagger out of the cockpit. The terrorist leader is shot when he releases a hand grenade that detonates in the front of the plane without damaging more than parts of the interior. The front toilet door is opened slightly. A gunshot is fired. The bullet hits the bullet-proof vest of one commando soldier. He returns the fire. Two more shots are fired at random by the terrorists, but they just hit the cabin ceiling. Then one of the female terrorists falls to the floor, bleeding from several wounds.

Five hundred meters away, the pilot who transported the commando troop describes the events to the management in Frankfurt. "The plane doors are open, the guys are getting inside, I can see 6, 7, 8, people of the hostages rushing out ... The soldiers have everything under control ... It is over. The action is finished."

From Frankfurt briefly comes the request: "We would like to know the number of killed and wounded." A few minutes later comes the answer:

"Three terrorists killed, the fourth badly injured."

"That is understood, OK" says Frankfurt. "Return to your base."

With the exception of the captain murdered earlier, all of the hostages survive the drama. The action in Mogadishu is later commented on, in a speech of the Federal Chancellor ...: "The event has made a deep, calming impression on our people."

Let us make a short summary of how the commando raid is carried through.

We can find five significant points:
— Accurate planning
— Timing
— Surprise
— Rapid control of the situation
— A quick withdrawal as soon as the surprise element has had the desired effect and has not lost its value.

Against this background we continue to describe our commission, operation Hot Cat, that in its methods, resembles the way commando soldiers execute their tasks.

Our "Hot Cat operation" was quickly manned. Three consultants were going to make a series of flying visits to the different units of the company. At the "base camp" we had one back-up consultant who was ultimately responsible for the operation.

Commando soldiers are led by military tactics. The clearer the management has fixed the strategy of an operation, the more independently the force can work. The individuals are also led by a military doctrine, i. e. a set of instructions shared by everyone. Thereby they develop a common moral attitude and behaviour pattern. The troop managers can, with full confidence, give operational responsibility to the leader of the troop without controlling in detail how the task is accomplished.

We ourselves had had our first training in something that later became a research program. We learned to work with organizational diagnosis in new, different and more fruitful ways. Through some meetings with the leader of the group we eventually acquired a common frame of reference. According to this approach, a culture diagnosis can serve as a starting-point for a development program where strategy and culture are brought into better agreement, i. e. strategy and culture will eventually cooperate to help the organization attain its goals.

In our design, the Commando model is in the first place a way to alternately gather and interpret cultural data. Simply a *technique* to gather and interpret data. It asks for rapidity, intensity and coordination together with a great adaptability in shifting situations. We have to be prepared to take time by the forelock when we gather our data. The data mostly comes from the 7 point model already described under the title "The cultural keys."

On the other hand, for us the adjacent concept Commando Consultants stands for a consulting style which means that you belong to a category of consultants whose professionality comes to be an advantage in flexible and complex situations.

The collecting and first interpretation was done during a short and intense period of time. The "Commando group" went out together to the units agreed upon. Our client had already informed the managers about our visit, and they had found a contact person at each unit for us. At our arrival we were shortly shown around and our presence was authorized. Every general manager had further prepared for our visit by ensuring that employees would be willing to be interviewed during the day. Important "bearers of culture" (public opinion moulders) were booked in advance and at our arrival we received a list with meeting schedules.

12.6.3 Three Steps

We arrive with cameras and taperecorders. After the first tour of inspection together with our contact person we spread out to work individually during the day.

All three of us in the group used the day for *individual data gathering*. We worked with private interviews and direct observations. Secondary material was mailed to us. In the evening we made an *individual analysis and interpretation* of the data we had gathered during the day. After that the group met to compare, control and put our material together in a *common interpretation*. This three-step pattern of individual and mutual work was used day by day during the collection of data. The positive side of this technique was that we had three independent bearings from the start.

At night, when the group had made its common interpretation, it reported the results to its "headquarters" and at the same time planned for the next day. New places to go, new units to visit.

When the data gathering and the first preliminary interpretation out in the field was done, we continued to look for patterns and characteristic points at home. The interpretation and report writing took about twice as much time as the gathering work did. Tapes had to be listened to, photos developed and all the material put together in a report. We made it all in ten days. Three days for gathering data, six days for analysis and interpretation and writing the report at home and one day for the typing of it.

The Commando model is only one dimension of the cultural diagnosis technique. It is a paradox in the way that it actually makes one think of a technical and instrumental view of organizational cultures. On the other hand, we have to remember that until now the Commando model has been tried, modified and refined through a handful of different cultural studies.

The strength of the Commando model is that it is a fast and lucid technique to find relevant cultural data. The shallowness has its own intrinsic value. We discover important features and turn the weakness of having few means and little time to our advantage. We get the overall picture and do not risk getting stuck in details. The organization obtains a foundation from which it can carry on and work.

12.7 Summary

We have given examples of how you, as uninitiated observer, could work when diagnosing an organizational culture. We also have described a concrete technique for gathering and interpreting cultural data, a fast and exacting technique. But it may be hard to find alternatives. If we investigate for a long time, we risk becoming part of the culture and not catching the snapshot views we find through the Commando model. We are translators, interpreting the things we hear and see as carefully as possible. We hope that our pictures create a knowledge that leads the organization forward, towards clearer goals and, in the long run, to higher accomplishments.

A cultural diagnosis with the help of the Commando model is a powerful intervention with lots of openings. It is important that senior managers, before we start the investigation, are prepared to continue the process once initiated. They do this by taking the consequences of the diagnosis. If they are not willing to do this, there is a risk that the positive effects of our work will not be felt. It is also important that the people interviewed and those who in other ways have given us help or support during our work, get the results of the study very soon and we feel it best to ask them to attend when we present our conclusions.

Appendix

Questionnaire Diagnosing and Furthering Corporate Culture Among Staff Members

Introductory questions

1. a. Managers
       Tell me about your career within the corporation. How did it start?
       Are there any key persons for you in your career?
    b. Others
       Tell me how you got where you are?
       How long have you been with the corporation?

The corporate saga

2. Tell me about the history of the corporation, how it all started?
3. Tell me about special epochs or remarkable periods within the corporation.
4. What events have been of special importance in its history?
5. What characterizes the current period?
6. What persons have been of special importance in the history?
7. Who are the heroes? Is there anyone you admire especially?
8. In what way have they influenced the enterprise?

Corporate progress/primary task

9. Please describe some of the most important reasons for the corporate success.
10. Can you describe the basic business idea of the corporation?
11. What will the corporation, in your opinion, be like in five years?

Rituals

12. Tell me about how you get your job done.
13. How are decisions made?

Ceremonies

14. Is there anything that is commemorated in a very special way?

Ethos (spirit)

15. If we talk about the general atmosphere within the corporation in terms of mind or heart, what would you say?

Rewards and punishment

16. To be successful, one shall ...
    To be successful, one shall not ...

The soul (metaphorical questions)

17. What would be your first move if tomorrow you were appointed Head at the HO?
18. If the corporation were an animal, what animal would you choose? Describe your animal.
19. If the corporation were a season, which would you choose? Describe your season.
20. If the corporation were an automobile, which brand would you choose? Describe your automobile.
21. If the corporation was a family, who would be the father, who would be the mother and who would be the children?

Final questions

22. Are there any questions you would add, change or take out?
23. Who can you suggest to help me like you have done in this interview?

References

de Board, R. (1984): *Våga lyssna*, Stockholm: Liber Förlag.
Dahlström, E. (1970): *Intervju- och enkätteknik*, Stockholm: Natur och Kultur.
Ehn, B. and Löfgren, O. (1982): *Kulturanalys*, Stockholm: Liber Förlag.
Eneroth, B. (1984): *Hur mäter man vackert?*, Stockholm: Akademilitteratur.

Goldberg, D. (1984): *Förstå och utveckla din intuition*, Stockholm: Svenska Dagbladets Förlag.

Hermann, K. and Kock, P. (1977): *Assault at Mogadishu*, London: Corgi Books.

Musashi, M. (1984): *De fem ringarnas bok*, Stockholm: Bonnier Fakta.

Peters, T. and Waterman, R. (1982): *In search of Excellence*, New York: Harper & Row.

Part IV
Style and Aesthetics

Chapter 13
The Collusive Manoeuvre: A Study of Organizational Style in Work Relations

Robert W. Witkin

13.1 Organizational Style

"It ain't what you do, it's the way that you do it"; the words of the song grant a significance, even a primacy to the concept of 'style' that contrasts with the lack of significance attributed to such a concept in organizational research. The concept of style is inextricably bound up with the sensuous, subjective and expressive aspects of social action and is explored in the sociological literature in relation to 'leisure culture' rather than 'work culture' (Hebdidge 1979; Willis 1978; Hall and Jefferson 1976). So far as the sociology of work and of organizations is concerned, there has certainly been a great deal of attention paid in recent decades to the human and subjective dimension of work (Argyris 1964; Herzberg 1972; Davis 1972). In the main, however, this interest in the subjective dimension has not involved serious attention to style and expression and to the problem of 'meaning' in work as distinct from motivation (Sievers 1984; Witkin 1986; 1987). Styles of work are often thought of as being personal and idiosyncratic, as oiling the wheels of functional interaction within the organization but as not being, in and of themselves, significant determinants of that interaction. My purpose in the present paper, however, is to reflect on the potential importance of the concept of 'style' for organizational research, to develop a framework for analysing 'work styles' in the context of organizations and to fill out some of these reflections with an account of an 'organizational work style' concerning a conflict over job evaluation drawn from a specific case study carried out in a large insurance company.

The work process in an organization is structured 'instrumentally' to achieve certain ends. Seen from this point of view, an organization is a rational-technical machinery. This perspective, essentially Weberian, predominates in organizational studies. What is often neglected in such studies is the fact that in the very process of structuring action as a rational-technical means for the attainment of given empirical ends, the organization must continuously revivify and recreate itself as a dynamic 'agency'. The work gets done by living actors who address each other in certain ways, observe certain niceties and rules of office etiquette and shape their encounters, relations and actions in ways designed to reinforce and revivify the 'organizational process' so that it is capable of delivering the action demanded in particular situations. While recurring patterns of action, developed in the work process, may well be 'instrumental' (means) for the achievement of definite extrinsic ends, those same patterns may also be viewed as 'styles' of action, as action, sensuously patterned, to realize (and express) *values intrinsic to the organizational process itself*.

Such styles of action are not merely an embellishment or adornment of the instrumental structure that would be to trivialise them. Rather, they serve to create and to disseminate a unity of *organizational being* out of the diverse variety of 'interests' that enters into the structure of organizational action. It is only through realizing values common to this diverse variety of interests that the organization, as a dynamic agency (we might even say, as an 'active subject'), can be made 'present' and 'affective' in the consciousness and actions of its members. A style of action is just such a sensuous realization of common values, of unity in diversity. It is in and through the cultivation of organizational styles that individual members manifest, at the level of their consciousness and action, an 'organizational presence' or 'organizational being'.

Quite apart from any specific training that an organization gives its recruits with respect to specific tasks and routines and ways of doing things, organizations also develop and disseminate a *modus vivendi*, an 'organizational being' or 'presence', in their members, which serves as a guide and basis for action in negotiating organizational encounters of all kinds. Such an 'organizational presence', insofar as it is developed within an individual member, provides the feeling for and understanding of situations from which organizational encounters derive their meanings. The design of the work process and the structure of work relations is fundamental in engendering an 'organizational presence' in the individual, an 'organizational being' which corresponds to his or her place within it.

The more that action approaches the routine, the habitual mechanical or repetitive, the less is it appropriate to speak of the actor in terms of his or her 'presence' or 'being' (Witkin 1986). The absence of discretion or autonomy in the performance of work is synonymous with an 'absence' of being rather than a 'presence'. Habit and repetition negates the subject as creative author of his actions: a number of writers have pointed up the gains in efficiency offered by autonomy in the labour process and the costs to organizations of the lack of it (Fox 1974; Friedman 1977; Katz 1973; Likert 1967; Edwards 1979). In claiming that the design of the work process and the structure of work relations is fundamental in engendering organizational presence in the members of an organization, I have in mind not the structure of work routines and habits of action as such but a special class of *recurring patterns of action* and relationship that require, for their realization, that actors exercise autonomy and discretion.

Notwithstanding the hierarchical and directed character of work processes in most organizations, all organizations have some interest in the development of autonomy and discretion in role performance, albeit to different degrees and in varying respects. Such discretion is a vital part of the organization's ability to orient itself in its external relations, to take the initiative in seizing market opportunities and so forth. It is also vital in the development of internal relations where competing interests must be negotiated as between departments, sections and units and effective allocation of resources must be made. Also, insofar as autonomy and discretion inheres in the performance of work roles of all kinds, it has a major part to play in reducing the costs involved in surveillance and control. Wherever role discretion is inherent in the design of a work process it is the very practice of that discretion which presupposes an integrity and coherence of value in the 'subject'.

The practice of role discretion and autonomy, however, is always a response to felt tensions that are in large measure structured by the situations in which actors find themselves in the organization. Each situation and organizational relationship has a problematic associated with it and the actors concerned are uniquely placed with respect to organizational resources and relationships in grappling with that problematic. Over time, patterns of action and relationship are evolved which prove more or less successful in resolving the recurring structured tension inherent in the situation. The fact that these patterns recur in the organization does not make them repetitions. Their production is not automatic or mechanical; it is always problematic. These patterns of action have to be skillfully accomplished, as though for the first time, in each realization. They may be likened to the invariant and recurring forms that appear in the works of art of a given artist, a given epoch or national culture, and which are subsumed under the concept of 'style'. Modigliani's women have been described as 'dying swans' and Lowrie's figures as 'matchstick men and matchstick cats and dogs'. Such phrases may describe recurring features of their respective styles of painting but on that account alone we would not regard a collection of the paintings of either painter as constituting a series of repetitions.

The tendency in writing about art is to emphasise the unique character of each work and to see no contradiction between doing so and, at the same time, recognising the genre or style to which the work belongs. It is precisely in this sense that I want to invoke the concept of 'style' to discuss those recurring organizational patterns of action that are realized by actors exercising autonomy and discretion in the performance of their roles. A style may be thought of as a set of values defining not only the sensuous/aesthetic qualities with which action is performed, its 'pitch', 'amplitude', 'rhythms' and 'harmonics' (whether these are discribed in terms of 'lightness of touch', 'slowness of deliberation' or 'smoothness' of delivery or in terms of types of speech, the use of certain words or grammatical structures etc.), *but also its more or less enduring patterning, form or structure*. Viewed in this way, we can go on to define the organizational being of an actor as an *incipient readiness* in organizational encounters to realize, in action, a set of organizational values — that is, to cultivate an organizational style. Just as an artist's work reveals consistencies peculiar or unique to himself as well as consistencies that his work shares with others of the same national culture, or the same artistic epoch, so the personal styles of members of an organizational contain elements unique to them as well as consistencies of a wider organizational kind. My interest, here, is in this wider level of consistency; that is, in the organizational styles realized in and through the personal work styles of members of the organization.

13.2 An Organizational Problematic

The present study concerns a large financial services company. The company, which re-located its head office away from the capital some thirteen years ago, has seen a substantial growth in business in recent times. Growth in financial services has been uneven with some parts of the business expanding at a much faster rate than others in accordance with the development of demand for their services. Taking these departments as constituent units, it is clear that development has been accompanied by a number of structural changes in the organization as a whole which have implications for the organization's overall problematic.

There exists, in this organization, a certain tradition of more or less tight corporate control and a sense of corporate identity. This has been strongly reinforced in the company's employment practices, job evaluation system, and the generous cultivation of what have been called 'hygiene factors', that is, the fringe benefits and 'perks' of organizational membership for the employees. Company growth, coupled with the uneven nature of expansion, has been accompanied by a growing autonomy of the separate departments as the latter have increased in size and complexity. The autonomy of the departments is rightly perceived as essential to the exploitation of opportunities for growth which demand innovation and flexibility of response in the development of work processes and departmental structures. However, this growing autonomy is in tension with the corporate control of the company exercised from the centre.

13.3 Material and Cultural Values in Job Evaluation

The tension is felt in a number of areas. The one that concerns me here is the company's job evaluation system. The company-wide system of discrete grades for levels of job responsibility is an important instrument of corporate control and corporate integration. Company growth means that there is a substantial degree of re-structuring and re-designing of jobs in the affected departments, as well as an overall increase in staffing. This in turn leads to submissions for up-grading of jobs within departments, ostensibly to take account of new responsibilities involved in those jobs. Submissions for re-evaluating jobs are made by department heads to a *job evaluation committee* which has a rotating membership of six individuals from various departments in the company. The one permanent member of that committee is the personnel manager. The company, of course, has a corporate interest in controlling the inflationary drift implicit in job re-design and re-evaluation. Staff costs are the company's major costs and there is continuing pressure to contain the rise in these costs, at least to levels that are justified by growth in the company's earnings.

However, the corporate interest in the job evaluation system extends beyond a simple concern with costs. The job evaluation system itself provides a common set of 'values' in terms of which all the myriad work processes constituting the organization can be expressed. One department is structured with so many 'grade twos', so many 'grade fours', so many 'grade sevens' and so forth. Another department is structured with different numbers of staff in the same (and therefore comparable) grades. To the company, the grading label may indicate simply a level in the organizational hierarchy which carries with it a certain entitlement to remuneration and perks. For the individual members of the company, the levels at which jobs are evaluated have symbolic significance. It is not just a matter of pay. The grade of one's job is literally a value that the company places on one's work; it locates one in the hierarchy of organizational values and serves as a basic of comparison with others on dimensions other than those of extrinsic rewards. Not surprisingly, individuals from other departments are frequently identified in conversations with colleagues with phrases like, "Oh, she's a grade five". The normal routes to improving grades are promotion to jobs carrying higher grades, or the re-design of jobs so that they carry new and enlarged responsibilities. Job evaluation, therefore, is not only a system of material values; it is also a system of cultural values bound up with the individual's sense of the personal autonomy and responsibility that inheres in the work process, together with the modes of relating to others that are made available in that work process and with the individual's sense of organizational statuses and organizational identities. Job evaluation is therefore bound up with the quality of the individual's 'organizational being'.

The job evaluation system is thus far more than an instrument of corporate cost control; it is a major element in the system of personal motivators and it plays a significant part in the creation and dissemination of meanings at the level of the work process. Not surprisingly, an increase in the autonomy of a department is bound to be accompanied by attempts to gain a departmental purchase on the job evaluation system. Indeed, it would seem to be implicit in the notion of departmental autonomy that the department has power over both the design of work and of the creation and dissemination of motivators and meanings in the work process. The greater the pressure for autonomy, the greater the inherent potential for bruising conflicts with the job evaluation committee. Not only is job evaluation a vital factor in the head of department's authority with, and management of, his staff. It is also an important part of the management of political struggles with other departments concerning share of scarce corporate resources since the upgrading of jobs in a department bestows organizational value on the department and not just on the individuals who are the direct beneficiaries of that upgrading. Furthermore, the manager who finds himself the loser in a struggle with the job evaluation committee may, in some way, lose face both with the staff dependent upon him and with other departmental heads.

The job evaluation system, therefore, becomes an important (not the sole) site within the company for a genuine conflict of interests between two *corporate* demands, the demand for local departmental autonomy and the demand for centralised company control. In this conflict, those managers with a primarily corporate and organizational function become key actors.

There are staff playing these roles in a number of different capacities in different companies. Departments of Organizational Development and Personnel Departments are obviously important locations for such staff in most companies. In the company that is the subject of this study, the personnel manager serves as an example of a manager playing a key organizational role. In the remainder of the paper, I shall use his account of his handling of one such clash of interests with a head of department over job evaluation to illustrate a management style that seems peculiarly well-fitted to riding both horns of this dilemma in the attempt to resolve what has been a long-running conflict. I have labelled the style the 'collusive manoeuvre'.

The illustrative data used here concerns a conflict within the company between the personnel manager and a business manager over the latter's failure to get approval for his proposals to upgrade certain jobs. It was recorded using a method for obtaining qualitatively rich data which I have described elsewhere (Witkin and Poupart 1986). Briefly, the method consists in inviting the subject to 're-live', imaginatively, a significant sequence of events that has actually occurred, and for which he can provide a precise time, place and situation. In the process of imaginatively 're-living' this sequence of events he is required to run a commentary on them *in the present tense* as though they are happening now. The present-centred nature of the discourse obtained is an important feature of the method. *There is no claim made, however, that the account given faithfully reproduces the events described. The relationship to real historical events remains undetermined. The authenticity of the account resides, rather, in the present-centred structuring of events disclosed at the time the account is given.* It is also important to note that the account given delineates the pattern of action in the perceptions and reflections of the personnel manager and there is no claim that these events would be perceived in the same way by the business manager with whom he is interacting. My concern is simply with the elucidation of a pattern of action, an organizational style, which a given individual cultivates in the context of a particular situation.

For the purposes of exposition I shall present an outline framework of the situational elements structuring the tensions experienced by the actors to which the collusive manoeuvre is a response. I shall then go on to describe the personnel manager's account in terms of two qualitatively distinct phases of the sequence of acts which goes to make up the pattern of action, the organizational style, realised in the events described. I shall call these phases *the blocking phase* and *the collusive phase*, respectively.

13.4 The Situational Frame

The situational elements structuring the tensions to which the collusive manoeuvre is a response, may be crudely summarised as follows:

13.4.1 Usurpationary Challenge

There is some attempt by an individual or department to undermine, railroad, or otherwise challenge or defeat a set of corporately imposed constraints upon his organizational freedom of action. Such challenges are perceived to be illegitimate by those wielding corporate power and they are defined as such.

13.4.2 Corporate Impediment

The usurpationary challenge is resisted through the imposition of a decisive corporate impediment, a set of actions or decisions by agents of the organization that prevent the challenge from being successful and which pose a more or less critical problem for the challenger.

13.4.3 Key Organization Personnel

There are present in the situation directly involved personnel having key roles with respect to both facilitating organizational and staff development throughout the company and exercising corporate discipline on behalf of the company. The effectiveness of such personnel depends largely upon the direct power they have with respect to both the imposition of the corporate impediment and to the lifting of that imposition.

13.5 The Blocking Phase

The business manager, Joe, has put in a submission to the job evaluation committee to have four jobs in his department upgraded from grade 3 to grade 4. The submission to the job evaluation committee argues that these jobs involve substantial new responsibilities justifying up-grading. The submission has been prepared with the assistance of a senior personnel officer from the personnel department. It has been entirely rejected by the job evaluation committee. The personnel manager, Brian, contacted Joe immediately after the meeting, knowing that he would be aggrieved and proposed that the two should meet to discuss the matter. The first meeting takes place in the personnel manager's office.

After the preliminary remarks, Joe expresses his surprise and concern at the rejection of his submission by the job evaluation committee in view of the fact that a senior personnel officer from Brian's department had been fully involved with one of his own managers in preparing the submission. The implied complaint is clear enough. If something was wrong with the submission then the personnel department were in some sense culpable because of their complicity in preparing the submission. Brian deflects the complaint:

"But I have reviewed it Joe and I find that I do not believe that your aspiration has failed to be achieved because of any failure or omission in the papers submitted. They were very well prepared. Jill and Mark had done an excellent job ... it was very clear indeed. It may seem ironic Joe, but it has nevertheless not contributed to your achieving the grades you aspire to."

Having deflected the complaint, Brian goes on to give the real reasons for the rejection as he sees them. In fact he offers two rather different reasons. The first is to suggest that Joe's perceptions of the differences between jobs in his department in terms of levels of skill and responsibility etc. may be legitimate from Joe's point of view but the job evaluation mechanism is a relatively crude one that cannot respond to the kinds of fine gradations he can perceive. The second reason he offers discloses the kind of challenge that Joe's submission poses to the corporate control over job evaluation exercised by the committee.

"You are building a structure like Topsy. You are not actually saying what enabling structure you need as a department. Yours is a very fast growing area and we have more submissions from your division than from any other in the company ... but the end result is you keep bolting bits on and the committee gets either confused or sees contradictions ... Now why are you then surprised that the committee is then resistant to that, feels that you are not telling the truth or that life isn't as you explain it to be."

Brian then goes on to make explicit what has really been implicit from the outset in the interview, namely that the path is effectively closed to any forward movement by Joe *acting alone* to achieve his aspirations for job evaluation. Of course, he can appeal but Brian makes it clear that the appeal will not succed —

"such was our strength of feeling and I have to say — from a personal point of view and not just as a committee member — looking at the structure, the way the jobs hang together, you are not going to achieve a grade 4 there. If you can accept that I suggest that we put the issue on one side ..."

In case there is still any lingering doubt in Joe's mind about the determination of the job evaluation committee, Brian invokes a whole history of conflict and dissatisfaction involving Joe's department and the committee who are "constantly being provoked by you into giving grades that you want whether or not they're valid."

13.6 The Collusive Phase

Brian's tone, throughout the interview (as reflected in the commentary), blends a quiet and patient reasonableness with a firmness of direction and purpose. In approaching Joe, he dons the mantle of the transcendent corporate being. It is reflected in the almost juridical character of the language used — "I have *reviewed* it Joe and I *find* that I do not believe ... such was the strength of our feeling and I *have* to say ..." In the second phase of the process, the collusive phase, Brian alters the perspective that he adopts in relation to Joe and, with it, the tone and language that he uses. The tone is both 'confidential' and 'mildly conspiratorial'. The language used is a vehicle for the 'bonding work' that is going on. Up until now he has been concerned to get Joe to accept both the illegitimacy of his approach and the impossibility of his achieving his aspirations using that approach. Now he demonstrates that he can see Joe as the injured party and he uses this to offer Joe an alliance, a way forward, provided that they work together.

"What you need is the ability not to have to come cap in hand to the job evaluation committee every time you want another job evaluated. That must be bloody frustrating for you. You must feel, sometimes, I am sure, that you are trying to manage a sharp end business operation and there's a whole bunch of idiots who don't really know what your business is about who are constraining you in that. *So I can try and see it through your eyes as well — what if we work together to determine what your framework structure of jobs and reporting relationships will be for 1988.*"

Brian then goes on to propose that the two of them collude to effect a radical re-definition of the situation, one that promises to achieve important gains in respect of job evaluation for Joe and one which has some real chance of success in obtaining company approval because it will have been produced by the two of them working together. Brian's power with respect to the committee and, therefore, the lifting of the corporate impediment, is an important factor here. His proposal is that the two of them work *together* on producing a job framework for the entire department which they will then submit for approval, as a whole, to the job evaluation committee. Joe will then be left free to move about the pieces in this structure at will without having to come back to the job evaluation committee for approval every time he wants a job changed. In effect, he will have obtained, from the job evaluation committee, an overall set of jobs at specified levels and he will be able to make use of this allocation as he pleases in re-structuring and developing work processes. Joe recognises that this is a radical change and asks whether they can get approval for it. Brian is confident that they can and draws on imagery depicting the conflict as occurring at the level of their bosses and pointing to the common interest that the two of them have in creatively resolving all such differences:

"My boss is acutely aware — because your boss keeps sticking him in the ear — that, you know, he's not very happy with the service he gets on job evaluation and he thinks we're a sort of millstone around his neck, so, perhaps this is a way of actually demonstrating to those two guys that you and I have got the ability to be creative and to solve some problems ... I'm prepared to aid you to maximise your position within that (the current corporate framework) ... not to give you what you want ... but to make sure you're getting a fair deal under it."

13.7 Analysis

It is important to note that what is on offer in the situation described above is an alliance, a process of collusion to obtain the lifting of the corporate impediment. Brian is not offering to negotiate or to strike a deal whereby Joe gives up certain of his aspirations in exchange for achieving others. That might indeed seem preferable to Joe. Certainly, striking a deal would be a less risky strategy. In a collusive alliance of this kind, Joe has to share some of his autonomy and his initiative with Brian. The latter makes it clear that his involvement will be of a wholly different kind from that of Jill, his senior personnel officer who assisted Joe's department in making the previous submission. He is not interested in simply preparing papers for the committee based on Joe's ideas. Rather, he proposes to work with the department in thinking through the structure required and arriving at the necessary generic job descriptions in the light of the functional requirements of each section.

Inevitably, this will put Brian in possession of a great deal of information about the entire management structure and work process design of the department. The more information that the centre possesses with respect to the departments, the more difficult it is for the latter to call the shots in bidding competitively with others for scarce organizational resources. Departments often find it prudent to be economical in supplying the kind of information that Brian will have as a matter of course. In addition to obtaining the necessary information, however, Brian's corporate perspective will be involved in a critical way in testing and developing the emerging structure and in harmonising is with corporate objectives. The end result will be the production of an enabling structure for the entire department which is the outcome of an initiative that is as much that of the organizational 'centre' as it is of the department.

This is the essence of the collusive manoeuvre, the direct involvement of organization personnel in steering the planning and development of departments, where it is understood that local initiatives are vital. The head of the department and his staff still retain the initiative in planning and structuring of the work process, but with an active 'corporate presence', an organization 'ally', to shape these initiatives into acceptable corporate structures.

The account given by the personnel manager of the second meeting, which took place in Joe's department with his senior staff present reveals him to be in exactly this situation. Joe sets up the meeting as a presentation of the department's work and structure, a presentation which takes an hour and a half. Following this he is questioned closely on it by Brian who then subjects both the logic of his claims and the manner of presenting information to criticism. Together they work out a way forward, with the department's managers, to building an overall 'enabling structure' for the department which will contain only generic job descriptions fully grounded in and supported by an analysis of sectional and departmental functionality. The effect of the collusion is that Brian's point of view and reasoning about the parameters of corporate development are made visible to the departmental managers in these encounters and are likely to operate as internalised constraints on their building of an enabling structure even when he is not present. Everyone has an interest in trying to assimilate his point of view since Brian is, in the very nature of the situation, key to their negotiation of the corporate impediment and to the realisation of at least some of their aspirations for control over staffing and job design.

It is important to distinguish between the structural constraints characteristic of the organization as a whole, which are conducive to the formation of definite working relations, and the structured tension inherent in those working relations. The conflict between the demands of corporate centralism and departmental autonomy provide an instance of the former. The situated tensions defining the relationship between Brian and Joe in the encounters referred to above offer an example of the latter. The organizational style realised by Brian in this situation, a style which I have called the "collusive manoeuvre" is really an attempt to resolve the tensions inherent in the structure of relations and encounters in which he is involved. These tensions are certainly precipitated by general structural constraints operating at the level of the organization as a whole but to discover anything of the manner of their precipitation would require a separate investigation and analysis. My argument here is simply that all situations in which organizational action takes place structure tensions for the actors involved such that the organizational styles cultivated may be profitably viewed as attempts (more or less successful) to resolve these structured tensions.

Furthermore, I would argue that these tensions should be seen as fully sensuous, as fully felt by the participants, even though they may not be explicitly formulated or understood at a cognitive level. It is possible to conceive of the tensions inherent in the situation described above as having been structured somewhat differently. They might have been structured, for example, in such a way as to preclude the formation of a collusive alliance and to effect a balance of interests through a direct and partisan conflict between the parties. There are many examples in industry where institutionalised conflicts of this kind constitute a basic style for resolving tensions. Much of the ritual, symbolism and argot of trade union and collective bargaining can be subsumed under this rubric. It is a culture in which the conflict that takes place between managers and workers preserves the integrity of the boundaries separating the parties in conflict. The conflict of interests is not negated but is used *positively* to achieve a mutual accomodation of interests, through negotiation, bargaining, etc.

The collusive manoeuvre belongs to a category of organizational styles of a wholly different kind. These effectively breach or permeate the boundaries between the parties to a given relationship and attempt to resolve conflict, not through a negotiated accomodation of interests but through *the establishment of a community of interest* and a negation of the conflict itself. The style adopted by Brian, in realizing this organizational pattern, calls upon him to transcend his role in imposing the corporate impediment and to disclose an understanding of Joe's position as well as an interest in facilitating

Joe's aspirations. For that to be credible Brian must adopt a *corporate* stance with respect to the interests of *both* central and departmental management. The firm opposition provided in the blocking phase of the manoeuvre is opposition to the 'unreconstructed departmentalist' in Joe. The sympathetic co-operation offered in the collusive phase of the manoeuvre is co-operation that presupposes a new 'corporate departmentalism' in Joe. Certainly, the collusive manoeuvre, like all organizational styles of action, is a complex cultural achievement. While it arises, in this instance, as an effort to resolve conflict between the demands of local initiative and departmental autonomy and those of corporate centralism, it points to the possibilities of a different type of management structure from that which exists at present. The practice of this kind of collusive alliance between department and centre on an ad hoc basis no doubt makes a contribution to easing the structural strains in the present development of the company but in the absence of any fundamental change in management structures it is likely to be relatively contained in its effects.

13.8 Conclusion

I would argue, therefore, that work styles, and the organizational styles realized in them, deserve the attention of all those interested in the development of organizational structures and that they have real implications for the most central aspects of organizational functioning. Firstly, there is an intimate connection between the sensuous qualities of action and the structure or 'form' of the action itself, that is, the kind of action that takes place. The very language used, its texture and nuances, the quality of gesture and expression, all are intimately bound up with the patterning of action and, together, they constitute its style. To adopt a 'confidential' and 'diplomatic' manner is one's dealings with others is likely to be more effective if the business at hand is diplomacy. Secondly, such styles may be seen as generated in response to the 'demand characteristics' of particular situations. And those situations, in turn, have to be seen as reflecting the interdependence of the organization as a whole and its overall problematic. Finally, contrasting styles of action may be equally effective in the same situation. Most organizations have known the situation in which a change of manager brings with it an entirely different style of operation. However, if the change is a true change of style, and not merely superficial, then it will be momentous. A true change of style represents a shift in the foundations of common value realised in an organizational style.

'Organizational styles' are not simply reducible to the personal qualities and attributes of the individual actors themselves. Such styles are emergent within and engendered by, the situations in which action takes place. The prolematic inhering in a given action situation 'cues' the organizational styles that provide the means of its resolution. Even where the actors are not directly aware of the overall problematic inhering in the structure of the organization, that problematic nevertheless operates as a real set of constraints upon action and upon the development of organizational styles in specific action contexts. Action situations within an organization are never isolated structures. They form part of a complex which may be vast, even extending beyond the boundaries of the total organization. The problematic inhering in a given situation is thus not determined purely locally and immediately but is shaped by the total complex of which that situation forms a part. Thus problems inherent in the overall structure of an organization are apt to reproduce themselves in a variety of different guises at the level of particular action situations. In this way, the specific problematics of selling a car, building a bridge, writing a contract, developing an insurance policy and so forth, are mediated by the overall problematics of the organizations in which they occur.

References

C. Argyris (1964): *Integrating the Individual and the Occupation*, New York: Wiley.

L. E. Davis (1972): Job Satisfaction Research: The Post-Industrial View, in L. E. Davis and J. C. Taylor (eds.), *Design of Jobs*, Harmondsworth: Penguin. New York: Wiley.

R. Edwards (1979): *Contested Terrain; The Transformation of the Workplace in the Twentieth Century*, London: Heinemann.

A. Fox (1974): *Beyond Contract: Work, Power and Trust Relations*, London: Faber and Faber.

A. Friedman (1977): Responsible Autonomy versus Direct Control, *Capital and Class*, London: Macmillan, vol. 1: 43 – 57.

S. Hall and T. Jefferson (1976): *Resistance Through Rituals: Youth Subcultures in Post-War Britain*, London: Hutchinson.

D. Hebdidge (1979): *Subculture: The Meaning of Style*, London: Macmillan Methuen.

F. Herzberg (1972): One More Time: How Do You Motivate Employees, in L. E. Davis and J. C. Taylor (eds., *op. cit.*

F. E. Katz (1973): Integrative and Adaptive Uses of Autonomy: Worker Autonomy in Factories, in G. Salamon and K. Thompson (eds.), *People and Organizations*, 190 – 224, London: Longman.

L. Likert (1967): *The Human Organization: Its Management and Value*, New York: McGraw Hill.

B. Sievers (1984): *Motivation as a Surrogate for Meaning*, Working Papers in the Department of Business Administration and Economics, no. 81, Bergische Universität, Wuppertal (Germany).

P. E. Willis (1978): *Profane Culture*, London: Routledge and Kegan Paul Ltd.

R. W. Witkin (1986): Cultural Engineering in Organizations as the Antithesis of the Creation of Meaning, *Proceedings of the International Conference on Organization Symbolism and Corporate Culture*, volume 2: 267–279, University of Quebec.

R. W. Witkin (1987): The Aesthetic Imperative of a Rational-Technical Machinery. A Study in Organizational Control Through the Design of Artifacts, *Dragon*, vol. 2 no. 4 — Special issue: *Art and the Organization*: 109–126.

R. Witkin and R. Poupart (1986): 'Running a commentary on imaginatively relived events: a method for obtaining qualitatively rich data.' In A. Strati, ed. *The Symbolics of Skill* Quaderno 5/6 Dipartimento di Politica Socials, Trento: University of Trento. 79–86.

Chapter 14
Aesthetics and Organizational Skill

Antonio Strati

The aesthetic dimension is of value for both the individual and for society. It passes beyond the bounds of economic well-being — although it belongs to it — to become a cultural and social good that relates different societies and different historical periods. How does it operate in organizations? The sentiment of beauty that organizations arouse, primarily in those who work for them but also in those who have dealings with them, provides the basis, I believe, for assessment of the analytical contribution that the symbolic approach can make to the study of organizations.

I shall begin this analysis by singling out the aesthetic dimension where it appears, as an organizational dimension, in the dynamics of the work process of three organizations. This subject of study is rather a mysterious one. I certainly cannot draw upon clearcut definitions of the aesthetic feeling, nor on any personal convictions on the matter. I have therefore been forced to rely on what the organizational actors themselves, within the organization or those acting on its behalf, have told me about their aesthetic values. And this complicates my analysis: neither the subject (the aesthetic dimension) nor the field of enquiry (the dynamics of the work process in organizations) display precisely definable features. There do exist a number of commonly used distinctions concerning the activities, organizations and environments where the aesthetic dimension is present, but how can we be sure that it is absent from other settings and structures? Problems such as these force the researcher to rely on the organizational actors' own insights and accounts.

I was reluctant to renounce my right to problematize, examine and understand in my own terms, and draw my own conclusions concerning the existence or otherwise of the aesthetic dimension. Therefore, I adopted as the guiding principles for my analysis that the aesthetic value should be described by numbers or small groups of informants; that it should have accompanying emphasis on the affective force that binds people and organizational values; and that it should be felt and recognized by many other members of an organization.

For safety's sake, I decided to examine this value in environments that were familiar to me (Van Maanen 1979), i.e. in organizations similar to the one in which I work. Thus, by conducting the analysis in three Italian university departments, I would be able to take advantage of the fact that, as a researcher belonging to the working community that I was studying, my presence in the department as a participating observer would be less obtrusive. By presenting myself as a colleague, I would be able to discuss my subject in a process of continuous and non-standardized feedback until I was able to recognize, evaluate and understand it properly.

Interviews between the researcher and the organizational actors were designed to bring out the aesthetic value and those organizational areas where this dimension was a forceful element in the relations among subject, work and organization. Techniques ranged from direct questioning and the use of imaginary doubles to the search for particular modes of expression like the mottoes and images of the organization, its layout and decorations/ furnishings, its architectural appearance, and the way people dress. All the material gathered in the first round of interviews was recycled in follow-up interactions with new informants in a continuous process of checks, illustration of fresh concrete elements and the construction of patterns and ways of perceiving the aesthetic dimension, the work process and the organization.

What I set out in the following pages cannot be directly assimilated into the tradition of organizational case studies; it is instead and more simply a series of reflections on the theme of the aesthetic dimension as an organizational value that have been generated by on-the-spot research. They are reflections, to tell the truth, developed jointly with the members of the organizations concerned and other scholars. Research is often a chorus of voices, which the expository style of the researcher may hide or not, as the case may be.

At an appropriate moment I asked my informants directly about the aesthetic dimension of their work. Not at the beginning of the interview but when the relationship between researcher and organizational actor had become warmer. And not always, since some informants were reluctant to talk about the subject.

"How would you describe the aesthetic dimension of the work of the members of your department?"
"Well, the fact that I work with material that is in itself aesthetic I find fulfilling. I don't think I could have done anything else in my life."

So answered a researcher in the university art department. The fact that she worked with material that was already intrinsically beautiful satisfied her sense of beauty. Aesthetic materials were part of her work environment, a physical relation and, also, the material source of her activity.

"If I were your double, what could I do?"
"Try and find out what your inclinations were. To overturn them, perhaps, or change them."

This was the answer given by another lecturer in the same organization. His personal preferences are revealing: they signal the reasons, largely incoherent, for his choice of career. And he expresses them in the conviction that he could not have done anything else in life. Many members of the department adduce a global dimension, broader than any view narrowly circumscribed by the work relationship. And their attitude to their work is to be interpreted in terms of their conception of beauty.

"This is a concept that should always be seen in terms of the cultural notions that artists create. The question of the perception of beauty is an imponderable one; it's so subjective," said another researcher.

On careful examination of personal preferences in terms of the attitudes of the subjects towards the aesthetic content of their work, it was evident that several lecturers in the department preferred the visual to the spoken or written image.

"In any case, you should never look at what is written below an illustration in a book. There are lots of techniques you can use. Mine is rather silly: for me, the first impression is the most important one, the one that matters most. Then you let your eye wander until it finds the detail that gives you an insight into the whole picture. Then you catalogue it, make a series of observations, open a file."
"You have to go and look at some architectural feature. As you approach, you distinguish between the animated surroundings and the inanimate: between the physical ... from people, from the social. I like to identify the spirit of a place from the signals conveyed by its people, their way of dressing, their way of speaking."

The above are two examples of the factors that guided me in my interpretation of the visual materials that the subjects in this organization worked with. Other lecturers and researchers in the department declared that they established this contact first through the written word and then went on to examine the visual image. These two approaches to the aesthetic content of the department's work seemed to be more indicative of personal preferences than of processes of socialization to work. They did not reveal particular forms of aggregation among the various members of the department; neither were there differences in the emotional intensity with which the subjects 'felt' what was beautiful to them. Both approaches reveal the vital and convincing presence of a relation between the subject and the material content of his/her work that was based on the aesthetic dimension.

This aesthetic relationship between the subject and the material substance of his/her work has been commented on by several authors (Jones 1980). In her study of an Oregon fishing community, Garson (1975) writes of the sensuous rapport between the cleaner and flesh of the fish she is gutting. Here the palpability of the fish unites with the variegated sheen of the fish-scales during the act of cutting and cleaning. Certain other scholars have described this sensuous bond between the worker and his/her physical environment, and Witkin (1987) insists on the sensuous (but problematic) nature of this relation, arguing that working life imposes an aesthetic discipline on people. However, most other writers on organizations have either ignored it or treated it as superfluous.

I tend to agree with them. I believe that, in many cases, the aesthetic dimension is of secondary importance in that it is an organizational fact. This is certainly not to deny the complex, multi-faceted network of relations (including the aesthetic) that intermesh around the perceptions and the behaviours of organizational actors in their relationships with their working environments. And this relational network is grounded in an awareness of an aesthetic value that is felt more in terms of humanity and society at large than of the organization.

In the art department, however, the aesthetic dimension was not of secondary importance. It was neither complementary nor additional, nor an embellishment. It was fundamental to the department's placement in the university's scientific environment. It was crucial to the choices of those members of the organization who did not work in the administration. Even the departmental librarian was a connoisseur of art.

For the lecturers and researchers, the visual appreciation of beauty was a decisive factor in their career choices, one that had led, in time, to their employment by different organizations and institutions. These were patterns of working life characterized more by the subjects' constant search for the aesthetic value than by the working environments of organizations. However, this is not to say that, because the aesthetic dimension constituted one of its organizational dimensions, the department represented the point of arrival of these careers; only that it was able to assess, select and accomodate such diverse perceptions of the aesthetic value from the academic community and the outside world and to exalt them as its own organizational fact.

In fact, the appreciation of beauty, a sentiment of beauty and personal preference provide the basis for: a) the desires and decisions that lead subjects to acquire the skills that qualify them for a job where they have the task of investigating aesthetic materials in order to suggest ways of conceiving what is beautiful; b) their submitting themselves to judgement by their peers and by other members of the academic community so that they can join this occupational community (Strati 1986; Van Maanen and Barley 1984), be assigned to the various university faculties, belong to the department; c) pass through the stages of an academic tenured career from researcher to associate professor to full professor. If we take a 'sign' to be something which can be assumed to be meaningfully substitutable for something else (Eco 1975), then the sign for the appreciation of the beautiful is the written word. Writing represented the final stage in a subject's relationship with the work process

"We have to work ... but to publish, as the law instructs us, to make a contribution to scientific knowledge. And, since the law tells us to publish, I suppose that this is our duty," said a researcher.

More than a written regulation, this is a documentary form for the expression, demonstration, communication and adjudication — above all by colleagues — of aesthetic expression. The statement by this researcher was also coloured by her defence of the identity that she had built out of her work and the deepest meaning of the pact that bound her to the university. The sign she used to defend herself (the publication of essays and articles documenting her research) was a verbalization of her feeling for the beautiful. And it was precisely this verbalization that rendered her work non-specific, indistinguishable from the work of her colleagues in the scientific community.

However, this was not an intrinsic feature of the verbalization process.

"There are descriptions that are superior in every sense to what they describe," warned one informant.

Calvino (1988) comments shrewdly on this subject. He describes his work as a process that frequently originates, at the ideational stage, in a visual image. This image comes to him charged with a meaning that he is unable to express in the conceptual terms of written discourse. The more he develops the image, the more it loses its visual impact and the more it becomes conceptual. He is determined to impose order and meaning: the verbal transcript becomes more and more important, and from this moment on the written word is "master of the field". He searches out equivalences for the original image, expressions to convey his initial insight. He leads his story in a direction where the verbal expression flows more freely until all you have to do is keep up with the visual imagination.

There was no work process reported in my interviews that had anything in common with Calvino's. Certainly no informant showed him/herself to be careless or slovenly in his/her speech or writing, but this was not a fact of prime importance. The aesthetic dimension of this aspect of the work process accompanied, but was not fundamental to, the subject's working identity. This, in fact, seemed to originate elsewhere: in the written word, the sign that indicated working membership in the academic community, that is that the subject belonged to the university as an institution. A subject's identity as an academic preceded his identity as a researcher into the aesthetic. Although the department members' relationship with the material content of their work was the metaphorical arena for the exercise of their talents and imaginations, in their relations with the organization they worked for competence prevailed. Although there was no denying the lecturers' and researchers' skill in feeling, understanding and appreciating beauty, there were no signs of its metamorphosis. Apparently, the process whereby a sense of belonging to the academic community is formed and a work identity is shaped progressively strips away the special and specifically aesthetic abilities of the organizational actors to reveal some sort of generalized identity of 'the academic' — an identity abstracted from the aesthetic dimension as an organizational fact. There was no lack of appreciation for stylistic elegance, although this was mere ornament and of no help to being an academic.

I provide further illustration of this below. First, a question which arose out of the fact that department members had previously worked with artists — the direct protagonists and creators of certain of the materials they studied.

"Why aren't artists members of the department?"

"They're too close to their work."

"Historically and artistically this is the experience of the Italian art colleges but not of the universities. The existence of art and music colleges has exonerated the universities of their duty to give technical instruction, which perhaps is not their duty anyway."

"There's no difference in quality between the colleges and the university? In theory an artist could teach here, although he would probably not be teaching how to interpret his works or the work of one of his pupils. That is, he wouldn't be an artist and would keep the critical aspect sharply distinct from the practical one. Then he should have the qualifications and training required to be able to teach."

"So the foreign bodies that had entered in experimental form were expelled?"

"They were foreign bodies, at any rate. In part, their duties were different. Above all, however, it was the public examination system, that settled the matter."

Second, analysis of the aesthetic dimension of the art department's work process seemed to reveal a contradictory dynamic among the constitutive values of the professional deontology of the academic identity of the members of this organization.

"Do you create things of beauty?"

When asked this question, informants tended to answer by shifting from the concept of the beautiful to the concept of the good, confusing and conjoining them to give their work a connotation of 'constructiveness'.

"I think that this job is only relatively useful, like any other. No-one will ever know who I was. My work will be catalogued, will become a name like so many others. Almost everyone, I think, is replaceable. However, many of the people working in a particular sector count for something, in the sense that they do a job that fits together with someone else's. Mine is useful insofar as it relates to the work of other people. Perhaps it creates a certain structure, which can be dismantled, of course."

One's name goes into a file, therefore; the creations of one's talent become part of the architecture of talents. But this process is stunted by the premises that deny specificity if not uniqueness to one's special talents. These premises constitute almost the extreme of anonymity and a leap (rather than a passage) into the narcissism of the collective creation of a special construction. Thus, although the theme is given reasonable, credible features, these do not enthuse or bring joy. It is abnegation. It alternates with and counteracts the aesthetic factor in the departmental organization and in the working community.

The terms of conflict rather than of co-presence that I have used to describe the dynamic between the aesthetic and ethical principles in the formation of the deontology of the lecturers and researchers in the art department were also emphasized by members of the education department. In this organization, too, I treated the aesthetic dimension as an organizational fact, beginning with analysis of this value in the work process.

"I believe that in some way there is an aspect of this sort ... an aesthetic reason why, at bottom, I enjoy doing research. Working, that is, at something that has no social usefulness. Being an academic allows you to do one of the very few jobs where this is possible: work as an end in itself, free of any externally imposed goal."

In this case, there is no contact with aesthetic materials that are institutionally and generally defined as such by society. And the lecturers and researchers in the education department did not refer to the aesthetic dimension when talking about the writings and verbalizations that constituted the substance of their work. They assigned the feeling for beauty associated with their work as academics to one fundamental area of their job: research as an end in itself.

Mukarovsky (1973) sees the absence of any reference to utility as a distinguishing feature of the aesthetic value. He argues that the difference between a work of figurative art and other types of product lies in the fact that, while the latter are produced to serve some specific purpose external to the object itself, a work of art is created as an autonomous, self-sufficient "sign". The object, the artistic product, is not subordinate to externally imposed ends. It does not acquire meaning through communication. Unlike language, it is not a sign-instrument.

A similar treatment of the diverse natures of language and art is to be found in Langer (1953). Art is presentational not representational. It is the creation of symbolic forms of human sentiment by means of indivisible symbols that refer only to themselves. In this they differ from spoken language, which employs conventional discourse symbols carrying external reference to the environment. Gombrich (1960) argues in similar fashion, even as regards more realistic art. There is never any compromise in the relationship between figurative art and external reality; there is only illusion. The concept of the naturalness of the vision, of the immediacy of the interpretation of visual data is nullified by figurative schemata that give the image the value of codification.

However, the literature of art is a complex corpus of historical, symbolic, sociological, anthropological, psychological and semiological studies. Various traditions interweave in it. I shall not dwell any further on this topic, except to point out that I have mentioned only a few, particular approaches among many to the artistic phenomenon. I would also cite here the work of Cassirer (1966), who considers expressive forms capable of manifesting contents not directly motivated by the natural appearance of the forms themselves. Cassirer's theory has provided the common matrix for various schools of art and aesthetic history. This has been recognized by Calabrese (1985), who also calls attention to the original insights of Mukarovsky's sociological writings. Mukarovsky dissociates himself from the sociological analysis that conceives of art as the outcome of the economic, social and cultural relationships operating in the society to which the artist belongs; an analysis which ignores the psychological factors that tie the work of art to the mental condition of its creator. He argues instead that the fluid distinction between an aesthetic value and a value of another sort can be drawn on the basis of the non-instrumental nature of the aesthetic sign: it is not subservient; it does not transmit messages; it does not invite thematic interpretation. On the contrary, it requires a complex, global, lived reading insofar as its function is to influence its perceiver's attitudes towards his/her environment through a process of evocation.

The environments in which the academic carries out his research work and an artist his creative activity are entirely different ones. I have not wished to use the image of art as a metaphor for the work process of the two organizations examined here. I have merely sought to set out for the reader, by means of elaborate simile, a personal approach to the aesthetic value in the organization. However, the image of the artist has already been used as a metaphor by Degot (1987) in his interpretation of the figure of 'the manager'. Degot begins his analysis with examination of the emergence of new criteria of business management such as worker satisfaction, improved corporate image and the present steady decline in the profit motive. Thus, by focusing on the transposition of the artistic world into the managerial one, he identifies the settings where emphasis on the idea of the entrepreneur as an economic agent may enable the manager's talents and personality to emerge. Managerial activities are kept distinct from administrative functions consisting of the application of a corpus of rules and instructions. In parallel fashion to what happens in an artist's studio, emphasis is placed on the 'posterity' of managerial artefacts. These are then classified according to genre, style and importance. Organizational studies could develop in the biographical direction already explored by Chandler (1981). This would change the form of the studies presently pursued by those seeking to become managers in organizations, which are presently dominated by so-called management science.

The most important aspect of this metaphor is that it assigns a central role to this organizational actor. This role has been undervalued by the rationalist tradition, which has emphasized instead the manager's ability to adapt to the more or less turbulent dynamics of the environment that surrounds and influences the organization. Degot uses his metaphor of the

Renaissance artist to identify the position that should be allotted to the manager: at the centre of things.

The infusion of the artistic into the organizational environment takes the two maps of the artistic and the organizational worlds and superimposes, splices and blends them together. If we look at this metaphor in reverse, it becomes one of the imaginary symbolic territories of the skills of the organizational actor and of the organization (Strati 1985; 1986).

Talent, craftsmanship and professionalism go beyond technical training, scientific knowledge or skills acquired through study and experience. They are the distinguishing features of organizational actors and of the nature of their skills. They are acquired through a process whereby their features are imagined before they can be experienced and possessed, whereby they are attributed a place and a meaning within particular groups and communities; whereby, therefore, the imaginary space of their dominion is mapped out. I would argue that this is well illustrated by the metaphor of art. That is, it reflects the main theme of my discussion here: the constant interrelations between the aesthetic dimension and the symbolics of the distinctive characteristics of organizations. This, therefore, is an appropriate moment to return to my investigation of the aesthetic dimension.

A lecturer in the mathematics department declared with enthusiasm:

"The definitive proof of a result is something that is extremely beautiful. Something from the age of the Renaissance. A problem that has remained unsolved despite who knows how many attempts. And then, with this theorem, you have the proof! And how! Comparisons are always stupid, but this is something comparable to a great symphony."

For this lecturer, and this was also the case of the academics in the art department, the materials he worked with were intrinsically aesthetic. However, the aesthetic nature of mathematical materials was not institutionally or generally recognized: not all the materials and products of the department were beautiful and, even if they were, not everyone recognized them as such.

Unlike what was commonly the case in the art department, here (in the mathematics department) a profound sense of participation in the result accompanied the emotional intensity of the description of the scientific product. This feeling further emphasized the difference between art and mathematics as manifested by the subjects' stance towards the production of the aesthetic value. The mathematicians acquired beautiful products as the materials of their work, and they also created them — or at least they were entitled to do so. When they achieved success, this depended above all on the ease with which the mathematical result had been arrived at. The mathematical author first identifies his main underlying ideas and then develops his argument by keeping to a line of generally geometrical reasoning.

Purely numerical intuition seemed to be very rare; it was much more common for the mathematicians to work with a visual image, a symmetrical or three-dimensional pattern as the graphic representation of a function. According to the descriptions provided by the lecturers and researchers in this organization, the nature of this intuited image seemed to be similar to the explorative process and result of mathematical thought. The mathematician was described as a "metaphorical animal". The metaphor served as a conceptual tool and, here too, the work process was based on evocation.

"A beautiful result is often one where the author gives a glimpse of, or proves more, than he says. Or one where he gives an idea of the proof. It may not work, but it's beautiful all the same."
"The idea conveyed by that mathematician was a beautiful one, a very good one. At bottom, he achieved a lot more than other results had, although proof was lacking. He said: "This is an idea." If he had kept it to himself, maybe he would have carried it to his grave. So, you see, he contributed a great deal."

Once again the sentiment for the beautiful interwove with the feeling for the good. We noted this in the other two organizations. Here, however, these feelings were not in conflict but blended together. If a conflict of principles did emerge in the work process, it was between beauty and truth. The principle of truth was seen as a fundamental, certain criterion. It established whether or not subjects and products belonged to the department, to the disciplinary community, to the university as an institution. This principle was used to evaluate the expertise of individuals and of the organization. It may have been breached by an act of homage to the imagination, which was equally important. It was seen as the ability to set up a problem, to conceive an idea, to intuit a result or a proof, to establish connections among apparently disparate areas of knowledge. A result that excluded this act of homage, because it was rigorous and cluttered by the enumeration of cases, was positive. However, it was no more necessary or useful than the result which — although it may not have been equally true — had an evocative capacity, instilled a sense of the unity of knowledge and its possessors, and revealed (almost as if it were a game) the talent of the individual, the skills of the department and the distinctive features of the disciplinary community.

"The aesthetic criterion is the criterion that the mathematician lives by," stressed a member of the department.

This feature marked out the department's work process and the working identity of the academic. The beautiful did not conflict with the principle of the good; neither did it replace the principle of truth. The aesthetic dimension was a crucial guide for the mathematician and illustrated how the symbolic frontiers of the working identities of the departmental members were the same as those that delineated the disciplinary community itself.

Disciplines, as we know, constitute a system for the drawing of distinctions within the community. They are separate and imaginary territories, inhabited by members with mutually distinct forms of expertise. This imaginary territory is, in turn, subdivided into further, smaller groupings. And subjects may also find themselves in conflict over the development and consolidation of the power (Frost 1987) of their disciplinary field in the academic world.

"Not all mathematicians care about the aesthetic side to their work. Indeed, recently it's been rather neglected."
"It's disappearing because of the use of the computer."
"But a mathematician is reluctant to give up the aesthetic, even when he's forced to," a number of informants complained.

Certainly, many interviewees maintained that it was difficult for those who did not belong to the disciplinary community to grasp the aesthetic dimension of its work and the results of its research. A guide was needed, even for the other members of the academic community. As in the case of the mathematician, a master was needed.

Analysis of the aesthetic dimension to the work process in the mathematics department showed how this value had discriminated among its produced and/or acquired objects, the forms of aggregation within the occupational community and the special skills attributed to the worker. It also showed that these features passed beyond the bounds of the departmental organization.

A feeling for and appreciation of the beautiful is not a general phenomenon; it does not belong to everyone. It is not merely the capacity of human beings to enjoy a sensuous rapport with their surroundings: it is an organizational fact, a strong bond. It singled out the most talented scholars and focused the attention of the other department members on them. It was a process of knowing and sharing, a way of perceiving one's work identity. It created audiences and circumscribed organizational forms that did not match the department's own − i.e. those based on the pupil-master as distinct from the member-director relation.

In Italy, departmental organization was introduced by law in 1980. The departments that I have described here were established around 1983 on the initiative of the lecturers and researchers who had previously been members of the institutes. In all three organizations this was the formalization of already existing aggregations, associations and sympathies.

"When we were an institute," said a lecturer in the art department, "it was wonderful, really wonderful. It was all a love story here, although now it's not that at all. Marriages, non-marriages, flirtations, jealousies, the institute was a meeting point. It's a pity that it no longer exists."

There were only a few members in the original institute. The department's first director was also its last. A man of great talent, a *maestro*, he and another outstanding scholar had now left the department. They, and a few others of the more distant past, were talked of as individuals of great intellectual fascination. Although very dissimilar in character, they both had great charisma. Their existential appeal, poetic talent, irresistible courage and exceptional scientific output were acknowledged by all members of the department, even by those who had not known them personally and who, with the foundation of the department, had "broken the mould".

"They were two individuals with the auras of *maestros*."
"Their abilities were even recognized abroad."
"The director of the institute was able to unite everyone," declared everyone who had been in the institute.

The informants warmly expressed the sense of beauty they felt in the organization that they themselves had dismantled. This organizational structure was beautiful.

Ramirez (1987 a), in his research study of three social organizations operating in the arts and entertainments sector, argues that subjects in these organizations saw them as beautiful purely as organizational forms. If we accept that the actual organization is able to arouse a feeling of beauty, it is possible to understand why certain individuals fall in love with the idea of joining a club, can find the work of a museum beautiful, can devote hours and hours of their time to voluntary work because they feel that a certain organization 'does beautiful things'. For Ramirez (1987 b), this perspective should be introduced into organizational studies, rather than have scholars focus their attention on the outcomes of organizational action, on objects, images and spaces.

Organizational studies have been principally concerned with these latter topics. Costa (1986) studies the name of the organization as a verbal sign; he analyses the verbal, graphic and chromatic features of trademarks in order to illustrate their semantic, aesthetic and emotional impact in the rapid communication of organizational identity. Schneider and Powley (1986) follow the changes taking place in the organizational culture of a large American company through analysis of changes in the visual imagery of its advertising, press releases, newsletters and other documentary material. Bolognini (1986 a) demonstrates the particularly aggregative effect of the use of photographs of successful racing cars when exploited within the organization. Dandridge (1986) observes the games-playing dimension inherent in organizational ceremonies. Berg and Kreiner (1987) draw a number of conclusions concerning those organizational studies that deal with the external and internal appearances of the buildings that house organizations. There is increased scientific awareness that inhabited spaces are not naked containers for organizational action. They focus attention on the symbolic conditioning of the organizational actor, and on the physical appearance of the organization as a symbol with a strategic purpose, as a symbol of status, potency and good taste, as packaging, as a sign of time, ideas and existence. Berg and Kreiner point out, however, that these studies still limit themselves to illustration of various ways in which physical structures can convey meanings and of certain of their effects on the behaviour of actors and their performances.

These are only some of the studies that have examined the relationships between organizational imagery, the aesthetic value in organizations and implicit organizational features. However, none of them takes the aesthetic dimension as its central theme. The researcher rarely mentions the physical nature of the organization, in the pretence that he/she had not noticed it. But art clothes the technology used by the organization, decorates the work environment: the architectural appearance of the buildings where the organization is located may be beautiful. The aesthetic appearance of these materials (which, in many cases, are already intrinsically beautiful) may emerge as an organizational fact that places the organizational actors in relation to the space they work in.

I do not think that this result contrasts with the findings of other scholars, with the exception of a few analyses like the study that Rusted (1987) conducted on the conflict that arose over the restoration of a number of old buildings in a Canadian town. Those who inhabited these buildings had other concerns than their aesthetic value; those who did not live in them wanted their original appearance to be preserved.

The buildings that housed the three university departments were certainly beautiful. However, this space did not by its mere appearance arouse a feeling of beauty among those who worked in it. For example, the building erected a twenty years previously for the mathematics department, on a design by a leading Italian architect, generally aroused feelings of indifference or incomprehension. Many remembered the name of the architect, and everybody knew that the building had been specially commissioned. The incomprehension was expressed over its rationality, modernity and function-ality — criteria which, as we have seen, are not the aesthetic criteria of the mathematician. Nevertheless, this building was seen as desirable by at least some members of the department who worked elsewhere. Distinguished scholars had worked on the premises; some of them were still working on the top floor. Many department members stressed the good fortune of a lecturer who occupied the same room as his father had done before him.

"This is the room where a great scholar used to teach," stated a lecturer in the art department, who had not been in the previous institute, "and where one of the greatest Italian poets and film-directors studied."

This bond with a particular place did not reveal the presence of the aesthetic dimension as a principle operating with any force in the relationship between organizational actor and space. Rather, it seemed to me, analysis showed that the sacral value attributed to places where individuals of great ability had worked revealed the mythical dimension of space. Places assume conno-tations of the sacred and the profane, claims Bolognini (1986 b) in his study of the maintenance department of an Italian steelworks. Bolognini writes of the difficulties that the subjects found in defining a neutral space, one without affective connotations and which could therefore serve as a meeting point for workers and technicians; a space that was free of expectations and not invested with complex significances.

Space is not always mythical. In the education department spaces arranged the layout of the disciplines in a similar but separate way. It was possible to observe the equilibria achieved in the metaphorical territory of the disciplines in the department's physical territory. Analysis and interpretation of these achieved equilibria could be developed much more. But this would not provide any further illustration of the theme I have pursued here.

This was not the case, however, of the space that made the art and mathematics departments tangible. It became mythical when it represented the material form of the organizations' skills.

"This is why this legacy is such a burden for me, for us. We've had some exceptional people, really exceptional people here," said a lecturer in the art department.

Individual talent and the skills of the organization alternated with each other in the subjects' descriptions. People, spaces, organizations and qualities intermeshed. One thing called forth another. The master-school-pupil relation in the work process and the organization as a place for meeting and union were the organizational skills that the interviews brought to light. These were not the only organizational skills of the university departments to emerge in the course of my study; they were merely those that were observable through examination of a specific, limited and metaphorical territory: that of the aesthetic value. This value operated differently in the three departments: it did not focus on the same objects; it did not apply to the same themes. The aesthetic dimension and organizational dynamics did not display precisely definable features. In confirmation of this I shall adduce a final element by referring once again to the "legacy" that the lecturer in the art department described in her interview. Another lecturer from the same department stressed that this was not only an awareness of an inheritance from the past; or, better, that this was not what was significant from the perspective of a sentiment for and an appreciation of beauty.

"It is an attempt at the nostalgic recovery of something; although we don't know what that something was. A certain nostalgia for a certain kind of relationship. The word 'nostalgia' could be a key one."

The analytical process moves once again towards the evocation of delicate and profound sentiments of organizational life. They constitute a fragment of organization (Weick 1987) that is reachable through an approach which lays stress not only on correct understanding but on more subtle understanding as well.

References

Berg, P. O. and Kreiner, K. (1987): *Corporate Architecture: Turning Physical Settings into Symbolic Resources*, 3rd International SCOS Conference, Milano.

Bolognini, B. (1986a): Images as identifying objects and as organizational integrator in two firms, *Dragon*, 2/3: 61 – 75.

Bolognini, B. (1986b): Il mito come espressione dei valori organizzativi e come fattore strutturale, in P. Gagliardi (ed.), *Le imprese come culture*, 79 – 101, Torino: ISEDI.

Calabrese, O. (1985): *Il linguaggio dell'arte*, Milano: Bompiani.

Calvino, I. (1988): *Lezioni americane. Sei proposte per il prossimo millennio*, Milano: Garzanti.

Cassirer, E. (1966): (1929) *Filosofia delle forme simboliche*, Firenze: La Nuova Italia.

Chandler, A. (1981): (1977) *La mano visibile. La rivoluzione manageriale nell'economia americana*, Milano: Angeli.

Costa, J. (1986): Toward a Signaletic Symbology of Identity in Corporate Communication, *Dragon*, 1/5: 5 – 16.

Dandridge, T. (1986): Ceremony as an Integration of Work and Play, *Organization Studies*, 7/2: 159 – 170.

Degot, V. (1987): Portrait of the manager as an artist, *Dragon*, 2/4: 13 – 50.

Eco, U. (1975): *Trattato di semiotica generale*, Milano: Bompiani.

Garson, B. (1975): *All the livelong day: the meaning and demeaning of routine work.* Garden City, N.Y.: Doubleday.

P. Frost, (1987): Power, politics and influence in F. Jablin K. Roberts and L. Porter (eds.), *Handbook of organizational communication*, 503 – 548, London: Sage Publications.

Gombrich, E. (1960): *Art and Illusion: A Study in the Psychology of Pictorial Representation*, London: Phaidon.

Jones, M. (1980): A feeling for form, as illustrated by people at work, in N. Burlakoff and C. Lindahl (eds.), *Folklore on Two Continents: Essays in Honor of Linda Degh*, 260 – 269, Bloomington: Trickster Press.

Langer, S. (1953): *Feeling and Form. A Theory of Art*, New York: Scribner's Sons.

Mukarovsky, J. (1973): (1966) *Il significato dell'estetica*, Torino: Einaudi.

Ramirez, R. (1987a): An aesthetic theory of social organization, *Dragon* 2/4: 51 – 64.

Ramirez, R. (1987b): The Relationship Between the Aesthetic Theory of Social Organization and Some Theories of Organizational Symbolism, *Dragon* 2/4: 65 – 84.

Rusted, B. (1987): *Housing as an Artifact of Organizational Communication*, 3rd International SCOS Conference, Milano.

Schneider, S. and Powley, W. (1985): The Role of Images in Changing Corporate Culture: the Case of A. T. & T., *Dragon* 1/2: 5 – 44.

Strati, A. (1985): *The Symbolics of Skill*, Booklet no. 5/6, Trento: Dipartimento di Politica Sociale.

Strati, A. (1986): Lavoro e simbolismo organizzativo, *Studi Organizzativi* 2/3: 65 – 85.

Van Maanen, J. (1979): The Fact of Fiction in Organizational Ethnography, *Administrative Science Quarterly* 24: 539 – 550.

Van Maanen, J. and Barley, S. (1984): Occupational Communities: Culture and Control in Organizations, *Research in Organizational Behavior* 6: 287 – 365.

Weick, K. (1987): Theorizing about organizational communication, in F. Jablin, L. Putnam, K. Roberts and L. Porter (eds.), *Handbook of organizational communication*, 97–122, London: Sage Publications.

Witkin, R. (1987): The Aesthetic Imperative of a Rational-Technical Machinery, *Dragon* 2/4: 109–126.

Part V
Whole Organizations

Chapter 15
Computers in Organizations: The (White) Magic of the Black Box

Jacques F. Brissy

15.1 Introduction

15.1.1 The Mysteries of Cybernetically-Based, Computer-Assisted Management Control

The focus of this paper will be on a variety of phenomena related to myths, magic, illusions, superstitions, mysteries, mystifications, and utopias concerning the *Computer* in organizations. These phenomena will be best understood in their relationships to each other, rather than analyzed separately as group stereotypes, distortions, ungrounded beliefs or mere superstitions.

These ideas and beliefs *all* revolve around the *same* anchor point: the computer. Shared, as well as conflicting meanings arise from experience of the same "reality" which is interpreted differently by various people using, being used by, fearing, admiring, ignoring, or having fun with the electronic weapon.

Since its creation in the late forties, the computer has often been referred to as a "black box," a "glorified adding machine," an "electronic brain," and so on. It is true that to many people, the computer operates in a foggy atmosphere, easily leading to such fantastic beliefs, beliefs which vary with the kind of encounter and relations we entertain with it. Let us not forget, however, that there is no magic without magicians, and that the broom is not the witch.

As in the past, the recent literature about computers continues to be primarily concerned with applications of computer technology from a business point of view (Coombs 1981; Kapor 1985; National Research Council 1985; Nivat 1983; Willmott 1985), with artificial intelligence research (Rose 1984; Winston and Prendergast 1984), and with the social consequences of the computer (Guile 1985; Nickerson 1986; Warner 1984; Briefs et al. 1985). If not completely absent, research from a symbolic point of view is extremely scarce, and psychological rather than sociological (Brod 1984; Demarne 1974; Ramsgard 1977; Deal and Kennedy 1982).

Over many years, my own investigations (Brissy 1979; 1984; 1986a; 1986b) of the impact of computers in complex organizations have led me to analyze the communication process, and the sharing of power and influence between producers and consumers of Electronic Data Processing (EDP) services. In this paper, I intend to shift from the "frontstage" to the "backstage" of computer operations, using a symbolic perspective for analyzing "soft" data collected mainly from participant observation, case studies, and in-depth, clinical interviews of various organizations members in six large U.S. corporations.

15.1.2 A Note on Microcomputers

At this early stage, an important qualification must be made. I want to make it clear that this study focuses on the lived experience by the users of *mainframe macrocomputers*. This may sound astonishing, considering the sudden outburst of *microcomputers*, but their omnipresence obscures in the public mind the enduring reality and predominance of the "data processing/management information systems organization" (Bair 1985: 61). Even their most enthusiastic partisans admit that micro-processors have not replaced the giant computer, though they have been added to it for different and very often insignificant purposes[1].

Discussing the present explosion of microcomputers, Ramsgard (1977: 234–35) observes that

[1] Apart from straightforward applications such as word processing, the actual potentialities of microcomputers remain vague to many observers: "Software producers are not driven by a careful analysis of market needs. Instead, they are driven by the need simply to figure out what to do with the personal computer. Because nobody knows what to do with these computers ... Right now PCs make a great deal of power available, but there are not many places for us to use that power yet (Thompson 1985: 4–5)."
To Diebold (1985: 12), microcomputers are a transitory fad: "They are bought through every conceivable means for all kinds of applications. Only a minimum number of these purchases are justified according to the sort of highly developed methodology that exists for conventional data processing ... The stand-alone personal computer is a transitory phenomenon, but it happens to dominate at the moment." Similarly, Kapor (1985: 31) says, "... nobody really understands what to do with a personal computer. We have this wounderful piece of technology for which creative people invent uses ... But for our target market of managers and professionals I don't think the applications of personal computer technology will occupy more than 5 to 10 percent of their time."
To Bair (1985: 61), their future is limited: "I now see the wave of office automation and personal computers dropping off and another wave coming. This next wave has already started with expert systems, knowledge systems, and robotics. Artificial intelligence will begin to take hold."

Data processing hardware has always been faddish, but Fads are still with us, nevertheless ... The common denominator of these 'fad' systems is that they process only very limited segments of the total information stream.

Concerning microcomputers, Long (1984: 275) claims that,

Up to this time, the main impact of the new technology has been simply to facilitate office operations as they are now being carried out. For example, the text editor replaces the typewriter; the microcomputer replaces the filing cabinet. While significant, these innovations simply increase the efficiency of work as it is now done.

Omand (1985: 72) considers that "Personal computing automates the function of the individual, not that of the department, the division, or the corporation." This involves mainly, according to Bennett (1985: 46 — 49):

automated spreadsheets, word processing, business graphics, and communications ... Such projects are outside the normal range of competence or responsibility of most data processing departments, and they are clearly limited in scope.

Accordingly, our discussion will focus on mainframe computers; microcomputers will be considered only very briefly below.

15.1.3 We Agree That It is There, but We Disagree on What It Means

Recently, cybernetics seems to have provided a new, original, and extraordinarily fruitful theoretical approach to *students* of organizations like, e. g., Stafford Beer (1966; 1972). Though many parallels could be traced between the "neurology of the firm" and the old "organicism," the cybernetic approach has a very distinctive component based on an unprecedented conception of *Control*.

Among organizational *participants* too, a new outlook is arising. It is not a "culture" yet; some will call it ideological or utopian. I think that presently, it is primarily based on magical (sometimes hysterical) beliefs. It is anchored to the shared experience of a new mode of management control: a mode of control which is *scientifically*-based on cybernetics, and *technologically*-assisted thanks to the computer.

We should realize that historically, in the field of sociology, it is not too often that both observers *and* members of organizations will agree on the reality of an analogy. In the 19th century, ordinary people of France or England were unaware of the works of Comte, Spencer, or Durkheim. Had they read their works, most of them would not have agreed, or approved of the idea of society as an organism. In 1984, organizational participants have not read the works of Beer either. However, they already share quite an impressive number of ideas, beliefs and meanings concerning the nature of the new system of control. The main reason, I think — and this is the topic of this paper — rests in the actual or supposed experience and interpretation by the participants of computerized management control.

This zone of agreement does not exclude basic disagreements about the new "cybernetically-based, computer-assisted management control." For instance, scientific observers, and some managers, claim that "this is how it should be, though it is not real yet"; organization members claim that "it is very real, though it is not how it should be."

This observation provides us with a preliminary line of inquiry: the observer's view has a utopian component, and the participant's view has a magical one (this is grossly oversimplified). The link between the two is the computer. That is why it will be necessary to introduce later a third kind of actor: those who can use the blackbook, the wand, and the other accessories, i.e., the witches, warlocks or wizards of the computer.

In the following analysis, I will first turn to the version of the analysts, the prophets and seers; for that purpose, I have selected Beer, whose prophetic tone and rhetorical performance make him one of the greatest apologists for computerized management.

Next, we will consider the heterogenous crowd of spectators, believers or witch-hunters, to be found among various organization participants. And last but not least, we will try to penetrate the perspective of the magicians and decide if it is black or white magic, to them and the others like the managers.

15.2 The Analyst: From Analogy to Model to Utopia

To analyse the observers' view, I will use Beer's work as an illustration of the cybernetic approach, because his presentation can be regarded as an 'ideal-type' of the perspective and also because the qualities of the work make it a 'classic'.

In *Brain of the Firm*, the *analogy* between the firm and the nervous system is constantly stressed[2]. Like the brain, the manager is in intelligent control[3]:

The contention ... is that neurophysiological and managerial systems ... are best understood in these terms, and that their basic elements — the neuron and the manager — both work on the model provided ... (Beer 1972: 88).

---

2 "There is a vital structural reason for this, which is detected in physiological structures such as nervous systems and in social structures such as company organizations" (Beer 1972: 42). "This book continuously compares the unfolding story of corporate regulation in the body with its manifestations in the firm" (id.: 100).

3 "In nature, and if we consider that most sophisticated control system the brain, this element might be identified as a single nerve cell — or neuron. In industry or government — indeed in any strongly cohesive social group — the element is some sort of manager" (id.: 84).

In summary, "The firm is something organic, which intends to survive ..." (id.: 99) thanks to "the brain of the firm, just like man's brain ..." (id.: 65).

From a mere analogy, Beer infers a *model*[4]: "Models are more than analogies: they are meant to disclose the key structure of the system under study" (id.: 99). The model, now superseding the analogy, is a "scientific" one:

Now the study of control is a science in its own right, known as cybernetics ... The main discovery of cybernetics ... is that there are fundamental principles of control which apply to all large systems ... This book is entirely concerned with the contribution which cybernetics, the science of control, can make to management, the profession of control (id.: 32).

However, cybernetical control requires the "electronic brain": "The question which asks how to use the computer in the enterprise, is, in short, the wrong question. A better formulation is to ask how the enterprise should be run given that computers exist" (id.: 31).

Quickly, the cold analyst gives way to the enthusiastic prophet[5]. The new *utopia* runs like this:

An end is rapidly approaching to the medieval dichotomy between the animate and the inanimate machine ... It is something which can be used as an extra lobe to the brain. There can now be, indeed at some point there certainly will be, some kind of merger between man and machine — a symbiosis (id.: 33).

Indeed, "it is time to start recognizing the sense in which man has invented a machine 'more intelligent' than he is himself" (id.: 72). The computers will not remain

the moronic slaves of their inventors. In fact we are telling them to learn; and giving them a training algorithm; but they learn more efficiently than we do and must pass us in the ability to achieve heuristic control (id.: 72—73).

We shall say what is a better and what a worse result, but the computer has to determine a better strategy, a better control system, than we ourselves know. And of course it can do it (id.: 71).

In summary Beer concludes that:

there exists today a capacity to cope with information vastly in excess of the human capacity, with the result that the manager must delegate this role to the electronic computer, just as he delegated other managerial prerogatives in the past — thereby losing them, be it noted, to people who were more expert than he but junior ... He

---

[4] "When we have eschewed the mystical-sentimental approach to biology ('isn't nature clever') we observe that nature is simply using its algorithms to specify heuristics" (id.: 71).

[5] Of course, Beer admits, the possibility may not be a reality yet: the tools of cybernetician's trade "... are not yet the tools of the manager's trade — although they ought to be" (id.: 102).

has to know how to organize computers to effect the firm's control; he has also to organize the firm so that it can be computed with (id.: 106).

15.3 The Participants: From Mystery to Magic to Alchemy

When discussing the *Brain of the Firm*, I now wonder if Beer had in mind the manager or the computer as the "real" brain. In society at large, the undifferentiated, predominant view is indeed simple *Anthropomorphism*. As a society, we are intrigued by the notion of "a machine with a mind, of the potential possibilities of 'artificial intelligence'", as Brod (1984: 9) observes:

[Society] has placed a machine as the central hero and metaphor of our time. *Time* magazine selected the computer as Man of the Year ('having the greatest influence for good or evil') for 1982. We idolize the computer's qualities − − − (Brod 1984: 14).

Anthropomorphism is so tempting that almost thirty years ago, a top executive at IBM handed his staff a dictum that forbade, on pain of being fired, anthropomorphising the computer. In "The Myth of the Computer," Rothery writes:

the moment the word 'computer' is mentioned we step into a mythological world as powerful as surrounded Homer and his ancestors. There is a meaning and power and even a sense of 'being' attributed to the computer. Programmers unhesitatingly attribute 'mind' to the computer. They know well that all they are talking about is an electronic control program that is residing, for as long as the power is switched on, inside the 'hardware' of the computer. *They do not really think it is a mind, but, and here is the rub, they find that the most convenient way to think about it, and to discuss it, is as if it were a being with a mind*[6] (Rothery 1971: 3).

Rothery's quotation above illustrates perfectly well what I call the "symbolic approach."

In the following pages, I will increasingly rely on a metaphorical language (witches, wizards and warlocks, magic, illusions, superstitions, mysteries, etc. ...) because most often, it is the one used by the participants themselves to describe their relations with the computer technology and the computer people. But the "computer's magic is not entirely benign" (Brod 1984: 3). The differential position of organization participants will enable us to identify a more profound variety of magical beliefs.

What is a computer? Many organization members do not know exactly what it is, how it operates and what it does. To many of them, the computer is "the machine that runs by itself" (Demarne 1974: 50 and 106). The

---

[6] Emphasis is mine.

computer is the unknown. And the meaning of the unknown ceases to be neutral as soon as we realize that we will have to cope with it. And everybody must at some time, at least in contemporary organizations. The primary experience of organizational participants, mainly for the *rank-and-file* people, is what the computer *does*: it is a job eater. Demarne (1974: 51) talks of the "men eater monster". It is going to replace you; it starts with the most routine activities, gnawing more and more, day after day. The computer is a *threat* (Warner 1984: 281; see Zeman and Russel (1980) for an overview).

To the *experts and middle-management* too, the primary threat of the computer is experienced through what it does. They see in it "a better gifted intellectual rival" (Demarne 1974: 50). However, such professionals are not scared for their "life"; they fear for their "soul", their skills and knowledge, i. e., their professional identity. They must abandon their ivory tower or control deck because the computer can do most of what they used to do, and it can even do it better, faster, and cheaper, they are told.

It is of importance that for the first time these changes due to Automation affect directly middle and even upper management. The modification of the traditional configuration — hierarchical or functional — challenges the vested positions and even career projects (Demarne 1974: 33).

Unable to protect themselves against the *curses*, they believe they are doomed.

As we climb up the hierarchy, the distance between the computer operations and the people decreases; but, the *mystery* increases. The question is no longer what the computer does, but *how* it does it, and *why*. The upper hierarchy will retreat, Demarne says (1974: 92) as to them "Information technology is the business of technicians." These are nasty questions to raise: they only show your ignorance and disrespect. The prevailing feeling is powerlessness, not just because you are afraid of the dark, but because you know with certainty that there is an enemy down there. And you realize that, like City Hall, you cannot fight the computer (Brissy 1984; 1986 a; 1986 b; Ramsgard 1977).

Up to now, the nature of the threat mainly has to do with the hidden but very real power of the computer: there must be some *magic: black* magic. "Certainly," Brod says (1984: 3), "the computer helps many of us to be productive; but its magic is not entirely benign". One step further on, the threat shifts from the computer to the computer people, the "*datacrats*," as Rose (1969) named them, or "the Great Sorcerers of the Computer" according to Demarne (1974: 64). "The computer nerd has been transformed into the computer wizard" (Brod 1984: 9). The mystery, the secret lies in the *algorithm*. "A caste systems has developed, by Brahmin systems analysts or ... systems 'czars'" (Ramsgard 1977: 226 and 232). People come to realize that there is no magic without magicians (see Ramsgard 1977: Chapter 6 "Magic School"). We should not be afraid of the magical cauldron: only of what is cooking, thanks to the sorcerers who know how to read and interpret the black-books, and who can even invent their own recipes!

Fascinated, some managers and professionals will even inquire about how to become magicians themselves, or at least, about how to learn to read the black-books and to be able to identify the ingredients. Many of them will give up at some time, disheartened by the esoteric "jargon." After all, magic is a profession, a vocation, not a hobby. The most stubborn ones will keep trying to communicate with the "spirits." They cannot be the medium or the officiant, but at least, they are no longer mere spectators, they are participants, they think, because they can feel the tables turning.

As for the *computer professionals*, they do not regard themselves as magicians. True, they will admit that some *alchemy* is going on; they will deny that they are trying to change metals into gold, but they will mention some elixirs for Management Information Systems that they are very proud of. "Computer people, even when trying to suppress all myths among the personnel, 'nevertheless consciously develop a definite mystery' around computer operations" (Demarne 1974: 50). *Other people*, they will say, hold to so many *superstitions* about their work. If there is some magic, they will keep explaining, it is certainly not black magic, but white magic. They have crystal balls, that nobody else can read, this is true. But they are innocent people, obeying organizational rules; they are "staff" people, offering a *service* to managers and to anyone they can help in the firm.

The high priest, or scribe, or clerk, sits in front of his model, feeds it with input data, extracts output data, and thereby controls the real life situation that the model represents (Rothery 1971: 64).

What I observed (Brissy 1984; 1986 a; 1986 b), but they would not admit it, is that they often come up with *answers* to *questions* that were never asked, and they spend a lot of time building up *solutions* to *problems* that were never there. And those of us who are professionally highly dependent on E.D.P. services suspect that sometimes, there is more than mystery: there might be some *mystification*, albeit unconscious and non deliberate on the part of the "datacrats" who collectively, have much more power and influence than they think consciously and individually.

The more detached, unimpressed, apparently "reasonable" group — at least, that is what it seems at first glance — is the *top management*: no fear of the machine, no fear of the mechanic either! "The speed with which it can perform ... seems both magical and practical" (Brod 1984: 9). They tried it and they liked it. At least some of them did.

There are probably two distinct viewpoints to be found among the top managers. Some are committed believers, others are disrespectful heretics. For the former, the computer and its acolytes constitute the promise of salvation and the way to redemption. We are now talking about the *fairy godmother*. This is the latest version of the technocratic *ideology*. Decisions, they say, are based on facts-and-figures; value preferences should be strained through a fine sieve, and fed into the system. This way, decisions can be properly manufactured, purified from the dangerous scoria of human passions, emotions and sentiments. According to Demarne (1974: 23 and 50) it is "the Information Messiah" ... "The General Management often treats the computer as the 'cherished baby', a 'plaything', 'much better than a sweetheart.''

The others, the "heretics," will not accept the orthodox view. They do not believe in the "Systems Analyst as Doctor of Business" (see Ramsgard 1977: Chapter 4). To them, the frivolous world of computers is the world of *illusion*: one can make appear only what was already there, and there is no magic, neither black nor white. They too, like the middle-management and the professionals, will be highly suspicious of possible mystifications, 'algorithmically' or 'heuristically' concocted by 'systems architects' or 'analysts', ignorant of or blind to the real-life conditions of business operations. The single computer principle that they will agree with is G.I.G.O. ("Garbage in, garbage out").

The computer is not just the unknown; it is mystery. It may engender fears and hostility, but it calls for respect and veneration. Beyond the various interpretations of the computer just discussed, one finds a set of shared meanings. All revolve around a common attitude: a *religious* attitude in Durkheim's sense.

In contrast to many *profane* organizational elements, the universe of the computer is the domain of the *sacred*, the separated, the untouchable, the inviolable. More specifically, the computer shelters the two contending principles of light and darkness, of good and evil; the creed is highly Manicheist in nature.

This dualism of the creed leaves room for different interpretations stressing one principle in front of the other. Further, as with many religions, the central creeds and rituals are often accompanied with, or superseded by various superstitions, magics, schisms or heresies. In the crowd of worshippers, one can find different degrees and styles[7].

---

[7] Although the problem of microcomputers is outside the intended scope of this paper, a quick word should be said about them. The extraordinary vogue for video games, for 'home' or 'professional' computers, is not just a passive response to clever advertising. It is in the world of microcomputers that one can find the *profane* counterpart of the religious attitude discussed above. To many people, microcomputing is conceived in opposition to, instead of in continuity with, macrocomputing. "Baby computers" are innocent, friendly, easy to communicate with, helpful and fun. They are "personal computers", to be enjoyed in our *private* life. By contrast, *organizational* computers seem threatening, impersonal, unapproachable,

15.4 Is There a Pilot in This Aircraft?

At the beginning of this paper, we discussed Beer's view of cybernetically-based, computer-assisted management control. It was also suggested that participants' views about the computer have a number of things in common with the "analyst's view." Two questions should be raised now. First, what is the extent of computerized control in complex organizations today? Second, does real or assumed computerized control affect the legitimacy of management power?

There is no straight answer to the first question. There is "some" form of computerized control in all organizations, but the nature and extent of such control varies immensely at e. g. Standard Oil., Pacific Telephone, or Bank of America. The effectiveness or rationality of such control is another issue. If "scientific observers" have divergent answers (see e. g. Winston and Prendergast 1984 versus Zimmerman 1985), can we expect managers to be in a better position to appraise the reality and effectiveness of cybernetically based, computer-assisted control?

Probably not, but it does not matter. What matters to us is whether or not employees *believe* in it. We remember that "what people define as real becomes real in its consequences." And it seems that many define computer control as real, *mainly because they are told so*.

This brings us to our second question: computerized management control as the latest version of the technocratic ideology. One could call it "data-cratic," in Rose's terms (1969). In summary, the datacratic ideology permits the merging of administrative authority *and* professional authority[8]. Decision making is thought to be a science. The computer, nourished with artificial intelligence, is expected to process the pertinent information, and manufacture decisions that are strictly rational. The "facts-and-figures" experts (Wilensky 1967) have ultimately vanquished. We should be entering the era of polity without politics (Jamous and Grémion 1978).

Cybernetically-based, computer-assisted management control, as Beer says, is entirely based on science and technology. Personal preferences, opinions of all kinds, have been eradicated. The system is both incorruptible and infallible. For the first time, we can truly speak of "Scientific Management." Automatic Data Processing yields automatic legitimacy.

---

heartless or boring. Brod (1984: 11 – 12) says: "The computer industry has developed the term 'user friendly' to assure everyone that computers are easy to use, accomodating, nonthreatening, and comforting companions with which to tackle problems ... In reality, computers can be frustrating and confusing to use and profoundly impersonal ... A computer is "bland, faceless, and unresponsive."

[8] A more detailed analysis of the datacratic ideology has been presented elsewhere (Brissy 1984).

For organization members, it is difficult to challenge the authority of the datacrats. Some will admit that human initiative and responsibility in decision matters have been transferred into the computer system, and that there is no longer any need for a human pilot in the aircraft. Others will still stress that no machine can operate without a mechanic, that there is no magic without magicians, but they too will agree with Beer's overall view that a better cookbook, and a better equipped kitchen can only make for a better cook.

References

Bair, James H. (1985): Personal Computers and the Office of the Future, in National Research Council, *Managing Microcomputers in Large Organizations*, 60–66, Washington D.C.: National Academy Press.

Beer, Stafford (1966): *Decision and Control*, London: Wiley.

– (1972): *Brain of the Firm: The Managerial Cybernetics of Organization*, London: The Penguin Press.

– (1979): *Neurologie de l'Entreprise*, Paris: Presses Universitaires de France.

Bennett, John H. (1985): Managing Uncontrollable Growth, in National Research Council *Managing Microcomputers in Large Organizations*, 45–51, Washington D.C.: National Academy Press.

Briefs, Ulrich, Kjaer, John and Rigal, Jean-Louis (1985): *Computerization and work; A Reader on Social Aspects of Computerization*, N.Y.: Springer.

Brissy, Jacques F. (1979): *The Sharing of Power and Influence between Bureaucrats and Datacrats*, Proceedings of the Illinois Sociological Association, Symposium on Occupations and Professions, Spring, Ill.

– (1984): La "datacratie": risque ou réalité? Conséquences de l'informatisation de la prise de décision dans les grandes organisations, in N. Delruelle-Voswinkel et Peeters, E. (eds), *Informatique et Société*, Editions de l'Université de Bruxelles.

– (1986 a): Users are Losers: Images of the Quantitative and Qualitative Aspects of the Division of Labor between EDP Specialists and Management Users, *Dragon: the Journal of SCOS*, vol. I, no. 4: 3–17.

– (1986 b): Expertise as a Handicap: The Professional, Social, and Organizational Skills of EDP Specialists versus Management Users, *Dragon: the Journal of SCOS*, vol. I, no. 8: 48–61.

Brod, Craig (1984): *Technostress: The Human Cost of the Computer Revolution*, Menlo Park, Cal.: Addison-Wesley.

Coombs, M. (1981): *Computer Skills and the User Interface*, New York: Academic Press.

Deal, T. E. and A. A. Kennedy (1982): *Corporate Cultures: The Rites and Rituals of Corporate Life*, Reading, Mass.: Addison-Wesley.

Demarne, André (1974): *La Greffe de l'Ordinateur*, Paris: Entreprises Modernes d'Edition.

Diebold, John (1985): The Organizational Issues, in National Research Council, *Managing Microcomputers in Large Organizations*, 11–16, Washington D.C.: National Academy Press.

Guile, Bruce R. (1985): *Information Technologies and Social Transformation*, Washington D.C.: National Academy Press.

Jamous, H. and Grémion, P. (1978): *L'Ordinateur au Pouvoir (Essai sur les Projets de Rationalisation du Gouvernement et des Hommes)*, Paris: Editions du Seuil.

Kapor, Mitchell (1985): Trends in Personal Computer Software, in National Research Council, *Managing Microcomputers in Large Organizations*, 28–35, Washington D.C.: National Academy Press.

Long, Richard J. (1984): Microelectronics and Quality of Working Life in the Office: A Canadian Perspective, in Warner, M. (ed.), *Microprocessors Manpower and Society*, 273–293, New York: St. Martin's Press.

National Research Council, Board on Telecommunications and Computer Applications, (1985) Commission on Engineering and Technical Systems: 1985. *Managing Microcomputers in Large Organizations*. Washington D.C.: National Academy Press.

Nickerson, Raymond S. (1986): *Using Computers: Human Factors in Information Systems*, Cambridge, M.I.T. Press.

Nivat, Maurice (1983): *Savoir et Savoir-faire en Informatique*, Paris: La Documentation française.

Omand, Alastair I. (1985): A Perspective for the Chief Executive Officer, in National Research Council, *Managing Microcomputers in Large Organizations,* 71–80, Washington D.C.: National Academy Press.

Ramsgard, William C. (1977): *Making Systems Work: The Psychology of Business Systems*, New York: John Wiley & Sons.

Rose, Frank (1984): *Into the Heart of the Mind. An American Quest for Artificial Intelligence*, New York: Harper & Row.

Rose, Michael (1969): *Computers, Managers, and Society*, London: Penguin Books.

Rothery, Brian (1971): *The Myth of the Computer*, London: Business Books Limited.

Thompson, John M. (1985): Vision and Value. Getting the Most out of Microcomputers, in National Research Council, *Managing Microcomputers in Large Organizations*, 3–10, Washington D.C.: National Academy Press.

Warner, Malcolm (1984): *Microprocessors, Manpower and Society*. New York: St. Martin's Press.

Wilensky, Harold L. (1967): *Organizational Intelligence*, New York: Basic Books.

Willmott, Thomas H. (1985): Faster, Smaller, Cheaper. Trends in Microcomputer Technology, in National Research Council, *Managing Microcomputers in Large Organizations*, 19–27, Washington D.C.: National Academy Press.

Winston, Patrick H. and Prendergast, Karen A. (1984): *The AI Business: The Commercial Uses of Artificial Intelligence*, Cambridge (Mass.): The M.I.T. Press.

Zeman, Z., R. Russell, (1980): The chip dole: an overview of the debates on technological unemployment, *C.I.P.S. Review* Jan/Feb, 10–14.

Zimmerman, Martin B. (1985): The User Era, in National Research Council, *Managing Microcomputers in Large Organizations*, 124–129, Washington D.C.: National Academy Press.

Chapter 16
The Organizational Sensory System

Klara Pihlajamäki

Marshall McLuhan pointed out in the 1960's that automation and new technologies have significant manifestations in the world of symbolism. "The Medium is the Message" was a symbolic statement by McLuhan. It emphasizes the effects of media as the hidden environment of our communications. Media — as metaphors — create modes of thought and communication. By extending our senses outside technologically, we — left inside — have created an environment that remains "hidden".

To understand this environment or context is to know "what sort of message a message is" (Bateson 1972: 199, 210). This is probably as difficult for us as it is for fish to realize water around them.

When we do not know what sort of message a message is there will be incompatibilities in our communications and — in an extreme case — schizophrenia. When our senses — our media — are not balanced there will be pathologies and waste of human resources.

16.1 Introduction

Our perceptions are mediated through senses. To communicate, to make ourselves understandable, we must express ourselves in "sense terms." Media technologies can be seen as extensions of our senses (McLuhan 1966). The communication media we have today stimulate, in the first place, eye and ear or both, i. e., the distance senses. Proximity senses, such as touch, smell and taste are not technologically developed to the same extent.

Media — as separate instruments — tend to isolate one or another sense from the others. At the same time, technologies have reciprocal effects upon one another, like the senses have. They interpenetrate, associate and condition each other. This is so especially today when different technologies get more and more integrated.

We get different types of information through different senses. Each one of the human senses is like a veil. These veils filter out many perceptions. Similarly, there are discrepancies in the message received through different media. Compare, for example, the same story mediated through film, radio, book and orally. Each medium — and each sense — offers a different perspective. The technological extensions of our senses make their own "space", visual or acoustic in the first place. Each of our senses are related to certain kinds of mental functions. By studying media — the extensions of senses — we can get an idea of where the attention is focused in an organization.

And just as a sense can hardly be separated from the whole sensory system, so a medium cannot be separated from the context in which it is operating. Experiences perceived through one set of culturally patterned sensory screens are quite different from the experiences perceived through other screens.

The hierarchy we have created among our senses is also reflected in our organizations; the visible goes before the invisible, distance is preferred to proximity, the newest is preferred to the old, differences go before resemblances. The ear is used as a tool of the eye — contrary to the order in nature. The oldest and the most fundamental sense — touch — is pushed into the very background and given the lowest status.

My purpose is to illustrate how the symbolism of senses can be applied to organizations. I will first describe some ways of thinking about visual and acoustic spaces in organizations and then apply that to the empirical case of my own research.

16.2 Visual and Acoustic Space

16.2.1 Visual Space

The eye focuses, pinpoints, abstracts and prefers one meaning at a time. The eye is concerned with boundaries, precision and unambiguity. It emphasizes a linear, sequential order between ideas and events. The eye minded person explains by a logical, sequential reasoning, following definitions. He/she connects by logic and is concerned about appearances, uniformity and respectability (McLuhan 1966). He/she easily imagines that there is a direct correspondence between input and output. He/she calls "rationality" the world of correspondences, matchings and repetitions (McLuhan and Fiore 1968).

Visual space is arbitrary, "either-or"; it either contains or excludes definable components or properties. It is connected by a logic, it is centre-margin oriented, with fixed boundaries, in continuous, sequential order. In visual space the cognitive aspects of communication are emphasized, enhancing the capacity of abstract thinking. Labels and classifications are typical for visual space. A divorce from concrete images leads to abstract generalizations.

In an extremely visual space there is a problem of information overload. By this people usually mean that there is too much paper to read. The problem is also, however, the imbalance between senses. The visual mode engenders a space which is uniform, continuous and connected. But pushed to its limits it can create fragmentation of experiences, schizophrenia. Schizophrenic communication is disoriented, autistically preoccupied, emotionally indifferent.

Learning in visual space is characterized by accuracy, the right answer to a specific question, technical know-how, discipline, formality, individually based evaluation, an ability to argue for one's knowledge and articulation of complex thought patterns. Individually based evaluation creates a need for secrecy and security. Knowledge becomes an individual commodity.

16.2.2 Acoustic Space

The ear is all embracing and can deal with sound from any direction. It is concrete and iconic. The ear is closely affiliated with emotional life, originally in terms of survival. We cannot automatically shut out sound as we can close our eyes to control vision. The acoustically minded person uses simultaneous, analogical relations. He/she relates by analogy (Nevitt 1982). He/she "acts out" experiences here and now. He/she does not "visualize" distant goals.

The acoustic space is a world of simultaneous relationships. It has no fixed boundaries, it is indifferent to background and without horizons. Everything goes on all at once all the time. Acoustic space lacks the precision of visual orientation and it has nothing surprising in it because it deals easily with opposites and paradoxes. It has no point of favoured focus. In acoustic space there are numerous simultaneous vistas of any topic whatsoever. The subject is looked at swiftly from many angles. We hear equally well from right and left, front or back, above or below. It is "both-and" space.

When everything affects everything else all the time there is a possibility that "terrorism" becomes common. When intolerance, insecurity and lack of identity increases there is a tendency to "we-them" thinking. Our "tribes" give some sense of security and sense of belonging. In an acoustic space, gossip and hearsay, tradition and taboo shape opinions and behavior. Every "tribe" has its *modus operandi* and "occult" ceremonies.

In acoustic space learning is informal; by imitation, listening, watching, doing. Concentration on audition increases the speed of learning but one also forgets more easily. The way small children learn foreign languages is an example of this. Learning is by sharing one's ignorance in a dialogue.

16.2.3 The Relationship Between Eye and Ear

Eye and ear, acoustic and visual spaces, are opposite and complementary at the same time through their effects.

What the ear gains in meaning, it loses in grammar (syntax). What the eye gains in grammar, it loses in meaning (semantics).

The ear is sensitive, the eye is cool and detached.

The ear is collectivist, the eye is individualist.

In acoustic space time is circular, in visual space time is linear.

The ear has ecological characteristics, the eye has logical characteristics.

The ear creates the meaning, the eye organizes the work.

The eye brings a man into the world, the ear brings the world into the man.

Visual space alone is flat, acoustic space alone is an empty sphere.

The ear attracts, the eye responds to the ear. The ear is negatively charged, the eye is positively charged.

Eye and ear cannot be separated without damage, because they complete, reinforce and condition each other. Acoustic stress can create visual effects, as music can be visually evocative. Music is also used to subserve the visual presentation. This is so because of the imaginary power of the ear. By hearing the voice we can tell the future ("speak so that I may see you"), by seeing it printed we can review the past.

When there is an extreme stress on one sense, the "tyranny" of that sense over the other makes any balanced interplay extremely difficult. In a situation like this, an overemphasis of the "lost" sense might be necessary to regain the balance. Today, in our western culture, we have a visual dominance, the ear being pushed to a background which is taken for granted. In nature the eye is the instrument of the ear, in our culture it is the other way round.

We cannot match the senses to each other because they are complementary. We can relate them to each other to see the patterns of connection and interplay between them. The patterns of the interactions determine the outcome. Bateson (1979: 22) writes that the right way to think about the pattern which connects is to think of it as primarily a dance of interacting parts.

16.3 Tactile Space

Tactility, sense of touch, symbolizes the highest quality of communication — total awareness. The skin as communication organ is highly complex and versatile with an immense range of functional operations and a wide repertory of responses. A human being cannot survive without a sense of touch. Tactual sensitivity is probably the oldest sensory process and in natal life probably the first one to become functional. The tactual mode of perceiving is sudden, but not specialist. It is total, synaesthetic, involving all senses. Touch always involves presence at once and inseparably.

Interplay between senses constitutes a sense of touch, a sense of integration, a sense of purpose or direction. The operational term for touch is "feeling". Tactility is achieved by using all modes of communication simultaneously. By using several senses/media simultaneously we increase learning capacity and the accuracy of information.

Without touch the modes of communication are doomed to imbalance. Imbalance occurs when there is over- or understimulation of any sense. The imbalance is even greater if only one aspect of visual or acoustic space is emphasized. The sense of touch — as with the other senses — is recognized by its effects.

Symbolically, vision takes note of what is ahead and reviews the past, hearing guides and directs, touch recognizes presence and responds to what is outside. If we do not know where we are now, what the presence is, we cannot perceive the future either.

16.4 Organizational Senses and Space

16.4.1 Senses

Media cannot be studied *ceteris paribus* because their effects are dependent on media interplay and on the specific context. However, to exemplify the idea of media as senses I here describe a couple of them — *ceteris paribus*.

The telephone is a audio medium; communication using it is analogous, informal, immediate, two-way, non-simultaneous (responses alternate), adaptive and unsynchronic. Written text or print is a visual medium; communication using it is formal, structured, standardized, sequential, one-way, organized in a linear order. Both of these media are quite opposite in their appearance. In their effects, however, they can be similar; space and time is enlarged through them, non-verbal and social cues are minimized and verbal communication is magnified. If only these two media are used, the consequences will be — *ceteris paribus* — more conceptual and anonymous relationships, abstracting of reality, homogeneity in communications. These are also the characteristics of bureaucracy, which is usually visually oriented.

The effects of telephone can be visual as the effects of a photograph are acoustic. A photograph is involving, all at once, "gestalt"-oriented.

Another instructive contrast is provided by computers and video or television. Computers are "active," they are logical, with menu-hierarchies and command systems. The computer is fast and accurate in its information processing. It has "users." Television is "passive", it is analogous and usually mediates the art of feeling. It is more right-brain oriented and it has "viewers." But computers also have some acoustic characteristics; their information processing is simultaneous and facilitates rapid, horizontal linkages. These two media together probably create more acoustic space.

McLuhan says that while a given form is latent and incomplete in its expression, it manifests itself under its opposition. The relation between appearances and effects is therefore complicated, we cannot study it by matching inputs and outputs. Human communication is by transformation, not by transportation. Sensory impacts are not sensory responses.

16.4.2 Spaces

We can recognize the following characteristics of organizations which correspond to visual acoustic space, based on the work of Nevitt (1982).

Visual Space	*Acoustic Space*
— high degree of specialization and hierarchy	— generalizing, integration predominant
— product oriented selling	— consumer oriented marketing
— quantitative forecasting	— qualitative forecasting
— pressure toward specific goals	— strategic planning
— "do-it-yourself" attitudes	— corporate identity and consensus
— leadership through stated goals and motivation programs	— leadership through participation, team orientation
— changes are induced according to the stimulus-response model	— changes are induced by reorganization of relationships
— communication is regarded as information transportation (via "pipelines" of hierarchy)	— communication is seen as transformation of messages (grapevine)
— learning through visual media, visual forms, explaining	— learning through roles, imitation, cultural manipulation, sharing of exoeriences
— rationality	— creativity

16.5 The Empirical Case

In the rest of this paper I will exemplify these theoretical issues by means of a case study conducted in a large wholesale company in Sweden between November 1987 and April 1988. Two of the company's about 30 "subdivisions" were studied. I call them here "House" and "Cloth". House dealt with household equipment and Cloth dealt mainly with clothes.

These subdivisions were like companies within a company; they were responsible for their financial results, but shared certain common administrative routines and procedures with the mother company. The decision making process was democratic and delegated to quite low levels in the organization. Both House and Cloth were divided into smaller groups that were each responsible for certain products and market segments. Every group had a buyer as a groupleader, 1 − 2 sellers and 1 − 2 clerks. Both House and Cloth had about 50 employees in total.

These subdivisions were chosen because of their apparent differences: different products, different markets, different office environment, different geographical location. In both House and Cloth a new computer based information system was introduced two months before this study started. My interest was focused on how the new medium might modify the balance of the sensory system.

16.6 Methodological Issues

16.6.1 Methodological Problems

We cannot "see" the interplay and multidimensional reality of our senses and media. Our predominantly visual mode of thinking is probably a hindrance to that. As we have noted McLuhan says that we are like fish that know nothing about water since we have no antienvironment which would enable us to perceive the element we live in. The mutual interaction of complex technological systems tends to produce − for us − unpredictable and paradoxical results because we do not fully perceive the character of these systems. Media cannot be studied merely by counting the frequency of use of different instruments or by comparing one medium with another in isolation from other media and their organizational context. It is better to study whole systems and their communication patterns, for patterns are in relationships, not in single quantities.

By listening to the stories of people in an organization we can get an idea of the pattern that binds people together. Only people can know where their attention is and how they perceive through their senses. It is therefore important to understand the perceptions and the stories of the people, to "step into their shoes." By comparing different organizations we can then more easily learn to see the "antienvironments".

16.6.2 The Applied Method

The method I have applied in this study is called "naturalistic inquiry" by Lincoln and Guba (1985). This method has similarities to, and is based on the "Grounded Theory" approach of Glaser and Strauss (1967).

Data collection and analysis are interwoven into each other during the whole research process. The final results never appear until the end of the research period or when there is a saturation of data. The research questions shift during the research process depending on the saturation and the importance of the subject matter in the field. This method is time consuming and requires tolerance of insecurity, because you never know what kind of questions might appear or how long it will take to saturate the data. The results must be grounded in the reality studied, by continuous feedback, both in the field and afterwards.

My core questions focused around the media; their use, importance, attitudes toward them. Simultaneously I studied the organizational culture, communication climate and information systems. I encouraged people to talk about their own path in the company and about the history of the whole company. What they said and how they said it were equally important.

In House I interviewed 37 persons and in Cloth 44 persons. Every interview took approximately $1,5-2$ hours. I also used a questionnaire, studied documents, participated in social activities and daily life as much as possible, and interviewed customers and suppliers.

16.7 Some Empirical Manifestations

16.7.1 Introduction

In my study I classified the organizations into
1) visual space with mostly visual characteristics
2) acoustic space with mostly acoustic characteristics
3) audio-visual space where both senses or spaces operate almost to the same extent but are not integrated, i.e., are seen as separate from each other
4) integrated space where the spaces/senses are integrated and the "sense of touch" is predominant. This kind of space could be seen as an ideal case today.

The over-all space of the subdivisions and the whole mother company was audio-visual. House was more visually oriented than Cloth which had changed its space from a predominantly visual one to a more acoustic one within the last five years.

House and Cloth classified their role or function somewhat differently; House emphasized buying and distribution more while Cloth emphasized selling and service. Both subdivisions were quite product oriented and the marketing function had a secondary place in the organization. Also leadership in both was classified as production oriented (as opposed to people oriented).

17.7.2 Media and Their Interplay

a) The Media Space

Of all the media, the face-to-face mode of communication was considered to be the most important in both subdivisions. Personal contacts are important in business.

When entering the organization one striking feature was the extensive use of telephone. The attitudes toward telephone were positive but somewhat ambivalent. Telephone and paper were considered important and were used almost to the same extent. There were a lot of calls in and a lot of paper out. This level of use and the attitudes toward these media made their effects more visual. Extensive personal contacts were used to balance this visuality.

Generally speaking, in both subdivisions the frequency of use of different media was about the same but attitudes and functions diverged somewhat. The employees in House felt that the use of all media had increased quantitatively and "linearly," so there was more of everything. In Cloth the employees felt there were more qualitative changes in media use.

According to McLuhan, if there is a regression in the use of a medium, a media balancing process is occuring. In Cloth there was such a "regression" in paper and meetings — their use had decreased relative to other media according to the employees. McLuhan says also that when a fast spin is put around a slower one, the slower one breaks down. Telefax and electronic mail were by-passing the old postal service because of their speed. The employees in both House and Cloth ascribed almost entirely negative attributes to the old, traditional postal service. It was, however, still considered necessary and important, and we still have to see if it will eventually break down.

Numbers — or quantities — and pictures dominated the information space of both subdivisions. In Cloth the employees emphasized also the importance of touch when determining the quality of clothes. "A suit can not be sold by telephone", they said. Orginally, numbers had both acoustic and visual as well as tactile dimensions (McLuhan 1966). There is, however, a difference between number and quantity (Bateson 1979). In this case it was more a question of sold quantities, quantity of orders, quantity of money etc.: in music number has a different quality. In both subdivisions writing and wordprocessing were considered secondary.

b) "In the Beginning Was The Word" — not Written, but Spoken

Most employees both in House and Cloth said that important information in the organization is mediated orally. "Important" information means things like "situation", personnel issues, relationships, atmosphere, what is going on, etc. It is the ambulance siren — not the blinker — that warns first. Because the ear is directionless, any sound from any direction can be attended to instantly. The ear is constantly alert to any sound in its boundless sphere.

Carpenter and McLuhan (1966: 69) write that preliterate — an acoustic — man was conscious of the auditory power to make present the absent thing (in magical ceremonies). Literate man — a visual man — annulled this magic and introduced a rival magic of making present the absent sound (in writing). We can balance auditory "magic" by visual "magic" and vice versa. In organizations, the effects of a grapevine or gossip (acoustic mode) can be powerful — no matter what people really see or know. A grapevine can be balanced by organized meetings or vertical information. How the meetings are organized has importance for their effects. In House the internal meetings were organized visually: every category (sellers, buyers, clerks) had their own meetings with the leaders. In Cloth the meetings had a more acoustic structure; they included everyone and were more team oriented. In both subdivisions the vertical and the horizontal communications were not quite balanced. In Cloth I was told that the horizontal communication had become better after the vertical communication had been improved.

c) Turning Senses On or Off Changes the Content of Organizational Drama

Visual media have different functions in an acoustic culture than in a visual culture. An eye medium in an ear space is somewhat "disturbing" until it finds its proper function. An introduction of an ear medium "turns off" the visual space and "turns on" the acoustic space. That kind of turning process can change power relationships.

Typewriters and the role of typists could be given as an example of this. Typing was given different attributes in House (which had a more visual culture) than in Cloth (with a more acoustic culture). In House the attitudes towards the typewriter were divided between typists and others. The former saw it more positively, the latter more negatively. In Cloth the attributes were more evenly distributed among all employees and there were different opinions about its present and future functions. When wordprocessing started to get more prominent the typewriter became a little bit "odd" in this culture. However, the typewriter also has acoustic characters; it gives, for example, a "melody" or a background to every word.

Clerks and typists usually live in an acoustic space, being "all in every-thing"; arranging information, contacts and meetings, making coffee, keeping up the social atmosphere, etc. The typist's work is quite "invisible" and very often taken for granted as a background work. Computer dataprocessing seemed to have "turned on" the acoustic space of clerical workers, especially in Cloth. The clerks felt that their position was changing and their work had become more important and more visible.

McLuhan says, however, that the impulse to get "turned on" is a simple Pavlonian reflex felt by human beings in an environment of electric informa-tion. It is the (hidden) environment that creates certain responses, not specific signals. Although man cannot be separated from his environment, we often do this in our relation to technology.

d) Narcissus Syndrome

Narcissus mistook his own reflection for another person and fell in love with his own image. "Falling" in love is a passive, uncritical acceptance of and adjustment to something or somebody in the hope of being taken care of in all circumstances. The Narcissus state creates a closed system that blocks perceptions and reduces self perception, but it might temporarily relieve stress. Our attitude towards new media is often something like the Narcissus syndrome.

In this organization, for example, the computers were considered necessary "to be able to survive." There had not been any collective discussions either in House or in Cloth about the new medium. All media that existed in the organization were considered necessary whether they were in use or not. To "cut off" any medium would be like cutting out a sense. That would create "phantom pain" or "drug withrawal symptoms."

The employees were "well adjusted" to the new medium, saw it positively and hoped that it would make their work easier in the future. But Bateson (1972: 224) "warns" that there is usually an "adjusted state" before schizophrenia becomes manifest. It is necessary, therefore, not only to adjust to the growing amount of media but to perceive their patterns to avoid the eventual fragmentation of experiences in schizophrenia.

16.7.3 Cultural Context

a) Hidden Eye

House had a big office landscape "without boundaries." At first sight this open office landscape seemed like a physical counterpart of the acoustic space for it was almost impossible to recognize any borderlines, physical or social. Cloth had more physical borderlines; there were different rooms, different furniture, etc. The appearance and "content" did not match, however. Lack of physical walls and doors does not mean a lack of psychological and social walls. The attitude toward the open landscape was more positive in House than in Cloth. The social hierarchy was recognized by the employees more easily in House than in Cloth. House was more visual than Cloth in this regard.

b) Culture is Communication

The unit of communication in acoustic space is a person or an individual. In visual space it is specific "jobs" or "skills" or some other "standardized replaceable part."

In my categorization of the organizational culture I used Handy's (1978) distinction between role, task, power and person culture. Role culture is visually oriented, based on specialization, bureaucracy and product orientation. It is a top-down culture and based primarily on written communication which deals with production matters in the first place. Task culture is acoustic. It is based on groups and has a bias toward oral communication with a minimum of formal rules. It is project oriented.

In House, 73 percent of employees considered their culture to be a role culture, whereas in Cloth, 43 percent of employees thought that it was a role culture, with a substantial number (35%) considering it as a task culture.

c) The Organizational Memory

In visual space the cultural memory is to a great extent "outside" the individual. "Eye organization" records itself essentially on the world outside — on paper, in the databank, whereas "ear organization" has a sort of instant, "collective", total memory inside itself.

Visual space reviews the past; printed information is always past information. The eye can "backspace" — as in reading — but the ear cannot. In acoustic space you view the present and "hear" the future. In both House and Cloth information was mainly built on past experiences, according to the employees.

Learning and memory are related. Learning through one's own mistakes, classroom learning and reading were the common modes of learning both in House and in Cloth. In Cloth the employees considered personal guidance ("imitation") as a learning mode to a greater extent than the employees in House did.

d) The Ear Hears Processes, The Eye Sees Events

The ear generates processes, the eye categorizes, generates events and reference points. Horizontal relationships are typical for ear space. The ear "talks" about relationships, the eye "talks" about facts, events, objects.

When people told their stories and the history of the company they often described events. The introduction of the new medium — the new computer system — was also seen as an "event." It came like a "parcel" from outside. People adjusted to it because it was considered something necessary. However, too much emphasis on (isolated) events makes it difficult to understand the present state of affairs, which is usually a result of several processes.

As already mentioned there was certain imbalance between the vertical and horizontal relationships and communication. Both in House and in Cloth horizontal communication was considered to be the dominant mode, but it was not considered to be satisfactory, or even sufficient. Rather, it was what it was because of lack of vertical communication. There was a need to balance vertical and horizontal communication and simultaneously improve the quality of the horizontal.

e) The Line of Success

Success in visual space is achieved by following a fixed "line" (upwards) or a set of rules. An undertaking must lead to something, to a goal or a desired end. Value is not put on the undertaking or the activity in itself or in the fulfilment of the self as such. The career usually goes upward in the social hierarchy. "Upper part" is considered better in our evaluations. We want to have somebody to look up to, etc.

If we do not succeed in following the line in our career, we have failed. In acoustic space — where the activity in itself is valuable — there is no failure or loss in the same sense as in visual space. In visual space one works for glory, in acoustic space one works for fun. The focus in acoustic space is on processes themselves, on discovery or creativity. Creativity has no necessary relationship to "success" in visual space.

In this organization the successful person was usually defined in visual terms: as one respondent said, "the one with skills and who follows the line". Other characteristics were ability to argue, "to keep one's feet visible," etc.

Rewards and punishments depend upon the line we draw to delimit the individual subsystem within an organization. They give additional information about the line of success and the balance of the system. In this organization many employees said that the work itself was rewarding and that the rewards came from outside, from customers. About 50 percent of the employees did not know how their performance was evaluated and about 30 percent did not know what the rewards were in this organization.

External reward often corrects for an internal change which could be punishing. I was told that if a person was externally very successful (made good business, appreciated by customers), but had problems internally, then he could reinforce his position but would have difficulty in making an internal career. External and internal success were not equivalent.

16.7.4 Space Dynamics

a) Eye Dominance

The eye is a tool to maintain and organize acoustic relationships. This is also often the function of the administrative, bureaucratic system. House and Cloth were a part of the larger mother company and thus a part of a larger bureaucracy. As in most large, bureaucratic organizations the employees also here complained of slow decision making, poor up-down information processing and extensive paper exercises.

b) Specialization Speeds up the Visual Space

One of the most common characteristics of visual space is specialization and this was quite prominent also in these subdivisions. Both groups and individuals were specialized in their specific products. It was difficult to replace people across groups — and even within the group. Specialization is a way to speed up learning, by ignoring the complex relationships which are the domain of acoustic space. Speed operates to extend and amplify. The speed of information enables one to centralize and to extend one's operations.

c) Integration Slows Down the Speed of Visual Space

When awareness of complexity arises, it "slows down" the achievement of expertness. Ear favours general knowledge and deals with paradoxes. In Cloth the integration of specialist knowledge was a parallel phenomenon to the specialization process. The integration was explained to be necessary because of the demand of the market; the integrated concept of clothes required integration of specialist groups to achieve maximum results.

The over-all organizational change programme also mentioned the importance of generalist knowledge.

d) Change of Organizational Brain Fields

Ellul (1980) states that technology interplay can change the field of the brain. Because of the short time period of this study I could not go deeper into the interplay between media and the cultural change in the organizations. There was, however, some kind of "brain field change" occuring in the organization.

The whole mother organization was going through a change programme that seemed to move it to a more visual space; coordination and control. Simultaneously there were strivings to hold the acoustic space; decentralization and the financial independence of subdivisions were also stressed. Cloth had transformed its space from a visual to a more acoustic space within five years. As I mentioned above their media culture was also changing more qualitatively — compared to House, which had kept its visual culture stable.

Translation from eye to ear means a gain in meaning but a loss of information. It might be that Cloth had gained more "meaning" because they did not experience loss of goals and the organizational ambiguity as a problem to the same extent as the employees in House did. This is, however, a very cautious conclusion.

To maintain dynamic balance, continuous changes are necessary on different levels — like in the case of the acrobat who maintains his/her balance by continual correction of imbalance.

e) Tribalization

When identity or relevance is missing, "tribes" start to appear. A natural response to confusion is a kind of "crisis", which is more often a quest for meaning than for specific goals. Whenever a group has an unique language or *modus operandi*, "tribal" boundaries start to appear. These boundaries can be abstract, psychological, social or physical. Tribalization creates "we-them" thinking, latent or manifest hostility between groups. Such a tribalization process can start when visual space is pushed to its limits, reversing its effects.

Because of the organizational changes, employees felt that the situation was somewhat confusing. Many employees complained that the whole company was lacking a "soul." The younger employees especially asked for a clearer profile and wished that the company would be more visible in the society, something to identify oneself with.

The members of the organization felt that the organization needed a new profile or "culture". Many employees considered the organization to be on the borderline between the old and the new, although they could not so easily define that "new".

One way to find out the possibilities of tribalization is to check the coorientation between groups; how coherently they define the problems, what they think of each other and how communication is between them. In House — which was visually oriented — the attitudes towards different issues were divided fifty-fifty. The attitudes were more coherent in Cloth. The employees considered that communication between groups should be better and more frequent. When I asked, for example, which group was best at the computers, I got different answers. Even when I asked which person knew most about computers, I got different answers. I did not notice any hostility between the groups in these subdivisions.

Tribalization means implosion of information space because of the mutual hostilities and defence of one's territory.

16.7.5 Organizational Tactility

a) Some Tactual Characteristics

Tactility is integrating. One important tactual characteristic of an organization is trust between people. Goldhaber (1983: 96−97) points out that trust and integration in an organization are interdependent. Honesty and trust belong together. When one tells the truth, all modes of communication — visual, acoustic, kinaesthetic — convey the same message. The truth is not in the "objective" statements but in the feeling of wholeness. The more ear and eye are balanced in communication the more truth there is. Lies express themselves in contradictory communication modes. Bateson (1972: 237) says that we have many double binds that rely on "lies" to maintain an illusion about what makes sense. Lack of trust is uneconomical, for it takes much time and energy to clear up all the misunderstandings that it creates. How easily conflicts are solved depends on trust between people.

Another tactual characteristic that is related to trust is the ability to listen. We achieve awareness — touch — by listening with all our senses simultaneously. We hear even through our skin. Handy (1978: 373) suggests that we need to encourage and promote the role of good listeners in our organizations. Listening means more than getting accurate meaning of the speaker's statements. It is sensing the underlying feelings and dimensions under what has been said.

The third tactual characteristic is humor. Humor is integrating. By means of humor we can shift our perceptions and information mode. Humor can release tension and give new insights. It is the oscillation between messages and metamessages that is amusing. Paradoxes become resolvable by means of humor. Lack of humor means lack of self awareness. Lack of self awareness means lack of awareness of others. We need also to cultivate corporate humor — to increase tactility and integration.

Lack of trust and humor was not a problem for the majority of employees in both House and Cloth. It was a somewhat bigger problem in House than in Cloth. About 30 percent of employees in House saw lack of trust as a bigger problem, the corresponding number for Cloth was 19 percent. Lack of listening and dialogue between people was experienced a bigger problem in House than in Cloth. For 40 percent of the employees in House it was a bigger problem, the corresponding number for Cloth was 21 percent. In House there was more of a split between opinions concerning listening and dialogue and the same kind of split appeared also concerning the clarity of goals.

b) Lack of Trust

Imbalance between eye and ear, or the denial of one of them, results in the feeling of guilt. Guilt is a sense of not doing what one should do. The sense of guilt is related to a lack of selfconfidence, to fear of failure and to fear of risks. Imbalance creates "pain", stress and "psychological poverty" (Nevitt 1985 b: 62, 76, 96).

The employees in both House and Cloth felt that visible work with paper and data took time from the invisible of keeping and creating contacts and of creativity, although this invisible work was considered more important. Making contacts does not create such immediate results as the paper work does.

If ear and eye deny each other strongly they cannot recognize each other, not even the fact that they are separated. The situation can develop to "adaptive indifference" where no one is concerned about the need to get in touch, to adapt to each other. There can be a lot of talk but little communication or dialogue between management and operating staff or between employees and customers. The administration creates its own life with no or very few contacts with the operating staff. "Parkinsons Law" is an example of "ungrounded" management. The relationship between eye and ear becomes inverse; the more bureaucracy or organization, the less meaning. As I mentioned before, eye organizes (administers) the work, ear creates the meaning. If eye creates something without cooperation from ear, it cannot stay manifested because it is not grounded (meaningless). In an extreme case a bureaucracy's own weight winds it down into a state where further useful work becomes almost impossible.

The denial between senses/spaces also causes time lags in the system. Tactility means skill of judging the right place and time. Judging means feeling when it is right. Bottlenecks and resistance arise, for example, if technological change is separated from the social and organizational change.

16.8 Concluding Remarks

By extending our senses technologically outside, we − left "inside" − have created an environment of which we are as little aware as a fish is aware of water around it. We often fall in love with technology as Narcissus fell love with his own image − without knowing that it is our own creation.

Communication and awareness are related to each other. To know "what sort of message a message is" we must know in which kind of context we are communicating.

Our relation to media reflects our mode of communication in organizations. "Survival" is not dependent on a specific medium but on the relationship "man-medium-environment." Narcissus' attitude combined with advanced media technology makes the likehood of survival "that of a snowball in hell" (expression of Bateson 1972: 462).

I think, the major incompatibility in our communications is not the incompatibility of different hardware/software components, but the incompatibility of our communication modes. The denial of this incompatibility and the failure to solve it may be a large source of tragic waste of human resources. The purpose of this study has been to identify some clues − by means of metaphors − that may help us to solve some of these incompatabilities.

To regard the visual and the acoustic modes as opposites or separate can be detrimental. It prevents the understanding of their cooperation and unity. To solve our communication problems we need to "get in touch". This requires that we see ears and eyes as integrated and supporting each other. We need to feel home in both visual and acoustic spaces. To translate eye and ear into one another's modalities creates complexity and confusion. Forcing one mode into the other distorts the wisdom of the system and made us even blind to that wisdom. To make people to fit by means of technology — like ancient Procrustes — may lead the 'fitted' to become the least fit for survival.

Even good memory is based on integration between ear and eye. It is confusing first to try to recall the material read by the eye and then to recall it both visually and auditorially. A good memory is "photographic" — all at once.

The idea of media interaction and the interaction of visual and acoustic spaces could also be seen as a kind of "self-organizing" principle in organizations. The "monopoly" of a sense can hasten development based on the other senses. But there is also "self-organizing" that can be conservative of a certain communication mode. Schizophrenic communication is sacred in a schizophrenic context.

The ability to switch modes of communication guarantees the overall balance, the sense of touch. It is said that the optimal learning capacity and intelligence is attained with the balanced use of all senses. We lack more systematic knowledge of the dynamic interaction between visual and acoustic spaces in organizations. We do not know how to integrate them, we do not even recognize them.

The context (subdivision) is affected by the wider context (the whole mother company) within which it has its being. There may be inconsistencies or conflict between context and metacontext. If there are continual traumata of this kind, the result can be schizophrenic corporate communication.

Evolution must be double defined — like Janus' face — both in visual and acoustic terms. Immediate gain in one mode can mean that the sign is reversed in the longer run.

The symbolism of ear and eye, acoustic and visual spaces, is the symbolism of corporate awareness. We can consciously balance our senses. "We can, if we choose, think things before we put them out," says McLuhan (1966: 49). We can choose to turn on and off our senses or our communication modes when perceiving their effects. Being aware of the effects of our communication modes we are also responsible for our choices of these modes.

In this study the employees classified all existing media in the organization as necessary or important — even if they were not in use. McLuhan (1966: 11) says that it is not use only that determines if an applepie, an atombomb or smallpox virus are "bad" or "good." Media — as metaphors — create modes of thought and communication, whether they are in use or not.

We cannot isolate the issues of humanity (human thought pattern) from the issues of technology. The unit of survival is the medium and the message (the effects) — "the Medium *is* the Message."

References

Gregory Bateson (1972): *Steps to an Ecology of Mind*, USA: San Francisco. Chandler Publishing Company.

Gregory Bateson (1979): *Mind and Nature*, Great Britain: Wildwood House.

Edmund Carpenter and Marshall McLuhan (1966): Acoustic space in Edmund Carpenter and Marshall McLuhan (eds.) *Explorations in Communications*, Boston: Beacon Press.

Barney G. Glaser and Anselm L. Strauss (1967): *The Discovery of Grounded Theory*, London: Weidenfeld and Nicolson.

Gerald M. Goldhaber (1983): *Organizational Communication*, Dubuque, Iowa: Wm. C. Brown Company Publishers.

Edward T. Hall (1973): *The Silent Language*, Garden City, New York: Anchor Books.

Charles B. Handy (1978): *Understanding Organizations*, Middlesex, England; Penguin Books.

Harold A. Innis (1972): *Empire and Communications*, Toronto: University of Toronto Press.

Yvonna S. Lincoln and Egon G. Guba (1985): *Naturalistic Inquiry*, Beverly Hills, California: Sage Publications.

Marshall McLuhan (1966): *Understanding Media*, New York: McGraw-Hill Book Company.

Marshall McLuhan (1969): *Counterblast*, New York: Brace & World Inc.

Marshall McLuhan and Quentin Fiore (1968): *War and Peace in the Global Village*, New York: Bantam Books.

Barrington Nevitt (1982): *The Communication Ecology*, Toronto: Buttersworths.

Barrington Nevitt (1985 a): *ABC-Prophecy*, Quebec: Libraire Renouf Ldt.

Barrington Nevitt (1985 b): *Keeping Ahead of Economic Panic*, Montreal: Gamma Institute Press.

John Short, Ederyn Williams and Bruce Christie (1976): *The Social Psychology of Telecommunications*, London: John Wiley & Sons.

Chapter 17
The Dynamics of Organizational States of Being

Ellee Koss

The Dynamics of Organizational States of Being is a work in progress that represents a new thesis in the arena of organizational theory. It links the success and productivity of an organization to the degree to which the organization creates, articulates and manifests its vision in daily practices. One might say that this work explores the extent to which organizations are true to themselves and the potential impact which this might have on the efficacy of organizations.

The setting for this work is a conceptual map, composed of three distinct states of being: vision, fusion/diffusion and confusion. This paper reviews the characteristics, operating principles and implications for managing of each of the three states. A major role of the research will be to explore the dynamics of interactions of the different states, looking, for example, at a subsystem of confusion within an overall context of a state of vision, and to develop a systematic theory of ordering. It is my intention to demonstrate that within these dynamics we may begin to shed some light on what it really takes to create an organization that is successful, spirited and a source of nourishment for the individuals that compose it. This research will not provide quick answers; rather it will provide a trail map which, when properly used, will guide the individual towards discovering a path to success in organizations.

As human beings we yearn for certainty. We would like to know precisely what tomorrow is going to bring so that we may sufficiently prepare ourselves and profit from this knowledge. At a macro level, this desire for certainty has manifested itself in the quantitative paths taken by most academic disciplines. On a personal level, when our risk-taking propensity is diminished and our ability to deal with change and the unknown seriously threatened, we look for answers instead of engaging in the rigour of thinking for ourselves and developing our intuition. In organizations, this has given rise to many systems, structure designs and ways of managing that promise 'success'. This has created an environment in which the system and not people are responsible for the successes and failures within and of organizations. Keeping all of this in mind, in this work I intend to create a context in which one can more effectively examine the determinants and dynamics of success within an organization.

Why is it that some organizations are consistently successful in acheiving their mission while others seem to fail miserably? Studies that consider this question tend to look for specific formulae for success that can be generally applied, with a very narrow definition of success. Success may be defined in many ways: for clarity we will define success as the accomplishment of intended results or objectives. For some organizations these results may be limited to profits, in others success may include the well-being and growth of people, and in yet others it may be the attainment of specific political or social objectives.

Definitions of success are inextricably linked to what we might call an organization's 'state of being'. For example, an organization that is coping with chaos and which sees itself as fighting for survival may not be capable of considering the well-being of its people as part of its success. However, in distinguishing between different 'states of being', one can begin to search for qualities that define and enhance the likelihood of success; qualities that transcend the structure and nature of an organization and that can be moulded to the character of a particular organization. Once these qualities are defined, it is important to consider how organizations might move from one state of being to another.

To understand the characteristics of organizational states of being it is helpful to distinguish three distinct states: *'vision'*, *'fusion/diffusion'* and *'confusion'*. *Vision* represents an organization that is clear about its purpose and remains true to itself through the inclusion of individuals. This clarity manifests itself by means of a succinctly articulated statement of mission and purpose that is translated into daily work practices; synergy; a sense of harmony and alignment; and a high degree of satisfaction and fulfilment among people within the organization — work is not a task or a chore, rather it is an opportunity to fully express oneself. *Fusion/diffusion* represents an organization that is either moving towards or away from a state of vision. Characteristics of a state of fusion/diffusion include a sense of something missing both individually and organizationally, and average yet acceptable results. The state of *confusion* represents an organization in which chaos and breakdown reign. A sense of vision is absent, satisfaction is seemingly non-existent and entropy appears to characterise the system.

If we are to use these three states of being to diagnose the condition of different organizations, we need to consider more fully the features of these states. The remainder of this paper elaborates some of the features which might be found in organizations in states of vision, fusion/diffusion and confusion.

17.1 Vision

17.1.1 Qualities and Characteristics

If you were to encounter an organization in a state of vision, many characteristics would be evident. Signs, literal and figurative, of a clearly and succinctly articulated vision would be present. The vision would manifest itself in a statement of a seemingly noble mission and purpose that embodies the qualities to which the organization is committed. These qualities remain consistent as they are translated into daily work practices. Moreover, there will be alignment of people towards this vision. A sense of harmony and of people working in concert towards the specific purpose prevails and communication will be open and flowing. An organization in vision tends to be action oriented, with a system of management and a system of acknowledgement that encourages this. Risk taking is promoted and, to reinforce this notion, mistakes and problems become regarded as opportunities. Consequently creativity tends to be high. The organization, as defined by its people, has the ability to allow ambiguity to exist and to engage with ambiguity until clarification and articulation of vision give rise to appropriate responses. The organization and its constituents have integrity: that is, they are being true to themselves. Each person, in such an organization, comes to see himself or herself as responsible for the overall success of the organization. The generative context of a vision organization is one of respect for the potential of human beings and a sense of being a 'winner'.

17.1.2 Operating Principles

The context of vision created in an organization is not worth anything unless there are positive, concrete, measurable results associated with it. In an operating state of vision, these efforts are likely to be rewarded with high productivity and growth. A typical operating principle is one of synergy: teamwork producing more than the sum of the team's individual parts. Change becomes transformational: people view themselves and the organization as co-creators of their own evolution.

17.1.3 Implications

The priority in a state of vision is empowerment: people then enable each other to produce beyond normal limitations while maintaining an excitement and enthusiasm for their work. The purpose of managing, therefore, is to create an environment in which people can express and realise simultaneously their own vision and the vision of the organization. Since paradox seems to govern this state, authenticity is extremely important. Attempts to manipulate or to control people will prove counter-productive. Action must be generated from the vision of what the organization can be and from a genuine concern for its people. Resources are available and provided as needed in order to accomplish an operating state of vision.

Table 17.1 Characteristics of Vision

Sense of vision	Clear and evident
Mission/purpose	Clearly articulated, consistent with vision
Daily works practices	Consistent with mission/purpose and vision
Alignment	Alignment around vision
Mood	Fulfilment, harmony, spirited, a sense of being a winner
Integrity	True to oneself and the organization
Communication	Open: leading to results, action-oriented
Commitment	High
Assumption about people	Highly committed, self-motivated and fully capable
Productivity	Synergy: $1 + 1 > 2$
Responsibility	Responsible for entire organization; accountable for own results
Ambiguity	Ability to exist and engage with until vision produces an appropriate response
Change	Transformational: co-creators of own evolution
Creativity	High: innovation and invention

17.2 Fusion/Diffusion

17.2.1 Qualities and Characteristics

In an operating state of fusion/diffusion an organization will display somewhat different characteristics than one in a state of vision. There is likely to be a sense of mission or purpose, but this may be rather vague, leaving room for personal interpretation and the emergence of results not in keeping with the vision. Or this vision, as manifested in the mission and purpose, may be inaccurate, out of date, or not representative of the current direction of the organization.

Some alignment of concerns may be present, but it will not be very clear in just what direction people are aligned. There will be a prevailing sense of something missing, although very few people will be able to identify what this is. People may be content but will generally not be fulfilled. There will tend to be a sense of resignation and acceptance that "this is the way it is supposed to be." At the same time, while some ambiguity may be tolerated, it will be accompanied by a strong need to clarify and resolve it as quickly as possible.

Integrity will be equated with honesty while responsibility will be reflected in accountability for personal results. Creativity will be acceptable, within limits, and will manifest itself primarily in the form of innovation. In fusion/ diffusion one may notice an absence of intentionality, an inability on the part of the organization to consistently produce the desired results. As the words imply, 'fusion' and 'diffusion' represent states of coming together and breaking apart.

17.2.2 Operating Principles

An organization in fusion/diffusion will tend to be productive, but not necessarily in a form which the organization would ultimately like to be. Synergy is unlikely to occur, so that one can expect results where "1 + 1 = 2" and nothing more. With regard to change, such an organization will take a pro-active stance: "Given that change is going to occur, how can we best make use of it?"

17.2.3 Implications

In fusion/diffusion, an organization needs to make a priority of revealing its current condition and commitments. Any work to improve its state of being without first doing this is likely to prove detrimental. Subsequently the organization will need to reconsider its vision, to restate its mission and purpose, and to create a new and more desired vision. It is helpful to involve

Table 17.2 Characteristics of Fusion/Diffusion

Quality	Characteristics in Fusion/Diffusion
Sense of vision	Some
Mission/purpose	Vague or inconsistent with vision
Daily work practices	Not completely consistent with mission/purpose
Alignment	Some: not clear towards what
Mood	Something missing; some satisfaction
Integrity	Equated with honesty
Communication	Open and closed
Commitment	Average
Assumption about people	Somewhat committed; competent but not self-generating
Productivity	Acceptable 1 + 1 = 2
Responsibility	Responsible for own results; sometimes accountable
Ambiguity	React with need to resolve
Change	Proactive: given that change is going to occur, how can we best use it?
Creativity	Medium; mostly innovation

the entire organization in this process, and outside consultants can be useful in developing vision and in aligning people with it. It is the job of the manager, the director or the equivalent committee to provide the rigour necessary to manifest vision in daily practices, although again, external consultants may be helpful as they can often 'see more clearly'. In a state of fusion/diffusion, managers need to be introduced to the notion of empowerment and trained to empower others. This can be started by shifting their presuppositions concerning the capabilities and commitment of people so that they assume that people *are* fully capable and naturally committed.

17.3 Confusion

17.3.1 Qualities and Characteristics

The operating state of confusion is, as it sounds, one of seeming disorder and chaos. Daily practices are inconsistent with any articulated mission or purpose. There is a general malaise; a lack of satisfaction that manifests itself through frequent complaining and low productivity. While people speak to each other, their communication does not lead to desired results. Problems and crises seem to be the order of the day. Ambiguity reigns, with little movement towards resolution. People experience a sense of being paralyzed and victimized by ambiguity and change. Integrity may manifest itself in the form of periodic dishonesty with people simply not telling the truth. Irresponsibility, or lack of trust, with people not keeping their word also seems to characterise this state of being. Perhaps the most serious symptom of confusion is a pervasive sense of hopelessness or resignation, concerning 'the way it is', a sense of being on a treadmill with no escape possible, or of drifting at sea being battered by the elements. People may view themselves as unable to affect the circumstances of their organization.

17.3.2 Operating Principles

As opposed to vision, where synergy seems to be the rule, confusion is governed by a degree of entropy. 'One' plus 'one' may yield no more than 'one', or it might even turn into 'minus one'. Productivity tends to be low, and in extreme cases, negative. Change efforts, in this operating state, can be described as reactive and survival oriented.

17.3.3 Implications

There are two priorities in confusion: to reveal the current condition and people's commitments within it, and to create a vision for the organization.

The first is perhaps the most difficult task, depending on how embedded the condition is. External consultancy or an influx of new leadership is necessary in all arenas. It is possible that once an initial group is trained sufficiently, that they can then replicate a similar process within their own working groups. Once the current condition is revealed, then an ongoing process needs to be introduced to create a vision for the organization. Coupled with this, such an organization must work to align people with this vision and to communicate in a way that leads to desired results. Creativity must be encouraged and not stifled throughout this process. One word of caution is needed — expect breakdowns during this process and use them to further learn what is missing in the organization.

Table 17.3 Characteristics of Confusion

Quality	Characteristics in Confusion
Sense of vision	None
Mission/purpose	Outdated and/or vague
Daily work practices	Inconsistent with mission/purpose
Alignment	None; chaos
Mood	Resignation
Integrity	Little and/or dishonesty
Communication	Complaining, closed
Commitment	Low
Assumption about people	Not committed, not trusted
Productivity	Entropy: $1 + 1 < 2$
Responsibility	Irresponsibility
Ambiguity	Pervasive with little movement towards resolution; sense of victim and paralysis
Change	Reactive: 'seat of the pants'
Creativity	Low, stifled

17.4 General Implications for Organizations

These organizational states of being: *vision, fusion/diffusion* and *confusion* represent the beginnings of a new approach to determining the success of organizations. If properly considered they can be used as a map to discover what is needed in particular organizations. Ultimately the success of a programme considering these states will lie in a person's ability to translate and nurture these qualities in his or her own organization and to manage the dynamics of moving from one state to another. Appropriate movement is dependent on a series of assumptions and theories concerning the values of different states of being and the factors that might govern the flow from one state to another. This will be addressed in the remainder of the paper.

17.4.1 Critical Assumptions

Several basic assumptions need to be made before considering the dynamics of organizational states of being. The first concerns what is the preferred state. For the purposes of this discussion we will assume that *vision* is the state of being preferred, either consciously or unconsciously, by people. The second assumption is that the attainment of the state of vision is limited by the collective structures of beliefs and presuppositions of the individuals who comprise an organization about the possibility of such a state and what it would really take to create an organization 'in vision'. Therefore not all people or organizations can or will opt to be in a state of vision at a particular moment. A related assumption is that there is an ordinal ranking system among the different states of being, with vision the state of the highest order of being, and confusion the state of the lowest order. A final assumption is that subsystems exist within the organizations concerned and will have an impact on the nature of the larger or contextual system. Keeping these assumptions in mind, let us now look at possible theories concerning the flow from one state to another.

17.4.2 Dynamic Principles

In an effort to understand how an organization may move to a state of vision from one of fusion/diffusion or confusion, we need to determine whether there might be any regularities that govern this process. If there are, it would be extremely valuable to know what they are. The following are three possible principles which could be tested empirically to help to explain the dynamic behaviour of organizational states of being, or why organizations grow and develop in different manners.

17.4.3 Entropic Principle

Ideas of entropy suggest that organizations will naturally degenerate to a lower order state. This implies that without conscious and intentional intervention, organizations will naturally devolve to a state of confusion. To move an organization to a state of vision, within this framework, requires constant attention and direction.

17.4.4 Evolutionary Principle

In an evolutionary view, growth and development are the expected rule: organizations will naturally move to higher order states. This implies that organizations will naturally move to a state of vision. Breakdowns are seen as temporary phenomena — natural indicators of where one has gone off course and of what needs to be done. One can argue that this approach calls for a hands-off approach to management on the assumption that people are also evolutionary and are naturally committed to growth.

17.4.5 'No Rules' Principle

If there are no universal rules that govern the system, there is no way of predicting the direction in which an organization is going to move. In order to move to a state of vision, a conscious and intentional effort is required. It is useful again to consider breakdowns as temporary indicators of loss of direction as in the Evolutionary Approach. Within this framework, flexibility, constant attention and direction with a sense of vision are necessary.

Table 17.4 Operational Implications of Dynamic Principles

Entropy	$\xrightarrow{\text{implies}}$	constant attention and direction needed to achieve vision
Evolution	$\xrightarrow{\text{implies}}$	hands off; belief that people are naturally committed and that organizations will evolve positively
No rules	$\xrightarrow{\text{implies}}$	flexibility; constant attention; sense of vision

17.4.6 The Dynamics of Subsystems

In addition to the dynamics of the overall organization, it is important that we consider the impact that subsystems may have on the entire larger system. What is likely to happen, for example, if a subsystem of confusion exists within a context of vision, or *vice versa*? Again we want to discover whether

Table 17.5 Operational Implications of Dynamic Subsystems Principles

Entropy	$\xrightarrow{\text{implies}}$	constant vigilance and attention
Evolution	$\xrightarrow{\text{implies}}$	hands off
Critical mass	$\xrightarrow{\text{implies}}$	be on guard; intervene consistent with belief in other principles
No rules	$\xrightarrow{\text{implies}}$	flexibility; sense of vision; do whatever is appropriate

there are any rules that govern these types of interactions. For the purposes of this discussion, I have considered four possible theories to explain the behaviour of sub-systems *vis-a-vis* the organizational state of being.

17.4.7 Entropic Approach

Since the Entropic Approach assumes that organizations will naturally degenerate to a lower order state and move towards chaos, this implies that without conscious and intentional intervention, a subsystem of a lower order will encourage the entire system to devolve to that state of being. If a pocket of confusion appears in a state of vision, the entire system will degenerate to a state of confusion. Similarly, in a state of confusion, a subsystem of vision will have no impact. Either to maintain or to move to a state of vision within this framework requires constant vigilance and direction.

17.4.8 Evolutionary Approach

The Evolutionary Approach assumes that evolution with development to a higher order state is the rule, so that, ultimately, organizations will move to a state of vision. When faced with subsystems of a higher order, movement toward vision may be accelerated — these manifestations may simply be taken as offering evidence that the larger system is already moving! In this model, confusion would have no impact in a higher order state of being.

17.4.9 Critical Mass Approach

The idea behind the Critical Mass Approach is that when a subsystem reaches a certain stage of development, when it has acquired a 'critical mass', it will have power over the larger system and therefore govern it. In the purest statement of this idea, the magnitude rather than the order of the subsystem has a bearing on the dynamics of the organizational state of being. Within this framework, confusion in a state of vision would only have an effect if the subsystem were of a critical size or influence. Empirical studies would be needed to assess what determines the critical mass in organizations. In the context of the Critical Mass Approach one would need to be on one's guard concerning the size and growth of subsystems. Also, since the approach may also be combined with either of the two previous ones, movement to a lower or a higher state will be a function of whether the subsystem has attained a critical mass and of whether evolution or entropy is at work.

17.4.10 'No Rules' Approach

The final possibility is that no rules govern the dynamics of subsystems and their larger systems. Unpredictability reigns — in one instance vision may give way to a state of confusion and in another confusion may dominate. To maintain or move to vision requires the ability to be flexible, to maintain a sense of vision, and to do whatever is appropriate.

17.5 Conclusion

While the research behind this discussion is controversial and by no means complete, it represents a new effort in the domain of organizational theory to illuminate the dynamics of organizations — the profit-making multinational, the worker-owned cooperative and the political action organization alike. While this work has been criticized as legitimizing manipulation, control and the pressure to conform, it is my belief that this type of behaviour can only take place in states of confusion or of fusion/diffusion, where complacency is acceptable. In a state of vision, this sort of behaviour can only prove counterproductive and lead to a movement out of vision. In a state of vision, individuals will be moved to action by what they want for themselves. It is out of their efforts and sense of individual vision that the organization, as a whole, can move to a state of *vision*. Again not all organizations will choose this path and that is entirely appropriate.

To solidify this research, we need to study individual cases to ascertain what theories may be accurate and what are the obstacles in moving an organization to a state of vision. Presently this approach may be used to explain why certain organizations are more productive or more desirable; and why others simply cannot get started, are constantly 'fire-fighting' or are just not particularly pleasant places to be. As opposed to more quantitative approaches, this work is steeped in the qualities and actions of human beings, for after all, organizations are simply groups of humans coming together for a common purpose.

Part VI
Against Conclusions: Comments on Theory and Post-Modernism

Chapter 18
Seeing Through: Symbolic Life and Organization Research in a Postmodern Frame

Andrew Travers

18.1 The Frame of "Seeing Through: Symbolic Life and Organization Research in a Postmodern Frame"

Travers in his essay "Symbolic Life" (my abbreviation) attempts to synthesize several controversial speculations, with a view to suggesting a frame for social research in general. His method is unusual, since he evidently would demonstrate in his textual performance the very possibilities he describes. And, contentiously, he concludes that, if the reader does no more than actually read him, then these possibilities are necessarily cogent.

The larger social world evoked to contextualize new sites of research is summarized as cyber-capitalism, whose most functional human collectivities are organizations. Put crudely, Travers's cyber-capitalism is an integration of the Baudrillardian notion of simulation not only with a cybernetic interaction model derived from Niklas Luhmann's *Love as Passion* but also with the frame analysis of Erving Goffman. Travers elaborates as follows:

Marx says that in societies principally organized for the production and consumption of commodities — which now means all societies — people themselves are seriously commodified. The most intensified form of the commodity is the sign (Baudrillard 1981),[1] whose principal producer is television, watched in the developed and semi-developed societies by silent majorities of (sign-consuming) people for as many hours as are worked (Williams 1974; Althiede and Snow 1979). Before they are anything else, then, most individuals today are micro sign-systems within a sign producing-consuming universe whose techno-science "seems to be a vanguard machine dragging

---

[1] See Kroker (1985 a) for an enthusiastic exegesis of Baudrillard's semiurgic Marxism. Baudrillard himself says: "... research — especially Marxist research — must come to terms with the fact that nothing produced or exchanged today (objects, services, bodies, sex, culture, knowledge, etc.) can be decoded exclusively as a sign, nor solely measured as a commodity; that everything appears in the context of a general political economy in which the determining instance is neither the commodity nor culture (not even the updated commodity, revised and reintegrated in its signifying function, with its message, its connotations, but always as if there still existed an objective substrate to it, the potential objectivity of the *product* as such; nor

humanity after it, dehumanizing it in order to rehumanize it at a different level of normative capacity" (Lyotard 1984: 63). Accelerating technologies of weapon and commodity production escalate the production (qualitatively and quantitatively) of individuals in the dehumanized form of ever more dedicated micro sign-systems geared to a similarly escalating total sign-environment within which, therefore, the principal mode of "normal" human activity is the reproduction — continuously, assiduously, remorselessly — of the self as an endlessly re-constituted unit which is equivalent to its complex, impersonal exchange-value identity. And this sign-identity, Goffman (1975) shows, is in every possible human interaction a copy of a copy, while the whole cyberprocess (or simulation of what are still called societies) runs as efficiently as it does by fostering fundamental illusions (false consciousnesses), many of which (a "real" self behind appearances, the "freedom" of democratic citizens etc.) would support a view that paragraphs of this stamp are hyperbolical.

Within Travers's hyperbolic space interaction can become mutual paranoia, as Travers describes:

Even a dyadic "love-system" (Luhmann 1986) in this "post-human" (Luhmann's epithet) world cancels the characteristics which could have been its basis and motive, for those characteristics are the "difference" between the two lovers, who, perceptually locked into each other, pathologize their love into a sort of paranoia when "every attempt to 'see through' the other person ends up in empty space, in the unity of true and false, of sincere and insincere, a vacuum for which there are no criteria of judgement" (Luhmann 1986: 178). Such "seeing through" happens because "the unity of the [love] code postulates the unity of the social system of intimate relationships, and the unity of this system is the unity of difference [between personal and impersonal relationships], which forms the basis of its information processing. One cannot 'found' anything on 'difference'. There is thus, as has always been maintained, no basis for love" (Luhmann 1986: 177).

What is perhaps most interesting in Travers's essay is his recourse to the emerging postmodern fiction paradigm of "metafiction" (Christensen 1981; Hutcheon 1980; Malmgren 1985; Rose 1979; Waugh 1984) and "cybernetic fiction" (Porush 1985). The essay argues that the "metafictional moment" is analytically demanded by a major inadequacy of Goffman's *Frame Analysis*. Goffman, Travers says, though depicting a social life that for each interactant is a never-ending transition from frame to frame, only bridges the gaps between frames (when indeed he does do this, which is rarely) with "negative experience" (Chapter 11 of *Frame Analysis*, 1975). In effect Travers contends — going beyond Goffman — that the negative experience of "frameless-ness" not only is not unframed in an absolute sense (as Travers pointed out

culture in its 'critical' version, whose signs, values, ideas are seen as everywhere commercialized or recuperated by the dominant system, but again as if there subsisted through all this something whose transcendence could have been rational-ized and simply compromised — a kind of sublime use value of culture distorted in exchange value)" (Baudrillard 1981: 147—148).

in Travers 1987) but also may be positive. So something like "positive negative experience" can initiate potentially emancipatory frames or, at the limit, moments of genuinely symbolic life.

Goffman, Travers would have it, is forced to downplay this positivity (of negative experience) by insisting that it is definitionally a contradiction to talk of a frame that isn't already on file in a "frame of frames" (Goffman's "cosmology" or culture). And one of the reasons for Goffman's conservative bias here is to be found in the source materials of Goffman's frame analysis (these mostly mass media materials Goffman calls "frame fantasies," celebrating beliefs about the world by being tailored, as "caricatures" of evidence, to demands for unity, pointedness, completeness, and drama in typifications rather than facts, thus evincing the "conventional understandings" that cope with "the furthest reaches of experience"). Travers as it were out-Goffman's Goffman by drawing on "second order" materials (analyses of metafiction) that heavily stress the burgeoning of new and original conventional understandings. And the proof of Travers's sociological speculations is that these materials already exist, having emerged, as Hayden White tells us, because it is already possible to read them.

Underlying the above is "the most fundamental assumption" of metafiction (shared by Travers) "that composing a novel is basically no different from composing or constructing one's reality" (Waugh 1984: 24), or, as Philippe Sollers laments, "perhaps the apotheosis of the civilized individual will be to live in an entirely novelized way" (1975: 62). However, metafiction, like every other discourse these days, is plagued by the problems of reference:

What has to be acknowledged is that there are two poles of metafiction: one that finally accepts a substantial real world whose significance is not entirely composed of relationships with language; and one that suggests there can never be an escape from the prisonhouse of language and either delights or despairs in this (Waugh 1984: 53).

In my opinion Travers hovers between Waugh's "two poles" (the very organization of his essay creates a "hovering Travers"), but Travers will not practise deconstruction, because he says that, while the metafictional moment certainly is a "de-framing," it is always followed by a "reframing," whereas deconstruction is an interminable deferring of any conceivable reframing. So we might align Travers with those metafictionalists who "finally" accept a "substantial real world," but with the proviso that Travers's "real worlds" must have the same ontological status as Goffman's frames, whose reality is simultaneously the understanding and the action that fits that understanding, both of these together generating a meaningful involvement (wherein the perception and the organization of what is perceived are isomorphic).

Perhaps Travers is unaware of how much his and Goffman's "real" simulation world matches the similar "realist" simulation and autopoietic worlds, respectively, of Baudrillard and Luhmann, who, without appealing to any fundamental ground (even in language), both manage to speak eloquently of postmodern human experience. It seems to me, however, that it is an open question as to whether or not the very practice of writing out of this paradox (that you only really are what you say you are) is precisely (as Travers would argue) what sufficiently simulates a reality that involves the reader in her or his reading.

Possibly Travers constructs his essay as he does because he believes with Brown (1980), White (1986), and Clifford (1986) that "conventional narrative only catches those fish that are already dead" (Brown 1980). So Travers — in his unconventional-but-becoming-conventional metafiction — manifests (and reduces) a pervasive anxiety that any discourse more projects the discursive practices of its culture than does justice to pretextual "scientific" analysed-data-to-be-reported.[2] But I am bound to conclude that such re-narrativization (or reframing) as Travers's may project the author no less, if not more, than any other frame she or he would use. Against this, Travers would say 1) that reframing practices are more relevant to cyber-capitalism than any other practices (such as Garfinkel's and Goffman's, where the reframing is a continuous, seamless performance in a highly idiosyncratic style unable to peel itself off the duller scholarly narrative it appears to be substituting for), and 2) that, in any case, he wants to produce not just frames but the vital metafictional moments that interpellate frames with promissory enlightenment.

18.2 It Is Impossible

Obviously Travers's essay "Symbolic Life," is only ever going to be its successive recapitulations and annotations. ... Here I have some comments that ignore that and bear on Section 1 (for convenience I am granting that Travers's "virtual" essay is possible and that the preceding summary is not a distortion of this essay). My comments take the form of reservations entered in the hope that Travers's essay would accomodate them in fact, accomodating them, I can't help it, through the agency of these reservations.

First reservation:

If "cyber-capitalism" is a Lyotardian "vanguard machine" with its own logic (I am reminded that Lyotard (1986) suggests a human telos of complexity for complexity's sake[3] which just so happens at this historical juncture

---

[2] See Filmer (1975) for an instructive emulative attempt to speak — like Raymond Williams and E. P. Thompson — in his own socially constitutive voice. Also Mulkay (1985) for a little reflexivity and some fascinating sociology of hard science practices. And anything by Hayden White is germane.

[3] This, like Lyotard's (1984) performativity principle, suspiciously resembles the kind of master narrative towards which, Lyotard says, postmodern works have an "incredulity."

to be best produced by a system which just so happens to be capitalism), how can Travers (or Lyotard, for that matter) escape it? What is the status of Travers's essay and what is the status of his primary resources (Baudrillard, Luhmann, Goffman, and metafiction analysts)? How can these texts defy their incorporation into the very system they seem to be trying to stand "outside"? How can these texts save themselves from becoming yet more products (sign-systems) inevitably geared to a complexity machine using them for ends other than the emancipatory ends that their authors (false consciously?)[4] imply?

Goffman (1975), at least, comes clean about where he stands, when he says that "since my analysis of frames admittedly merges with the one that subjects employ, mine, in that degree, must function as another supportive fantasy." Baudrillard, on the other hand

("No more subject, focal point, centre, or periphery: but pure flexion or circular inflection. No more violence or surveillance: only 'information,' secret virulence, chain reaction, slow implosion and simulacra of spaces when the real-effect comes into play" (Baudrillard 1983: 53 – 54)),

feels that our going beyond the social through the uncontrolled production of commodities and signs is only to be challenged by seduction, "the form which remains to language when it has nothing more to say" (Baudrillard 1979, quoted in Morris 1984). Meanwhile Luhmann, so long as he confines himself to his "epistemological constructivism" or the autopoiesis of "second-order cybernetics," obviously sees himself — presumably in the process of being de- and then re-humanized "at a different level of normative capacity" — as a complicit theoretician whose theory if "sufficiently complex" will "recognize which of its assumptions it has to change or differentiate if it is able to recast ... [historical] facts in its own theoretical language" (Luhmann 1986: 7). Travers's own self-legitimation I quote at length:

Albrecht Wellmer (1985) provides, in my opinion, the best available provisional advice for meaningful narration in philosophy. He [Wellmer] situates Lyotard and Adorno (the latter "read against the grain as a postmodernist") in a Wittgensteinian language-as-life-form frame and argues for the " 'sublation' of the one reason in the interplay of plural rationalities" (366). Wittgenstein's language games (the driving metaphor of Lyotard's The Postmodern Condition, through now jettisoned by Lyotard) are readable as Goffman's frames, which I think are more comprehensive than games (by virtue of their inclusion of nonverbal signs and also because Goffman explores — far

---

[4] Lukes says: "The radical ... maintains that men's wants may themselves be a product of a system which works against their interests, and, in such cases, relates the latter to what they would want and prefer, were they able to make the choice" (1974: 34). But he too does not consider how the radical also may be a product of a system which needs her or him for motives that could be described in terms that make the radical radically conservative.

more than Wittgenstein explores games — both their internal reflexions and their definitional, ongoing constitution of human conduct). Frames, like games, as Wellmer says (of games), precede "every possible convention and every possible rational discourse" (352) so that reason (and reasonable or legible conduct too, in Goffman) can't and shouldn't catch up with itself, any more than society can be "transparent to itself" (352) in abstract formulations. In this view reason must accept that it can only write such "operating fictions" (Goffman 1975: 26) as frames and their analyses (by research). Thus there is a possible freedom for demystifying society in actual research much more than there is a possible freedom, whether this is by Rortyesque pragmatism or recycled Critical Theory, in pure philosophizing.[5]

This is as much as to say that action can create a truth, and that this truth can only create action. Presumably the "escape" then is effected by not even conceiving a sign-universe in the first place?

Second reservation:

If the essay is a demonstration of a felt oppression by signs of symbols, and if it lays the blame for this oppression at the door of cybercapitalism, may the reader not be excused for feeling that since the essay claims that it represents the best that symbols can do then the problem of the oppression is not to be solved by essays but by direct political action against capitalism outside of texts?

Or is Travers "saying" that saying is improbably exotic, and is he only saying that, in this way because it's the best way?

Third reservation:

I believe Travers fetishizes the word fiction. He sees all self-presentations and discourses, theoretical ones too, as fictions. Admittedly Goffman is conducive to this view: that which involves (i. e., what is real, what is therefore framed) is to a certain degree fictional since fictions have the greatest capacities of all phenomena to involve people as readers of the social. But can we say that the self, sociology, philosophy even, are merely fictions? Doesn't this pull the rationale out from under our serious intellectual enterprises? Not if the fictions we have in mind are Dostoyevsky's or Marx's, Travers would say. Well? Let him have *that* point. But let him accept as a consequence that if everything is fictional — this section also — the word

---

[5] Habermas tries to overcome the poverty of philosophy by absorbing some raw social science into a theory that has now become so cumbersome and fraught with self-contradiction (Alford 1987; Ferrara 1985; Livesay 1985) that it is more a beautifully measured self-destruct colossus than a fieldworker's pocket compass. By contrast, D'Amico's Marx "now stands somewhere between a possible social science and an interpretation of culture;" and, narrower and more delimited than Habermas, as well as less internally systematic, Marx's interpretive conception of society "makes it possible for society to become an object of explanation." Maturana (1988) in a prose that is harder to follow than Garfinkel's puts the autopoietic case (almost a paraphrase, in part, of Wellmer) in pure form.

fiction becomes redundant every time it is used about social phenomena, and repetitively saying that all is fiction is hardly more illuminating than saying (after deconstruction) that words are words. Nevertheless, I do think that there is one strong argument for Travers's fictionalizing of the world (or his autopoietic soliloquizing). He could claim that the descriptor "fiction" is politically motivated to debunk the reifications of "gospel truth," "realism," "scientifically proven facts," and so on. Travers could proceed to contend, then, that if we interpret social practices as being too imaginary to be real yet too real to be imaginary (Iser 1979), we accept a Goffmanian ontology and so can assert confidently with Sukenick (1984 b) that "the act of composing a novel is basically not different from that of composing one's own reality ..." So the Traversian "turn" has to accent composition: in the end we can and do make new frames (Goffman's "operating fictions," no less).

18.3 What Is Metafiction?

After the first two sections (frames) of Travers's "Symbolic Life" essay I'm still not sure what metafiction is. For instance, does metafiction start from the Beckettian premiss that, in an infinitely diffuse "social" whose unification is impossible, "any attempt to break out of the communicational dilemma [of expressing the meaninglessness of mass-catastrophized discourse] remains therefore nothing but the 'apotheosis of solitude'" (Bruck 1982)? Or is Beckett by being a vanishing point also a point of departure "in whose works there is a constant conflict between narrator, narrative voice, the main character, and the limits of the medium" (Pearce 1975)? And venturing forwards from Pearce can it be said that fictions in drawing attention to their fictionality liberate the reader in order that she or he may confront the issue of "how man [and woman] develops fictional systems" (McCaffery 1984)? And is the difference between metafiction (categorized by Waugh (1984) and McHale (1987) as only one form of postmodern fiction) and unselfconscious fiction the difference between "an imposed order and one that develops as it goes along — 'occurs as it occurs,' as Stevens would say, 'by digression,' as Laurence Sterne would put it, or, in terms of jazz, by improvisation" (Sukenick, 1984 a)?

Other questions occur. ... Does Travers agree with Hutcheon (1980) that the metafictional mimesis is of its process of simultaneous (metafictional) interpretations (that can be representations)? And does Travers further agree with Hutcheon that nineteenth-century realism (which still (Marcus and Cushman, 1982) dominates ethnographic accounting) is a discrete convention crowned by Modernism with compulsive allusion, parody, lyricism, and reductions to absurdity, and then succeeded by metafictions that are "a continuing of that ordering, fiction-making process that is part of our normal coming to terms with experience" (Hutcheon 1980: 89)? Does Travers's essay then assume, as does Hutcheon's book, that the novel (and, in Travers's case, theory too) "is experientially or 'vitally' significant *because* it insists on its own reality, confronting the reader, constructing and composing his [or her] experience, operating upon his [or her] consciousness" (op. cit. 140)? Or does Travers accept Charles Newman's (1985) judgement that the reflexivity (of metafiction) is a subordinate technique lamely producing unparodiable textual responses to inflated, hyper-pluralist, fragmented critical discourse? Or does Travers, unlike Newman but like Alan Wilde (1981: 154), approve of a normatively ironic mode since 'generative' irony "attempts to activate consciousness as a whole, making of its relationship with the world something dynamic, kinetic, and reciprocal"?

Would Travers then endorse David Porush (1985) when he declares:

I conceive of cybernetic fiction as at once a battleground for these ideas [that a machine will be human when it says it is, or — Travers's logical corollary — that a human will be a machine when it says it is] and as a final weapon in defence of the differences between human and artificial intelligence (70)?

Or would Travers provisionally say yes to Patricia Waugh's definition of a "creation/description paradox" (so defined to collapse McHale's (1987) premiss that while the problems of modernism are epistemological (consolidating by directly attacking an ultimate ground) the problems of postmodernism are ontological (how or whether to write any ground as plausible or possible)):

... the ontological status of fictional objects is determined by the fact that they exist by virtue of, whilst also forming, the fictional context which is finally the words on the page. Such language has to be highly conventional in order to perform simultaneously the function of creating a context and that of creating a text. Metafiction, in laying bare this function of literary conventions, draws attention to what I shall call the *creation/description* paradox which defines the status of *all* fiction (Waugh 1984: 88).

Finally would Travers resort to citing those anthropologists (such as James Clifford) who, metafictionally agonizing over their ethnographies, accept that since ethnography cannot be more than allegorical (a representation that interprets itself), ethnographers no longer can say "this means that" but must confess "this is a story about that" (Clifford 1986)? And would Travers then go so far as to look for validation in Michael Fischer's study of "natives'" ethnic autobiographical writing, which, says Fischer, for some time has been using meta-discourse, whose intention is to "activate in the readers a desire for *communitas*, while preserving rather than effacing differences?" And would Travers feel he was making a crucial point by quoting this from Fischer:

Ethnic autobiographical writing parallels, mirrors, and exemplifies contemporary theories of textuality, and of knowledge, and of culture ... They are postmodern in their deployment of a series of techniques: bifocality or reciprocity of perspectives, juxtaposing of multiple realities, intertextuality and inter-referentiality, and comparison through families of resemblance (Fischer 1986: 230)?

I have no answers on Travers's behalf but this: that the questions by being questions create a yes/no metafictional space until they are answered.

18.4 Seeing Through?

Though I am sympathetic to the previous section's plea for a metafictional definition, I feel that we are overdue for a clearer account of how Travers approaches Luhmann's (1986) description of the dyadic "love-system" by way of Goffman's (1975: 562) well-known idea that "everyday life, real enough in itself, often seems to be a laminated adumbration of a pattern or a model [a fiction] that is itself a typification of quite uncertain realm status ..." For Travers does seem to be assenting to Goffman's verdict that "life may not be an imitation of art, but ordinary conduct, in a sense ... belongs more to make-believe than reality." Thus Travers must read Goffman's "social life" as the incessant reproducing of individuals' experiences (of monitoring their own and others' performances of equivalent monitoring experiences) as nothing but a collusive mimicry, with emotions to suit, of subjective objectifications (usually denying their realm status). So Travers, in this version, would seem to be saying that Marx, Goffman, Baudrillard, and Luhmann all imply systems of constantly cycling simulations. And certainly Luhmann does say that lovers pathologize their love-system into a sort of paranoia when "every attempt to 'see through' the other person ends up in empty space, in the unity of true and false, of sincere and insincere, a vacuum for which there are no criteria of judgement" (Luhmann 1986: 178). (Much the same — Travers would say — could be said about my attempt here to "see through" Travers.) In Luhmann the ultimate interpersonal vacuum is a consequence of the love-system being founded on "artificial" difference (between the personal and the impersonal), for as a result of this difference the love-system can't have a unity unless even in the "post-human" world both lovers have a regressive "neo-humanist, Romantic concept of a worldly individual who constitutes his or her own world" (Luhmann 1986: 177) as well as a regressive "notion of self-reference, of love for love's sake ... [which] prescribes that, in the area of intimacy, systems themselves have to produce those conditions which are necessary if they are to come about and be reproduced" (Luhmann 1986: 177).

Now one might hypothesize that Travers would be of the opinion that Luhmann's post-humans ("see-through people") are as they are because capitalism has advanced to a multi-national phase (Jameson 1984; 1985) from the monopoly phase of F. R. Leavis' day when Leavis could write in all seriousness that a fiction by D. H. Lawrence faces the reader like the typical Lawrentian lover faces his or her male or female beloved, as "a 'door'; an opening into the 'unknown,' by which the horizon, the space of life, is immensely expanded, and unaccepted limits that had seemed final are transgressed" (Leavis 1967: 115).

Or perhaps like Goffman "Travers" is neither a vacuum nor a transgressive unknown but a textual epiphenomenon trapped in Goffman's "corpus of cautionary tales, games, riddles, experiments, newsy stories, and other scenarios which elegantly confirm a frame-relevant view of the world," when "the human nature that fits with this view of viewing does so in part because its possessors have learned to comport themselves so as to render this analysis true of them," such that "in countless ways and ceaselessly, social life takes up and freezes into itself the understanding we have of it" (Goffman 1975: 550). And in "Baudrillard's," "Goffman's," and "Travers's" case interaction may be a declining activity, increasingly replaced by the watching of TV, since this better performs interaction's "more traditional way of incorporating its [the world's] incorporation of us" (Goffman 1975: 550).[6] Yet for the metafictionalists and for Travers the Luhmannesque autopoiesis and the Baudrillardian simulation are not the only alternatives to Goffmanian "understandings," for an ever open option is always more metafiction. ...

18.5 Travers in One of His Own Voices

A disposable metafictional definition of metafictional interaction can be essayed at this point: it is nothing other than the de-framing of any possible frame. This isn't the same as surrealism, Burroughs's cut-ups, Beckett's auto-solipsism, or deconstruction. It is simply an interaction practice that Garfinkel (1967) and McHugh (1968) call "breaching." But, where the side-effect of breaching is discomfort for the interactants, metafiction has an opposite life-enhancing "main-effect," since it engages interactants at a higher level of meaning than "members' practices" or premeditated fictions. So, unlike breaching and unlike other programmatic procedures designed to destroy the grounds for their own possibility, metafiction is, contrariwise, very dependent on those very grounds, if it is allowed that grounds are always socially-constructed exemplary forms.

This is to say that the person in interaction who initiates a metafictional moment opens a window of pure possibility, which of course — that social

---

[6] For an exuberantly nihilistic account of this process see Kroker (1985 b).

life might go on intelligibly — almost immediately becomes opaque, though, once the interactants have gone through the window of opportunity so to speak (this process engendering the opacity), they are perfectly able to perform the same process again, ad infinitum. And the metafictional writer does just this: she or he constantly problematizes an unproblematic narrative sequence, the better to be read as writing that interacts with the reader. Naturally the metafiction writer, as opposed to an interactant, is marooned in a solitary communion with a putative reader, and that's her or his difference from an interactant in practice, though not in form (and it is arguable — by Richard Brown (1980) for one and, at far greater dialectical length, by Adorno for another — that all interactants anyway in "postmodern society" are similarly marooned).

One major *differance* from deconstruction should be noted. Deconstruction, especially in its most thoroughgoing, but not so inimitable, proponent, Jacques Derrida, chronically refuses to reframe, while metafiction must be the copula of every framing and reframing cycle.

Metafictionality as so far defined could be swallowed whole as a topic and as a practice by Goffman's *Frame Analysis*, were it not for its essentially distinguishing feature, that it is wilfully productive of a frame-that-will-not-be-a-frame. In *Frame Analysis*, however, non-frames (except when they are totally engrossing performance, an eventuality left unanalysed by Goffman) are definitionally "negative experience," inducive of instant remedial reframings. But the transient non-frames of metafiction constantly strive (in writing and in life) to become "positive negative experience," compelling an involvement which requires that they be sustained to the limit of their possibility. Elsewhere (Travers 1981; 1982) I have criticized Goffman's interaction theory for its analytical neglect of the very rituality it enrolls so that its interactions may function at all, a neglect expressed in Goffman by his homeostatic reading of rituality as a constant quantity merely to be restored to its *status quo ante* if fallen below because of rudeness or offence. In this essay I find another weakness of Goffman in his evaluation of negative experience as being inevitably negative (that is, painfully meaningless, or "embarrassing" because an individual cannot be but must be two, three, or more coherent persons at once (Goffman 1972)).

In interaction, of course, there is a possible coincidence of boosted ritual power (Travers 1982) and metafictional expertise (though some of postmodernism's levelling irony belies this to the degree that it does in fact level), the one feeding the other. But for analytic purposes, here, the former (ritual power) can be bracketed so as to emphasize the rather too structural analytico-phenomenon of metafictionality.

A metafictional non-frame has to have a very short lifespan, for its comprehension and social assimilation depend on its being quickly reframed. But there is a definite and necessary space (or time gap) prior to reframings (the domestication of "wild" practice), and it is this conceptualized space, alongside and merging with the space of ritual power, which prompts its analysis, for here, if anywhere, is a space for free human interpretation of conduct. Here, if anywhere, is a site for human re-creation otherwise not ordained, and this space itself, even, may accrue ritual power, just because of its potential transcendence in formal-structural *as well as* primarily emotional figurations.

Obviously metafictional practices are subjunctive interactional moods and therefore the only possible locations (Victor Turner 1980) wherein to actualize new symbols. But unlike Turner's subjunctive praxis, they will be fleeting and manifold rather than phases of a communal sociality, and they are not a guarantee of symbols — more often I would expect signs not symbols to be produced — nor of these symbols being 'good' symbols, or 'bad', or 'dysfunctional' (in whatever functionality is schematized). However, by definition, their life will be more enrapturing than the life of residual symbols that have had longer to disintegrate in the capitalist vanguard machine.

One such symbol would be the word postmodern itself. Increasing numbers of those people who feel suffocated by the past and threatened by futures they cannot control are trying to invest postmodernism with some symbolic meaning, in a word, with hope, as I do here, modestly or immodestly.

Beyond this, there is, I believe, an elided possibility in *Frame Analysis:* that all reframings — in Goffman reframing is virtually continuous — anyway imply some sort of analytico-phenomenal gap before the new frame is experienced for what it is. Goffman, though, closes this gap in advance, and thus glosses his own analytic potential for metafictional praxis. It also seems to me (from my understanding of this essay's Section 2) quite likely that insistent metafictionality is directly related to insistent cyber-framing, the more repressive the cyber-framing the more — equally and oppositely — the occasions for metafictionality, though, as Angela McRobbie (1986) observes, Baudrillard, Eco, and Jameson mostly refuse the possibility of this reciprocity.

18.6 The Writing on the Wall

I have now read the major part of Travers's essay "Symbolic Life," and I do have a few thoughts of my own, which might not be a second-guess or read-out of Travers's subtext but which are necessary if — as he would — Travers intends installing the metafictional moment at the heart of interaction. Very briefly, by way of a quote from Donald Barthelme, I sketch "the human metafiction" that flows from Travers's intention:

Goals incapable of attainment have driven many a man to despair, but despair is easier to get to than that — one need merely look out of the window, for example.

Following Barthelme I would assert, metafictionally, that there is a window in every frame, through which is a new frame, with a new window, and so on. And, as Goffman shows, any frame can be reframed (during a moment of metafictionality, of course) at any instant. Goal-oriented beings, surveying this prospect instead of peering towards the light or goal at the end of their infinitely long and dark tunnels, may be delivered into post-natal despair by this prospect of frames but the prospect does suggest that people are neither necessarily carceral, finite sign-systems nor irresistibly propelled along assembly- and dis-assembly lines. However, it should be acknowledged that frames (as ritual realms) can become hopelessly carceral (Travers 1987) if the requisite ritual power and the requisite skill to reframe are too enfeebled.

That then is the human metafiction to date. Narcissistically but unreasonably hopeful, it is bent over its own ironic reflections (in a silent pool or on a blank page or in a video screen) disturbed only by its own dabbling cyberfingers, and, in the marketplace (that phantasmal referent), surfacing, as Newman (1985) has it, in the form of unfinished masterpieces, unfinished by readers stupefied and barbarized by literary theory. This may or may not be the image of postmodern woman or man, whether reading books or reading situations or reading the writing on the wall of a fellow interactant's face. The writing on this particular textual wall, however, still perseveres in saying that there is no necessary wall, or that, if there is, there is a window of opportunity in it, metafictionally constituted and not inevitably blocked by bricks of non-human indifference cemented there, as often as not, by the blank stare of the person who has given up on exits.

18.7 Research

The title of Travers's essay promised that it would offer ideas about actual research, which ideas, no doubt, he would say now do not need saying in so many words, such as these that follow. It is clear that Travers is in favour of research even to the extent of organizing his thoughts as data in and for and of themselves. His research, I think, both here and in the field, must succeed or fail according to whether it locates and honours the analytico-phenomenon metafictionality (the research automatically fails if metafictionality cannot be located, but, more importantly, it fails in the reading if it is not itself metafictional and/or ritually powerful). Metafictionality, Travers says in effect, is where symbols may be nascent, liminal forms (and Travers's essay is an example of a pre-symbolic metafiction). Research reporting of actual fieldwork, therefore, would be an honorific writing that at its best (learning from James Agee, George Orwell, Tom Wolfe, and V. S. Naipaul) would elude sign-equivalence through the symbolic exchange Baudrillard negatively defines in his early work.

Such reporting would create itself ambivalently as a non-exchangeable, altruistic gift that obligates the reader-recipient (if she or he accepts — does not haggle over — the gift) not to pretend that she or he could have received more or less the same thing from an equivalent researcher.[7] (It should be remembered in this context that the gift, the latent symbol, the amniotic symbolization, is a form of life extinguished when sign and commodity fetishism, manifesting itself on the verbal level by neo-conservative descriptions of society as "the economy," turns terrorist by unemploying its (sociological) critics.) Travers himself has this to say about research:

Organization research could resuscitate itself by focusing on (boot-strapping) metafictional moments not only in interaction but also in the frames and ritual realms that metafiction promotes in social lore. These moments may be writable, but only research — patient anthropological sensitivity to (centrally meaningful) possible and actual trans-rational symbolization — will show how. This is not necessarily to anticipate an elimination of metafictionality in practice, by the practices of researching and then writing in (sociological) languages. For if metafictionality is a viable notion and if it is an equal and opposite reaction to cyberprocessing, such research itself, the fieldwork and the writing both, can only be the occasion for more metafiction (because such writing — if it is symbolic — breeds the symbols that bring people back to life rather than recycling the purely informational signs that dehumanize them). ... Goffman's *Frame Analysis* partakes of frames and frame conduct borrowed from the fictions of his era. Similarly the metafictionality of Travers borrows from students of current (and so already in a sense "historical") metafictional cultural-entertainment novels.[8] It may be that already as much as can be done in this direction has been done by the writing of this essay. And there may be no call to go beyond this point. Or the way of going beyond it might be purely textual (as it is in Goffman's case) by referring to other postmodern practices in what-the-avant-garde-would-be-if-it-could-be-an-avant-garde. But I don't think, at present, that the roads radiating out from

---

[7] This to escape Wilden's (1972) disenchantment: "Whereas the worker is alienated in the classical sense because he does not share in the fruits of his labor, the academician is alienated because his labor is, in general, quite fruitless. His products — books, papers, 'communications', courses, footnotes in other people's products — become the objects of a reified form of symbolic exchange. The alienation of the relationships between people which this process implies is a measure of the impotence of the scholar as opposed to the ruthless efficiency of the university machinery. The units of knowledge may have no use value, but they certainly have exchange value. Thus they are indeed useful — as CURRENCY. Unfortunately this currency was devalued by the inflation of knowledge long ago."

[8] To sample the full implications of the phrase "cultural-entertainment novels" see Huyssen (1980) and Burger (1984).

here are all piers or cul-de-sacs, since the very nature of metafiction is that it is always emergent from current practices, and in perpetual self-transformation: that is its logic and its performance in life.

It is relevant to note here that Baudrillard says there is no possible site of resistance to exchange equivalence except in non-equivalent symbolic exchange (other sites of resistance have been nominated: schizophrenia by Laing and by Deleuze and Guattari; desire, by Lyotard; ideal speech situations, by Habermas; suicide, by those who commit suicide; and, latterly, hyperconformism by Baudrillard himself). Baudrillard writes: "Only total revolution, theoretical and practical can restore the symbolic in the demise of the sign and of value. Even signs must burn" (1981: 163). Goffman − more radically, it would appear − thinks that signs already burn:

... once the exchange of words has brought individuals into a jointly sustained and ratified focus of attention, once, that is, a fire has been built, any visible thing (just as any spoken referent) can be burnt on it,

and

conversation can burn anything ... the conventionalized inter-personal rituals through which we put out these fires or add to the blaze are not themselves sentences in any simple sense, having speech-act characteristics quite different from, say, assertions about purported facts (Goffman 1981: 37−38).

Fire, of course, is only a metaphor, though as Porush (1985: 120) has it, "metaphors are apt metaphors for the human situation," and so fire, even in sociological texts, still bespeaks something more than monological, centripetal, techno-rational informationality. It is a symbol of life.

Robert D'Amico (1981) has no nose for smoke or fire and thinks Baudrillard too optimistically pins his emancipatory hopes on an impending subjective sign-exhaustion, which D'Amico says (rightly, Travers believes) indicates a considerable under-estimation of late capitalism's power to reinvest an exhausted and grovellingly grateful subjectivity in status or money equivalence, and this is also Luhmann's and Livesay's (1985) systemic view, based, in Livesay's critique of Habermas, on the theory that capitalism's human products are increasingly narcissistic, increasingly incapable, therefore − because their other-orientation alternates between corrosive contempt and insatiable greed for admiration − of relating in Habermasian consensual communicative rationality. Against this background (and this is why I limned it in) Goffman emerges on the side of life and that must underscore his appropriateness for new symbolic practices, as Travers indeed maintains. But only time will tell whether there is a future for symbolic life in organizations and their research, or whether this particular Traversian frame for it is a good enough one, which is as much to construct here, against the spirit of reframing, a semantically deteriorating Derridean "possible that is presently impossible."

So I close this section concerning actual organization research by stating a possibility which — in this closure — is presently not impossible: that is, the possibility of there being more to learn from interactions with other people (however role-bound, however much, even, they may be those of "researcher" meets "subject") than from theory and metafiction theory (a view I believe to be shared by Barry Turner (1988)).

Finally (as it were standing upright behind a lectern on a podium, and speaking with ironic, parodic gravity) I believe that a condition for such research in an organization is to know the degrees and modes of the prevailing fictionality (which always are the relevant determinative frames of experience) or else, literally (except on the rare occasions of full ritual interaction), there will be Goffman's negative experience of intolerable meaninglessness. I also believe that Travers shows how "positive negative experience" is real only in terms highly resistant, in principle, to modification, especially the modification that research can't help producing as "findings," and that therefore new forms of scientific reportage should be tried and tested for their yields of metafictional moments and of ritual power.

Lastly, I do not forget that Travers's essay is just one more text among very many thousands of other organization texts with no more meaning for the reader than that she or he might weave it into some other story or metafiction of her or his own making. Thus nemesis is foretold as impotent ambivalence or potent possibility in the fluorescent nowhere of libraries.

References

Alford, C. Fred (1987): Habermas, Post-Freudian Psychoanalysis, and the End of the Individual, *Theory, Culture & Society* vol. 4, no. 1: 3—29.

Althiede, David L. and Snow, Robert P. (1979): *Media Logic,* Beverly Hills: Sage Publications.

Baudrillard, Jean (1979): *De la Seduction,* Paris: Denoel-Gonthier.

Baudrillard, Jean (1981): *For a Critique of the Political Economy of the Sign,* St. Louis, Missouri: Telos Press.

Baudrillard, Jean (1983): *Simulations,* New York: Semiotext(e).

Brown, Richard Harvey (1980): The Position of Narrative in Contemporary Society, *New Literary History,* vol. 11, no. 3: 545—550.

Bruck, Jan (1982): Beckett, Benjamin and the Modern Crisis in Communication, *New German Critique,* 26: 159—171.

Burger, Peter (1984): *Theory of the Avant-Garde,* Minneapolis: University of Minnesota Press.

Christensen, Inger (1981): *The Meaning of Metafiction: A Critical Study of Selected Novels by Sterne, Nabokov, Barth, and Beckett,* Bergen: Universitetsforlaget.

Clifford, James (1986): On Ethnographic Allegory, in Clifford, James and Marcus, George E. (eds.), *Writing Culture: The Poetics and Politics of Ethnography*, California: University of California Press.
D'Amico, Robert (1981): *Marx and Philosophy of Culture*, Gainesville, Florida: University Presses of Florida.
Ferrara, Alessandro (1985): A Critique of Habermas' Diskursethik, *Telos*, no. 64: 45—74.
Feyerabend, Paul (1975): *Against Method*, London: NLB.
Filmer, Paul (1975): Sociology and Stratification. Issues of Reflexivity and Tradition, in Sandywell, Barry; Silverman, David; Roche, Maurice; Filmer, Paul; Phillipson, Michael, *Problems of Reflexivity and Dialectics in Sociological Inquiry: Language Theorizing Difference*, London and Boston: Routledge and Kegan Paul.
Fischer, Michael M. (1986): Ethnicity and the Post-Modern Arts of Memory, in Clifford, James and Marcus, George E. (eds.), *Writing Culture: The Poetics and Politics of Ethnography*, California: University of California Press.
Garfinkel, Harold (1967): *Studies in Ethnomethodology*, Englewood Cliffs, New Jersey: Prentice-Hall.
Goffman, Erving (1972): Embarrassment and Social Organization, in *Interaction Ritual: Essays on Face-to-Face Behaviour*, Harmondsworth: Penguin University Books.
Goffman, Erving (1975): *Frame Analysis: An Essay on the Organization of Experience*, Harmondsworth: Penguin.
Goffman, Erving (1981): *Forms of Talk*, Oxford: Basil Blackwell.
Hutcheon, Linda (1980): *Narcissistic Narrative: The Metafictional Paradox*, Ontario, Canada: Wilfrid Laurier University Press.
Huyssen, Andreas (1980): The Hidden Dialectic: The Avant Garde — Technology — Mass Culture, in Woodward, Kathleen (ed.), *The Myths of Information: Technology and Postindustrial Culture* London: Routledge & Kegan Paul.
Iser, Wolfgang (1979): The Current Situation of Literary Theory: Key Concepts and the Imaginary, *New Literary History*, vol. 11, no. 1: 9—20.
Jameson, Fredric (1984): Postmodernism, or the Cultural Logic of Late Capitalism, *New Left Review*, 146: 53—92.
Jameson, Fredric (1985): Postmodernism and Consumer Society, in Foster, Hal (ed.), *Postmodern Culture*, London: Pluto Press.
Kroker, Arthur (1985a): Baudrillard's Marx, *Theory, Culture & Society*, vol. 2, no. 3: 69—83.
Kroker, Arthur (1985b): Television and the Triumph of Culture: 3 Theses, *Canadian Journal of Political and Social Theory*, vol. 9, no. 3: 37—47.
Leavis, F. R. (1967): *D. H. Lawrence: Novelist*, London: Chatto & Windus.
Livesay, Jeff (1985): Habermas, Narcissism, and Status, *Telos* no. 64: 75—90.
Luhmann, Niklas (1986): *Love as Passion: The Codification of Intimacy*, Cambridge: Polity Press.
Lukes, Steven (1974): *Power: A Radical View*, London: Macmillan.
Lyotard, Jean-Francois (1984): *The Postmodern Condition: A Report on Knowledge*, Manchester: Manchester University Press.
Lyotard, Jean-Francois (1986): Defining the Postmodern, in Appignanesi, Lisa (ed.), *Postmodernism: ICA Documents 4*, London: ICA.

McCaffery, Larry (1984): Fiction-Making and the Metafictional Muse, in Pütz, Manfred and Freese, Peter (eds.), *Postmodernism in American Literature*, Darmstadt: Thesen Verlag.

McHale, Brian (1987): *Postmodernist Fiction*, New York and London: Methuen.

McHugh, Peter (1968): *Defining the Situation: The Organization of Meaning in Social Interaction*, Indianapolis: Bobbs-Merrill.

McRobbie, Angela (1986): Postmodernism and Popular Culture, *Journal of Communication Inquiry*, vol. 10, no. 2: 108 – 116.

Malmgren, Carl Darryl (1985): *Fictional Space in the Modernist and Postmodernist American Novel*, Lewisburg: Bucknell University Press.

Marcus, George and Cushman, Dick (1982): Ethnographies as Texts, *Annual Review of Anthropology*, vol. 11: 25 – 69.

Maturana, Humberto R. (1988): Reality: The Search for Objectivity or the Quest for a Compelling Argument, *Irish Journal of Psychology*, vol. 9, no. 1: 25 – 82.

Morris, Meaghan (1984): Room 101 Or a Few Worst Things in the World, in Frankovits, Andre (ed.), *Seduced and Abandoned: The Baudrillard Scene* Australia: Stone Moss Services (PO Box 81 Glebe NSW 2037).

Mulkay, Michael (1985): *The Word and the World: Explorations in the Form of Sociological Analysis*, London: Allen & Unwin.

Newman, Charles (1985): *The Postmodern Aura: The Act of Fiction in an Age of Inflation*, Evanston: Northwestern University Press.

Pearce, Richard (1975): Enter the Frame, in Federman, Raymond (ed.), *Surfiction: Fiction Now … And Tomorrow*, Chicago: Swallow Press.

Porush, David (1985): *The Soft Machine: Cybernetic Fiction*, London: Methuen.

Rose, Margaret A. (1979): *Parody//Metafiction: An Analysis of Parody as a Critical Mirror to the Writing and Reception of Fiction*, London: Croom Helm.

Sollers, Philippe (1975): The Novel and the Experience of Limits, in Federman, Raymond (ed.), *Surfiction: Fiction Now … And Tomorrow*, Chicago: Swallow Press.

Sukenick, Ronald (1984 a): Thirteen Digressions, in Pütz, Manfred and Freese, Peter (eds.), *Postmodernism in American Literature*, Darmstadt: Thesen Verlag.

Sukenick, Ronald (1984 b): The New Tradition, in Pütz, Manfred and Freese, Peter (eds.), *Postmodernism in American Literature*, Darmstadt: Thesen Verlag.

Travers, Andrew (1981): The Stalking Ground: Some Varieties of Human Conduct Seen in and Through a Frame of Ritual, PhD University of Bath; England.

Travers, Andrew (1982): Ritual Power in Interaction, *Symbolic Interaction*, vol. 5, no. 2: 277 – 286.

Travers, Andrew (1987): Social Beings as Hostages: Organizational and Societal Conduct Answering to a Siege Paradigm of Interaction, in Mangham, I. L. (ed.), *Organization Analysis and Development*, Chichester: John Wiley.

Turner, Barry A. (1988): The Rise of Organizational Symbolism, in Hassard, John and Pym, Denis (eds.), *The Theory and Philosophy of Organizations: Critical Issues and New Perspectives*, London: Routledge.

Turner, Victor (1980): Social Dramas and Stories About Them, *Critical Inquiry*, vol. 7, no. 1: 141 – 168.

Waugh, Patricia (1984): *Metafiction: The Theory and Practice of Self-Conscious Fiction*, London: Methuen.

Wellmer, Albrecht (1985): On the Dialectic of Modernism and Postmodernism, *Praxis International*, vol. 4, no. 4: 337–362.

White, Hayden (1986): Historical Pluralism, *Critical Inquiry*, vol. 12, no. 2: 480–493.

Wilde, Alan (1981): *Horizons of Assent: Modernism, Postmodernism, and the Ironic Imagination*, Baltimore: John Hopkins University Press.

Wilden, Anthony (1972): *System and Structure: Essays in Communication and Exchange*, London: Tavistock.

Williams, Raymond (1974): *Television: Technology and Cultural Form*, London: Fontana.

Chapter 19
Organizational Bricolage

Stephen A. Linstead and Robert Grafton-Small

19.1 Organizational Bricolage

Organizational bricolage is a way to proceed in organizational analysis. It is also the process by which organizational members (and members of societies at large) make sense of and order the world about them, inventing schemes and places and personal identity against a background of material and social constraint. It is less specific than a method, less comprehensive than a philosophy. It is applicable to the analysis of industrial societies, to professional disciplines, to actual events in everyday life. It is, in short, the way *we* proceed in organizational analysis.

In terms of the philosophies which inform it, we would consider it to be a post-structuralist development rooted in Levi-Strauss's structuralism and semiotics, but as a critical revision and even a reversal. It is characteristically post-modern in that it is reflexive: we are aware that we use the same means in making sense of our world as our "subjects" use in making sense of their world, and in both our making sense of their world and our making sense of their sense-making. There is no condescension or privilege of perspective implied in our position as analysts. "They" are just as complicated as "we" are. The methodological underpinning of our procedure is discussed by Linstead (1988; Linstead and Grafton-Small 1986) but we regard the nature of organizational understanding as being fundamentally fictional. We attempt to de-construct the fictions of others, but nevertheless both participate in those fictions and "bricolate" them into pieces of our own, and need to be constantly aware of the need to reflexively de-construct our own fictions in turn. Paradoxical and often contradictory though the theorizing may appear, it is rooted in action, understanding and the everyday: though theorists we may be, we have dirty hands, and metonymically dirty minds.

19.2 What Is Bricolage?

"Bricolage" — a form of do-it-yourself — was a term first used in an anthropological context by the French structuralist thinker, Claude Levi-Strauss (1976). Levi-Strauss concentrates much of his work on the savage mind, and the processes by which primitives make sense of a problematic world. He claims that 'savage' thought is quite as rigorous as 'scientific' thought, but is a different sort of logic. This different sort of logic Levi-Strauss calls *bricolage*. The term bricolage:

... refers to the means by which the non-literate, non-technical mind of so-called 'primitive' man responds to the world around him. The process involves a 'science of the concrete' (as opposed to our 'civilised' science of the 'abstract') which far from lacking logic, in fact carefully and precisely orders, classifies, and arranges into structures the *minutiae* of the physical world in all their profusion by means of a 'logic' which is not our own. The structures, 'improvised' or made up (these are rough translations of the process *bricoler*) as ad hoc responses to an environment, then serve to establish homologies and analogies between the ordering of nature and that of society, and so satisfactorily 'explain' the world and make it able to be lived in (Hawkes 1977: 51).

This capacity for homologically based analogical thought Levi-Strauss felt was lost to civilised man with the advent of writing, and indeed some of the most telling criticism of his work has been Derrida's exposure of his nostalgic preference for speech above writing, a phonocentric longing for a lost 'golden age'. But it has been argued that this form of thought has not been entirely forgotten by modern man. Hebdidge examines the significance of style in the creation of the meaning of subculture, particularly in 'spectacular' subculture involving punks, rastafarians, and Teddy boys in 'pop' culture. *Homology*, Hebdidge says, following Willis (1978) describes:

the symbolic fit between the values and lifestyles of a group, its subjective experience and the musical forms it uses to express or reinforce its focal concerns ... contrary to popular myth which presents subcultures as lawless forms, the internal structure of any particular subculture is characterized by an extreme orderliness: each part is organically related to other parts and it is through the fit between them that the subcultural member makes sense of the world (Hebdidge 1979: 113).

Hebdidge cites hippie culture, but possibly a better example would be that of the Hells Angels — outwardly aggressive and lawless to the stereotype, but inwardly observing rank, rules and procedures strictly. Subcultural members radically adapt, subvert and extend prominent social forms of discourse in *bricolage*:

Together object and meaning constitute a sign, and, within any one culture, such signs are assembled, repeatedly, into characteristic forms of discourse. However, when the bricoleur relocates the significant object in a different position within that discourse, using the same overall repertoire of signs, or when that object is placed within a different total ensemble, a new discourse is constituted, a new message conveyed (Clarke 1976, in Hebdidge 1979: 104).

The Teddy boys' transformation of the fashionable early 50's Edwardian revival style of dress; the mods' appropriation of the business suit, the Crombie overcoat and the motor-scooter; the punks' revaluation of the school uniform were all transformations of what were in one culture icons of respectability. Through "perturbation and deformation" meaning was reorganized.

Although the process of bricolage usually makes chosen objects "reflect, express and resonate ... aspects of group life," with considerable consistency, they need not, and in the punk culture at least, they did not become iconic.

If we were to write an epitaph for the punk subculture, we could do not better than to repeat Poly Styrene's famous dictum, 'Oh Bondage, Up Yours!' or somewhat less concisely: the forbidden is permitted, but by the same token, nothing, not even these forbidden signifiers (bondage, safety pins, chains, hair-dye etc.) is sacred and fixed. (Hebdidge 1979: 115).

As Hebdidge points out, there is no 'key' to punk style. Despite the existence of homology, attempts to be too literal in ascribing meanings to objects utilised by the culture tend to founder. Some signifiers (e. g. the swastika) were exploited simply because of their potential for deceit, for empty effect. Yet it could be argued that by this bricolage, with its resistance to ossification and incorporation, the homology that identified the subculture was established. Levi-Strauss in this way can be seen both to have over-estimated the impact of writing on the civilised mind, and to have contributed considerably to contemporary cultural studies by his identification of the processes of the 'savage' mind.

In its reliance on symbolic reason, however, our culture is not radically different from that elaborated by the 'savage mind'. We are just as logical, philosophical and meaningful as they are. And however unaware of it, we give to the qualitative logic of the concrete as decisive a place. Still we speak as if we had rid ourselves of constraining cultural conceptions, as if our culture were constructed out of the 'real' activities and experiences of individuals rationally bent upon their practical interests ... Everything in capitalism conspires to conceal the symbolic ordering of the system (Sahlins 1976: 220).

Perhaps unsurprisingly, the exploration of organizational bricolage we place at the heart of our explorations of the organizational "text."

19.3 Sperber and Symbolism

An important development in our understanding of the symbolic process, and hence bricolage, is Sperber's argument that Levi-Strauss and others, following a semiological model, have a tendency to limit symbolic meaning to a set of codings or decodings.

Sperber puts forward a challenge to such semiological approaches which see symbolism as merely a decoding process. Without denying that humans use codes, he challenges whether the pairings of symbols with commentaries, proper uses or other symbolic phenomena, or customary interpretations are always paired in such a way as to constitute a relationship of message-code (symbol)-interpretation. He suggests that semiological decodings, and he is particularly critical of Geertz and Levi-Strauss, habitually simplify the 'meaning' of symbols in such a way as to make them banal. To do this, he argues is to misrepresent the nature of the symbolic and to subordinate it to the conceptual code:

The one single condition that would permit the consideration of symbolism as a code is not fulfilled: no list gives, no rule generates, a set of pairs (symbol, interpretation) such that each occurrence of a symbol finds in it its prefigured treatment (Sperber 1975: 16).

What symbolism does, he argues, is organize an otherwise random environment around 'landmarks' which *evoke* associations and meanings and are open and shifting, with some similarity to the post-structuralist text. Anything can set this evocation in motion, and nothing appears to be able to stop it, although he does suggest that particular *evocational fields* can be preferred, which allows him some contact with Foucault (1980).

Symbolic thought is capable, precisely, of transforming noise into information: no code, by definition, would be able to do this ... in contrast to what happens in a semiological decoding, it is not a question of interpreting symbolic phenomena by means of a context, but − quite the contrary − of interpreting the context by means of symbolic phenomena (Sperber 1975: 67−68).

This leads him to put forward his criticism of Levi-Strauss' treatment of the process of bricolage:

To return to Levi-Strauss' image the symbolic mechanism is the bricoleur of the mind. It starts from the principle that waste-products of the conceptual industry deserve to be saved because something can always be made of them. But the symbolic mechanism does not try to decode the information it processes. It is precisely because this information has partly escaped the conceptual code, the most powerful of the codes available to humans, that it is, in the final analysis, submitted to it. It is therefore not a question of discovering the meaning of symbolic representations but, on the contrary, of inventing a relevance and a place in the memory for them despite the failure in this respect of the conceptual categories of meaning. A representation is symbolic precisely to the extent that it is not entirely explicable, that is to say, expressible by semantic means. Semiological views are therefore not merely inadequate; they hide, from the outset, the defining features of symbolism (Sperber 1975: 113).

Sperber's approach to symbolism is closer to the post-structuralist approach. This does not mean, however, that he rejects semiotic work, but rather that he understands it differently, and one of the concepts which both he and Levi-Strauss recognise as important in approaching the symbolic is that of *bricolage*. Sperber adds, however, the central concepts of *evocation* and *landmarks* to our understanding.

19.4 The New Semiotics

Sperber as we have noted is critical of semiotics, and indeed semiotics has moved through some critical stages of development. Blonsky (1985) identifies three stages, and most commentators external to the semiotic endeavour probably identify "semiotics" with one of its earlier stages of development. Blonsky's criticism of the third stage of *semiotics in anxiety* might well apply to the work of such organizational semioticians as Broms and Gahmberg (1987).

It was so preoccupied with the manufacture of meaning that it failed to take into account that concepts, themes signified might be undone, that within the obvious or unobvious statements made by an utterance are murmured meanings from "between the words" words under words.

In contrast, Blonsky (1985: XVII) argues "semiotics at the crossroads" should proceed by trying:

to grasp the culture's bloodstream as sign *and* secret practices, as the language of our rationality and also silent, infinitesimal procedures. Semiotics must not weigh on a part, whether literature, politics, commerce or social life, without awareness of the flow of the process in which that part was immersed and in which it lived Blonsky (1985: XIX).

With this awareness, Eco offers a framework for beginning to grasp "the flow of the process."

19.5 Eco and Anthropology

Any symbolic act or utterance draws upon, or is interpreted in terms of, a background weft of cultural phenomena which Eco (1976: 21) sees as having communicative effects that are not normally acknowledged as such.

If the term 'culture' is applied in its correct anthropological sense then we are immediately confronted with three elementary cultural phenomena which can apparently be denied the characteristic of being communicative phenomena: (a) the production and employment of objects used for transforming the relationship between man and nature; (b) kinship relations as the primary nucleus of institutionalized social relations: (c) the economic exchange of goods.

These phenomena can be considered remarkable in that they convey meaning about man's relationship to nature, to his fellows, and to his social institutions and yet are not regarded as communicative.

With Eco, we do not wish to make the assumption that culture is *only* communicative (1976: 22) nor do we wish to follow the aforementioned semiotic pursuit of identifying interpretative codes. We do wish to affirm the importance of these phenomena in the evocation of social relations and social structures, or customary relations (Golding and Linstead 1984). The 'transmission' of information is achieved through the 'bricolage' of those who read, but this occurs within a context and history of previous bricolations and evolving material circumstance.

With regard to the first, we live in an environment which is mediated by the goods, tools and buildings with which we populate it. Our sense of time, of space and productivity, our consciousness of place and possibility, are enabled and constrained by these things. Things and places are important for thinking — indeed, Levi-Strauss talks of 'goods to think with'. Kinship relations we see as being transformed and decentred in our post industrial civilization, and alongside the family we see *professional* kinship groups and *organizational* kinship groups as exercising sometimes conflicting gravitational fields on organizational members (Galimberti et al. 1985). Finally, not only do goods communicate through their cost, availability, style, etc. but they are symbolically available even to those who cannot afford to participate in them — they can be traded *indexically* and used to mark the limits of the system in which trading does take place. Even those who produce goods and services far beyond their own means can thus consume them and participate in their use symbolically (Linstead and Grafton-Small 1987 a and b).

These three sets of phenomena, and the ways in which they are symbolically appropriated, form the background weft against which meaning is created.

19.6 Textuality

We have elsewhere outlined the development of the concepts of "organizational fictionality" and "textuality" and what follows is a paraphrase of those discussions (Linstead and Grafton-Small 1986; Linstead 1988). However, it is important that although our discussion so far has been of symbolic signs and sign systems, some specific attention must be paid to linguistic formulations, as these are likely to furnish much of our organizational data. We should observe that material conditions, rhetorical techniques, historical relationships and patterns of representation can through the medium of language (though not exclusively):

a) Effect the link between *knowledge and power*, to the extent that power may constitute knowledge (Foucault 1980).

b) Habitually prefer certain *accounts, readings* and offer a limited range of *subject-positions* (responses) to readers and interpreters.

c) Seek to establish patterns of *legitimacy, hegemony and domination*, usually through the determination of the boundaries of *rationality* (Foucault 1972; Daudi 1985).

d) Occasion as a response different *forms of resistance* to the overt and discursive (although these do not disappear) as the prevailing order seeks to become the *natural* order, suppressing movement at the social/organizational boundary (Cooper 1985; Linstead 1985; Lyotard 1984; Power 1986).

Our experience of everyday and organizational life is fictional because it is based on an inevitably false version of the natural world, mediated through perception, memory, interest, social experience and language. Our fictions, offered in place of testimony from a silent object-world, are confirmed, disconfirmed and re-created by our audiences, where they compete with other fictions to be recognized. Within every such fiction there is a "play of possibilities" of meaning (though not necessarily an equal play) or an "intertextuality" (Kristeva 1980). Our accounts, even scientific ones, ultimately rest on the order of experience and the degree of self-recognition that they induce in the "reader."

Giddens (1979) with some relevance to our project, examines the qualities of texts which may be relevant by analogy to social life. We summarise:

1) Texts are the outcome of a *process of production* involving the reader, rather than being merely a fixed form of the author's intentions.

2) Texts have an *artful quality* — they are constructed, consciously or unconsciously, and exploit knowledge, skill, rhetoric, rationalization, and conceptions of competence in readers and organizational members.

3) Texts are both *productions of authors* and produce those authors. To study a text is to study the production of its author, the process of the production/consumption duality. An author is therefore more than either a bundle of intentions or a series of traces in the text.

4) Texts are *situated productions* which have a life of their own independent of the author. They are reproduced as part of the life of the reader and in specific historical contexts, and are subject to extra-discursive effects (power relationships etc.). Burton and Carlen (1981) propose that texts or discourses have *discursive effects* which constitute:

a) the *author* is a position rather than a person,

b) the *reader*, similarly,

c) the *object* of the discourse, i. e. what it does, what it seeks to establish, deny, justify, etc. In organizations, the focus would be on the boundary it seeks to preserve.

d) The *Other* of the discourse i. e. the opposition, albeit silent, which makes the *object* necessary (justification, negation, presentation). The potential alternative, disorganization, or that which threatens the Organization.

e) The *Imaginary* of the discourse, i. e. the image of the world which the discourse seeks to establish as unitary and natural. In organizational discourse this becomes the *Organizational-Imaginary*. The discourse or organization cannot attempt to propagate its imaginary version of the world without recognizing the Other, the alternative, the potential or actual opposition which makes this exercise necessary. The seeds of contradiction lie at the heart of every such attempt.

We suggest that organizational cultures should be studied with regard to the fictional nature of organizational and social life and with attention to the features outlined above. The attempt to *interpret* organizational cultures should be replaced by the attempt to *interrupt* them, to expose their inevitable contradiction, and to reveal their constitution as effects. That meaning resides in the *readings* which members and others give to these cultures, and the ways in which these readings are constituted should be emphasised, with an awareness of the duality of production/consumption. It should be remembered that readings *can* be privileged by discursive and extra-discursive effects, material effects included, particularly with regard to Eco's three cultural phenomena. Finally it should be remembered that control is always out of the hands of the creator, subject to the processes of evocation, bricolage and other forms of symbolic and actual resistance. The nature of organizational culture is such that "engineering" or even "design" are inappropriate metaphors: the duality and productivity of cultural phenomena require a different frame of reference which the post-structuralist model of the text makes available (cf. Linstead 1988; Young 1981; Linstead and Grafton-Small 1986).

In illustrating our analysis of various fragments of organizational data, we can proceed by focussing on the two frameworks we have outlined above. We present below two examples of our analyses which cohere around an examination of the symbolic importance of Eco's anthropological phenomena. The first relates directly to our everyday life: in fact it is taken from our everyday academic lives. The second moves from the immediately material and social to the world of images, and in looking at a particular piece of advertising (a field which has been well-ploughed by structural analysts) seeks to trace the impact of these phenomena on a more generalized process of trading on sexuality.

19.7 One Green Bottle

Our first incident occurred during a conference at which we were presenting a paper which was based on a series of discussions with marketing managers. In considering them as professionals, we treated them as members of a "nascent profession" (Walker 1976). As such, they attempted to manage their individual and group identity through the production of skilled performances, and of skilled representations of those performances. We examined the ways in which they used symbols, created accounts, and identified and 'solved' problems to establish themselves as a distinct group, yet having a specific authority in relation to wider society.

Within the conference we had met a number of new and interesting people with whom we were evolving friendships. We were invited to join a small group of Italians for an evening meal at a restaurant, only one of whom, Carlo, was a fluent speaker of English. None of the English speakers spoke Italian, although one was bilingual in French, another in Swedish. When we arrived at the restaurant at the appointed time, it was closed, and a note on the gate from Carlo gave us directions to another restaurant nearby.

We entered through the bar and reached the restaurant down a short flight of steps. The cellar was warm, candle lit and walled by shelves of bottles of wine. Our friends were seated at a table for four: as the four of us joined them, the waiter moved up another table to enlarge the group. As we moved through the twilight to our seats, Linstead accidentally dislodged a bottle of red wine from its place on the shelf behind him. It sundered with the usual crash, dispersing glass and wine over a wide area, and causing those of us about to be seated to stand hurriedly. His stark horror at his own ineptitude could be seen to receive some form when related to Eco's phenomena.

19.7.1 The Production and Employment of Objects Used for Transforming the Relationship Between Man and Nature

The bottle of wine itself was already the product of a series of modifications to the relationship between man and grape, man and silica, and other natural objects. But it had been produced for the specific purpose of transforming the consumer's relationship with his/her environment and his/her fellows, through taste, bouquet, colour and not least alcoholic content. To employ such a product for the inappropriate purpose of washing the floor, or destroying it, would be a demonstration of intentional or unconscious social ineptitude: he had done both. This assumed even greater significance in a group whose relationship was as yet unformed — was such a person as he really to be embraced as warmly as the original hospitality of the Italians had indicated?

Additionally, he had no way of accounting for his action or influencing the symbolic interpretations of his act in language, as only one of our hosts would have followed.

The bottle itself, however, was a special one. As he attempted to pick up some of the pieces, he noticed the date on the label, 1967. *1967*! The transformation between man and nature to be effected by this object was so rare that it had lain for 18 years unopened waiting to accomplish it. He had dashed the cherished object to the ground.

19.7.2 The Economic Exchange of Goods

Although the phenomena are not to be considered sequentially, there is narrative logic in considering the importance of economic exchange here. Not only was the bottle of wine one which could be expected to have pleasant and significant social effects, but this was reflected in its valuation. He recalled that the last time he had seen a bottle of similar age in his home town it had cost almost £ 25 — virtually a full day's accommodation and subsistence allowance from his employers. It represented a level of participation in the economy which he was yet to attain — the upper reaches of the bourgeoisie may well carry cases of this wine home in their BMW's but he could not aspire to the merest sip. He was suddenly very aware of his socio-economic place.

19.7.3 Kinship Relations as the Primary Nucleus of Institutionalized Social Relations

It was interesting that our interpretation of 'kinship' in our work elsewhere was one embracing wider relations than blood relations: our Italian friends had argued from a different psychological perspective that familial relationships had been replaced by others in organizational and business life (Galimberti et al. 1985).

Linstead's membership of the nascent 'kinship group' had been rendered problematic by his demonstration of incompetence in breaking the bottle. Additionally, the breakage occurred as the group was being *physically* brought together and resulted in our *physical* sundering. On a symbolic level too, the physical cause of the breakage was sundering his membership, at that moment a doubly fragile thing. Perhaps a more overpowering threat was the overlap with the economic consequences of the act. Who should repair the damage? Would the *group* be asked to pay? If so, he would have imposed on the goodwill of his new friends and materially damaged their pockets. If he had been asked to pay, it would have so damaged his carefully budgeted finances that he would have been unable to continue to participate in the activities of the group.

What we hope that this sort of demonstration makes clear is the inter-penetration of these aspects of symbolic life. Any intervention in one (e. g. breaking the bottle) immediately affects the 'meaning creation' process through the others. The lack of an immediately available means of negotiating the reconstruction of such meaning in this case (i. e. the language barrier) perhaps brings this aspect into stark relief. In the event, he was unable to explore the interpretations of the consequences by his fellows, and he did not broach the subject of payment with our genial host for fear of offending his hospitality.

Our argument in the paper was that professionals manipulate the symbolic evocations of the above phenomena skilfully to prefer interpretations which preserve and establish their distinctiveness as a *kinship group* different from lay society, yet permeable to lay understandings and wider social tensions. As should be apparent however, the degree of control or success in influencing this process is of its nature partial, fluctuating, and subject to the existence of multiple realities. As we left, he finally plucked up the courage to ask Carlo what had happened about the breakage as it had not appeared on the bill.

"It's all right" he said "The waiter says he does it all the time."

19.8 The Name of the Roses

Photographs quote from appearances. The taking-out of the quotation produces a discontinuity, which is reflected in the ambiguity of a photograph's meaning. All photographed events are ambiguous, except to those whose personal relation to the event is such that their own lives supply the missing continuity. Usually, in public the ambiguity of photographs is hidden by the use of words which explain, less or more truthfully, the pictured events (Berger, Mohr and Philibert 1982: 128).

Up to this point, part of our argument has been that goods are used as a sense-making device, as landmarks around which the world is "made" symbolically (Sperber 1975). As a result of this process, a series of coding possibilities develops, without being a pre-requisite for the process. Semiotics has, as a result of the analysis of these linguistic and cultural codings, developed into a mature discipline, and the "slippage" of the double herme-neutic between analysts and encoders has meant that a new reflexive aware-ness has developed amongst advertising copywriters, architects, designers and others who work in overtly symbolic modes. As Williamson (1983) observes in the fourth edition of *Decoding Advertising*, she may not be responsible but since the publication of her original text, advertisers and copywriters have become more sophisticated and play with meaning to a greater extent than ever before. Even post-structuralism has begun to influ-ence the conscious creation of the surface artefact and the consideration of effect.

In post-structuralist analysis, the impossibility of determining an "inten-tion" as a source, combined with the concept of an "intention" being viewed as an explanatory rather than a telelogical phenomenon, produces a shift of emphasis from this area which has been of some importance to social scientists in the past. In our unpickings of the following advertisement, we are aware that our object has been consciously crafted, and that human intention played a part in its creation. However, that part is not the sole determinant of effect, as we shall see: contrary or conflicting discourses are an inevitable and necessary complement to any attempt to create meaning. Every statement carries with it the possibility of its own negation, otherwise it would not be necessary.

The advertisement which is the focus of our attention appeared in the July 1986 edition of *Executive Travel: The Frequent Flyer's Friend*, a monthly magazine primarily aimed at the British business traveller and therefore designed for an essentially middle-class, middle-aged and, in social terms, powerful, male audience. The ad begins with a visual and verbal paradox — the question "What can four hours in a Guy Salmon Daimler do to a dozen roses?" is answered by the split photograph. However, the traverse from "stale" to "fresh" reverses our expectation, and if we are to resolve the paradox, and find out what is so unusual about the Guy Salmon Daimler, then we must read on.

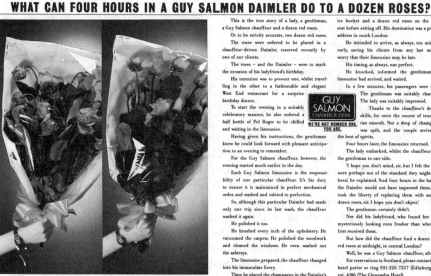

The advertisement was provided by courtesy of Guy Salmon Car Rentals.

One important feature here is that the "product," the Daimler, though specifically branded, does not appear in the advertisement. The roses, although *a* product, packaged and presented, are not *the* product being sold. Neither, of course, is the Daimler, although it is the artefact over which money changes hands. The product on sale here is *service*, the concept of service, the crucial *transformation* of the customer's *order of experience*. It is the transformation of the roses we are being sold, not the roses or the Daimler. The products act as signifiers for the service, hence quality, or even magic, as in the artful reversal of natural entropy, is important.

The *products* are important for the transformation of the relationship between man and nature. The car itself enables time to be revalued: the theatre is a matter of minutes away, and may be attained in a leisurely fashion. The champagne is a fairly expensive (about £ 20 a bottle) brand with a distinctive taste — the choice of a discerning drinker, especially in the half-bottle size, a measure of control which would otherwise denote relative poverty. There is a sense of attenuated luxury in the way all of these products are used; the car is cleaned whether it needs it or not, the car which is capable of well over 100 m.p.h (160 k.ph.) is driven with such care that "not a drop was spilt." Indeed, the products are identified and used with such care and discernment that a sense of the appreciation of worth, a desire for luxury which stops short of excess, is created. The lavish care and attention serves to create *order, perfection*, which, once attained, is sufficient. Notice the use of expressions: strictly accurate; perfect, perfection, ordered, suitably, immaculate, fashionable, elegant, standard, improved. Everything must be suitable: the product which is not (the roses) will be replaced.

The sense of order and stability conveyed by the use of the product also carries with it the *kinship* dimension, which in this case has both *class* and *gender* aspects. It may well be our supposition that this advertisement appeals to the upper middle-class, but it affirms kinship in definite ways. The branding of the products, which according to their differentiated characteristics conveys a specific sense of both quality and cost, is blended with the generalised reference to a "fashionable and elegant" West End restaurant and a "private address in South London." It *could* be Brixton, but we know it's not. The branding is usually, as Fussell (1984) points out, a gesture characteristic of the middle-class, riddled as they are with psychic guilt and "status panic," the need to reaffirm class identity. The mixture here of the specific with the general, where generalised statements such as "drinks" or "an address in South London" would normally be born of the assurance of the upper class, creates an unevenness. The advert perhaps tries *too* hard, in using the vocabulary of "private," "fashionable," "elegant" — if it were truly to establish itself as an upper middle-class document, these things would be understood, would go without saying. But of course, this is to neglect the role of the *author* as created as an effect of the discourse. The advertisement is a description of what happened, by a tradesman, the *supplier of the vehicle*, and hence a member of the servant class, although an exalted one. And indeed, the not-quite-perfect vocabulary adds to the sense of deference: the chauffeur as an onlooker who can make things possible but cannot participate, and cannot even find a vocabulary other than the banal to convey the grandeur of the occasion. But he can relate to products.

The use of artefacts, in combination with the lexicon, produces our dual awareness of the controlled luxury of the upper middle-class and the deferential civility and efficiency of the service class. And this is ironic, because although the upper middle-class attitude is one of relaxed assurance, or order prevailing, the service class is necessary to make its considerable efforts to preserve that order. Perfection needs help from the less than perfect if it is to be attained, and hence failure or disorder is always a threat.

The chauffeur here appears in the role of *helper*, as in many classical myths, where the hero, despite his own marvellous qualities, attains the goal of his quest only with the intervention of a "good" assistant. What here is our hero's quest?

An innocent interpretation may well be simply that of a "good night out," a birthday celebration, but that would ignore the sexual discourse present. We are witnessing a seduction, working on both modern and classical lines. In the first place, we have a number of aggressively male and predatory symbols, the car, the red roses of passion, the champagne as intoxicant. But these are mediated with softer, rounder, more feminine qualities: the car is not a Jaguar, but a Daimler, the more luxurious and less sporty equivalent, the champagne is a brand of discernment not of excess, and the roses are placed in the back seat to be discovered not presented. And of course, they weren't perfect. The driving was done by a third party, which further symbolically distanced the male from the car as expression of libido. The car was driven so that the "course of true love ran smooth" and "not a drop was spilt." The ambiguity is relevant here. Order and restraint is necessary so that consummation may occur when everything is completed and in place; a courtship ritual if not a ceremonial occasion.

The apparent yielding of male aggression to more feminine qualities is both superficial and temporary. The issues of sexuality/power are intertwined and relate in the concept of the *economic change of goods*. The man purchases the services of the chauffeur and car, and has the power to bend their subtle skills and qualities to his will, and to structure the experience of his companion of the evening towards its inevitable conclusion.

However, before this goes any further, we should consider the significant moral undertow. A certain form of culture is clearly intended when the purchaser demonstrates his 'honourable intentions' — you might get bought but you won't get raped — by bringing the unknown woman drinks but not trying to get her drunk; intoxicated with pleasure, perhaps, but that's another matter.

Of course, this propriety is not simply a question of moral behaviour. The entire interplay between text and reader, between artefact and theory, depends upon an understanding of goods as appropriate symbols for ideas of masculinity and femininity which nevertheless enable the debate and composition of exactly these qualities. This understanding also accepts that it is moral for those who debate such interpretations and have the "power to speak" (Clastres 1977) to assert their view of these symbols through social and commercial exchange.

Whilst Levi-Strauss (Leach 1970) has long insisted on goods, food and women as three different aspects of just such a means of communication, others, particularly those from Marxist and feminist backgrounds, have seen these forms of communication as structures of social and sexual dominance. The Guy Salmon ad admits all of these possibilities and exploits them openly.

The service on offer is, in effect, a medium of exchange whereby an implicitly wealthy, powerful and potent man can offer a woman an array of goods and services of great social and symbolic worth in exchange for herself. Furthermore, the text assumes that it is right and proper for the chauffeur to be male yet not considered as such; he is an artefact, a functionary with prescribed, and therefore proscribed functions. To be good at his job, he must not only sublimate his own sexuality, and so enhance that of his immediate employer, but in so doing, he must also reassure readers who are potential customers, those who might want him as a driver but not as a rival.

For these people, the text is an open invitation to imagine themselves participating in everything on offer, having been written with the male executive in mind and not chauffeurs or lesbians or those of a Platonic nature. Business women notwithstanding, this notion is so pervasive that, in the Guy Salmon ad, the obscure object of desire is excluded from the photographs yet we can infer her significance from the hand that holds the roses, that wears a Cartier and is clearly much sought after. Indeed, the passive partner has become an accessory to her own accessories for she wears her watch in a way which is of no use to her at all, being on the outside of her right wrist and upside down.

The inversion is nevertheless deliberate. It shows the reader that this is, after all, a true story as four hours really have gone by, through from 7.30 to 11.30 and not, as the text would have it, from 8 p.m. until midnight, the witching hour when things are no longer what they seem. This timely volte-face also presents the reader with the clearest possible picture of the otherwise unreadable face and thereby establishes the watch as nothing less than a Cartier. Once again, the terrible insecurity over artefacts and their significance, the same "status panic".

Naturally, the eternal threat to this sexual manoeuvering is disorder, the unexpected failure, or failure to consummate, for whatever reason. Power and fertility/virility must go together. This is enhanced by the replacement of waning, fading roses with fresh ones. And the symbolism grows overt — not only do the roses grow more erect, but so does the arm which holds them, and which is identifiably female.

The patriarchal discourse unfolds then to affirm our advertiser as the supporter to the potentially flagging power/virility of the upper middle-class male, bon viveur and Lothario though he be. And the Other, the image of chaos is also present, because although the powerful image of the potential client has been sustained there remains the unspeakable question: What if my roses fade? What if I can't get it up? The resourceful chauffeur may resort to a little mysterious magic to answer the first, which symbolically answers the second. And if the second has to be answered in *reality*? He is a Guy Salmon chauffeur, after all!

19.9 After the Fact, as Theory Arose

After a seminar in which we first presented our analysis we were called upon to deconstruct our own analysis when Richard Whittington questioned our interpretation of the hand in the picture as the hand of the woman in the text. He wondered "why could it not be the hand of the shop assistant?"[1]

We felt that the evocation of the shop assistant was inappropriate because the artefact which Richard wanted to rework, that is, the mystery of the roses, was better understood as a product of obscurity if it were interpreted in terms of the theme of the story. We might also add that the rigour of our analysis, which requires us to follow *only the text and the contradictions within the text*, accords no justification for such an exegesis. Nor do we feel any compelling need for Levi-Straussian symmetry whereby the shop assistant might be invoked as a female counterpart to the chauffeur in his role as a sexual and functional intermediary.

We have no indication that there *was* a shop assistant and in any case, we believe that shop assistants with Cartier watches, especially upside down Cartier watches, may well be too subtle, too ambiguous a possibility for the rest of the text to bear. We have also to consider the explicitly persuasive purpose of the advertisement and its implicit dependence on status goods as means of evoking those everyday understandings of class and power that it serves to reinforce.

However, we then discovered that according to our own rules, the hand could not be the hand of the lady in the story *either*. She only handled fresh bunches of roses. At neither 7.30 or 11.30, when the roses were handed to her, were they faded. Indeed, if the text is to be believed, the image of faded

---

[1] The seminar took place as part of the Standing Conference on Organizational Symbolism Conference, *The Symbolics of Artefacts*, June, 1987. Richard Whittington lectures at the University of Warwick.

roses at 7.30 must be entirely false. Nor would the shop assistant have ever handled any faded roses: yet still there is the problem of time. Who, in particular which woman, other than the recipient, would have handled the roses at 11.30 p.m.? What is perhaps more important is the fact that, symbolically, the faded roses must be kept from the view of the desirable lady because revitalisation is a *male* domain.

We must conclude that this contradictory signifier is impersonal, not a literal representation or even a symbol capable of narrow interpretation, save that it must be a female rather than a male hand. However, our recidivism, our own lapse into 'modernist' habits, led us to interpret it as *personal*; that is, having a source, or a metonymic function, a logos, a 'story' of its presence in its current form, and a connection with the 'story' of the text.

The hand with the wilted roses is, in fact, an *empty* signifier. It is the hand of no-one which nevertheless draws attention to itself as a creation, an artefact − part of a visual discourse which *cuts across* that of the text. Of course, as an artefact, with all its attendant inconsistencies of interpretation and recreation, the photograph is also subject to the vagaries of those who had a hand in its 'creation'. Perhaps the copywriters or the 'creatives' at the advertising agency were so used to using female models to represent or re-present products that they failed to notice any contradiction in treating these artefacts as entirely interchangeable, in failing to see the model as a person.

It is also more than possible that the 'creators' of the text were misled in the same way as we, the re-creators of the text, were misled, for the hand with the wilted roses may be seen as both a product and a function of the story's compelling logic, even though the story is itself illogical. This paradoxical proposition is nevertheless persuasive because the advertisement in question is itself ambiguous. It is known to be fiction yet understood and accepted as an unavoidable, even unremarkable, part of the everyday world. Accordingly, the propriety of our critique is based on the exclusion of the improper world beyond the text just as Richard's critique of our text is properly based on the impropriety of any attempt at a conclusion to either the text or the world.

19.10 Against Conclusions

It certainly seems that it is impossible as a project to control meaning, as it is impossible to speak without contradiction. It may be that forms of articulation become dominant, naturalized, and organization members, 'decked out in another's language' enthusiastically participate in the construction of their own prison. If it were not so perhaps our paper would not be necessary. Additionally, if it were not also true that the converse is frequent and inescapable then our paper would not be possible. We too are tangled in our own evocative paradox, but are at least aware of the reflexive necessity to deconstruct it. The reader might feel the need to *construct* the paper as a relative broadside against the stultifications of functionalism; alternatively it might be seen as a badly constructed anecdotal tirade of unprofessional assertion lacking the rigour of an academic argument, and appropriate for *destruction*. We wish to usurp the privilege, and in reflexively *deconstructing* our work exemplify the post-modern predicament in the face of the problem of meaning/non-meaning — that what we achieve is created as much by what we do not accomplish as what we do accomplish. This is perhaps the most important characteristic of the shift from modernist ethnomethodology to a post structuralist fictionality — from meaning to non-meaning. Hence we leave the problem of cultural determinism with an image of the organizational member suspended in 'webs of signification' in which the holes may be more important than the strands; in a quivering warp of structuration and a weft of evocation; caught against a background in which we attempt to control Nature as Environment, Human Nature as Culture (Cooper 1985). We must resist being strapped too tightly to a particular version of "reality" to allow "objectivity" to take over. To bricolate Blonsky's admonition: "Beware, you are not taking in evidence."

And finally, Eco offers us some comfort amidst a world exploding with oppositions and contradictions (1986: xii).

There is no rule; there is only the risk of contradiction. But sometimes you have to speak because you feel the moral obligation to say something, not because you have the "scientific" certainty that you are saying it in an unassailable way.

References

Berger, J., Mohr, J. and N. Philibert (1982): *Another Way of Telling*, London: Writers and Readers Publishing Co-operative.

Blonsky, M. (1985): *On Signs*, Oxford: Basil Blackwell.

Broms, H. and H. Gahmberg (1987): *Semiotics of Management*, Helsinki: Helsinki School of Economics Publications.

Burton, F. and P. Carlen (1981): *Official Discourse*, London: Routledge & Kegan Paul.

Clarke, J. (1976): "Style" in *Resistance Through Rituals* (S. Hall et al. eds.), London: Hutchinson: 175–191.

Clastres, P. (1977): *Society Against the State: The Leader as Servant and the Human Uses of Power amongst the Indians of the Americas*, Oxford: Mole Editions, Basil Blackwell.

Cooper, R. (1985): *Organisation/Disorganisation*, unpublished paper, University of Lancaster: UK.

Daudi, P. (1985): *The Discursive Legitimation of Managerial Practice*, paper presented to SCOS Workshop on Corporate Image and Corporate Culture Antibes, France.

Eco, U. (1976): *A Theory of Semiotics*, Indiana: University Press.

— (1986): *Faith in Fakes*, London: Secker and Warburg.

Foucault, M. (1972): *The Archaeology of Knowledge*, London: Tavistock.

— (1980): *Power/Knowledge*, Brighton: Harvester.

Fussell, P. (1984): *Caste Marks: Style and Status in the USA*, New York and London: Heinemann.

Galimberti, C. et al. (1985): *Families like Firms and Firms Run as Families*, paper presented to SCOS Conference Workshop on Skill Trento, Italy.

Giddens, A. (1979): "Structuralism and the Theory of the Subject" in *Central Problems in Sociological Theory*, London: Macmillan.

Golding, D. and S. A. Linstead (1984): *The maintenance of customary relations in organisations*, paper presented to the Annual Conference of the British Sociological Association on Work, Employment and Unemployment, University of Bradford, April.

Hawkes, T. (1977): *Structuralism and Semiotics*, London: Methuen.

Hebdidge, D. (1979): *Subculture; The Meaning of Style*, London: Methuen.

Kristeva, J. (1980): *Desire in Language*, Oxford: Basil Blackwell.

Leach, E. (1970): *Levi-Strauss*, London: Fontana.

Levi-Strauss, C. (1976): *The Savage Mind*, London: Weidenfeld and Nicholson.

Linstead, S. A. (1985): One Green Bottle: A Look at the Cultural Creation of Meaning, *Notework*, vol. 4, no. 3: 12—15.

— (1988): Fictions — A Methodologocal Discussion, *Dragon*, vol. 2, no. 5: 51—76.

Linstead, S. A. and R. Grafton-Small (1986): Reading the Organizational Text, *Dragon* 2, vol. 2, no. 1: 93—126.

— (1987 a): Artefact as Theory: All Roses Lead to Milano, paper presented to SCOS Conference *The Symbolic of Artefacts*, Milan, June.

— (1987 b): Theory as Artefact: The Monicker of the Glen, as above.

Lyotard, J. F. (1984): *The Postmodern Condition*, Manchester: Manchester University Press.

Power, M. (1986): *Modernism, Post-modernism and Organisation*, paper presented to conference on Aspects of Organisation, Lancaster.

Sahlins, M. (1976): *Culture and Practical Reason*, Chicago: Chicago University Press.

Sperber, D. (1975): *Rethinking Symbolism*, Cambridge: Chicago University Press.

Walker, D. (1976): *The Professionalization of Marketing in Britain*, Ph.D. Thesis, University of Aston: Birmingham.

Williamson, J. (1983): *Decoding Advertisements* (4th ed.), London: Marion Boyars.

— (1986): *Consuming Passions*, London: Routledge & Kegan Paul.

Willis, P. (1978): *Profane Culture*, London: Routledge & Kegan Paul.

Young, R. (1981): *Untying the Text*, London, Routledge & Kegan Paul.

Authors' Biographical Notes

Guy B. Adams earned his doctoral degree in public administration at George Washington University. He has taught at George Washington University, California State University-Hayward and the Evergreen State College, where he is currently Member of the Faculty. With *Ingersoll* (see below) he has been engaged in research on organizational symbolism and culture for the past six years. Their research has been published in "Administration and Society", "Dragon", and in Frost, et al. "Organizational Culture" (Sage, 1985). Their book "The Tacit Organization" is currently under publisher's review.

Omar Aktouf (born in Algeria in 1944), Associate Professor HEC, Montréal; M.S. Psychology and Business and Development Economics (Algeria); M.B.A. and Ph.D. Business Administration (Canada); for ten years Manager in Petroleum and Project management; since 1972, Teacher and Researcher in "Management." "Project Management," "Organizational Culture," and "Research Methodology."

Jacques F. Brissy (born in 1942) is "Licencié en Sciences Sociales" (Université Catholique de Louvain, Belgium), M.A. and Ph.D. in Sociology (University of California at Berkeley, U.S.A.). Between 1974 and 1979 he was Assistant Professor at the University of Illinois at Urbana-Champaign, U.S.A. Since 1979, he is Associate Professor in Sociology at the Université Libre de Bruxelles, Belgium, and co-director of the Centre de Méthodologie du Traitement des Données at the Institut de Sociologie of the same university. His research work is mainly in the field of organizational behavior, management ideologies, computers and society, and symbolic consumption.

Barbara Czarniawska-Joerges (born in 1948) holds an M.A. in Social Psychology at the University of Warsaw (1970) and an E.D. from the Central School of Planning and Statistics, Warsaw (1976). Until 1981, she was Assistant Professor at the Faculty of Psychology, University of Warsaw. At present she is Associate Professor at the Stockholm School of Economics, Sweden. Books in English: "Controlling Top Management in Large Organisations: Poland and U.S.A." (Gower, 1985), "Ideological Control in Nonideological Organizations" (Praeger, 1988), and "Economic Decline and Organizational Control" (Praeger, 1989).

Lars D. Edgren is a graduate of the Department of Business administration at the University of Lund where he now lectures on consulting methodology.

He has been employed in a number of senior administrative posts in Swedish industry, and during the past decade he has worked as a Senior Consultant for Albatross 78 Consultants in Lund, and, more recently for SMG Corporate Consultants in Stockholm, concentrating on corporate portraits, corporate culture diagnosis and industrial and organizational analysis. He has a number of academic and business publications: the latest, "Stena's People: A Corporate Portrait of a Shipping Company" appeared in December 1988.

Ellis Finkelstein (born in 1942); B.A. Northeastern University (1968); M.A. Manchester University (1971); Bristol University (Ph.D. cand.); employed as a probation officer in England since 1975.

Pasquale Gagliardi (born in 1936) is Professor of Organizational Behaviour and Director of ISTUD-Instituto Studi Direzionali, Belgirate, Italy. He graduated in law from the Università Cattolica del Sacro Cuore in Milan. After working in private industry, he joined the "Centro di organizzazione aziendale" of the University of Padova where he taught organizational behaviour from 1964 to 1969. Professor Gagliardi is a consultant to many large Italian corporations. His current research concerns organizational culture and cultural change. *Mailing Address*: ISTUD-Instituto Studi Direzionali, Via Mazzini 127, 28040 Belgirate (Novara), Italy.

Henrik Gahmberg, Ph.D. (1946) is Associate Professor of Organization and Management in the Swedish-speaking School of Economics and Business Administration in Helsinki, Finland. His research interests are organizational culture and strategic management. He has published books on organizational communication and on the values of strategic managers. Together with his colleague, Dr. Henri Broms, he has published a book and several articles on the semiotic study of organization and management. Address inquiries to: Henrik Gahmberg, the Swedish School of Economics and Business Administration, Arkadiagatan 22, 00100 Helsingfors, Finland.

Dr. Robert Grafton-Small (University of Strathclyde) The source of this suspicion is of Scots and English descent though raised on the Welsh Marches and currently in a basement in Glasgow. Dr. Grafton-Small is a tenured academic in the Biggest University Department of Marketing in Europe. His background, his nature and his education in various Victorian cities, including Sheffield where he was first over-whelmed by Stephen Linstead, have left him ideally suited to a life-long pursuit of the arcane and the ambiguous. Dr. Robert believes himself to be a bachelor and in this, if little else, he is probably right.

Virginia Hill Ingersoll earned her Ph.D. in communications and organizational psychology at the University of Illinois, and has taught at the University of Illinois, the Annenberg School of Communications at the University of Pennsylvania and The Evergreen State College, where she is currently Member of the Faculty. For research activities see *Adams* above.

Egbert Kahle (born in 1943) studied Business Management and Sociology in Hannover and Göttingen. Dipl.Kfm. 1969 Göttingen, Dr. rer. pol. 1973 Göttingen, Habilitation 1977 Göttingen; from 1969 to 1982 Assistant Professor University of Göttingen, Institute for Production Research, interim 1981 Visiting Professor University Kassel, since 1982 Full Professor for Business Management especially Organization and Decision Theory University of Lüneburg. He has published five books and 30 articles on various topics.

Krzysztof Konecki is an Assistant Lecturer in Sociology in the Institute of Sociology, University of Lodz. He has published articles on: organizational culture, redefinitions of self in concentration camps, ridiculing rituals and the conception of work in interactionist sociology. His current research is concerned with the meaning of 'face' in organizational settings. He graduated from Lodz University in 1983 and is just completing his doctorate at Warsaw University.

Ellee Koss (born in 1952) earned a Ph.D. in Economics, specializing in Economic Development, from Boston University. Dr. Koss' research has evolved from highly technical and empirical work in the area of productivity to, most recently, qualitative and conceptual work on the role of vision and change in organizations and societies. In the past ten years, she has taught at several universities in the Boston area. Ellee has created and taught such diverse courses as "The Creation and Leadership of Change," "Global in Nature: To Thrive in the 21st Century," "Economic Development," and "Values and Creative Thinking." As founder and directer of PEOPLEWARE, Dr. Koss is currently consulting to individuals and organizations around issues involving vision, change and globalization.

Dr. Stephen A. Linstead (Expert Training Systems). A thoroughbred Yorkshireman with experience as an Industrial Baker and semi-professional folk singer, Dr. Linstead has, in addition to his prodigious range of academic and professional qualifications, recently been appointed as Principal Course Director with a prominent firm of Management Educators. Previously the Head of a local Polytechnic Department of European Business, Stephen is very much at home in Barnsley with his wife Eileen, their three children and the nagging suspicion that something, somewhere has been left undone, probably by his co-author.

Klara Pihlajamäki (born in 1947) gained a B.Mc. in Social Sciences and Business Administration from the University of Stockholm, where she is now a teacher in Business Administration. She is presently working on a doctoral dissertation dealing with organizational communication. She has worked in different countries and cultures, in Saudi Arabia, Finland and the U.S.A. in management and organizational development, both in the public and the private sector.

Michael Rosen (born in 1956) is the President of Sundered Ground, Inc., a real estate development firm specializing in residential construction projects in New York City and New England. Michael Rosen received his Ph.D. from The Wharton School and teaches on an adjunct basis in the Management Department at New York University. His academic writings primarily focus on radical understandings of power, control, and domination in formal organizations. His research methodology is primarily rooted in ethnography.

Burkard Sievers (born in 1942) is since 1977 professor of Organization Development in the Department of Business Administration and Economics at Bergische Universität Wuppertal in Germany. In addition to his academic work he is consulting to enterprises as well as to non-profit institutions. He also is Scientific Director of the 'Standing Conference for the Promotion of the Learning of People and Organizations (MundO)', a network in the tradition of the Group Relations Programme of the Tavistock Institute of Human Relations.

Antonio Strati is Researcher at the Dipartimento di Politica Sociale, University of Trento, Italy. He was educated at the Universities of Trento and Florence, and received his action research training at the Tavistock Institute of Human Relations in London. He is a founder-member of the Standing Conference on Organizational Symbolism, and has been editor of "SCOS-NoteWork". He has researched and published on the temporal dimension in organizations, on the symbolic approach and on the cultural analysis of work and organizations.

Andrew Travers completed his Ph.D. (a development of Goffman's ritual frame) at Bath University's School of Management in 1981. Currently he is an Honorary Fellow in the Department of Sociology at the University of Exeter, and his present fieldwork interest is "creativity" in the culture of advertisers. Work in progress includes a postmodernism reader (with a comprehensive annotated bibliography) and (with Paul Oldfield) a Goffmanian extrapolation of Jean Baudrillard subtitled "Postmodern Sociology and Literature after Baudrillard."

Barry A. Turner is Reader in the Sociology of Organizations at the University of Exeter. He has had for many years an interest in the cultural features of organizations and also in the organizational causes of large-scale accidents. He is currently engaged on a study of Safety Culture at the EC Joint Research Centre, Ispra, Italy, where he is a Visiting Scientist. He was one of the founder-members of the Standing Conference on Organizational Symbolism, and he is currently Chairman of that association.

de Gruyter Studies in Organization

An international series by internationally known
authors presenting current research in organization

Vol. 12

**Management in China during and after Mao in Enterprises,
Government, and Party**

By *Oiva Laaksonen*
1988. 15.5 x 23 cm. X, 379 pages. Cloth. ISBN 3 11 009958 6; 0-89925-025-4 (U.S.)

Vol. 13

Innovation and Management
International Comparisons
Edited by *Kuniyoshi Urabe †, John Child* and *Tadao Kagono*
1988. 15.5 x 23 cm. XX, 371 pages. Cloth. ISBN 3 11 011007 5; 0-89925-294-X (U.S.)

Vol. 14

**Leadership and Management in Universities:
Britain and Nigeria**

By *Titus Oshagbemi*
1988. 15.5 x 23 cm. XX, 249 pages. Cloth. ISBN 3 11 011514 X; 0-89925-426-8 (U.S.)

Vol. 15

**Boards of Directors Under Public Ownership:
A Comparative Perspective**

By *Miriam Dornstein*
1988. 15.5 x 23 cm. X, 166 pages. Cloth. ISBN 3 11 011740 1; 0-89925-496-9 (U.S.)

Vol. 16

The State, Trade Unions and Self-Management
Issues of Competence and Control
Edited by *György Széll, Paul Blyton* and *Chris Cornforth*
1989. 15.5 x 23 cm. X, 362 pages. Cloth. ISBN 3 11 011667 7; 0-89925-475-7 (U.S.)

Vol. 18

**Strategies for Retrenchment and Turnaround: the Politics
of Survival**

by *Cynthia Hardy*
1989. 15.5 x 23 cm. XII, 222 pages. Cloth. ISBN 3 11 011612 X; 0-89925-452-7 (U.S.)

WALTER DE GRUYTER · BERLIN · NEW YORK

Genthiner Strasse 13, D-1000 Berlin 30, Phone (0 30) 2 60 05-0, Telex 1 83 027
200 Saw Mill River Road, Hawthorne, N.Y. 10532, Phone (914) 747-0110, Telex 64 66 77